WITH THE
GRAIN
OF THE
UNIVERSE

WITH THE
GRAIN
OF THE
UNIVERSE

THE CHURCH'S WITNESS
AND NATURAL THEOLOGY

BEING THE GIFFORD LECTURES
DELIVERED AT THE
UNIVERSITY OF ST. ANDREWS
IN 2001

Stanley Hauerwas

Brazos Press
A Division of Baker Book House Co
Grand Rapids, Michigan 49516

Published by Brazos Press
a division of Baker Book House Company
P.O. Box 6287, Grand Rapids, MI 49516–6287

Printed in the United States of America

Library of Congress Cataloging-in-Publication Data

Hauerwas, Stanley, 1940–
    With the grain of the universe : the church's witness and natural theology : being Gifford lectures delivered at the University of St. Andrews in 2001 / Stanley Hauerwas.
      p.   cm.
    Includes bibliographical references.
    ISBN 1-58743-016-9 (cloth)
    1. God. 2. Natural theology. I. Title
BT102.H366 2001
230—dc21   2001035721

For current information about all releases from Brazos Press, visit our web site:
http://www.brazospress.com

To Paula
for the beauty
and gracefulness of
her witness

The point that apocalyptic makes is not only that people who wear crowns and who claim to foster justice by the sword are not as strong as they think—true as that is: we still sing, "O where are Kings and Empires now of old that went and came?" It is that people who bear crosses are working with the grain of the universe. One does not come to that belief by reducing social processes to mechanical and statistical models, nor by winning some of one's battles for the control of one's own corner of the fallen world. One comes to it by sharing the life of those who sing about the Resurrection of the slain Lamb.

John Howard Yoder,
"Armaments and Eschatology"

Contents

Preface

To give the Gifford Lectures was not for me the fulfillment of a dream. I never dreamed that I would be asked to give the Gifford Lectures. Theologians did not have a conspicuous role in the Gifford Lectures in the second half of the twentieth century. Moreover, I am not even a proper theologian but a representative of the even more disreputable field called Christian ethics, and it is not clear that I am a competent worker in that "field" because it is not apparent what constitutes competence in Christian ethics. I am part philosopher, part political theorist, part theologian, part ethicist, but I have no standing in any of the "parts." I am not complaining but only suggesting why, given the eccentric nature of "my work," it never occurred to me that I would be asked to give the Gifford Lectures.

So it was with the delight that comes only from an unimagined gift that I received the invitation to be the Gifford lecturer at the University of St. Andrews in 2000–2001. At least part of the gift was to be asked four years in advance, giving me ample time to think through what I wanted to do, as well as to increase my general worry captured in the thought: "What have I gotten myself into?" Of course it has become apparent for many years, apparent even to me, that God has blessed me with a sublime absence of self-protective strategy. I often go where angels fear to tread. I should like to be able to attribute my "recklessness" to courage, but I do not have the appropriate fear to so name it. Rather, I become so possessed by what I think needs to be said that I begin to understand, and to count the costs of, what I have said only after it is too late.

I do not pretend, therefore, that what I have attempted in *With the Grain of the Universe* is modest. The Gifford Lectures are, I think, best done on a large canvas. My aim is nothing less than to tell the theological story of the twentieth century by concentrating on three of the greatest Gifford lecturers—William James, Reinhold Niebuhr, and Karl Barth. I argue that Karl Barth is the great "natural theologian" of the Gifford Lectures because he rightly understood that natural theology is impossible abstracted from a full doctrine of God. Mine is a thesis clearly aimed to get attention, but more important, it is one that I think true.

I wish I could say that because I had four years to work on these lectures that this book is different—more thoughtful, more fully argued—than my past work (a description, I might add, that I dislike because it presumes that the way I have worked is not "careful"). But this is not the "big book" that many of my friends and critics have suggested I should write. Indeed, if this book is different than my past work, I hope the difference is simply that here I make clear why I do not think theologians, particularly in our day, can or should write "big books" that "pull it all together." Any theology that threatens to become a position more determinative than the Christian practice of prayer betrays its subject. At best, theology is but a series of reminders to help Christians pray faithfully. So if this book does anything different than my past work, it does so only to the extent that it displays why my work cannot help but be as occasional and unfinished as Barth's *Church Dogmatics*. Of course, I do not pretend that my work has the power of Barth's extraordinary performance. I can only follow at a distance.

Some of the more friendly readers of earlier drafts of the lectures have expressed disappointment that there is not more of "me" in it. They feel that, particularly in the last lecture, I should have returned to my emphasis on the church and the difference the church makes for reflection on war, peace, suicide, abortion, the mentally handicapped, baseball, and Trollope. These readers want me to show how the work I have done in *With the Grain of the Universe* requires the kind of redescriptive display present in what might be called "my casuistry." Those readers who would have me end differently think that to conclude with a discussion of the difference Christian practice should make for the knowledge that constitutes the university is to end with a whimper not a bang. All I can say is that I saw no reason to go over well-plowed ground. Moreover, given the challenge that Lord Gifford's will presents to the Gifford lecturer, I did not think that I could or should avoid the question of the kind of knowledges that constitute the practices of the modern university and determine for many what counts as "rationality."

This book is like my past work not only in its refusal to pull everything together, but in its display of my dependence on others. Alasdair MacIntyre was particularly helpful when I was trying to think through the overall conception of the lectures. Discussions with Alasdair helped me map the main outlines of the argument I wanted to make with my focus on James, Niebuhr, and Barth. Of course, my indebtedness to MacIntyre has been apparent for many years, though, needless to say, he is not to be held responsible for the way I may use his work to come to conclusions that he may well find quite foreign.

Peter Ochs has from the beginning to the end been a wonderful friend and critic. I wish I was as competent a Christian philosopher and theologian as he is a Jewish philosopher and theologian. Bruce Kaye was also an extremely helpful questioner in the early stages of my work. We discussed "Why Barth?" during a wonderful vacation that Paula and I enjoyed with Bruce and Louise in the American West. Barth, I should like to think, would have enjoyed knowing that his work was being questioned amid the grandeur of Colorado, Utah, and Arizona. I often observe that being a Christian in our time makes the world small just to the extent that we actually bump into one another. Knowing that Bruce and Louise pray for us means that Australia does not seem so distant.

As usual, I have relied on a wide community of friends to read and criticize what I have written. Listing their names is an insufficient indication of how much I owe them, but it is the best I can do. They are Michael Quirk, Terry Tilley, Scott Davis, Frank Lentricchia, David Aers, Jim and William Buckley, Mark Nation, Bill Werpehowski, Joe Mangina, Jim Burtchaell, David Burrell, Ralph Wood, Rusty Reno, Hans Reinders, Bill Hart, Reinhard Hütter, Arne Rasmusson, Travis Kroeker, Sam Wells, Nicholas Adams, Rob McSwain, Charlie Reynolds, Bruce Marshall, Robert Jenson, John Bowlin, Fergus Kerr, Catherine Wallace, Russ Hittinger, Robert Richardson, Glen Stassen, Gary Dorrien, Tommy Langford, and Jim McClendon. Tommy died before I finished the lectures, but his advice was invaluable for revision of the first lecture. And a few days before his own death, Jim McClendon called me for the last time to urge me to take a stronger stance in the last lecture. I miss them both.

My life has and continues to be gifted by past and current students who make me better than I am. I have relied on them for criticism at various stages of my work. They include Mike Cartwright, Mike Baxter, Charlie Pinches, Steve Long, David Matzko McCarthy, Phil Kenneson, John Berkman, Bill Cavanaugh, Dan Bell, Jim Fodor, Scott Williams, Alex Sider, Charlie Collier, Chris Franks, Peter Dula, Tom Harvey, Jeff McCurry, Roger Owens, Richard Church, and Joel Shuman—to name only those who read and commented on the text of the Giffords. Of course, what I have done in this book depends on learning from all the students who have trusted me with their lives.

I am grateful to the Louisville Institute for making it possible for Martin Copenhaver, John McFadden, Dale Rosenberger, David Wood, James Gorman, and Carl Becker to read *With the Grain of the Universe* and to attend the last week of my lectures. Having ministers—who are in the trenches, so to speak—read the text gave me some idea how what I have done may or may not help face the challenges of the church in our day. Richard Neuhaus was kind to convene a session of the Dulles Col-

loquium in which the first and last of my lectures were discussed. Joe
Mangina gave me an opportunity to test what I had done by having a
class at Wycliffe College, Toronto, read an earlier version of the lectures.
I learned a great deal from these opportunities.

I am grateful to the Luce Foundation for awarding me a Luce Fellow-
ship. That support made it possible for me to have the time to put the
lectures into their final form. Duke University has been extremely sup-
portive, and I am grateful to John Strohbehn and Peter Lange for the
support they provided from the office of the provost. Colleagues and
students in Duke Divinity School were wonderful companions during
the time I worked on the lectures, but I owe a special debt to my friend
and dean, Greg Jones. He not only read and criticized the lectures in various stages but made wonderfully constructive suggestions about how
to make them better. What a gift it is to have a dean who is at once
smart and good.

Rodney Clapp made this book possible by imagining Brazos Press.
Not only is Rodney an old friend, but he has the extraordinary ability
to give institutional form to the dream many of us have for a revitalized
and faithful church. Moreover, I think it is a wonderful thing for a native of Oklahoma to name the press after a river—a river I have crossed
and recrossed many times—in Texas. Rodney and his fellow conspira-
tors at Brazos also gave me a great gift by having David Toole copyedit
this book. David—also a former student, as well as the author of the extraordinary book *Waiting for Godot in Sarajevo*—went well beyond the normal responsibilities of a copy editor to help me clarify as well as
strengthen my argument. It is rare indeed to have a copy editor with
David's philosophical and theological skills.

The manuscript would have never gotten to the stage of being copy-
edited if it were not for my secretary, Sarah Freedman. It always feels a
bit odd for me to call Sarah "my secretary" because Sarah is simply too
wonderfully complex to be called a secretary, and in particular "my secretary." She has her own views about much that I write and is never
hesitant to tell me when she thinks I may have it wrong. Yet Sarah has,
with her normal wacky sense of humor, endured without complaint
the various revisions of the text. I thank her for putting up with me.

Finally, I must thank those at St. Andrews who not only invited me
to be the Gifford lecturer but provided such wonderful hospitality over
the month I delivered the lectures. I am particularly grateful to Mrs.
Elaine McGonigle and Mrs. Joyce Scott of external relations at St. Andrews for the work they did to make Paula's and my stay at St. Andrews so delightful. Dr. Brian Lang, Principal of St. Andrews, and Ron
Parent, Head of the Divinity School, were wonderful hosts. Philosophy
professors John Haldane and John Skorupski were extremely gracious
just to the extent that they were willing to take me seriously. Alan

Torrance, Chris Seitz, Trevor Hart, and Richard Bauckham made theological conversations rich as well as fruitful. St. Andrews can rightly be proud not only of their students but of the kind of serious training in theology the Divinity School in St. Mary's College represents.

St. Andrews is a charming and lovely town on the coast of Fife facing the North Sea. I enjoyed my stay at St. Salvator's College and was honored to be asked by Rev. Dr. James Walker to preach in the University Church, St. Salvator's. I confess I was a bit apprehensive when I learned that I was to be locked in the pulpit stall until I preached the gospel, but I am glad to report I was let out. Paula and I were in St. Andrews at the beginning of Lent. We are particularly grateful to All Saints Episcopal Church of Scotland and to Rev. Jonathan Mason for making possible our participation in the wonderful liturgies at All Saints. To begin Lent with the Great Litany followed by evensong and the benediction of the Eucharist made this a memorable Lent for us. It is surely a good thing for a Gifford lecturer to come to the end of his lectures confronted with Christ's cross.

1

God and the Gifford Lectures

God, at least the God whom Christians worship, has seldom held center stage in the Gifford Lectures. That the god of the Gifford Lectures is rarely the Trinity is not surprising, given the conditions of Lord Gifford's will and the times and circumstances in which the Gifford Lectures have been presented. The god that various Gifford lecturers have shown to exist or not to exist is a god that bears the burden of proof. In short, the god of the Gifford Lectures is usually a god with a problem. That some Gifford lecturers have actually tried to show that something like a god might exist seems enough of a challenge. For a Gifford lecturer to maintain that the God who exists is the Father, Son, and Holy Spirit seems wildly ambitious, if not foolish.

Yet the heart of the argument I develop in these lectures is that natural theology divorced from a full doctrine of God cannot help but distort the character of God and, accordingly, of the world in which we find ourselves. The metaphysical and existential projects to make a "place" for such a god cannot help but "prove" the existence of a god that is not worthy of worship. The Trinity is not a further specification of a more determinative reality called god, because there is no more determinative reality than the Father, Son, and Holy Spirit. From the perspective of those who think we must first "prove" the existence of god before we can say anything else about god, the claim by Christians that God is Trinity cannot help but appear a "confessional" assertion that is unintelligible for anyone who is not already a Christian.

That God is Trinity is, of course, a confession. The acknowledgment of God's trinitarian character was made necessary by the Christian insistence that the God who had redeemed the world through the cross and resurrection of Jesus was not different from the God of Abraham, Moses, and the prophets. God has never not been Trinity, but only through the struggle to render its own existence intelligible did the church discover God's trinitarian nature. Accordingly, Christians believe rightly that few claims are more rationally compelling than our confession that God is Trinity. Of course, our knowledge that God is Trinity, a knowledge rightly described as revelation, only intensifies the mystery of God's trinitarian nature.

I am acutely aware that claims about God's trinitarian nature seem to be no more than sheer assertion for those whose habit of thought has been nurtured in modernity. Surely there must be a better, or at least more polite, way to begin the Gifford Lectures? Yet I assume that a Gifford lecturer is rightly held to say what he or she takes to be true. And I am a Christian theologian. As such, I am not trying to think a new thought or to rethink an old one in a new way. Rather, I must show why Christians, even Christians who are theologians, can be no more than witnesses. And the very character of that witness is an indication not only of who God is but of why that which exists, that is, God's created order, cannot avoid witnessing to the One who is our beginning and end.

John Milbank has observed that "the pathos of modern theology is its false humility."[1] Theologians, particularly theologians who are paid by universities, too often do theology in a manner that will not offend the peace established by the secular order. Given the requirements of that order, theology cannot help but become one more opinion, one more option, to enliven the dulled imaginations of those who suffer from knowing so much that they no longer know what they know. I hope Milbank's warning about false humility explains why I cannot help but appear impolite, since I must maintain that the God who moves the sun and the stars is the same God who was incarnate in Jesus of Nazareth. Given the politics of modernity, the humility required for those who worship the God revealed in the cross and resurrection of Christ cannot help but appear as arrogance.

That Christian humility cannot avoid appearing arrogant is an indication of why the argument I develop in these lectures entails a politics and an ethics. I show that the very idea that we might know God abstracted from how God makes himself known was the result of the loss of a Christian politics called church. Put in the categories we have

---

1. John Milbank, *Theology and Social Theory: Beyond Secular Reason* (Oxford: Basil Blackwell, 1990), 1. It is extremely important to note Milbank's observation that the problem facing theology is a "false humility." Theology done rightly requires humility just to the extent that the theologian's work is possible only if the theologian submits to authority. Heresy is but the manifestation of pride. See, for example, Alasdair MacIntyre's account of Abelard in *Three Rival Versions of Moral Enquiry: Encyclopaedia, Genealogy, and Tradition* (Notre Dame: University of Notre Dame Press, 1990), 90–91.

learned to use in modernity, I show why ethics cannot be separated from theology. In terms more appropriate to the Christian tradition, I show why the truthfulness of theological claims entails the work they do for the shaping of holy lives.

The title of these lectures, *With the Grain of the Universe*, is a phrase from an essay by John Howard Yoder. The passage that frames this phrase appears as the epigraph to this book, and it is worth repeating here:

> The point that apocalyptic makes is not only that people who wear crowns and who claim to foster justice by the sword are not as strong as they think—true as that is: we still sing, "O where are Kings and Empires now of old that went and came?" It is that people who bear crosses are working with the grain of the universe. One does not come to that belief by reducing social process to mechanical and statistical models, nor by winning some of one's battles for the control of one's own corner of the fallen world. One comes to it by sharing the life of those who sing about the Resurrection of the slain Lamb.[2]

The attempt to develop a natural theology prior to or as grounds for subsequent claims about God cannot help but be mistaken to the extent such a project fails to help us see that there can be no deeper reality-making claim than the one Yoder makes: those who bear crosses work with the grain of the universe. Christians betray themselves as well as their non-Christian brothers and sisters when in the interest of apologetics we say and act as if the cross of Christ is incidental to God's being. In fact, the God we worship and the world God created cannot be truthfully known without the cross, which is why the knowledge of God and ecclesiology—or the politics called church—are interdependent.

Such are the bare bones of the position that I develop in these lectures. Only in the last three lectures will I turn to these claims explicitly, but I state them at the beginning, without argument and qualification, because these are the convictions that have informed the way I have approached these lectures and that have shaped the story I tell. I realize that by stating my views so baldly I risk losing those people who have already decided such theological claims cannot be defended. To these people, I can say only that the proof is in the pudding, and I ask them to have patience—a virtue Christians share with many traditions, but also one that we believe has been given particular form by the worship of the God who would rule all creation from Christ's cross.[3]

---

2. John Howard Yoder, "Armaments and Eschatology," *Studies in Christian Ethics* 1, no. 1 (1988): 58.

3. For a wonderful analysis of patience and the forms it can take, see John Howard Yoder, "Patience as Method in Moral Reasoning: Is an Ethic of Discipleship Absolute?" in *The Wisdom of the Cross: Essays in Honor of John Howard Yoder*, ed. Stanley Hauerwas, Chris Huebner, Harry Huebner, and Mark Thiesson Nation (Grand Rapids: Eerdmans, 1999), 24–42.

Keeping Faith with Adam Gifford

The question remains whether or not the lectures I am about to give are in fact the Gifford Lectures. In this respect, I am at least in good company. Alasdair MacIntyre begins his Gifford Lectures with the same question.[4] MacIntyre observes that the Gifford lecturer is someone who should try to implement the conditions of Lord Gifford's will. Yet MacIntyre does not share Lord Gifford's presumption that a nontraditioned account of rationality is sufficient to make natural theology a subject analogous to the natural sciences. Put more accurately, MacIntyre does not think Adam Gifford's understanding of the natural sciences should be a model for natural theology because Gifford's view distorts the character of science. I suspect that MacIntyre also thinks that our knowledge of God is more certain than the knowledge secured through the natural sciences. To that extent his own views cannot help but be at odds with the assumptions that shaped the provisions of Lord Gifford's will.[5]

The clause from Lord Gifford's will that best indicates the distance between MacIntyre and Gifford says that "the lecturers shall be under no restraint whatever in their treatment of their theme." MacIntyre characterizes this clause as Adam Gifford's "reckless generosity" and uses it to justify his being a Gifford lecturer.[6] From MacIntyre's perspective, to "be under no restraint" is but an indication that we have lost the

---

4. MacIntyre, *Three Rival Versions*, 9.

5. I cannot document this claim, but I make it on the presumption that MacIntyre is a follower of Aquinas on these matters. For example, in response to the question whether sacred doctrine is nobler than the other sciences, Aquinas notes that since sacred science is partly speculative and partly practical, it transcends all other speculative and practical sciences. Sacred science surpasses all other speculative sciences in matters of certitude because the other sciences derive their status from "the natural light of reason, which can err," whereas sacred science derives its certitude from the light of divine knowledge, which cannot be misled. The practical sciences are hierarchically ordered according to the purposes to which they are ordained. Since the purpose of sacred doctrine is eternal bliss, the purpose of every practical science gains its ultimate intelligibility from that end. St. Thomas Aquinas, *Summa Theologica*, trans. the Fathers of the English Dominican Province (Westminster, Md.: Christian Classics, 1948) part 1, question 1, article 5. It may be objected that Aquinas in this article is not dealing with natural theology but with sacred doctrine. But to the extent that natural theology has an integral part in sacred doctrine, I think Aquinas would maintain that the knowledge of God's existence is more certain than what we can know from the other sciences.

A note about references to the *Summa:* hereafter I will offer only the numerals; thus the reference above would appear as 1.1.5. As those familiar with the *Summa* know, it is divided into three parts, and the second part is itself divided into two parts; furthermore, each article is divided into objections and replies to objections. Thus the reference 1-2.3.4.5 would be to the first part of the second part, question 3, article 4, reply to objection 5 (likewise, 2-2 indicates the second part of the second part).

6. MacIntyre, *Three Rival Versions*, 30–31.

possibility of rational argument. Accordingly, MacIntyre traces the increasing incoherence of the modern university to the loss of religious tests for appointments to the professorate.[7] MacIntyre attributes the success of the natural sciences in modern universities to their informal and unstated policy of limiting questions through exclusion. Thus the sciences continue to enjoy a confidence in their ability to tell us the way things are because scientific disciplines do not correspond to Lord Gifford's understanding of rational inquiry. In comparison to the sciences, moral and theological inquiry are now at a disadvantage because the ideological effect of Gifford-like accounts of rationality have relegated such subjects to private opinion.

However, just to the extent MacIntyre is concerned to keep faith with Gifford's will, he honors what I take to be Gifford's concern that those who give the Gifford Lectures should attempt to help us understand how any account of the moral life cannot be divorced from our understanding of the way things are. In Lord Gifford's words, the Gifford Lectures are dedicated to:

"Promoting, Advancing, Teaching, and Diffusing the Study of Natural Theology," in the widest sense of that term, in other words, "The Knowledge of God, the Infinite, the All, the First and Only Cause, the One and the Sole Substance, the Sole Being, the Sole Reality, and the Sole Existence, the Knowledge of His Nature and Attributes, the Knowledge of the Relations which men and the whole universe bear to Him, the Knowledge of the Nature and Foundation of Ethics or Morals, and of all Obligations and Duties thence arising."[8]

MacIntyre hopes that if Lord Gifford were alive today, he *might* be able to recognize as his own MacIntyre's attempt to provide a quite different account of moral rationality and its relation to natural theology.[9] It is quite remarkable that, unlike MacIntyre, many Gifford lecturers have not thought it necessary to attend to the provisions of Gifford's bequest. I take this lack of attention to Gifford's will as a confirmation of MacIntyre's account of the philosophical developments over the cen-

---

7. Ibid., 17–18. MacIntyre does not assume that such tests in themselves are sufficient to sustain rational argument; rather, such tests are effective only if they safeguard agreements that are themselves the result of hard won judgments that constitute a tradition. Such tests are no doubt subject to abuse and may be complicit in wholesale injustice against certain groups (thus the exclusion of Jews from the Scottish university), but the very naming of such injustice requires participation in a tradition that makes such tests at least a possibility. The last chapter of *Three Rival Versions of Moral Enquiry* is a wonderful account of the effects of the loss of such tests on the Scottish university.

8. "Lord Gifford's Will," in Stanley Jaki, *Lord Gifford and His Lectures: A Centenary Retrospective* (Macon, Ga.: Mercer University Press, 1986), 72–73.

9. MacIntyre, *Three Rival Versions*, 25–26.

tury in which the Giffords have been given. In a world in which you can no longer trust your knowledge of how things are, it is unclear why you should keep trust with trusts.

I have called attention to MacIntyre's attempt to justify his Gifford Lectures as the Gifford Lectures because my arguments are even more foreign to the purpose of the Gifford Lectures than MacIntyre's. At the very least, MacIntyre shares with Gifford a profound commitment to philosophy as a master science.[10] Yet I am a theologian. Even worse, I am a theologian who has been profoundly influenced by the work of another Gifford lecturer, Karl Barth. My problem becomes even more acute because I will try to convince you that Karl Barth is the great natural theologian of the Gifford Lectures—at least he is so if you remember that natural theology is the attempt to witness to the nongodforsakenness of the world even under the conditions of sin.[11]

I am aware that this claim will strike many people as problematic at best, and some may even think such a claim borders on being intellectually dishonest. Indeed, I believe it might make Stanley Jaki apoplectic. In

10. I am not suggesting that Gifford would understand philosophy as a master science in the same manner that MacIntyre does, but rather that at least they share the Scottish commitment to philosophy as a way of life. It is not accidental that in the "Introduction" to *Three Rival Versions of Moral Enquiry,* MacIntyre references the work of George Elder Davie for his wonderful accounts of the struggle to maintain philosophy as indispensable for the maintenance of the Scottish tradition (3). MacIntyre observes in *Whose Justice? Which Rationality?* (Notre Dame: University of Notre Dame, 1988) that the title of professor of moral philosophy became central to those who sought to maintain a distinctively Scottish cultural tradition "just because the peculiar and distinctive principles of Scottish law, Scottish education, and Scottish theology depended for their survival on the elaboration of philosophical theories and theses which could underpin those principles and provide for their defense in public debate within Scotland as effectively as the Calvinist Aristotelianism of Baillie had done, but which had also come to terms with the philosophical debates of late seventeenth-century and early eighteenth-century modernity" (258). The hold of that tradition is wonderfully witnessed in Lord Gifford's life, particularly as we learn of his last years in John Gifford's "Recollections of a Brother," in Jaki, *Lord Gifford and His Lectures,* 77–99. John Gifford suggests that it may surprise his friends that Adam Gifford's "heart was never entirely with his profession"; rather, his first love was philosophical theology (95–98). But it is hard to see how anyone who had come through the Scottish educational system would have been surprised that such was the case.

11. In the "Introduction" to the new edition of *Marxism and Christianity* (London: Duckworth, 1995), MacIntyre explains that Christianity had become problematic for him due to his mistaken assumption that the terms in which theology was to be understood were those provided by Karl Barth. "But what Barth's theology proved unable to provide was any practically adequate account of the moral life, and, although I should have known better, I mistakenly took what is a defect in Barth's theology to be a defect in Christianity as such. This judgment seemed to be confirmed by the platitudinous emptiness of liberal Christian moralizing in which the positions of secular liberalism reappeared in various religious guises. And this liberalism, the moral and political counterpart and expression of developing capitalism, I rejected just as I had done in 1953 and for the same reasons" (xx). Although I am sympathetic to MacIntyre's criticism of Barth, I hope to show that Barth's

his overview of the Gifford lecturers, Jaki treats most of the lecturers with respect. He even praises antitheistic Gifford lecturers such as Dewey and Ayer for "touching off a hunger for something more solid and elevated on the part of judicious readers."[12] Jaki shows no such respect for Barth, whom he characterizes as "alone among Christian Gifford lecturers in inveighing against natural theology. He and his followers seem to be strangely myopic to a facet of the much heralded onset of a post-Christian age through the alleged complete secularization of the Western mind."[13] The only thing positive Jaki can say about Barth is that he serves as a witness "to the reluctance of most Christian theologians to cut their moorings from reason, for fear of undercutting their very credibility."[14]

Jaki was equally unimpressed by the lectures given by Reinhold Niebuhr. He notes that from the "viewpoint of philosophy" there is little significance to be gathered from Niebuhr's lectures. "The 'Christian' interpretation which Niebuhr tried to give to the nature and destiny of man was deprived of philosophical foundations and breadth by the short shrift given in his Barthian neo-orthodoxy to metaphysics and epistemology."[15] However much it may seem from the "viewpoint of philosophy" that Niebuhr is a Barthian, it will be the burden of my lectures to show that the difference between Niebuhr and Barth is exactly the difference between a theology that has given up on its ability to tell us the way the world is and a theology that confidently and unapologetically proclaims the way things are—a distinction that is unintelligible if the God Christians worship does not exist.

Like MacIntyre, I hope that in spite of my distance from Lord Gifford's theological convictions, he might recognize what I try to do in these lectures as a trustworthy attempt to keep faith with the provisions of his will.[16] Although I lack MacIntyre's brilliance and learning, I am going to try to do in these lectures something like what he did in *Three Rival Versions of Moral Enquiry.* In those lectures, MacIntyre told the philosophical story since the endowment of the Gifford Lectures. I am going to try

theology has resources that provide for the development of a more adequate ethic. I owe the phrase "nongodforsakenness of the world" to Joe Mangina.

12. Jaki, *Lord Gifford and His Lectures,* 39.

13. Ibid. Jaki's criticism of Barth was voiced earlier by Brand Blanshard, when he was giving the Gifford Lectures at St. Andrews in 1952. His criticism of Barth was reported in *The Scotsman* (April 9, 1952), which occasioned a fascinating exchange of letters between Blanshard and T. F. Torrance. I will discuss their exchange later.

14. Ibid.

15. Ibid., 26.

16. In "Recollections of a Brother," John Gifford reports that Adam Gifford admired Spinoza but denied that he was a pantheist, marking the distinction thus: "Spinoza holds that everything is God. I hold that God is everything; if I were to assume a name descriptive of my belief, I should be called a Theopanist." Jaki, *Lord Gifford and His Lectures,* 98. I confess that I take this to be a case of a "rose by any other name is still a rose."

to tell the theological story. By so doing, I hope to show, like MacIntyre, that Lord Gifford was right to think that the truthfulness of our theological convictions is inseparable from questions of how we are to live.

I hope it will be evident not only from the form but from the substance of these lectures that I have learned much from MacIntyre. I should make clear, however, that as much as I would like to use MacIntyre to support the position I develop, to do so would be unfair. MacIntyre and I differ, and not simply due to my pacifism (though that is not unrelated). Rather, we differ in our understandings of the relationship between philosophy and theology. For example, in response to the suggestion that his most recent philosophical positions conceal a reassertion of Christianity, MacIntyre declares:

> It is false, both biographically and with respect to the structure of my beliefs. What I now believe philosophically I came to believe very largely before I reacknowledged the truth of Catholic Christianity. And I was only able to respond to the teachings of the Church because I had already learned from Aristotelianism both the nature of the mistakes involved in my earlier rejection of Christianity, and how to understand aright the relation of philosophical argument to theological inquiry. My philosophy, like that of many other Aristotelians, is theistic; but it is as secular in its content as any other.[17]

I have no stake in denying that philosophy has a history that can be told in a manner that separates the work of philosophy from theology, or that philosophy as a discipline, particularly in the modern university, has its own canons of excellence. Nor do I think that philosophy has no other purpose than to be a handmaid to theology. Yet the strong distinction MacIntyre maintains between philosophy and theology—such that philosophy represents a secular discipline—does justice neither to

---

17. Alasdair MacIntyre, "An interview with Giovanna Borradori," in *The MacIntyre Reader,* ed. Kelvin Knight (Notre Dame: University of Notre Dame Press, 1998), 265–266. MacIntyre gave this interview in 1991. In the new "Introduction" to *Marxism and Christianity,* MacIntyre explains that what he discovered in Aristotle was how any account of rationality requires an articulation of the embodiment of concepts presupposed by practices, as well as how "such concepts themselves need to be understood in terms of their functioning within just those same modes of practice." Having adopted this Aristotelian standpoint, MacIntyre discovered "that I had thereby discarded philosophical assumptions that had been at the root of my difficulties with substantive Christian orthodoxy. And the removal of these barriers was one, even if only one, necessary stage in my coming to acknowledge the truth of the biblical Christianity of the Catholic church." MacIntyre notes that he also came to understand better that in spite of much that was right about official Catholic condemnations of Marxism, Catholic theologians failed to see that Marx was right to focus on the close relationship of theory to practice. Marxists rightly see that any type of theory, whether scientific or theological or political, when divorced from the practical contexts in which it is at home, becomes too easily a free-floating body of thought

the complex relationship between philosophy and theology in Aquinas, the thinker MacIntyre most admires, nor to MacIntyre's own historicist commitments.[18]

I do not think that to be valid, philosophy—or any other science—must be shown to "depend" on our knowledge of God. Aquinas certainly did not construe the relationship between theology and the other sciences in this way:

> The principles of other sciences either are evident and cannot be proved, or are proved by natural reason through some other science. But the knowledge proper to this science comes through revelation, and not through natural reason. Therefore it has no concern to prove the principles of the other sciences, but only to judge them. Whatsoever is found in other sciences contrary to any truth of this science, must be condemned as false: "Destroying counsels and every height that exalted itself against the knowledge of God." (2 Cor. 10:4–5)[19]

Bruce Marshall observes that Aquinas did not think that we can or should deduce what we ought to believe about medicine or architecture

---

that is apt to be transformed into an ideology. "So when Catholic theology is in good order, its peculiar work is to assist in making intelligible in a variety of contexts of practice what the church teaches authoritatively as the Word of God revealed to it and to the world." According to MacIntyre, when theology does not subordinate itself to that teaching it cannot help but become one more set of religious opinions. Such opinions may be interesting, but they function quite differently from theology in service to the church (xxviii–xxix). It will become obvious that I share MacIntyre's understanding of practice, but exactly because I do, I find it hard to understand why he seems to make such a sharp distinction between the work of theology and the work of philosophy.

18. MacIntyre's strong claim for the independence of philosophy from theology is all the more puzzling in that it seems to put him on the side of Scotus. In *Three Rival Versions,* he criticizes Scotus who, in contrast to Aquinas, set the stage for the autonomy of philosophy (155–156). Nor does MacIntyre explain what he means by "secular," but I take him to mean no more than "not revelation." Yet such a view of the secular, which is surely to be distinguished from any views that would defend the self-sufficiency of the secular, is not innocent. My worry is that MacIntyre's understanding of the secular may be analogous to some of the neo-Scholastic accounts of nature that resulted in making grace little more than an "add-on."

I am aware that MacIntyre's "historicism" is not easily characterized. See, for example, Robert Stern's, "MacIntyre and Historicism," in *After MacIntyre: Critical Perspectives on the Work of Alasdair MacIntyre,* ed. John Horton and Susan Mendus (Notre Dame: University of Notre Dame Press, 1994), 146–160. In his response to Stern, MacIntyre expresses appreciation for Stern's constructive defense of his work, but contrary to Stern, he does not believe his historicism requires elimination of the place of truth as part of any inquiry. In this context, I wish only to question whether a history of philosophy as a self-justifying activity is, on MacIntyre's own grounds, possible. Such a history of philosophy seems to be the result of the professionalization of philosophy in the modern university, which has led to the kind of specialization against which MacIntyre's whole project is advanced.

19. Aquinas, *Summa Theologica,* 1.1.6.2.

from the articles of faith. The reasons we have for holding the vast majority of our beliefs need not be derived from the basic principles of the faith. Yet, according to Marshall, exactly because Aquinas presupposes Aristotle's understanding of science "as a set of interpreted sentences tied in logically tight ways to other interpreted sentences which are themselves either proven or beyond proof and doubt alike," Aquinas rightly maintained that *sacra doctrina* could and must stand in judgment on the other sciences.[20]

I am not suggesting that MacIntyre disagrees with Aquinas's claim that *sacra doctrina* can and must judge the other sciences, including philosophy. Indeed, I assume that MacIntyre believes his statements about the secular character of philosophy are but restatements of Aquinas' own views. Yet if theology (which is not the same as *sacra doctrina*) can stand in judgment of philosophy, then the relation between philosophy and theology is at least more complex than MacIntyre's stated views suggest.[21] My disagreements with MacIntyre may appear to be simply a quibble, but at stake is the very status of theological knowledge. The strong distinction MacIntyre seems to make between philosophy and theology threatens to underwrite the modern presumption that in com-

20. Bruce Marshall, "Faith and Reason Reconsidered: Aquinas and Luther on Deciding What Is True," *The Thomist* 63 (1999): 18–19. Marshall says the practices of medicine and architecture do not need theological justification, but he does not say that about philosophy. It would be a mistake to make too much of this point, but at the very least I think the absence of philosophy suggests that what philosophers do, which can be done independent of theology, often appears to be more similar to theology than to medicine and architecture. It is my own view, however, that medicine and architecture are determinative philosophical disciplines, or at least entail philosophical questions, which suggests that it is important for theologians to attend to them as disciplines that often raise theological questions.

In a fascinating footnote, Marshall argues that Aquinas thought that the *principia per se nota* are subject to theological judgment just to the extent that we can decide whether we have a principle known only in itself or by seeing whether the belief in question is consistent with the articles of faith. I am indebted to Marshall for the illuminating account of Aquinas he has developed not only in the quite remarkable series of articles he has published over the years, but now in his book *Trinity and Truth* (Cambridge: Cambridge University Press, 2000).

Alfred Freddoso develops an account of the relation of philosophy to theology that I find quite compatible with my own views in his essay "Two Roles for Catholic Philosophers," in *Recovering Nature: Essays in Natural Philosophy, Ethics, and Metaphysics in Honor of Ralph McInerny*, ed. Thomas Hibbs and John O'Callaghan (Notre Dame: University of Notre Dame Press, 1999), 229–252.

21. Perhaps the point I am trying to make can be put more clearly in terms of MacIntyre's understanding of the virtues. For example, in his *Dependent Rational Animals: Why Human Beings Need the Virtues* (Chicago: Open Court, 1999), MacIntyre observes that Aquinas treats *misericordia* as one of the effects of charity, and since charity is a theological virtue, "an incautious reader might suppose that Aquinas does not recognize it as a secular virtue. But this would be a mistake. Charity in the form of *misericordia* is recognizably at work in

parison to our other beliefs about the way things are, theology cannot help but be question-begging.[22]

For example, Aquinas's characterization of the knowledge that is proper to theology—that is, knowledge that "comes through revelation"—seems to name for many today a knowledge that is incapable of rational defense. Yet Aquinas assumes the opposite. For Aquinas, knowledge attained by "natural reason" is not more certain than that attained by revelation; "natural" and "revelation" do not name epistemological alternatives.[23] Thus, those who attempt in the name of Aquinas to develop a "natural theology"—that is, a philosophical defense of "theism" as a propaedeutic for any further "confessional" claims one might want to make—are engaged in an enterprise that Aquinas would not recognize. I do not assume that MacIntyre's understanding of the rela-

---

the secular world and the authorities whom Aquinas cites on its nature, and whose disagreements he aspires to resolve, include Sallust and Cicero as well as Augustine. *Misericordia* then has its place in the catalogue of the virtues, independently of its theological grounding" (124). Though accurate, MacIntyre's point here fails to attend to Aquinas's claim that charity is the form of the virtues just to the extent that without charity, *misericordia* will be disordered, if it is not, as all the virtues require, properly ordered to its proper end. Of course, Christians expect to discover the virtues in our non-Christian brothers and sisters. Moreover, in this time when we are all "wayfarers," the embodiment of the virtues in the lives of Christians cannot help but be disordered. But the difference between those who are Christians and those who are not is that Christians have been made part of God's economy sufficiently to locate for one another the disordered character of our lives. So we cannot assume that the *misericordia* made possible by God's grace, although certainly analogous to the pity we find characteristic of others, is the "same" virtue, since every virtue is determined by its relation to the other virtues.

22. The crucial issue for many people today, of course, is not whether theology can tell you anything about the way the world is, but whether any discipline, and in particular philosophy, can pretend to tell us anything about the way the world is. In these lectures, I do not pretend to do justice to the technical philosophical issues required for any close arguments in defense of how some propositions, particularly as they are considered in relation to other propositions, can tell us something about the way things are. I do think, however, that the arguments I will develop are defensible. See, for example, Grady Scott Davis's defense of Yoder's understanding of theology in the light of James Gustafson's challenge: "Tradition and Truth in Christian Ethics: John Yoder and the Bases of Biblical Realism," in *The Wisdom of the Cross*, 278–305. At the very least, I hope the argument I am trying to make is sufficient to show that the contrast between "theology based on reason alone" and "revealed theology" is a false alternative just to the extent that "reason" draws on the conceptual resources that are given to it through traditions of inquiry. Accordingly, there is no contrast that can be drawn between theology that is "natural" and theology that is "something else." I am indebted to Michael Quirk for helping me see better how the contrast between revealed and natural theology is implicated in questionable epistemological assumptions.

23. As I will indicate below, it is, of course, from MacIntyre that I learned not to read Aquinas as an "epistemologist." Fortunately, the history of medieval philosophy that has been shaped by the presumption that medieval theologians maintained a sharp distinction between faith and reason (where those categories are assumed to name epistemologi-

tionship between theology and philosophy is implicated in such a mis-understanding of Aquinas, but I fear that his views may give aid and comfort to those who assume that theology is beyond reason.

On the Unnatural Nature of Natural Theology

Lord Gifford expressed the wish for "the lectures to treat their subject as a strictly natural science, the greatest of all possible sciences, indeed, in one sense, the only science, that of Infinite Being, without reference to or reliance upon any supposed special exceptional or so-called mirac-ulous revelation."[24] Given what I have said so far, it should be clear that I do not agree with Lord Gifford's understanding of natural theology. Lord Gifford had every reason to think that his understanding of natu-ral theology was unexceptional; but in fact his understanding of natural theology as a necessary prolegomenon to test the rationality of theology proper was a rather recent development.

For example, though Aquinas's Prima Pars of the *Summa* is often iden-tified as "natural theology," Aquinas never so described his work. George Hendry observes that it is seldom noticed that the so-called proofs for the existence of God were perfected at a time when the exist-ence of God was barely questioned. Calling attention to what he calls Aquinas's "little coda" that ends each of the five ways—"and this every-one understands to be God"—Hendry notes that the problem in the time of Aquinas "was not really to persuade people to believe in God, but to help them to relate their belief in God to the nature and condi-tions of the world and to see that their belief in God and their under-standing of the world mutually illumine each other."[25]

---

cal alternatives) is increasingly being called into question. For example, see John Inglis, "Philosophical Autonomy and the Historiography of Medieval Philosophy," *British Journal of the History of Philosophy* 5, no. 1 (1997): 21–53; *Spheres of Philosophical Inquiry and the Historiog-raphy of Medieval Philosophy* (Leiden: Brill, 1998). Inglis rightly argues that none of the great medieval theologians—for example, Aquinas, Scotus, or Ockham—maintained a strict dis-tinction between philosophy (reason) and theology (faith). According to Inglis, they sim-ply had no interest in speculative inquiry into human understanding for its own sake. Calling attention to Aquinas's *De Veritate*, Inglis observes in his article that Aquinas explores questions of human understanding only as a way to show how "human self-understanding is *analogous* to divine self-understanding because when human beings reflect on their own intellectual activity, they analogously represent the self-referential understanding of God" (46). MacIntyre would seem to agree with Inglis's account, which makes all the more puzzling his strict distinction between philosophy and theology. I am indebted to Professor Terry Tilley for calling my attention to Inglis's important work.

24. "Lord Gifford's Will," 74.

25. George Hendry, *Theology of Nature* (Philadelphia: The Westminster Press, 1980), 14. The "little coda" is, of course, found in *Summa Theologica*, 1.2.3. Cornelius Ernst, O.P., de-

In a similar fashion Nicholas Wolterstorff argues that

> the medieval project of natural theology was profoundly different from
> the Enlightenment project of evidentialist apologetics. It had different
> goals, presupposed different convictions, and was evoked by a different
> situation. It is true that some of the same arguments occur in both
> projects; they migrate from the one to the other. But our recognition of the
> identity of the émigré must not blind us to the fact that he has migrated
> from one "world" to another.[26]

Wolterstorff characterizes "evidentialist apologetics" as the frame of
mind that assumes that unless one has good reasons for one's theistic beliefs, one ought to give them up. According to Wolterstorff, evidential-
ists hold that "belief is assumed guilty until it proves its innocence by
evidence."[27] Locke, according to Wolterstorff, is the great representative
of the evidentialist perspective just to the extent that Locke sought to defeat Enthusiasm by shifting the burden of proof to those who claimed
certainty. Locke thought it important to defeat Enthusiasm because
from his perspective the Enthusiasts were socially pernicious. According to Locke, not only did the Enthusiasts threaten social disruption,
but they put forward an account of religion that violated one's dignity
as a human being.[28] Locke sought to defeat the Enthusiasts by developing what Wolterstorff characterizes as a foundationalist theory of justified belief, that is, the theory that a belief can be a rational belief only if
it is grounded in certitude, whether immediately or mediately.

Wolterstorff argues that this kind of foundationalist project makes
sense only in our modern situation. Without religious and moral pluralism, foundationalism would lack social urgency or relevance. The secularization of society is therefore the breeding ground for the attempt to
develop foundationalist epistemologies and for the correlative fear that
if we surrender the assumption that our beliefs can be grounded, then

---

scribes what Aquinas was doing with the "proofs" in this way: "Our ordinary contexts for
'God' (prayer, ritual, even swearing) are ways of life and behavior which are discriminated
from ways of life and behavior which are tacitly identified as everyday and which count
to make the language which belongs to them 'literal.' The point of the five ways was to
show how one might go on speaking of 'God' in the ordinary world." See *Multiple Echo:
Explorations in Theology*, ed. Fergus Kerr, O.P., and Timothy Radcliffe, O.P. (London: Dalton, Longman, and Todd, 1979), 74.

26. Nicholas Wolterstorff, "The Migration of the Theistic Arguments: From Natural
Theology to Evidentialist Apologetics," in *Rationality, Religious Belief, and Moral Commitment:
New Essays in the Philosophy of Religion*, ed. Robert Audi and William Wainwright (Ithaca:
Cornell University Press, 1986), 39.

27. Ibid., 38.

28. Ibid., 43. By "Enthusiasm" Locke meant forms of Christianity that were based in
the emotions rather than in reason.

"anything goes." As Wolterstorff puts it: "Foundationalism or antinomianism: that gaunt *either/or* has seemed obviously true to most reflective modern intellectuals. The alternative to grounding is thought to be arbitrary dogmatism."[29]

The alternative between foundationalism or antinomianism simply did not exist for Aquinas. In MacIntyre's terms, Aquinas was not an "epistemologist."[30] Rather, what we now call Aquinas's natural theology was intrinsic to his understanding of Aristotelian science and how such a science must proceed if we are to avoid making God but another item among the things in the world.[31] God, the creator of all that is, cannot be—as the evidentialist enterprise assumes—part of the metaphysical furniture of the universe. In the words of John of Damascus: "God does not belong to the class of existing things, not that God has not existence but that God is above all things, no even above existence itself."[32]

Aquinas's account of our natural knowledge of God is an exploration of the implication that the divine essence cannot be a genus because of the very way in which essence is found in God. As Joseph Bobik puts the matter, for Aquinas *"what God is* is Existence, i.e., the Divine Essence is Existence."[33] Accordingly God can be known only through effects, which means that our knowledge of God is not just accidentally analogical but necessarily so. As Aquinas puts it: "Although we cannot know

29. Ibid., 55. Wolterstorff observes that one of the striking facts about the Enlightenment mentality is that though science no more fits the foundationalist canons than does religion, many people continue to assume that something about science makes Christianity problematic.

30. MacIntyre notes that in *Aeterni Patris,* epistemological questions are never raised; as a result Leo XIII remained true to Aquinas. That was not the case, however, with those who responded to *Aeterni Patris.* Too often they followed Kleutgen, whose revival of Thomism was done in Kantian terms. "And in so doing they doomed Thomism to the fate of all philosophies which give priority to epistemological questions: the indefinite multiplication of disagreement. There are just too many alternative ways to begin." *Three Rival Versions of Moral Enquiry,* 75.

31. Eugene Rogers has helped us see how Aquinas used Aristotle's "scientia"; see *Thomas Aquinas and Karl Barth: Sacred Doctrine and the Natural Knowledge of God* (Notre Dame: University of Notre Dame, 1995), 17–70.

32. Quoted in William Placher, *Domestication of Transcendence: How Modern Thinking about God Went Wrong* (Louisville: Westminster/John Knox, 1996), 10.

33. Joseph Bobik, *Aquinas on Being and Essence: A Translation and Interpretation* (Notre Dame: University of Notre Dame Press, 1965), 215. Bobik's work on Aquinas is as important as it is unknown; unfortunately, his work has been ignored. Aquinas repeats his argument in the *Summa Theologica,* 1.3.4: "Since in God there is no potentiality, it follows that in Him essence does not differ from existence. Therefore His essence is His existence. Just as that which has fire, but is not itself fire, is on fire by participation; so that which has existence but is not existence, is a being by participation. But God is His own essence; if, therefore, He is not His own existence he will be not essential, but participated being. He will not therefore be the first being—which is absurd. Therefore God is His own existence, and not merely His own essence."

in what consists the essence of God, nevertheless in this science we make use of His effects, either of nature or of grace, in place of a definition, in regard to whatever is treated of in this science concerning God; even as in some philosophical sciences we demonstrate something about a cause from its effect, by taking the effect in place of a definition of the cause."[34]

From Aquinas's perspective, if we could have the kind of evidence of God the evidentialist desires, then we would have evidence that the God Christians worship does not exist. But one may well ask: If this account of Aquinas is right, what are we to make of the arguments for the existence of God in Question Two of the Prima Pars? The answer is simple, given Aquinas's understanding of science and how such science contributes to our happiness as creatures of a good God.[35]

For Aquinas, the best order of human learning is the order of existence. But this does not mean, as is often presumed this side of modernity, that Aquinas begins with as minimal account of God as possible in order to then "add" thicker theological descriptions. The *Summa* is, as Timothy L. Smith argues, trinitarian from beginning to end. Aquinas's ordering principle, *ordo rerum*, does not require that he must first establish God's existence by philosophical argument in order then to make claims about God's trinitarian nature. Rather,

> the unity of this science, *sacra doctrina*, demands that all remain under or within the *ratio* of being divinely "revealable." As Thomas attempts to find a rational basis for some of those beliefs, he is pursuing a deeper under-

34. Aquinas, *Summa Theologica*, 1.1.7.1. Aquinas's understanding of rationality was nicely exemplified in an exchange of letters in the *New York Review of Books* 46, no. 3 (February 18, 1999) concerning the rationality of Thomas Kuhn's understanding of science. A philosopher of science, Alex Levine, wrote protesting an article by Steven Weinberg that seemed to suggest that Kuhn's account of the history of science made science an irrational process. In response, Levine, I think rightly, argued that that was not Kuhn's view because the very claim that science is irrational would depend on a prior account of rationality. "But for Kuhn, ever the scientist, our best hope of understanding what rationality is resides in the study of *paradigm cases* of rational activity. Since science is the best such case, the claim that science is irrational is, for him, not only objectionable, it is downright incoherent" (49). I suspect that Professor Levine might think theology is irrational, but his account of Kuhn's understanding of rationality follows the same logic as Aquinas's claim that sacred doctrine is more noble than the other sciences (*Summa Theologica*, 1.1.5). The presumption in our times that theology is at a disadvantage in comparison to science for helping us understand the way things are is at least partly due to deficient accounts of the activity of science.

35. Wolterstorff rightly argues that for Aquinas the exploration of our natural knowledge of God is part of the believer's desire to, as Aquinas puts it, "think out and take to heart whatever reasons he can find in support thereof." Of course not every believer has the time or inclination to follow this path, but that some do is a good thing. To demonstrate some of the things we "unseeingly took on faith, so that now we 'see' them to be true, that is a step toward felicity." Wolterstorff, "Migration of the Theistic Arguments," 71.

standing with the belief that the object of faith is intelligible in itself if not to us in this life. The reasoning upon the faith will typically but not exclusively involve the manifestation of that faith where reason cannot attain of its own accord. Revelation, however, provides the more certain and complete knowledge. The argument from authority never gives up its place to rational argument, though rational argument may be employed where the authority of revelation is retained. As one commentator puts it, the whole of the first 43 questions of ST 1 are "a single and unified treatise of revealed theology called 'De Deo.'" The argument from authority, that is, from the authority of revelation, always reigns as the more certain and complete.[36]

For Aquinas, arguments from revelation carry more authority, but we are creatures created to desire God, which means that God is implicated in desires as fundamental as satisfying hunger and as complex as the longing for friendship. Thus, even without revelation, we all have some intimations of God. But Aquinas says that to pursue these intimations solely through reason is not sufficient:

> The truth about God such as reason could discover would only be known by a few, and that after a long time, and with the admixture of many errors. Whereas man's whole salvation, which is in God, depends upon the knowledge of the truth. Therefore, in order that the salvation of men might be brought about more fitly and more surely, it was necessary that they should be taught divine truths by divine revelation. It was therefore necessary that, besides philosophical science built up by reason there should be a sacred science learned through revelation.[37]

The existence of God, then, which can be known by natural reason, is rightly understood as a preamble to the articles of faith, but "preamble" does not mean that the truthfulness of the articles of faith must await for such preambles to be established before their truth can be known.[38] Indeed, Aquinas even doubts whether unbelievers can be said to believe in "a God," since Christians understand such belief in relation to the act of faith. "For they do not believe that God exists under the conditions that faith determines; hence they do not truly believe in a God, since, as the Philosopher observes (Metaphysics, 9, 22) 'to know simple things defectively is not to know them at all.'"[39]

36. Timothy L. Smith, "Thomas Aquinas's *De Deo*: Setting the Record Straight on His Theological Method," *Sapientia* 53, no. 203 (1998): 135–136.

37. Aquinas, *Summa Theologica*, 1.1.

38. For Aquinas's discussion of the so-called proofs as preambles, see *Summa Theologica*, 1.2.2.1.

39. Aquinas, *Summa Theologica*, 2-2.2.2.3. Indeed, Aquinas explicitly notes that the Platonists said that there is one supreme god, the cause of all things, yet this did not prevent them from worshiping heavenly bodies and demons. According to Aquinas, "natural the-

This brief account of Aquinas's understanding of the status of our natural knowledge of God does not do justice to the complexity of his understanding of the status such knowledge has for Christian theology. I will take up these matters in much greater detail when I turn to Barth. I have sought at this stage simply to raise some questions about Lord Gifford's assumption, an assumption widely shared, that something called "natural theology" is a given that can clearly be distinguished from theology proper. I intend to show that Christian theologians' acceptance of Lord Gifford's account of natural theology is one of the reasons that Christian theology in our time suffers from the pathos of false humility.

What Happened to Make Natural Theology Seem So Natural?

If I am right that Lord Gifford's understanding of natural theology is anything but natural, the question remains: What happened so that anyone who thinks otherwise now seems to bear the burden of proof? The shorthand answer is something called "modernity," whose agent is identified as "The Enlightenment." Behind these developments lies (what Protestants call) the Reformation—which is often credited with creating, at least for Europe, the "problem of pluralism." That problem, as Wolterstorff notes, set the agenda for Locke and the many followers of Locke who try to secure a peace between the warring religions, insuring that we share something in common more determinative than our particularistic convictions about God. Equally important, if not more so for the development of natural theology, has been the rise of science and, in particular, the social sciences correlative to the development of capitalist political economies, for which God can appear only as an "externality."[40]

I do not pretend to have the erudition or insight to make the connections necessary to tell the full story that has made natural theology seem so natural for us. The argument I develop in these lectures will betray the influence of those like MacIntyre, Milbank, and Funkenstein, who have helped us understand better the world that inhabits us.[41] In

ology" is to be associated both with those who maintain that the whole world, by which they mean the world-soul, is to be worshiped and with the views of the Platonists. From Aquinas's perspective, such "natural theology" is but a form of idolatry. *Summa Theologica*, 2-2.94.1. I am indebted to Russell Hittinger for reminding me of Aquinas's understanding of idolatry.

40. This way of putting the matter obviously reflects my debt to the argument John Milbank develops in *Theology and Social Theory*.

41. The difficulty of putting it all together (so to speak) can be illustrated by simply asking how one can understand the similarities and differences between MacIntyre's,

what ways I get the history of these developments right is best tested in the light of the overall story I tell. It is important, however, that I make clear that I do not assume my account of modernity is necessarily one of declension. Though I admire and am attracted to many of the movements and figures we associate with what we call the Middle Ages, I do not assume the latter to be some golden age from which modernity names a fall.

My reasons for not making the story of our time the story of "the fall" are theological. The gospel, the good news Christians have been given, the good news that we believe is embodied in the church, is not "at home" in this world. The assumption that the Middle Ages represents a time when Christians "got it right" not only does an injustice to the complexity of the times and places so named, but also betrays the gospel requirement that even in a world that understands itself to be Christian, faithful witness is no less required for the truth that is Christ to be known. When Christianity is tempted to become a civilizational religion in a manner that makes witness secondary to knowing the truth about God, Christians lose the skills necessary to make known to themselves and others how what we believe is true to the way things are. The very attempt to tell the story of modernity as one of decline from a genuinely Christian world ironically underwrites the assumption that the story that Christianity *is* is inseparable from the story of Western culture.

I have earned what I hope is a well deserved reputation for attacking modernity, but in some ways modernity is an appropriate protest against Christian presumption.[42] The protest against God in the name

---

Milbank's, and Funkenstein's accounts of the transition to modernity. [With the latter reference, I am referring to Amos Funkenstein, *Theology and the Scientific Imagination from the Middle Ages to the Seventeenth Century* (Princeton: Princeton University Press, 1986)]. Charles Taylor's *Sources of the Self: The Making of Modern Identity* (Cambridge: Harvard University Press, 1989) must also be taken into account in order to try to get some understanding of where we are.

42. Some people may think my attacks on modernity lack a complex view of the reality "modernity" seeks to name, but I am ready to take that risk. Too often, attempts to characterize modernity die the death of countless qualifications. I am, however, not without allies in support of my understanding of modernity. For example, Matthew Bagger, in his *Religious Experience, Justification, and History* (Cambridge: Cambridge University Press, 1999), argues that "the rise of human self-assertion following the breakdown of the medieval world-view captures the central features of modern thought and culture. Modernity represents the outcome of a dialectic motivated by contradictions within medieval theology. Self-assertion requires that humans give to themselves the standards of thought and action rather than seeking them from an external source, like God" (212). Bagger's view is significant because he thinks this is a good development that is now so completely entrenched in the institutions of modernity that it has become "irrational" to believe in God. Bagger's argument is admirable for its epistemological humility—that is, all he claims is that this is the way it is for those of us who share the common features of modern life.

of humanity was and continues to be a tragic and misguided, but perhaps necessary, attempt to humble Christians whose lives have been constituted by a pride incompatible with the humility that should come from the worship of a crucified God. One of the forms of the price we pay for that protest is called natural theology.

A detailed account of how natural theology came to seem so natural would certainly include the story Michael Buckley tells in his magisterial book *At the Origins of Modern Atheism*.[43] Just as Milbank rightly reminds us at the beginning of *Theology and Social Theory* that once there was no "secular," so Buckley reminds us that once there was no atheism with the correlative demand to develop a response called natural theology.[44] Buckley is surely right that the great curiosity of our time is how the issue of Christianity versus atheism became a purely philosophical one. I think he is also right to suggest that this curiosity has everything to do with developments in Christian theology in which it was assumed that the reality of God must be secured on grounds separate from Christology.[45] According to Buckley, Leonard Lessius and Marin Mersenne prepared the way for deism (and the atheism only deism could produce) in an attempt to develop an apologetic strategy that assumed a Stoic conception of a mechanistic universe in which a god was still necessary to the extent some comprehensive principle is necessary for such a world.[46]

There is a great dispute about how to explain this development of an account of the universe in which God has no place, as well as about who is to be blamed for it. If what I have argued concerning Aquinas's understanding of our natural knowledge of God is correct, then I think Buckley is wrong to suggest that Aquinas is the culprit. Buckley alleges that Aquinas began the *Summa* assuming he must develop philosophically a doctrine of the one God.[47] Following David Burrell, Milbank

---

Of course, one of the reasons I admire Bagger's atheism is that he makes clear why I must contend that the argument I am making in this book cannot be divorced from a politics and an ethics. For example, Bagger observes that we have no epistemological or metaphysical guarantee that epistemic values could not change, thereby making possible supernatural explanations that might once again become rationally acceptable. Bagger, however, is quick to note that "such a turn of events defies the imagination" (227). I hope to show, if not convince Bagger and those who share his position, that Barth has helped us see what a Christian "defiance" must look like—a defiance, for example, that denies that Bagger's distinction between the natural and the supernatural makes sense.

43. Michael Buckley, S.J. (New Haven: Yale University Press, 1987).

44. I am referring to the opening line of the first chapter of *Theology and Social Theory*, 9.

45. Buckley, *At the Origins of Modern Atheism*, 47.

46. Ibid., 37–66.

47. Ibid., 66. Buckley is no doubt right to suggest that some read and continue to read Aquinas in this fashion. But such a reading requires a studied inattention to the first question of the Prima Pars. Nicholas Lash has rightly challenged Buckley's reading of Aquinas;

rightly argues that Aquinas's understanding of analogy and his correlative understanding of the creature's participation in God mean that Aquinas's philosophical analysis is always in service to his theology.[48] According to Milbank, it was John Duns Scotus, not Aquinas, who set theology on the path that culminated in Lessius, just to the extent that Scotus distinguished metaphysics as a philosophical science concerning being from theology as a science concerning God. As a result, being was understood univocally because Scotus argued that to insure our knowledge of God, existence must be an attribute of God as well as of God's creatures. Milbank argues that to understand existence in this way leaves no room for an analogical relationship between God and God's creation, nor between one creature and another, and thus fails to account for the only difference that matters, namely, that between God and God's creation. On Milbank's reading, Scotus prepared the way for the nihilism that comes to full flower in modernity.[49]

Others, following the trail that led to Descartes, think the problems that currently confront us began with Cardinal Cajetan's assumption

---

see "When Did the Theologians Lose Interest in Theology," in *Theology and Dialogue: Essays in Conversation with George Lindbeck,* ed. Bruce Marshall (Notre Dame: University of Notre Dame Press, 1990), 131–147.

48. Milbank refers to David Burrell's *Analogy and Philosophical Language* (New Haven: Yale University Press, 1973), 95–119. Burrell's work over the years has been a wonderful development of the argument he began in this book.

49. Milbank, *Theology and Social Theory,* 302–306. Milbank's arguments have been developed further by Catherine Pickstock in *After Writing: On the Liturgical Consummation of Philosophy* (Oxford: Blackwell Publishers, 1998), 122–125; see also, Phillip Blond, "Introduction" to *Post-Secular Philosophy: Between Philosophy and Theology,* ed. Phillip Blond (London: Routledge, 1998), 3–9. I confess that I have not done the hard work necessary to confirm or criticize these accounts of Scotus's alleged "mistakes." Fergus Kerr at least makes clear that the story is much more complex; see "Why Medievalists Should Talk to Theologians," *New Blackfriars* 80, nos. 941 and 942 (July/August): 369–375. Kerr rightly suggests that Scotus's understanding of predication is more complex than either Milbank or Pickstock suggests. Also, the story Inglis tells in *Spheres of Philosophical Inquiry and the Historiography of Medieval Philosophy,* particularly his critique of the alleged dichotomy between reason and revelation in the Middle Ages, rightly makes the gross generalization about the difference between Aquinas, Scotus, and Ockham problematic. In his appreciative but critical review of Pickstock's *After Writing,* David B. Hart echoes Kerr's worry. In particular, Hart suggests that Pickstock's reading of Scotus is wrong because Scotus had no universal ontology. Rather Scotus, in the Franciscian-Augustianian tradition, understood being as the "coincidence of the transcendentals in God's utterly transcendent *esse verum.*" So, according to Hart, Scotus did not elevate being over God or assume that God and creatures *are* in the same way. See David B. Hart, "Review Essay: Catherine Pickstock, *After Writing," Pro Ecclesia* 9, no. 3 (summer, 2000): 367–372. The quotation can be found on page 370. Perhaps more important, Hart raises issue with Pickstock's assumption that Plato is an alternative to Derrida, noting that both represent regimes of power that attempt to police the flow of time. I am indebted to my colleague and friend David Aers for trying to keep me straight on these issues.

that the doctrine of analogy was just that, a doctrine, which required something like Scotus's account of being.[50] It is then Francisco Suarez who is usually blamed for compounding Cajetan's error by attempting to defend an attributive account of analogy to insure our knowledge of God.[51] MacIntyre thinks Suarez's distortion of Aquinas is even more fundamental to the extent that Suarez presents Aquinas's work as a finished system that makes Aquinas's indebtedness to his sources an accidental feature of his position. As a result, Suarez makes possible an interpretation of Aquinas as an epistemologist, so that it appears that Aquinas is trying to present a finished "system." Joseph Kleutgen's Kantian recovery of Aquinas made this interpretation of Aquinas all the more persuasive, just to the extent that Suarez thinks "the mind in apprehending necessary truths about possible essences apprehends what may, but need not, exist." This cannot help, according to MacIntyre, but lead to Descartes' assumption that some foundation is necessary to secure the transition from our apprehensions of essence to judgments of particular existence.[52]

For the argument I make in these lectures, it is not necessary for me to take sides in these debates about "when it was done and who did it." Although I am sure that ideas matter and that it may take centuries for the results of a mistaken idea to bear fruit, I remain suspicious of attempts to lay the birth of modernity at the door of Scotus or Suarez. That we live in an age in which the church is but another voluntary agency and theology, at best, one subject among others in the curriculum of universities is the result not just of mistakes in the thirteenth century but of the effect of innovations such as the clock that intellectuals (exactly because we are intellectuals) are prone to discount. (Of course, I am aware that clocks are also the result of ideas.)[53]

50. I learned this criticism of Cajetan first from David Burrell in his *Analogy and Philosophical Language*, 9–20.

51. William Placher provides a useful overview of these developments in *The Domestication of Transcendence*, 71–87. It is often assumed that Ockham is behind the developments associated later with Suarez. However, David Aers argues that Ockham's God is not a God of arbitrary power, as is often said. Aers notes, for example, that in *Quodlibetal Questions* Ockham says that God "is an absolutely perfect being and consequently he moves things intelligently and rationally." See David Aers, *Faith, Ethics, and Church: Writing in England, 1360–1409* (Woodbridge, England: D. S. Brewer, 2000), 9–12.

52. MacIntyre, *Three Rival Versions of Moral Enquiry*, 73–76. The story of the influence of Suarez cannot be confined to Catholic theology. John Platt tells a fascinating story of Suarez's influence on the development of natural theology in Protestant thought; see *Reformed Thought and Scholasticism: The Arguments for the Existence of God in Dutch Theology, 1575-1650* (Leiden: Brill, 1982). In a fascinating chapter, Platt traces the development of natural theology among the Calvinists to an abridgment of Calvin's *Institutes* that gave some Calvinist theologians warrant to develop a more robust natural theology than Calvin would have thought possible.

53. By calling attention to the development of the clock, I mean to suggest that how time was understood changed once time could be measured "exactly," and that this change

What interests me about these debates is what they suggest about how certain metaphysical developments led to what I can call only the epistemological overcoming of theology.[54] That "overcoming" I take to be a correlative of the temptation to cast Christianity as a truth separable from truthful witness—a temptation always present in attempts to make Christianity at home in the world. At least one name for this temptation is "Constantinianism." As a result of the attempt to make Christianity anyone's fate, the truth that is God is assumed to be available to anyone, without moral transformation and spiritual guidance.

Such a view stands in marked contrast to Aquinas's contention that the truth about God that reason can discover comes mixed with many errors. Aquinas says the same thing about our knowledge of the natural law, because some propositions are evident only to the wise. That is why in matters of our knowledge of God and our knowledge of God's law, we need training from one another. The *Summa* was Aquinas's attempt to provide an aid for such training, but for it properly to do its work we must submit to schooling by all of it, which means the *Summa* must be read as a theological, not a philosophical, text.[55]

---

contributed to the eventual marginalization of the church. Jacques Le Goff observes that only with the organization of commercial networks in the twelfth century did time become an object of exact measurement. First, the merchant communes acquired the right to have bells marking the day differently from the monastery. This development was the forerunner of the manufacture of more accurate clocks that signaled that the unit of labor would be the hour rather than the day. According to Le Goff, this change separated the time in which the merchant worked professionally from the time in which the merchant lived religiously. Le Goff suggests that the church, at least for a while, was able to keep the times together by prohibiting usury, just to the extent that the prohibition depended on the presumption that time could not be sold since time was a gift held in common. Increasingly, however, the clock undercut the presumption that time is a common good not to be bought or sold. See Jacques Le Goff, *Time, Work, and Culture in the Middle Ages*, trans. Arthur Goldhammer (Chicago: University of Chicago, 1977), 29–52. Joel Kaye makes matters even more complex with his account of the interrelated developments of a money economy and the quantitative measurement necessary for developments in science; see *Economy and Nature in the Fourteenth Century: Money, Market Exchange, and the Emergence of Scientific Thought* (Cambridge: Cambridge University Press, 1998). I am indebted to David Aers for calling Le Goff's and Kaye's work to my attention.

54. I am obviously playing with the title of John Milbank's chapter "Only Theology Overcomes Metaphysics" in his *The Word Made Strange: Theology, Language, Culture* (Oxford: Blackwell, 1997), 36–54.

55. For Aquinas's account of natural law, see *Summa Theologica*, 1-2.94.1, and 95.1. Aquinas is equally insistent in his *Summa Contra Gentiles* that "even though God has inserted into the minds of men a natural appetite for knowledge," only those who are willing to undergo the labor of inquiry have such knowledge rightly. Moreover, to "undergo" such labor requires direction from the wise because it is from the wise that we learn the proper order of studies of which metaphysics is the last part. *Summa Contra Gentiles* 1.4, trans. Anton Pegis (New York: Image Books, 1955). For this understanding of the *Summa Contra Gentiles*, I am much indebted to Thomas Hibbs, *Dialectic and Narrative in Aquinas: An Interpretation of the Summa Contra Gentiles* (Notre Dame: University of Notre Dame, 1995).

I am not suggesting that metaphysical questions are irrelevant for the display of the truthfulness of theological claims. Indeed I am quite sympathetic to Étienne Gilson's account of the transformation in metaphysics occasioned by Aquinas. Gilson notes that the supreme thought of Aristotle could not be "He who is," that is, it could not give existence because the world of Aristotle was not a created world. I think Gilson is right to suggest that the true metaphysical revolution was achieved by Aquinas, who understood that all the problems concerning being had to be translated from the language of essences into that of existences.[56] The problem is not that kind of metaphysical testing but is, rather, when metaphysics becomes an attempt to secure the truth of Christian convictions in a manner that makes the content of those convictions secondary. Such a project, I fear, has been legitimated for some time in the name of natural theology and, accordingly, has found its natural home in the Gifford Lectures.

Varieties of Theological Work

The suggestion that the Gifford Lectures represent a metaphysical or, more exactly, an epistemological overcoming of theology may seem an odd way to characterize them. Many of the scholars that have given the lectures have thought metaphysics to be at least as doubtful an enterprise as theology. Buckley identifies the source of this suspicion of metaphysics:

> Descartes had begun with ideas and established god as a guarantor of nature. Newton had begun with the phenomena of nature and established god as a force by which the phenomena were structured so that they could interact. In both systems, god entered as a causal necessity. In both physics, god gave movement or design to nature. Diderot had eliminated this inferred necessity by positing movement not as an effect upon matter, but as an effect of matter. Matter was reflexively responsible for its own movement.[57]

After Diderot, any theistic affirmation required an inversion in the understanding of everything in the universe: Nature was now a self-enclosed causal nexus requiring no explanation beyond itself. Such a view of nature was Kant's inheritance, and his response became the mode for most Christian theology after him. Under Kant's influence, Christian theologians simply left the natural world to science and turned to the only place left in which language about God might make sense, that is, to the human—and not just to the human, but to what makes the human

---

56. Étienne Gilson, *God and Philosophy* (New Haven: Yale University Press, 1941), 66–67.
57. Buckley, *At the Origins of Modern Atheism*, 277.

"moral." Kant became the exemplary Protestant theologian, and *Religion Within the Limits of Reason Alone* became the great text in Protestant moral theology.[58] In the words of George Hendry: "When Kant gave priority to the ethical over the natural as the gateway to God, he provided a city of refuge to which harassed theologians fled from their philosophical and scientific pursuers in increasing numbers in the nineteenth century."[59]

That city of refuge took many forms inhabited by names such as Ritschl, Schleiermacher, and Troeltsch; but each in his own way underwrote the presumption that there is no alternative to Kant's "solution." That is the story I tell in these Gifford Lectures. In short, I want to show that the very social and intellectual habits that shaped Lord Gifford's understanding of natural theology left Christian theologians devoid of the resources needed to demonstrate that theological claims are necessary for our knowledge of the way things are and for the kind of life we must live to acquire such knowledge.

No Gifford lecturer better exemplifies this conundrum than that figure who for many people continues to represent the greatest, or at least the most famous, Gifford lecturer: William James. In a world in which theology could no longer pretend to tell us anything significant about the way things are, James attempted, without leaving the world of science, to show how religious experience might at least tell us something about ourselves.

I begin these lectures with James partly because he has such interesting things to say that help us understand the challenges facing Christian theology. Indeed, his pragmatism is not entirely without interest for helping Christians understand how they must live if they are to make clear for Christians and non-Christians alike the way things are. Yet I also begin with James because he provides the necessary background for my account of Reinhold Niebuhr. Next to James, Niebuhr is *the* Gifford lecturer (at least in the United States), and he is often thought to stand in marked contrast to James. Niebuhr allegedly challenged the humanism James represented. I will argue, however, that Niebuhr's account of Christianity stands in continuity with James's understanding of religion, and that this continuity indicates why Niebuhr's way of trying to do Christian theology cannot help but be misguided.

Niebuhr provides an opportunity to develop more fully a theme I can only suggest with James, namely, how the truth-fulfilling conditions of Christian speech have been compromised in the interest of developing an ethic for Christians in liberal social orders. Niebuhr had no use for the kind of metaphysics attributed to Scotus and Suarez, but Niebuhr as-

58. Immanuel Kant, *Religion Within the Limits of Reason Alone*, trans., with an introduction and notes, Theodore Greene and Hoyt Hudson (New York: Harper and Brothers, 1960).

59. Hendry, *Theology of Nature*, 15.

sumed that the truth of Christianity consisted in the confirmation of universal and timeless myths about the human condition that made Christianity available to anyone without witness. So conceived, Christianity became a "truth" for the sustaining of social orders in the West. In an odd way, James and Niebuhr offer accounts of religion and Christianity, respectively, that make the existence of the church accidental to Christianity. My criticism of Niebuhr will allow me to begin to develop the argument that any attempt to provide an account of how Christian theological claims can tell us the way things are requires a correlative politics. In theological terms, such a politics is called "church."

Often when you are telling a story it is wise to keep your audience in suspense about how the story will end. However, my ending is so counterintuitive that I should at least warn you how the story will come out. As I have intimated, I will argue that the great natural theologian of the Gifford Lectures is Karl Barth, for Barth, in contrast to James and Niebuhr, provides a robust theological description of existence. The *Church Dogmatics,* as I read it, is a massive theological metaphysics that provides an alternative to the world in which Lord Gifford's understanding of natural theology seems reasonable.

Moreover, I will argue that Barth—in a way not unlike Aquinas—rightly assumes that the vindication of such a theological program is to be found in the way Christians must and should live. Barth's language for how we "must live" is witness. For Barth, witness is intrinsic for any understanding of what it means to hold that Christian convictions are true to the way things are. Accordingly, Barth kept faith with Lord Gifford's trust just to the extent that he provided the account necessary to understand how our knowledge of God and the way we should live are inextricably bound together. It remains an open question whether or not Barth's ecclesiology is sufficient to sustain the witness that he thought was intrinsic to Christianity.

As I tell this story, I hope it will become clear that it is an argument. There is a presumption in modernity that an argument is something different than a story. Thus, I must show why my argument—that is, why any Christian account of the way things are requires a full doctrine of God—cannot help but take the form of a narrative. Of course, James, Niebuhr, and Barth represent lives and positions so large that no single set of lectures could hope to do justice to any one of them. That I propose to give an account of each of them as well as how they need to be understood in relation to one another not only indicates that my account of their lives and work is selective, but also illuminates how and why the truth of theological claims is inseparable from lives well lived.[60]

60. I should like to think a useful comparison could be made between the argument I am making in these lectures and that made by Steven Shapin in *A Social History of Truth:*

Each of these figures needs to be understood in light of the other be-cause, for example, Barth's quite extraordinary accomplishment can be appreciated more fully in the light of James's work. I am certainly not suggesting that Barth was a closet pragmatist. Such a claim not only would be unfair to Barth, but would be, as I hope to show, a mistaken account of pragmatism. If pragmatism names a theory that must be ap-plied, then clearly it is not the pragmatism James thought worthy of de-fense.[61] Rather, I hope to show that James's understanding of truth helps us appreciate why Barth's way of doing theology should com-mand the attention even of those who may think the entrance fee to Barth's world is too high.

I decided to deal not only with the works of James, Niebuhr, and Barth but also with their lives because in lectures that argue that lives matter, I could hardly afford to ignore the lives of William James, Reinhold Nie-buhr, and Karl Barth. The lives of each of these larger-than-life figures are intrinsic to my argument because I think they represent, for all their indi-viduality, admirable alternatives that cannot help but be in tension.

Overly simple though my portrait may be, William James represents for me the paradigmatic philosophical life to the extent that philosophy for James was not just another subject in the university but a passion, a way of life; James was committed to the criticism of criticism for the sake of living well.[62] Alternatively, Reinhold Niebuhr's life was a polit-ical life in which all convictions were tested in terms of their signifi-cance for sustaining the democratic enterprise. In contrast, Barth's con-victions were tested by their ability to sustain service to God. For Barth, all that is—what we know and what we do—was finally determined by this service. Few people could better represent the demands of a life committed to theology than Karl Barth.

Civility and Science in Seventeenth-Century England (Chicago: University of Chicago Press, 1994.) Shapin shows how the development of seventeenth-century science depended on the trust between gentleman. Therefore, it was impossible to separate the truth, for example, of what was being learned about icebergs from the trustworthiness of the one investigating ice-bergs. Shapin's account, like mine, is meant to suggest that how and what we know may challenge what we have learned from trustworthy agents. Such a challenge will also involve, as Shapin puts it, the ineradicable interdependence of "people-knowledge" and "thing-knowledge." I am sure Shapin is right to insist that all knowledge entails moral pre-sumption, and in particular trust, but my emphasis on the necessity of witness for the knowledge of God is not simply Shapin's point in a different key. "Witness" names a quite particular form of life determined by a quite different content than "science."

61. John Patrick Diggins fails to understand this most basic of points about pragma-tism in his otherwise quite wonderful book, *The Promise of Pragmatism: Modernism and the Crisis of Knowledge and Authority* (Chicago: University of Chicago Press, 1994).

62. I am indebted to my friend Michael Quirk for this understanding of what a philo-sophical life entails. He attributes such a view to Dewey, though I think that may be giv-ing Dewey too much credit.

Of course the lives of James, Niebuhr, and Barth are "messier" and more ambiguous than these characterizations.[63] Yet I think my descriptions of their lives are useful insofar as they help us see that the issues at stake in the Gifford Lectures are not just "intellectual" but are about the very character of our lives. To the extent I am able to sustain that claim, I trust that Lord Gifford would find that my lectures fulfill the purpose of his endowment.

63. To say that philosophy, politics, and theology name lives is my way of indicating how these designations name moral possibilities of a way of life. Such lives, in a manner similar to MacIntyre's account of "characters," are objects of regard by some significant segment of a culture. For MacIntyre's account of "characters," see *After Virtue: A Study in Moral Theory*, 2d ed. (Notre Dame: University of Notre Dame, 1984), 27–31.

2

The Faith
of William James

James's Religion

William James never entertained the presumption that the God of Israel might exist. The problem for James was not God's existence but the significance of human existence. Therefore, in his Gifford Lectures, James did not try to prove God's existence; rather, he attempted to provide an account of the human condition in which our very existence is an indication that life is not pointless. Unlike many who have found it impossible to believe in God, James thought he needed to explain the persistence of religion if he was to give an adequate account of the human. Thus it is important to remember that his positive account of religion in *The Varieties of Religious Experience* is rightly subtitled *A Study in Human Nature*.[1]

The Varieties of Religious Experience has proved to be James's most enduring popular work.[2] That it has been popular surely must indicate that James's account of religion continues to strike a chord in many who are attempting to survive modernity. No doubt the continuing popularity as well as persuasiveness of James's case for religion helps some people continue to believe that they can be religious without taking "institutionalized" religion

1. William James, *The Varieties of Religious Experience: A Study in Human Nature*, foreword Jacques Barzun (New York: Mentor Book, 1958).

2. The editors of the Modern Library listed *The Varieties of Religious Experience* as the second best English-language work of the hundred most important nonfiction works published this century. Only Henry Adams's *The Education of Henry Adams* was deemed more significant. "Publishers Names Top Nonfiction of Century," *The Herald-Sun* (Durham, N.C.), April 30, 1999, A12.

seriously. Therefore, no matter how foreign James's understanding of religion may be for those of us who consider ourselves orthodox Christians, we cannot afford not to take what James did seriously.

I confess, however, that I find it difficult to enter sympathetically into James's project. His account of religion as "the feelings, acts, and experiences of individual men in their solitude, so far as they apprehend themselves to stand in relation to whatever they may consider the divine," I take to be but an expression of pietistic humanism.[3] What bothers me is not so much the humanism as the piety. James acknowledges that such a view arbitrarily ignores aspects of the institutional side of religion such as ecclesiastical organizations and systematic theology, but he thinks this view is justified to the extent that all such institutions derive originally from "personal religion."[4] Yet that is an empirical claim incapable of verification, as is James's equally problematic assumption that something called "religion" can be shown to exist.

According to James, churches once established live secondhand on tradition, "but the *founders* of every church owed their power originally to the fact of their direct personal communion with the divine. . . . So personal religion should still seem the primordial thing, even to those who continue to esteem it incomplete."[5] Of course *The Varieties of Religious Experience* was written to substantiate such a claim, so it is perhaps unfair to say that James's account of the personal basis for all religion is sheerly assertorial. Still, even after attending to his arguments, I find them unconvincing,[6] which makes it all the more important for me to try to understand why his account remains for so many, if not persuasive, at least haunting.

3. James, *Varieties,* 46.
4. Ibid., 44. For a devastating critique of James's attempt to separate the individual experience of religion from the corporate, see Nicholas Lash, *Easter in Ordinary: Reflections of Human Experience and the Knowledge of God* (Charlottesville: University Press of Virginia, 1988), 52–58. Lash observes that James's views on "religious experience" may entail that he deny that "all human experience is formed and shaped by the institution of language" (58). Richard Gale substantiates Lash's charge, noting that James's commitment to an in-principle private language in *The Principles of Psychology* became fully explicit in his last publication, *Some Problems of Philosophy.* Gale notes that James's commitment to the view that an individual can decide whether to call, for example, a sensible quality white or not earned James "the distinction of being the major whipping boy of the later Wittgenstein." Richard Gale, *The Divided Self of William James* (Cambridge: Cambridge University Press, 1999), 164–165. James's account of belief at least qualifies what I can regard only as his inadequate understanding of language, but it is nonetheless the case that his view of "experience" remains a problem not only for his views about religion but for his wider philosophical views.
5. James, *Varieties,* 45.
6. Lash rightly criticizes James for his account of religion as "feeling," by which Lash takes James to mean the "flow of consciousness" before thought has intervened. Lash accuses James of remaining, in spite of his stated position, "Cartesian." *Easter in Ordinary,* 64–70. Robert Jenson criticizes James in a similar fashion, observing that James is a paradigmatic example of the modern effort to "deny the face value of our experience, with its inner deferral, and insist that the Ego I can know and describe is somehow itself the transcenden-

One of the reasons *The Varieties of Religious Experience* remains persuasive for many people is what I can describe only as the profound seriousness with which James approaches his subject. Though he wrote as a self-described scientist, seeking to create in effect a new discipline to be called the psychology of religion, his work betrays an undeniable passion and humanity. James, moreover, understood his work to have a "religious" character. Writing to Miss Frances R. Morse on April 12, 1900, James described the purpose of *Varieties* in terms of his own religious passion:

> The problem I have set myself is a hard one: *first*, to defend (against all prejudices of my class) "experience" against "philosophy" as being the real backbone of the world's religious life—I mean prayer, guidance, and that sort of thing immediately and privately felt, as against high and noble general views of our destiny and the world's meaning; and *second*, to make the hearer or reader believe, what I invincibly do believe, that, although all the special manifestations of religion may have been absurd (I mean its creeds and theories), yet the life of it as a whole is mankind's most important function. A task well-nigh impossible, I fear, and in which I shall fail, but to attempt it is *my* religious act.[7]

Such passages can be quite misleading to the extent that they invite a psychological or biographical reading of *Varieties*. James and his family are fascinating people who make ready subjects for biographical portrayal, but it is a mistake to interpret what James did in his Gifford Lectures as an attempt to work out his own religious anxieties.[8] Santayana's oft quoted remark that James "did not really believe; he merely believed

---

tal unity from which I grasp it." Jenson observes that James not only provides the classic statement of the effort to turn consciousness back on itself in hope of catching a glimpse of the "I" that I know and will myself, but also is the typical victim of such an effort. He is so just to the extent that consciousness for James remains a mere postulate that can be "verified" introspectively only as the occurrence of one "pulse" of consciousness after another. Such "pulses" hang together by various "phenomenal relations," and such a contingent fact, as James admirably shows in the *Principles of Psychology*, is as far as the quest for the "I" can go. Robert Jenson, *Systematic Theology: The Works of God*, vol. 2 (New York: Oxford University Press, 1999), 101–103.

7. Quoted in Henry Samuel Levinson, *The Religious Investigations of William James* (Chapel Hill: University of North Carolina Press, 1981), 67–68. Ralph Barton Perry also calls attention to this letter in his *The Thought and Character of William James* (Cambridge: Harvard University Press, 1948), 257.

8. Perry's wonderful book, *The Thought and Character of William James*, remains one of the best accounts of the interrelation of James's life and work, partly because Perry simply is not tempted to speculate on James's inner life. Gerald Myers, *William James: His Life and Thought* (New Haven: Yale University Press, 1986), is surely the most thorough account of James's work since Perry. The James family cannot help but attract attention, not only because of the stature of William and Henry but also because their father and grandfather are of great interest—in themselves and because their lives tell us so much about the changing character of America. R. W. B. Lewis provides a wonderful account of the

in the right of believing that you might be right if you believed" fails to appreciate the significance of what James was trying to do in *Varieties,* but it rightly challenges those who think James was simply describing his own religious views.[9]

James's most explicit account of his religious views was expressed in a letter in 1904 to psychologist James Leuba:

> My personal position is simple. I have no living sense of commerce with a God. I envy those who have, for I know that the addition of such a sense would help me greatly. The divine, for my active life, is limited to impersonal and abstract concepts which, as ideals, interest and determine me, but do so but faintly in comparison with what a feeling of God might effect, if I had one. This, to be sure, is largely a matter of intensity, but a shade of intensity may make one's whole centre of moral energy shift. Now, although I am so devoid of *Gottesbewusstsein* in the direct and stronger sense, yet there is *something in me* which *makes response* when I hear utterances from that quarter made by others. I recognize the deeper voice. Something tells me:—*thither lies truth*—and I am sure it is not old theistic prejudices of infancy. Those in my case were Christian, but I have grown so out of Christianity that entanglement therewith on the part of a mystical utterance has to be abstracted from and overcome, before I can listen. Call this, if you like, my mystical *germ.* It is a very common germ. It creates the rank and file believers. As it withstands in my case, so it will withstand in most cases, all purely atheistic criticism.[10]

I have no doubt that James drew on his own experience in his famous characterization in the *Varieties* of "The Sick Soul." He had experienced what he called *anhedonia,* that is, a melancholy so deep one lost the capacity for joyous feeling.[11] That James's account was autobiographical, moreover, became accepted once it was learned that the famous description translated from French of the person who suddenly experienced "a horrible fear of my own existence" was in fact a disguised account of James's own panic

---

family in his *The James: A Family Narrative* (New York: Anchor Doubleday, 1991). The most recent biography of James is Linda Simon, *Genuine Reality: A Life of William James* (New York: Harcourt Brace and Co., 1998).

9. Georges Santayana, *Character and Opinion in the United States* (New York: Charles Scribner's Sons, 1920), 77. I think Santayana, however, is right when later in his portrait he notes that James "liked to take things one by one, rather than to put two and two together. He was a mystic, a mystic in love with life. He was comparable to Rousseau and to Walt Whitman; he expressed a generous and tender sensibility, rebelling against sophistication, and preferring daily sights and sounds, and a vague but indomitable faith in fortune, to any settled intellectual tradition calling itself science or philosophy" (94).

10. Quoted in Perry, *The Thought and Character of William James,* 266.

11. James, *Varieties,* 136–138. This aspect of James's life has been subject to the greatest speculation concerning what may have been at the root of James's melancholia. No doubt the tension between his father's desire to have him become a scientist and his own artistic

attack.[12] The subsequent image of the epileptic patient, "entirely idiotic, who used to sit all day on one of the benches, with his knees drawn up against his chin, moving nothing but his black eyes and looking absolutely non-human" certainly is the kind of horror that could strike in James the conclusion: "That shape am I."[13] Yet, whatever mood James may or may not have been in at various times of his life, the argument of *The Varieties of Religious Experience* would be belittled if interpreted as an attempt to make sense of his life. James's target was more ambitious because he sought within the restraints of science to show the significance of human life (of course, by extension, he also sought the significance of his own life).[14]

Such an ambition accounts a hundred years later for the continuing power of James's *Varieties*. In that book, James gave voice to the haunting but unacknowledged sense that the human project no longer matters.

---

ambitions contributed to his inability to choose what he would do with his life. I think Perry takes the wisest course when at the end of his book he refrains from making what he calls any "clinical diagnosis." Perry observes that James was at once a tough-minded accepter of facts and a tender-minded respecter of principles. Yet he is surely right to suggest that James "transcended his own classifications in the act of creating them." *The Thought and Character of William James*, 359–360. Richard Gale, I think, has most acutely described the interrelation of James's life and thought: "The best way to characterize the philosophy of William James is to say that it is deeply rooted in the blues. It is the soulful expression of someone who has 'paid his dues,' someone who, like old wagon wheels, has been through it all. Whereas its immediate aim is to keep him sane and nonsuicidal—'to help him make it through the night'—its larger one is to help him find his way to physical and spiritual health. In this respect James is very much in the Nietzschean and Wittgensteinian mold. His is not a nihilistic V.D. blues of the 'I have had my fun, if I don't get well no more' variety, but rather of the 'I can get well and have my fun' sort. The deep difference between James and Dewey is that Dewey couldn't sing the blues if his life depended on it." *The Divided Self of William James*, 1.

12. James, *Varieties*, 147–148.

13. For the most complete analysis of this famous passage and its relation to James's work, see Louis Menand, "William James and the Case of the Epileptic Patient," *New York Review of Books* 45, no. 20 (December 17, 1998): 81–93. Menand rightly raises questions about the chronology that would have James reading Renouvier and then deciding his first act of free will was to believe in free will.

14. In spite of my criticism of those who would interpret James's account of religion biographically, I do think James was passionately and personally engaged in the project represented by the Gifford Lectures. Levinson is right to suggest that James saw his science of religions as a mechanism for the solution of his own religious problem, once you see that James's "problem" was what he took to be anyone's problem, given the world in which he found himself. Levinson is also right, I think, when he observes that, for James, the science of religion was an enterprise aimed at disciplining its practitioners to keep an open mind about the determinants and consequences of religious experience. "If James was convinced that neither he nor his culture could live without the personal consolations and social additions that religious life brought, he was just as certain that credulousness and tribal instinct had to be displaced by a willingness to respond to new information with an open mind and by a strenuous toleration of tolerant peoples. He thought partici-

Toward the end of *Varieties,* in what can be called only an extraordinary chapter in the history of human egoism just to the extent that the most primitive as well as the most sophisticated religions assure individuals that the divine meets them on the basis of their personal concerns. Yet according to James, the work of science utterly repudiates the personal point of view. Science records its laws and constructs its theories, ignoring their bearing on human fate:

> Though the scientist may individually nourish a religion and be a theist in his irresponsible hours, the days are over when it could be said that for Science herself the heavens declare the glory of God and the firmament showeth his handiwork. Our solar system, with its harmonies, is seen now as but one passing case of a certain sort of moving equilibrium in the heavens, realized by a local accident in an appalling wilderness of worlds where no life can exist. In a span of time which as a cosmic interval will count as but an hour, it will have ceased to be. The Darwinian notion of chance production, and subsequent destruction, speedy or deferred, applies to the largest as well as the smallest facts. It is impossible, in the present temper of the scientific imagination, to find in the drifting of the cosmic atoms, whether they work on the universal or on the particular scale, anything but a kind of aimless weather, doing and undoing, achieving no proper history, and leaving no result. Nature has no one distinguishable ultimate tendency with which it is possible to feel a sympathy. In the vast rhythm of her processes, as the scientific mind now follows them, she appears to cancel herself. The books of natural theology which satisfied the intellects of our grandfathers seem to us quite grotesque, representing as they did, a God who conformed the largest things of nature to the paltriest of our private wants. The God whom science recognizes must be a God of universal laws exclusively, a God who does a wholesale, not a retail business. He cannot accommodate his processes to the convenience of individuals. The bubbles on the foam which coats a stormy sea are floating episodes, made and unmade by the forces of the wind and water. Our private selves are like those bubbles,—epiphenomena, as Clifford, I believe, ingeniously called them; their destinies weigh nothing and determine nothing in the world's irremedial currents of events.[15]

---

pation in his science of religions *required* training in these dispositions" (*The Religious Investigations of William James,* 159). Thus *Varieties* is not just a book about religion but a religious book designed to produce a certain kind of person. Such a tolerant person no doubt can appear quite admirable from a non-Christian perspective, but from a Christian perspective, the well-trained reader James sought to produce cannot help but suffer from the sin of pride. Such a judgment may seem harsh, but it is confirmed by Richard Gale's description of James's philosophy as Promethean. According to Gale, James, to sustain his view that we humans must create meaning and value out of the "big, blooming, buzzing confusion" that confronts us, drew on the American myth of the pioneer who carves a human habitat out of the wilderness (*The Divided Self of William James,* 7–9). Gale develops this point wonderfully throughout his book.

15. James, *Varieties,* 406–408. This understanding of our place in the world remains persuasive for many in our time. For example, in his recent book *Edward Said and the Religious*

The Varieties of Religious Experience is James's attempt to claim more for our lives than that they are but bubbles of foam on a stormy sea. It is extremely important to note that James's attempt to secure human significance is his response to a quite different understanding of science than that of Adam Gifford. Gifford's confidence in science led him to ask that natural theology be considered "just as astronomy or chemistry is."[16] For James, Darwin's work had made Gifford-like confidence in science problematic. As the passage above suggests, James thought that after Darwin it was impossible to think that the world represented an orderly order. That we exist is an accident, and our ending will be equally accidental. Chance, not purpose, rules. Accordingly, science itself can no longer offer certainty and/or proof but only probable and persuasive explanations.[17]

James understood his task in *Varieties*, indeed it was the task of all his

---

Effects of Culture (Cambridge: Cambridge University Press, 2000), William Hart expresses his own skepticism about all attempts of metaphysical humanism to make beings more than complex animals. As Hart puts it, in a passage that echoes James, "On our view, *homo sapiens* are one more species, however complex, doing the best it can, responding to the pressures of natural selection like the amoeba or the coral reef. We mortals do our best within the orders, disorders, and accidents of the natural process. Were we to ascribe intentionality to that process, we would say that nature is indifferent to our beliefs, desires, hopes, and fears. But strictly speaking such anthropomorphic language, while generally harmless, is a mischaracterization. Nature, apart from our attributions, is not cold and indifferent. It just is. To think otherwise is to anthropomorphize. On the other hand, if nature has the quality of serendipity, it is only because we have the language to imagine it so. There is no goal, destiny, or *telos* other than those we have imagined. Our imaginative investments are often sublime, but they are our investments. We should not imagine that some one else or some thing else is paying attention. Pragmatic naturalists do not think less of these investments because they are ours, rather than God's, Being's, or Nature's. We are not disturbed by a cosmos forever mute, which is indifferent (not hostile or sympathetic) to value and truth. We do not begrudge the fact that we share a common fate with the amoeba, although we can understand why animals such as us might be tempted. That our life cycle is only a complex variation on the simplest form of animal life is a source of wonder and awe. Wonder, awe, dependence, and gratitude come close to exhausting our religious affections; beyond these, we feel no desire to worship, which is not to say that this is not another way of worshiping" (166–167).

16. "Lord Gifford's Will," in Stanley Jaki, *Lord Gifford and His Lectures: A Centenary Retrospective* (Macon, Ga.: Mercer University Press, 1986), 74. MacIntyre suggests that Gifford's views about science were more or less those of the Ninth Edition of the *Encyclopaedia Britannica*. According to MacIntyre, such a view of science had four constitutive elements—facts, unifying conceptions supplied by methodical reflections on the facts, methods of confirmation, and continuing progress in supplying ever more comprehensive schemes. Alasdair MacIntyre, *Three Rival Versions of Moral Enquiry: Encyclopaedia, Genealogy, and Tradition* (Notre Dame: University of Notre Dame Press, 1990), 20–21.

17. Paul Jerome Croce provides the best account of which I am aware of this extremely important development in debates surrounding the reception of Darwin in America. See his *Science and Religion in the Era of William James: Eclipse of Certainty, 1820–1880* (Chapel Hill: University of North Carolina Press, 1995). Croce documents the influence of Chauncey Wright on James through their participation in the Metaphysical Club. Trained in mathematics, Wright, who had an animus against traditional religion, nonetheless maintained

work after *The Principles of Psychology*, to do nothing less than to reclaim the human from the impersonality of chance. By chance we exist, and by chance we know that we exist. The knowledge of our existence, a knowledge that often takes the form of religious experience, is at least an indication that even in a world of chance, we matter. In fact it is bad science to deny our experience, just to the extent that our experience is a fact that science cannot ignore if it is to be science. This understanding of the relationship between science and experience leads James to the astounding suggestion that we should "agree, then, that Religion, occupying herself with personal destinies and keeping thus in contact with the only absolute realities which we know, must necessarily play an eternal part in human history."[18]

The Will to Believe

To appreciate appropriately what James attempted in the *Varieties* requires an understanding of the much misunderstood argument he developed in *The Will to Believe*.[19] Only by attending to this earlier book will we be able to understand how the kind of science James thought he was performing in the *Varieties* is part of a wider philosophical project. Contrary to the oft made criticism that James was defending a view that we can make of the world whatever we like, he was attempting to show

---

that "Atheism is speculatively as unfounded as Theism" (170–171). Accordingly, Croce observes that for James the "fallibility of scientific and religious knowledge was a chief lesson of his education; finding a way, despite those limitations, to attain truth and its positive fruits was the challenge of his adulthood. James devoted himself both personally and philosophically to the search for the benefits of certainty without an epistemology of certainty" (229).

18. James, *Varieties*, 415. James's understanding of science is extremely interesting, if for no other reason than that he seems to have assumed an account of science that has increasingly been influential since the work of Kuhn. For example, in his *Talks to Teachers on Psychology* (Cambridge: Harvard University Press, 1983), James observes: "The whole progress of our sciences goes on by the invention of newly forged technical names whereby to designate the newly remarked aspects of phenomena,—phenomena which could only be squeezed with violence into the pigeonholes of the earlier stock of conceptions. As time goes on, our vocabulary becomes ever more and more voluminous, having to keep up with the ever-growing multitude of our stock of apperceiving ideas. In this gradual process of interaction between the new and the old, not only is the new modified and determined by the particular sort of old which apperceives it, but the apperceiving mass, the old itself, is modified by the particular kind of new which it assimilates. . . . In this way, our conceptions are constantly dropping characters once supposed essential, and including others once supposed inadmissible. The extension of the notion 'beast' to porpoises and whales, of the notion of 'organism' to society, are familiar examples of what I mean" (99).

19. William James, *The Will to Believe* (New York: Dover Publications, 1956). *The Will to Believe* is a collection of essays that constitutes a coherent position. When I am referring to an essay in the collection other than the title essay—"The Will to Believe"—I will offer the title.

why what he called religious experience is crucial for discovering the way the world is. By attending to the argument in *The Will to Believe,* I hope to show that James's account of "faith," in spite of what I can regard only as a cavalier dismissal of basic Christian beliefs, should remain of great interest to those of us committed to providing an account of what it might mean to claim that our beliefs about God are true.

The Will to Believe *was published five years before James gave the Gifford Lectures. The book represents James's "coming out" as a philosopher. Of course much of the work done in *The Principles of Psychology* is properly (particularly from our contemporary perspective) described as philosophy.[20] But in *The Will to Believe* James began to work as a philosopher on the problems that would dominate his work to the end of his life. That James would return again and again to the questions he began to explore in *The Will to Believe* creates a certain difficulty for anyone trying to treat James fairly, for to concentrate on the position he takes in this "early" book might fail to do justice to his more mature views. Yet I think it is important to understand the argument in *The Will to Believe.* Not only is the position James began to explore in this book important for understanding his later work, but also some of James's arguments in defense of the will to believe are promising for helping us understand how theological claims require a transformed character, if we are to understand how such claims work to tell us the way the world is.

One of the problems presented by *The Will to Believe* is indicated by its subtitle—*And Other Essays in Popular Philosophy.* Like Lord Gifford, who wanted the lectures he endowed to "be public and popular" because the subject "lies at the root of all well-being,"[21] James was determined to make his work accessible to those who were not professional philosophers or scientists. James's attempt to reach a wider audience was not just a protest against the increasing professionalization of the university but also a necessary correlative of the position he began to develop after the work he had done in the *Principles of Psychology.*[22] David Hollinger rightly observes that part of James's project was to "vindicate the right of

---

20. In her introduction to the republication of Perry's *The Thought and Character of William James* (Nashville: Vanderbilt University Press, 1996), Charlene Haddock Seigfried observes that by treating *The Principles of Psychology* as a classic in the discipline of psychology, Perry unwittingly trapped James within conventional disciplinary categories. She notes that Perry had good grounds for such a classification, not the least being James's own self-understanding, but Seigfried rightly argues that such a classification delayed the recognition "of the radical nature of the paradigm shift pragmatism inaugurated" (xiii).

21. "Lord Gifford's Will," 74.

22. James's work as a philosopher contributed to making philosophy a strictly professional discipline, which ironically turned out to be a development he despised. In *A Pluralistic Universe* (Lincoln: University of Nebraska Press, 1996), he decries the development of technical philosophy, which he characterizes as the habit of mind that only values work that has been thought before. "You must tie your opinion to Aristotle's or Spinoza's; you

the average man and woman to resist the directives of the self-appointed spokespersons for science."[23]

James's determination to write in an accessible manner made him vulnerable to criticisms that often were as unfair as they were irritating to him. Ralph Barton Perry notes that James wrote a friend in 1902 to the effect, "I want now if possible to write something serious, systematic, and syllogistic; I've had enough of the squashy popular-lecture style."[24] But as any pragmatist could have told James, habits are hard to break, so he never got around to writing a philosophical work comparable to the *Principles of Psychology*.[25] Still, criticisms that arguments in *The*

---

must define it by its distance from Kant's; you must refute your rival's view by identifying it with that of Protagoras. Thus does all spontaneity of thought, all freshness of conception, get destroyed. Everything you touch is shopworn. The over-technicality and consequent dreariness of the younger disciples at our American universities is appalling. It comes from too much following of German models and manners. Let me fervently express the hope that in this country you will hark back to the more humane English tradition. . . . In a subject like philosophy it is really fatal to lose connexion with the open air of human nature, and to think in terms of shop-tradition only" (16–17). James, whose only earned degree was an M.D., began to doubt the value of the Ph.D. just to the extent that the developing university culture of America thought the degree more important than the person. See, for example, his "The Ph.D. Octopus," in *The Moral Equivalent of War and Other Essays,* ed., with an intro., John Roth (New York: Harper Torchbooks, 1971), 25–33. Linda Simon provides an informative account of James's increasing unease with the developments to professionalize the philosophy department at Harvard; see *Genuine Reality,* 325–335. Simon observes that James's favorite students were like him, "undisciplinables."

23. David Hollinger, "James, Clifford, and the Scientific Conscience," in *The Cambridge Companion to William James,* ed. Ruth Anna Putnam (Cambridge: Cambridge University Press, 1997), 69. That James succeeded is clear from reports of the effect that *The Will to Believe* had on people's lives. For example, Geoffrey Wainwright, in his biography of Lesslie Newbigin, reports that reading James's *The Will to Believe* prevented Newbigin from losing his faith. Newbigin's faith, of course, turned out to be more robustly orthodox than James would have thought justified. Newbigin was later attracted to the thought of Michael Polanyi but seems never to have explored how James and Polanyi might be compared. See Geoffrey Wainwright, *Lesslie Newbigin: A Theological Life* (New York: Oxford University Press, 2000), 3, 21, 30.

24. Quoted in Perry, *The Thought and Character of William James,* 272. In *Pragmatism and the Meaning of Truth,* intro. A. J. Ayer (Cambridge: Harvard University Press, 1996), James mocks himself, noting: "Readers who admit that satisfactoriness is our only *mark* of truth, the only sign that we possess the precious article, will say that the objective relation between idea and object which the word 'truth' points to is left out of my account altogether. I fear also that the association of my poor name with the 'will to believe' (which 'will,' it seems to me ought to play no part in this discussion) works against my credit in some quarters. I fornicate with that unclean thing, my adversaries may think, whereas your genuine truth-lover must discourse in Huxleyan heroics, and feel as if truth, to be real truth, ought to bring eventual messages of death to all our satisfactions." In contrast, James argues for what he takes to be the true idea about truth: "The maximal conceivable truth in an idea would seem to be that it should lead to an actual merging of ourselves with the object, to an utter mutual confluence and identification" (252–253).

25. Seigfried observes that the complaint of pragmatist philosophers that they are misunderstood is matched in frequency only by their critics' claim that pragmatists are un-

Will to Believe are sloppy often fail to appreciate what James was trying to accomplish in that essay. Certainly Moore's and Russell's criticisms, which became all the more influential through thoughtless repetition by others, were wide of the mark.[26] Moreover, such criticisms often overlook James's defense of his position in the *Essays in Radical Empiricism,* published after his death by Perry.[27]

Although I want to defend James against criticisms that rest on what I can characterize only as misreadings of *The Will to Believe,* I should note that he bears some of the responsibility for these misreadings. His book, at least since his death, has been read in the light of the famous passage in his diary (April 30, 1870) that reports the effect the reading of Charles Renouvier had on him. There he said: "I think that yesterday was a crisis in my life. I finished the first part of Renouvier's second *Essais* and see no reason why his definition of will—'the sustaining of a thought *because I choose to* when I might have other thoughts'—need be the

---

clear and unnecessarily obscurantist. Other philosophers, such as Nietzsche, have taken paths pioneered by the pragmatists, and it is easier to see how their very originality makes understanding difficult. "Nietzsche, for example, was acutely aware of the pitfalls of using a language forged in metaphysical dualism in arguments meant to undermine this common-sense point of view. By alerting readers to this incongruity, he anticipated charges of inconsistency and clarified his own position. James's alternative decision to pour new wine into old bottles without reflecting on the consequences had the unfortunate result that while it was soon recognized that he was not answering old questions very well, the fact that he was forging a new set of questions and answers often went unnoticed" (from the introduction to *The Thought and Character of William James*, xii–xiii).

26. James wrote a very effective response to Russell's critique. See his "Two English Critics," in *Pragmatism and the Meaning of Truth*, intro. A. J. Ayer (Cambridge: Harvard University Press, 1996), 312–319. T. L. S. Sprigge provides a helpful analysis of the critiques of Moore and Russell and of James's response; see his "James, Aboutness, and His British Critics," in Putnam, *The Cambridge Companion to William James*, 125–144.

27. William James, *Essays in Radical Empiricism*, intro. Ellen Kappy Suckiel, preface Ralph Barton Perry (Lincoln: University of Nebraska, 1996). James is partly responsible for those who see no connection between the pragmatism implicit in his defense of the will to believe and his empiricism. In the preface to *Pragmatism and the Meaning of Truth*, he notes that "there is no logical connexion between pragmatism, as I understand it, and a doctrine which I have recently set forth as 'radical empiricism.' The latter stands on its own feet. One may entirely reject it and be a pragmatist" (6). James may be correct to say that there is "no logical connexion," but that does not mean, as I shall argue in the next lecture, that there is no connection whatsoever. Gary Dorrien has pointed out to me that in James's last years, he defended pragmatism as a step toward radical empiricism. As Dorrien observes, what made James's empiricism "radical" was his insistence, as James puts it in *Essays in Radical Empiricism*, that "the relations that connect experiences must themselves be experienced relations, and any kind of religion experienced must be accounted as 'real' as anything else in the system" (42). Accordingly, James understood himself to be radicalizing the empiricist tradition just to the extent that Hume and Mill tried to do away "with the connection of things" in favor of insisting "most on the disjunction" (43). From James's perspective, the latter way of seeing the world invites rationalism to return through the back door, so to speak.

definition of an illusion. At any rate, I will assume for the present—until next year—that it is no illusion. My first act of free will shall be to believe in free will."[28] This passage not only gives the impression that James was more of a voluntarist than he was (he certainly did not think we could just "choose" our beliefs), but also, with its closing sentence, underwrites the assumption that James believed we could make the world be whatever we want it to be by "willing." Yet even a cursory reading of *The Will to Believe* will not sustain such an interpretation.

Too often, I fear, some scholars who interpret James's defense of the will to believe in voluntarist terms forget that the same James who defended the will to believe also wrote the chapter on habit in *The Principles of Psychology*.[29] What James means by "will" and "belief" must be understood as further specifications of his understanding that our life, insofar as it is governed, is shaped by passion-formed habits. A belief—which James, following Alexander Bain, understood to be that on which we are prepared to act—is but a rule of action that has become habitual.[30] As James observes in *Talks to Teachers of Psychology:* "All our life, so far as it has definite form, is but a mass of habits—practical, emotional, and intellectual—systematically organized for our weal or woe, and bearing us irresistibly towards our destiny, whatever the latter may be."[31] In defending the will to believe, James certainly was not implying that the will is some "third" thing to be distinguished from passion, belief, or habit.[32] Rather "the will to believe" names a resource made possible by our capacity to be habituated.

28. Quoted in Perry, *The Thought and Character of William James*, 121. In *William James: His Life and Thought*, Myers comments helpfully on James's appeal to Renouvier by observing that James used Renouvier to underwrite his presumption that we have a moral obligation to ameliorate the obvious deficiencies of our world. What makes such an obligation seem onerous is not only the objective obstacles to such a task, but the feeling that what we do ourselves has such little chance of altering the big picture. By adopting Renouvier's injunction, James was doing no more than expressing a belief in freedom as part of commitment to make sense of his understanding of our duty (422).

29. William James, *The Principles of Psychology* (Cambridge: Harvard University Press, 1981), 109–131.

30. See, for example, Richard Gale's extremely informative analysis of James's understanding of belief, in *The Divided Self of William James*, 50–71, 158–159. Of course, I am not suggesting, against Gale's analysis, that James's account of the will is free of problems. Rather, I am simply arguing that James's psychology makes those who would interpret him as a voluntarist absurd. Gale attempts to defend James's account of the will to believe from an analytical point of view, but he fails to develop James's understanding of passion, without which there is no willing. For this point, I am indebted to Mr. Chris Franks for his extremely helpful paper, "Passion and the Will to Believe."

31. James, *Talks to Teachers on Psychology*, 47.

32. See, for example, James's account of the will in his *Talks to Teachers on Psychology*, 101–114. In his *Religious Experience, Justification, and History* (Cambridge: Cambridge University Press, 1999), Matthew Bagger observes that James is often criticized for not reflecting on the revolution in philosophy that was beginning during his lifetime, namely, the (re)dis-

It is certainly true that James, as he says in the preface to *The Will to Believe*, sought to defend the legitimacy of religious faith, but he rightly says that he did not think anyone reading his essay could accuse him of preaching a reckless faith.[33] James observes that some people will think such an enterprise foolhardy because most of humanity is all too ready to follow faith unreasonably. However, James notes that he is not addressing the Salvation Army but those who have been captured by a peculiar form of mental weakness instilled by the assumption that there is something called scientific evidence by which they can "escape all danger of shipwreck in regard to truth. But there is really no scientific or other method by which men can steer safely between the opposite dangers of believing too little or of believing too much."[34]

James wrote his essay "The Will to Believe" in response to W. K. Clifford's famous essay "The Ethics of Belief." Clifford, often taken (not without some evidence) to be a positivist, had argued that it was immoral to believe anything on insufficient evidence. Positivism aside, Clifford's primary concern was to maintain the importance of truth for sustaining a decent civilization.[35] David Hollinger criticizes James for

---

covery of the importance of language. Bagger, however, observes that James says in *A Pluralistic Universe* that our experience, that flux of sensation, is "shot through with adjectives and nouns and prepositions and conjunctions," thus indicating that he realized the close relation between experience and language. Bagger develops this point by calling attention to James's account of habit as the means he might use to show how our perceptions are shaped by our linguistic habits. Bagger, therefore, thinks James is not subject to Wilfrid Sellar's famous attack on the "myth of the given" (28–38). I have great sympathy with Bagger's reading of James, but I remain unconvinced that the "straws" Bagger finds in James to support his interpretation are sufficient to sustain a suggestion that James actually used his understanding of language constructively. It may well be true that James's understanding of "pure sensation" is an abstraction, but his distinction between religious experience and "over-beliefs," as I will suggest in the next chapter, depends on a problematic distinction between "experience" and language. Bagger rightly maintains, however, that James's understanding of habit provided the means to split the difference, so to speak, between the idealist and empiricist accounts of knowing. As Bagger puts it, James saw that "the natural, habitual character of perception causes perception to feel immediate and direct" (38).

33. James, *The Will to Believe*, x–xi.

34. Ibid.

35. See, for example, Van Harvey's defense of Clifford in his "The Ethics of Belief Reconsidered," *Journal of Religion* 59: 406–420. Harvey calls attention to Clifford's example of the shipowner who sent a vessel with immigrant passengers to sea although he had received troubling suggestions that the ship was unseaworthy. The shipowner relied on his faith in providence (as well as insurance), but the ship sank anyway. Harvey takes Clifford's condemnation of the shipowner to be the heart of Clifford's position, noting that Clifford's alleged positivism is but a form of his more profound moral commitments. Richard Rorty also defends Clifford from James's characterization of him as a positivist. Rorty argues that Clifford and James were not far apart, since neither thought the demand of evidence to be a demand for something that floats free of human projects; it is, rather, simply the demand to be intellectually responsible to people with whom one is

ignoring the moral aspect of Clifford's argument, but in fact James was no less concerned than Clifford about the importance of truth for the maintenance of a humane world.[36]

For example, in the preface to *The Will to Believe,* James observes that some people may take his argument to be but a plea for the right of the individual to indulge in a personal faith at their own risk. James notes that no scientist, in an age of toleration, will actively try to interfere with someone's religious faith as long as we "enjoy it quietly with our friends and do not make a public nuisance of it in the market-place."[37] But James thinks it would be a great mistake to leave the matter there because it is exactly in the market place that such views should be tested, if we are to be free of falsehood. Thus if religious hypotheses about the universe are in order at all, "then the active faiths of individuals in them, freely expressing themselves in life, are the experimental tests by which they are verified, and the only means by which their truth or falsehood can be wrought out."[38]

James's criticism of Clifford is not that Clifford is a positivist but that Clifford is not sufficiently an empiricist. In particular, Clifford fails to appreciate the desire for the kind of truth that brings about its own existence. In James's words: "There are, then, cases where a fact cannot come at all unless a preliminary faith exists in its coming. *And where faith in fact can help create the fact,* that would be an insane logic which should say that faith running ahead of scientific evidence is the 'lowest kind of

---

joined in a common practice. Richard Rorty, "Religious Faith, Intellectual Responsibility, and Romance," in *The Cambridge Companion to William James,* 86–87. For a wonderful collection of essays on the ethics of belief that includes essays on Clifford, James, Harvey, and many others, see *The Ethics of Belief Debate,* ed. Gerald McCarthy (Atlanta, Ga.: Scholars Press, 1986).

36. Hollinger, "James, Clifford, and the Scientific Conscience," 69–83. Hollinger criticizes James for suggesting that on Clifford's grounds we would never be able to act because too often we must act where our knowledge is only probable, at best. He argues that in fact Clifford's and James's positions are closer than James acknowledges.

37. James, *The Will to Believe,* xi. James's position about the public character of religion seems confused because he did not distinguish between "publics." He certainly thought our religious convictions should be tested for truthfulness, but even if they pass that test, they should remain private in the political sphere. James thought, as we shall see in the next lecture, that if democracy is to work, it must privatize religion politically.

38. Ibid., xii. James assumes, in this respect, that evolution provides for the appropriate pragmatic testing. Religious hypotheses are tested like scientific hypotheses in terms of what works best, so we see through religious history that one hypothesis after another has crumbled at contact with widening knowledge of the world. The most favorable condition for the competition of the various faiths with one another is the open market under which the survival of the fittest can proceed. Therefore faiths should not to lie hidden, each under a bushel, indulged in private between friends, but "they ought to live in publicity, vying with each other" (xii). James obviously did not seek to protect faith from public scrutiny.

immorality' in which a thinking being can fall.'[39] This was not a new position for James. He had argued in "The Sentiment of Rationality," written in 1879 and included in *The Will to Believe,* that *"there are then cases where faith creates its own verification.* Believe, and you shall be right, for you shall save yourself; doubt, and you shall again be right, for you shall perish. The only difference is that to believe is greatly to your advantage."[40]

It is extremely important to note that James is not suggesting that all we know involves such "faith." He observes:

> In our dealings with objective nature we obviously are recorders, not makers, of the truth; and decisions for the mere sake of deciding promptly and getting on to the next business would be wholly out of place. Throughout the breadth of physical nature facts are what they are quite independently of us, and seldom is there any such hurry about them that the risks of being duped by believing a premature theory need be faced.[41]

The movement of the stars or the facts of past history, James declares, are determined once and for all whether we like it or not. In such matters, subjective preferences have no part and can only obscure judgment.[42]

Hollinger suggests that James's acknowledgment of such an "objective order" indicates that when he wrote *The Will to Believe* he remained committed to a too strict separation between the spheres of religious and scientific cognition.[43] To be sure, James had not yet fully developed his understanding of truth, but I think the basic outline of his views is present in *The Will to Believe,* and I do not think these views presume the

39. Ibid., 25. Bagger nicely describes James's views as a "pragmatic analysis of explanation" as "explanations consist in contextually relevant descriptive answers" (*Religious Experience, Justification, and History,* 23).

40. William James, "The Sentiment of Rationality," in *The Will to Believe,* 97. The similarity and difference between Pascal's wager argument and James's position would be a study in itself. James mentions Pascal's argument in different contexts in his work in a manner that suggests he was never impressed with it as an argument. As he observes in *The Will to Believe:* "It is evident that unless there be some pre-existing tendency to believe in masses and holy water, the option offered to the will by Pascal is not a living option" (6). Robert J. O'Connell, S.J., provides a extremely useful discussion of James's use of Pascal's wager; see his *William James and the Courage to Believe* (New York: Fordham University Press, 1997), 33–52. O'Connell points out that Pascal did not mean his argument for "hard-hearted" unbelievers but for the torpid who unreflectively plod on to death without a sidelong glance at how such a death will affect them (43). In other words, Pascal (and James) used the argument not to prove God's existence but as a reminder that the question of God matters.

41. James, *The Will to Believe,* 20.

42. James, "The Sentiment of Rationality," 97. James's view that "the facts of past history" are just there seems to indicate he had an unjustified confidence in the developing discipline of history.

43. Hollinger, "James, Clifford, and the Scientific Conscience," 79–80.

separation of spheres that Hollinger suggests. Instead, Hilary Putnam gets it right when he characterizes James as a direct realist about perception, but not about conception.[44] James's account of the will to believe was his attempt to develop the notion—represented by contemporary philosophers such as John McDowell, John Haldane, and Putnam—that conceptions are like capacities for representing rather than representations.[45] "Will" was, I think, James's name for such capacities.[46]

Such capacities have to be acquired, but they are anything but arbitrary. To properly understand what James means by "will" one must attend to his account of the difference between options that are living or

44. Hilary Putnam, "James's Theory of Truth," in *The Cambridge Companion to William James,* 175. In fairness to Hollinger, it should be noted that Putnam is characterizing James's views from his later work, but I think the essential position is present in his essay "The Sentiment of Rationality," in *The Will to Believe.* Of course, every essay in *The Will to Believe* gives some indication of James's developing position.

45. In his article, Putnam explicitly associates McDowell and Haldane with James (184). I hope Putnam is right about this, but there is a lingering "individualism" in James's epistemology that does not seem consistent with Putnam's, Haldane's, or McDowell's emphasis on what McDowell calls "second nature." It is hard, for example, not to think of James's individualism when McDowell observes, in relation to Kant's attempt to deal with the real connection between concepts and intuitions, that "this strain to which Kant's thinking is subject, when he tries to find a place for the essential insight about experience in the lethal environment of a naturalism without second nature, [has] . . . another historical influence: the rise of Protestant individualism. That brings with it a loss or devaluation of the idea that immersion in a tradition might be a respectable mode of access to the real. Instead it comes to seem incumbent on each individual thinker to check everything for herself" *Mind and World* (Cambridge: Harvard University Press, 1996), 98. This, of course, is one of the decisive differences between James and Peirce. James never quite got beyond the presumptions that make the conflict between empiricism and idealism intelligible. Peirce's great achievement was to refuse to accept that alternative.

46. In *Essays in Radical Empiricism,* James defends the view that the true is that which gives the maximal combinations of satisfactions. Truth, in these terms, requires a sense of consistency, and James defends this view by asking: "And are not both our need of consistency and our pleasure in it conceivable as outcomes of the natural fact that we are beings that develop mental *habits*—habit itself proving adaptively beneficial in an environment where the same objects, or the same kind of objects, recur and follow 'law'?" (262). Robert O'Connell, S.J., provides a defense of James along the lines I am suggesting in *William James and the Courage to Believe.* According to O'Connell, James was trying to show "that only the thinker of developed moral character can be expected to 'see' our universe in appropriate moral terms." O'Connell asks rhetorically, "In short, is James dusting off a modern version of the old traditional stress on 'knowledge by connaturality'?" O'Connell, I think rightly, answers his question with the reply, "To some extent" (3). At the very least, James's understanding of the habituated form of the will means that he is open to the kind of analysis exemplified in Linda Trinhaus Zagzebski's, *Virtues of the Mind: An Inquiry into the Nature of Virtue and the Ethical Foundations of Knowledge* (Cambridge: Cambridge University Press, 1996). Zagzebski tries to show that a virtue-based epistemology is preferable to a belief-based epistemology for the same reasons that, as she puts it, a virtue-based moral theory is preferable to an act-based moral theory. My disquiet about Zagzebski's project involves her assumption that it is necessary to develop something called a "pure virtue theory" in order to make her case.

dead, forced or avoidable, momentous or trivial. At the time he wrote
The Will to Believe, these distinctions were analytic machinery that James
used to distinguish those aspects of our lives for which the will to believe is rationally required. For an option to be alive, it must be perti-
nent to an individual's life; for it to be forced, the option *must* be chosen;
for it to be momentous, the option must be significant and irreversible.[47] For James, what the will to believe names is the unavoidability of
recognizing that I cannot not acknowledge that I exist and that I care
that I exist.

As he puts it in "The Moral Philosopher and Moral Life":

> Wherever minds exist, with judgments of good and ill, and demands
> upon one another, there is an ethical world in its essential features. Were
> all other things, goods and men and starry heavens, blotted out from this
> universe, and were there left but one rock with two loving souls upon it,
> that rock would have as thoroughly moral a constitution as any possible
> world which the eternities and immensities could harbor. It would be a
> tragic constitution, because the rock's inhabitants would die. But while
> they lived, there would be real good things and real bad things in the uni-
> verse; there would be obligations, claims, and expectations; obediences, re-
> fusals, and disappointments; compunctions and longings for harmony to
> come again, and inward peace of conscience when it is restored; there
> would, in short, be a moral life, whose active energy would have no limit
> but the intensity of interest in each other with which the hero and hero-
> ine might be endowed.[48]

The will to believe is, therefore, not some irrational effort on our part
to make the world what it is not, but the rational acknowledgment that
we are part of that which makes the world what it is.[49] The discovery
of the unavoidable moral character of existence is but one aspect of the
equally unavoidable discovery of the religious character of our existence. "A man's religious faith," according to James, is "essentially his
faith in the existence of an unseen order of some kind in which the rid-
dles of the natural order may be found and explained."[50] "Religion" is

47. James, *The Will to Believe,* 2–8. For a good discussion of the significance of James's
analysis of these alternatives for his account of religion, see Ellen Kappy Suckiel, *Heaven's
Champion: William James's Philosophy of Religion* (Notre Dame: University of Notre Dame
Press, 1996), 27–37.

48. William James, "The Moral Philosopher and Moral Life," in *The Will to Believe,* 197.

49. For the most careful analysis as well as defense of James's understanding of the will
to believe, see Gale, *The Divided Self of William James,* 93–116. Gale avows that James's doctrine
of the will to believe, at least as reconstructed by Gale, is one of the great contributions to
the history of philosophy. That may well be true, but anyone who has read Aristotle or
Thomas Aquinas cannot help but think that they not only anticipated James but may well
have provided a more defensible view of the relation of virtue and knowledge.

50. James, "Is Life Worth Living?" in *The Will to Believe,* 51.

simply James's way of naming the fact that our minds are teleological mechanisms that constitute our difference from the brutes.[51]

For James, therefore, theism does not involve the claim that something like God exists, but rather that no account of the world is adequate that denies the aspect of human existence that led us to believe in a god or the gods. In terms reminiscent of the ontological argument, James observes that his ambition is to show that a god, whether existent or not, is the kind of being that, if it did exist,

> would form *the most adequate possible object* for minds framed like our own to conceive as laying at the root of the universe. My thesis, in other words, is this: that *some* outward reality of a nature defined as God's nature must be defined, is the only ultimate object that is at the same time rational and possible for the human mind's contemplation. *Anything short of God is not rational, anything more than God is not possible,* if the human mind be in truth the triadic structure of impression, reflection, and reaction.[52]

James, then, understands his investigations in *The Will to Believe* to be continuous with a rigorous empiricism that discovers the unavoidability of subjectivity as constitutive of the world. Theism is in congruity with our nature as thinkers. "God," he observes, "may be called the normal object of the mind's belief," and to inquire into such belief is but to investigate a chapter in the natural history of the mind.[53] Such an investigation is exactly what James undertook in *The Varieties of Religious Experience.* That book takes the form of a phenomenology of religious experience, but we can now see it as part of James's continuing argument for (or investigation into) the claim that although our existence may be an accident, we cannot rightly live as if we are accidents with no purpose.

By saying that we cannot live as if we are accidents, James means that we are quite literally forced to recognize ourselves as moral and religious animals. Just as James thought that determinism cannot be true if we are creatures capable of regret, so it is that we learn from our regret that we cannot be other than religious. We might, for example, at some point in our development, erroneously regret what may turn out to be good, but our error in regretting might itself be good, on one simple condition:

> That the world must not be regarded as a machine whose final purpose is the making real of any outward good, but rather as a contrivance for deepening the theoretic consciousness of what goodness and evil in their intrin-

---

51. James's description of the mind as teleological is found in "Reflex Action and Theism," in *The Will to Believe,* 117. He distinguishes humans from the brutes in the same essay (131).

52. Ibid., 115–116.

53. Ibid., 116.

sic natures are. Not the doing of good or of evil is what nature cares for, but the knowing of them. Life is one long eating of the tree of *knowledge*.[54]

The Varieties of Religious Experience

Defenders of James's account of religious experience are often embarrassed by (or at least ignore) his psychical research as well as his "great man" view of history. Yet the evidence of this sort that James sought to marshal in *The Varieties of Religious Experience* is, as with his understanding of the will, but a development of reflections he had begun in *The Will to Believe*. Already in this book, he had addressed the role of great men in history, as well as the possibility of some people having the ability to make contact with the dead.[55] That James included long essays on these topics in *The Will to Believe* is sufficient evidence to suggest that he did not think of them as secondary to his more properly philosophical work.

Indeed, some of James's most extended reflections on the importance of Darwin occur in his essay "Great Men and Their Environment," which appears in *The Will to Believe*.[56] James argues that just as Darwin must accept spontaneous variations as a given, so we must accept geniuses as data. The only questions, from Darwin's as well as James's point of view, are how the environment affects such men and how they affect their environment. The answers, according to James, cannot be given in principle but depend on the conditions into which the genius

54. James, "The Dilemma of Determinism," in *The Will to Believe*, 165. James had what can be described only as an optimistic faith in the evolutionary process for weeding the good from the bad. He thought the course of history was nothing but the story of the struggle from one generation to another to discover a more inclusive order. In another essay in *The Will to Believe*—"The Moral Philosopher and the Moral Life"—James suggests that society—which he seems to have identified with the people with which he was associated—had moved from one relative equilibrium after another by a series of discoveries analogous to those of science. Thus polyandry, polygamy, slavery, private warfare, judicial torture, and arbitrary royal power have succumbed to aroused complaints (205). James recognized that such a view means that you cannot dismiss advocates of anarchy, nihilism, or free love; rather such practices must be viewed as experiments concerning the amount of good that might be gained through them. He argued that in cases of conflict, the presumption must always be in favor of the conventionally recognized good; but that does not mean that such experiments are to be judged *a priori* as wrong. Instead they are to be judged "by actually finding, after the fact of their making, how much more outcry or how much appeasement comes about" (207). The most charitable interpretation of such a view is that James surely cannot have thought these matters through.

55. James was by no means unique in his fascination with psychical research. Henry Sidgwick was perhaps even more involved in investigating such phenomenon. James never approached his study of this phenomenon uncritically. Indeed, as Linda Simon makes clear, James never thought after twenty years of research that he had succeeded in verifying such phenomenon; see *Genuine Reality*, 366–369.

56. William James, "Great Men and Their Environment," in *The Will to Believe*, 216–254.

comes. Thus geniuses can come too early or too late, depending as they do on the results produced by previous genius—"after Voltaire, no Peter the Hermit; after Charles IX and Louis XIV, no general protestantization of France; and so on."[57] From James's perspective, any view of history that denies the vital importance of individual initiative is "utterly vague and unscientific conception, a lapse from modern scientific determinism into the most ancient fatalism."[58]

The Varieties of Religious Experience is, therefore, but a continuation of James's study of genius. His refusal to engage in reductive accounts of religion—that is, theories that would "explain" religion in terms of sex or other functions—is part of his general view that such reductive accounts are not properly scientific.[59] James also refused to explain religion by trying to find its essential character in our fear of the unknown or in feelings of absolute dependence.[60] Rather, as I noted at the beginning of this lecture, personal religion for James was a "primordial thing" and was thus the source of all institutional forms that religion might take.[61] In *The Will to Believe*, James had described religion as a belief in an unseen world. In *The Varieties of Religious Experience*, he elaborates and

---

57. Ibid., 230.

58. Ibid., 245.

59. James, *Varieties*, 30–31.

60. James had some knowledge of developments in Protestant liberal theology. He seems to have read Adolf Harnack's *The Essence of Christianity*, and his allusion to the "feeling of absolute dependence" suggests he had some knowledge of Schleiermacher. Indeed, Robert Richardson, who is writing a biography of James, says (in personal correspondence) that James met Dilthey in Germany in 1867, when Dilthey had published the first volume of his *Life of Schleiermacher*. Richardson also notes that Schleiermacher appeared on one of James's 1869 reading lists, and that on at least one occasion James made some notes on Schleiermacher, so James no doubt knew something of Schleiermacher. There is also this passing reference to Schleiermacher in "Reflex Action and Theism," in the *Will to Believe*: "Among all the healthy symptoms that characterize this age, I know of no sounder one than the eagerness which theologians show to assimilate results of science about universal matters. One runs a better chance of being listened to today if one can quote Darwin and Helmholtz than if one can only quote Schleiermacher or Coleridge" (112). Richardson has documented Schleiermacher's influence on the Transcendentalists in his "Liberal Platonism and Transcendentalism: Shaftesbury, Schleiermacher, and Emerson," *Symbiosis*, 1.1 (1997), 1–20.

61. James, *Varieties*, 45. That James never doubted that religion describes something in common between different religions as well as forms of life that are not explicitly religious cannot help but strike us as naive. But in his defense, it should be observed that it has been only recently that attempts to secure some common account of religion have been decisively called into question. See, for example, Talal Asad, *Genealogies of Religion: Disciplines and Reasons of Power in Christianity and Islam* (Baltimore: Johns Hopkins Press, 1993), in which Asad criticizes attempts to claim that religion has some kind of universal function (46). Asad's observation that attempts to account for something called religion are an indication of how marginal religion has become in modernity makes one think he was writing with James in mind. That he was not suggests just how widespread James-like views are. James's presumption that a "science of religion" should be developed that discrimi-

speaks of the "added dimension of emotion, this enthusiastic temper of espousal, in regions where morality strictly so called can at best but bow its head and acquiesce. This sort of happiness in the absolute and everlasting is what we find nowhere but in religion."[62]

James's identification of religion with an attitude toward the whole universe that is necessary to provide for "healthy-mindedness" is the background for the development in *Varieties* of what might be called "religious characters," that is, "the sick soul" and "the divided self," as well as "the converted." These "characters," however, were but James's mechanism for organizing what otherwise he thought of as "data." Therefore James's phenomenology of religious conversion, as well as his subsequent accounts of saintliness and mysticism, interesting though they may be, were not meant to provide the basis for assessing the truth of religious claims.[63] "I do indeed disbelieve," he declared, "that we or any other mortal men can attain on a given day to absolutely incorrigible and unimprovable truth about such matters of fact as those which religion deal."[64] Rather, all James sought, through what I can describe only as the piling up of religious narratives, was to show that religion is but another name for the hope necessary to sustain a modest humanism. That he was not unsuccessful can be measured not only by the popular-

---

nates the "common and essential from the individual and local elements of the religious beliefs" (378) has obviously become as problematic as the presumption that something called religion exists.

62. James, *Varieties*, 58–59. James observes that personal religion, even without theology or ritual, embodies some elements that morality pure and simple does not contain. He seems to mean that religion supplies a sense of happiness, but it is not clear why morality itself does not involve such an attitude. In the passage in which he contrasts morality with religion, he seems to associate the former with Stoicism and the latter with Christianity. He therefore reads Stoicism as a "drab discolored" mode of resignation in contrast to the happiness of the Christian saint (53–54). Such an account is surely prejudicial to Stoicism, but it also fails to do justice to his own understanding of how Christianity is by no means immune from the "sick-soul." James's identification with "religion" is nicely suggested by an insightful inscription he made in a copy of *Varieties* he sent to Professor Francis G. Peabody: "You will class me a Methodist, *minus* a Savior." Perry, *The Thought and Character of William James*, 259.

63. In many ways, *The Varieties of Religious Experience* is one of James's less interesting books on religion. Richard R. Niebuhr is surely right when he observes: "All in all, *Varieties* is a transitional book, exhibiting description and spiritual judgments, psychology and incipient metaphysics, intertwining in James's mind." "William James on Religious Experience," in *The Cambridge Companion to William James*, 223. Niebuhr quite rightly calls attention to the importance of James's lectures on mysticism as the climax of the phenomenology of religion he sought to provide. At the start of the chapter on mysticism, James observes that "one may say truly that personal religious experience has its root and centre in mystical states of consciousness," but since they are ineffable and transient, the knowledge they represent, while persuasive for the one who has had the experience, cannot be veridical.

64. James, *Varieties*, 284.

ity of *The Varieties of Religious Experience,* but by what appears to be the basic acceptance of James-like accounts of Christianity by allegedly more orthodox Christian theologians, not the least being Reinhold Niebuhr.

All of this makes James an extraordinarily frustrating figure for theologians who rightly refuse to have fundamental Christian convictions relegated to Jamesian "over-beliefs." In summing up his analysis of James, Nicholas Lash vents his frustration, observing that even if we leave theological considerations to one side, James's preoccupation with pattern setters—those who live their lives at "firsthand" and not (like most of us) merely at "secondhand"—depends on an arbitrary and unsustainable disjunction between personal and institutional existence, and between personal existence and intellectual activity:

> By banishing the institutional and intellectual orders to the wastelands of the *im*personal, both politics and theory are reduced to matters of mere mechanism or technique, unconstrained by considerations of personal responsibility. And so, by seeking for sense and safety in the wrong direction—at some center of our individual privacy rather than in the public realm of common action, common understanding, and shared experience—we merely succeed in bringing nearer the day when darkness and destruction have the last word. To put the point theologically: if we would find ourselves in the presence of God, we are ill advised to pursue strategies which exacerbate the conditions of his absence from our world.[65]

If, as Lash contends, to follow James is to seek safety in the wrong direction or, more pointedly, to provide for the conditions of God's absence, then why have James's views been so influential, particularly among Christians? The answer, I think, is that James gave voice to the character of Christianity in modernity: Christianity makes sense only as disguised humanism. That Christianity might make sense as something else is a possibility that James rejected. For those of us who think that in fact Christianity makes sense only as something other than what modernity has made of it, it is imperative that we understand James's rejection of what he took Christianity to be. That will be my task in the next lecture.

---

65. Lash, *Easter in Ordinary,* 88–89.

3
God and
William James

James, Pragmatism, and Christianity

In the last lecture I gave as sympathetic an account as I could of James's attempt to save human significance in a world of chance. James's account of religion was part of his strategy to sustain a hope sufficient to promote the human endeavor. James's humanism cannot help but be extraordinarily seductive for those of us who continue to find our lives located in religious traditions, just to the extent that we are able to recognize ourselves in his extremely sympathetic portrayals of the healthy-minded, the twice born, the saint, and the mystic. Yet James presents a seduction that must be resisted because his account of religion, in spite of his disclaimers, is reductionistic.

James's reductionistic account of religion is all the more seductive because it is so subtle. For example, at the end of the lecture on saintliness, James calls attention to those who surrender all before God. Rather than dismissing those who would make such a sacrifice, James chastens his readers, saying that they must have "been there" to understand what such a sacrifice means. Just as an American can never understand the loyalty of a Briton toward the king, "how much more is this the case with those subtler religious sentiments which we have been considering! One can never fathom an emotion or divine its dictates by standing outside it."[1] Yet, as we shall see, James does not extend the same sympathy to those

1. William James, *The Varieties of Religious Experience: A Study in Human Nature*, foreword Jacques Barzun (New York: Mentor Book, 1958), 275–276.

who have claimed and continue to claim that following Christ might require such a sacrifice.

James's sympathetic account of religion is exemplified by his contention that prayer is the very soul and essence of religion. "The genuineness of religion," he observes, "is indissolubly bound up with the question whether the prayerful consciousness be or be not deceitful."[2] Whether the God to whom prayer is directed exists does not seem to bother James. What makes prayer authentic is not the status or character of the one to whom one prays, but the subjectivity of the one who is praying. The difficulty, of course, is whether James's understanding of such subjectivity is the same as the understanding of the one who is in fact doing the praying, given that the latter at the very least assumes that there is a God to whom he or she prays.

James thought he was providing a nonreductive account of religion, of matters such as sacrifice and prayer, because of his commitment to the pragmatic method. Moreover, he thought that method was commensurate with the best insights of the representatives of religious convictions, such as Jonathan Edwards: "By their fruits ye shall know them, not by their roots. Jonathan Edwards' Treatise on Religious Affections is an elaborate working out of this thesis. The *roots* of a man's virtue are inaccessible to us. No appearances whatever are infallible proofs of grace. Our practice is the only sure evidence to ourselves we are genuinely Christian."[3]

Toward the conclusion of *Varieties,* James expands this initial account of pragmatism by drawing on Peirce's famous article "How to Make Our Ideas Clear."[4] Following Peirce's account of beliefs as rules for actions habitually embodied, James argues that any aspect of our thinking that makes no difference in the practical consequences of our lives cannot be considered of significance:

> To develop a thought's meaning we need only determine what conduct it is fitted to produce; that conduct is for us its sole significance; and the tangible fact at the root of all our thought-distinctions is that there is no one of them so fine as to consist in anything but a possible difference of practice. To attain perfect clearness in our thoughts of an object, we need then only consider what sensations, and what conduct we must prepare in case the object should be true.[5]

2. Ibid., 386.

3. Ibid., 37. For a fascinating linkage of Edwards and James, see Martha Gail Hamner, "Habits of a Christian Nation: An Alternative Genealogy of American Pragmatism" (Ph.D. diss., Duke University, 1997), 229–289. Hamner also provides a helpful account of Peirce in comparison to James.

4. James, *Varieties,* 368–369.

5. Ibid., 369. It is not necessary for my purposes to try to clarify the similarities and differences between Peirce and James over the meaning of pragmatism. Peirce was no

In a similar vein, James says in *Pragmatism: A New Name for Some Old Ways of Thinking* that theological ideas will be true if they have a value for concrete life. But he also says that the truth of some ideas "will depend entirely on their relations to other truths that also have to be acknowledged."[6] That some ideas are true only in relation to other ideas is an extremely rich suggestion, and it helps us see how, for example, the Christian understanding of God cannot be abstracted from what it means to pray to Jesus. I am not suggesting that James had in mind such an example of how "ideas" must be understood in relation to one another. My point is that on his own grounds James has no reason to dismiss theological claims simply because they seem to have no immediate pragmatic significance. Indeed, if, as James says, some ideas are true only in relation to other truths (and thus not in relation to any

---

doubt right to distance his own views from those of James, but I do not think the difference between them is as exaggerated as some have suggested. See, for example, Christopher Hookway, "Logical Principles and Philosophical Attitudes: Peirce's Response to James's Pragmatism," in *The Cambridge Companion to William James,* ed. Ruth Putnam (Cambridge: Cambridge University Press, 1997), 145–165. Hookway contrasts Peirce's realism to James's nominalism. That James was a nominalist about some things is no doubt true, but it is not clear how much it helps to understand James by calling him a nominalist or a realist. For example, in *The Meaning of Truth* (Cambridge: Harvard University Press, 1996), James argues that for the pragmatist "there can be no truth if there is nothing to be true about. Ideas are so much flat psychological surface unless some mirrored matter gives them cognitive lustre. This is why as a pragmaticist I have so carefully posited 'reality' *ad initio,* and why, throughout my whole discussion, I remain an epistemological realist." James suspects that the reason he has been misunderstood is that his critics confuse truth with reality. "Realities are not *true,* they *are;* and beliefs are true *of* them" (272). Perhaps James gave an inadequate account of how his pragmatism is consistent with such a realism, but it is clearly wrong to argue that he was intentionally an antirealist. Hilary Putnam has provided an account of James's realism in his "Pragmatism and Realism," in *The Revival of Pragmatism: New Essays on Social Thought, Law, and Culture* (Durham: Duke University Press, 1998), 37–53. Putnam acknowledges that there are certainly antirealist elements in James's thought, but to defend what he calls James's natural realism, he rightly draws on James's *Essays in Radical Empiricism,* intro. Ellen Suckiel, preface by Ralph Barton Perry (Lincoln: University of Nebraska Press, 1996). John Smith's *Purpose and Thought: The Meaning of Pragmatism* (New Haven: Yale University press, 1978) remains one of the most informative comparisons of Peirce, James, and Dewey.

6. William James, *Pragmatism and the Meaning of Truth,* intro. A. J. Ayer (Cambridge: Harvard University Press, 1996), 40–41. In his quite appreciative account of James, Ayer suggests, using James's own categories, that James was at once tough-minded in his empiricism and tender-minded in his attitudes toward free will, morals, and religion. He sought, according to Ayer, to make reason "more flexible" to accommodate his tender-minded beliefs.

James's pragmatism is misunderstood if one assumes that it can be defined as the position that our thoughts are true only if they have an immediate "cash value." In *Essays in Radical Empiricism,* James notes that most of our knowing is never completely nailed down. What "pragmatism" names is how to go on when a dispute arises. James is well aware that our ability to continue to think is usually justified without "our knowing in the completed sense" (67–76).

practical consequences they might have in isolation from these other truths), then his refusal to consider substantive religious convictions as true cannot help but appear arbitrary and reductive.

James's arbitrary judgment concerning what is essential and non-essential for assessing religious truth is evident in his assertion that "feeling" is the deepest source of religion. James makes this assertion in a manner that renders philosophical and theological "formulas" secondary. James calls such formulas "over-beliefs," suggesting that they are speculations of the intellect building on directions that come originally from religious feeling.[7] By calling attention to such beliefs, James does not mean that they are unimportant. Indeed, he declares that the most interesting and valuable things about a person are usually her over-beliefs.[8] Yet James's assumption that such beliefs are important does little to help us understand what makes any belief an over-belief.

James confesses that his own over-beliefs, which he acknowledges as the somewhat pallid kind that befit a critical philosopher, consist in the conviction that there is an altogether other dimension of existence behind the sensible and understandable world.[9] In "Pragmatism and Religion," the last chapter of *Pragmatism: A New Name for Some Old Ways of Thinking*, James says that he cannot begin a whole theology, but he then pleads:

> I have written a book on men's religious experience, which on the whole has been regarded as making for the reality of God, you will perhaps exempt my own pragmaticism from the charge of being an atheistic system. I firmly disbelieve, myself, that our human experience is the highest form of experience extant in the universe. I believe rather that we stand in much the same relation to the whole universe as our canine and feline pets do to the whole of human life. They inhabit our drawing-rooms and libraries. They take part in scenes of whose significance they have no inkling. They are merely tangent to curves of history the beginnings and ends and forms of which pass wholly beyond their ken. So we are tangents to the wider life of things. But, just as many of the dog's and cat's ideals coincide with our ideals, and the dogs and cats have daily living proof of the fact, so we may well believe, on the proofs that religious experience affords, that higher powers exist and are at work to save the world on ideal lines similar to our own.[10]

7. James, *Varieties*, 358–359.
8. Ibid., 424.
9. Ibid., 415.
10. James, *Pragmatism*, 143–144. James's use of animal examples nicely illustrates his mood swings between healthy-mindedness and what he called *anhedonia*. For example, in his essay "Is Life Worth Living?" in *The Will to Believe* (New York: Dover Publications, 1956), James observes that our "whole physical life may lie soaking in a spiritual atmosphere" that we have no way to apprehend. We are, he suggests, like dogs who are in human life but not of it. In this case, however, the dog in question does not inhabit the library or the

James never pretended that his "over-belief" was compatible with orthodox Christianity, but he saw no difficulty in identifying his over-belief with God.[11] Indeed, in *Varieties,* he even goes so far as to say:

> God is the natural appellation, for us Christians at least, for the supreme reality, so I will call this higher part of the universe by the name of God. We and God have business with each other; and in opening ourselves to his influence our deepest destiny is fulfilled. . . . I only translate into schematic language what I may call the instinctive belief of mankind: God is real since he produces real effects.[12]

Yet it is extremely unclear on what basis James can count himself a Christian, as he obviously does in this quotation, or why he thinks he has the right to name his over-belief "god." As we shall see, James was acutely aware that his god, a finite god, has little in common with what he understood to be the God of Christianity.[13]

---

drawing room but is "a poor dog whom they are vivisecting in a laboratory. He lies strapped on a board and shrieking at his executioners, and to his own dark consciousness is literally in a sort of hell. He cannot see a single redeeming ray in the whole business; and yet all these diabolical-seeming events are often controlled by human intentions with which, if his poor benighted mind could only be made to catch a glimpse of them, all that is heroic in him would religiously acquiesce. Healing truth, relief to future sufferings of beast and man, are to be bought by them. It may be genuinely a process of redemption. Lying on his back on the board there he may be performing a function incalculably higher than any that prosperous canine life admits of; and yet, of the whole performance, this function is the one portion that must remain absolutely beyond his ken" (57–58). That James placed his dog in the library in *Pragmatism* nicely illustrates his mood in the last decade of his life, but I do not think he ever forgot the dog being vivisected. In *The Divided Self of William James* (Cambridge: Cambridge University Press, 1999), Richard Gale provides an extremely interesting account of James's defense of vivisection. If, as James suggests in the quotation above, the heroic dog would religiously acquiesce in his sacrifice, then asks Gale rhetorically, on what grounds could James argue against the justification of human sacrifice? Gale argues, I think rightly, that to make such an argument, James would have had to qualify his view that the essence of the good is simply to satisfy demand (37–49).

11. In "Is Life Worth Living?" James declares that on the whole he assumes it to be a gain that the naturalistic superstition, that is, the worship of the God of nature, has begun to lose its hold on the "educated mind." Indeed, he goes so far to say that "the initial step towards getting into healthy ultimate relations with the universe is the act of rebellion against the idea that such a God exists" (44). In this passage, James does not identify "the God of nature" with the God Christians worship, but as I show below, he seems to assume that the Christian God and the God of nature are the same.

12. James, *Varieties,* 425.

13. In *A Pluralistic Universe* (Lincoln: University of Nebraska Press, 1996), James provides his most extended defense of his notion of a finite god. James understood such a god to be a correlative of his humanism. In "The Essence of Humanism," in *Essays in Radical Empiricism,* James says: "I myself read humanism theistically and pluralistically. If there be a God, he is no absolute all-experiencer, but simply the experiencer of widest actual conscious span" (194). It is not clear to what extent James's views about such a god changed or developed over the last twenty years of his life. The god of *Radical Empiricism,* for example,

Perry calls attention to a letter that James wrote in 1884 to Thomas Davidson in which he despaired of any "popular religion of a philosophical character." James found himself wondering if there could be any

> popular religion raised on the ruins of the old Christianity without the presence of . . . a belief in new *physical* facts and possibilities. Abstract considerations about the soul and the reality of a moral order will not do in a year what the glimpse into a world of new phenomenal possibilities enveloping those of the present life, afforded by an extension of our insight into the order of nature, would do in an instant.[14]

One cannot help but wonder if James, almost in Platonic fashion, was not attempting to supply an account of religion that would allow the "common man" to continue to believe in the God associated with Christian practice while changing the substance of that belief.[15] In other

---

may not be the "thou" of *The Will to Believe*. In the latter work, James suggests that it is essential that god be conceived as the deepest power in the universe, and under the form of mental personality. He notes, however, that "intrinsically" attributing personality to god need not mean anything more than that which is involved in holding certain things dear, but "extrinsically." "God's personality is to be regarded, like any other personality, as something lying outside my own and other than me, and whose existence I simply come upon and find" ("Reflex Action and Theism," in *The Will to Believe*, 122). For James's reflections concerning how theism requires a movement from the "it" to the "thou," see "Reflex Action and Theism," 134.

14. Ralph Barton Perry, *The Thought and Character of William James* (Cambridge: Harvard University Press, 1948), 257.

15. In an obscure passage from *A Pluralist Universe*, James asks his readers to distinguish the notion of the absolute from what he describes as "another object" with which it is liable to become heedlessly entangled. "The other object is the 'God' of common people in their religion, and the creator-God of orthodox theology. Only thoroughgoing monists or pantheists believe in the absolute. The God of our popular Christianity is but one member of a pluralistic system. He and we stand outside of each other, just as the devil, the saints, and the angels stand outside of both of us. I can hardly conceive of anything more different from the absolute than the God, say of David or of Isaiah. *That* god is an essentially finite being *in* the cosmos, not with the cosmos in him, and indeed he has a very local habitation there, and very one-sided local and personal attachments" (110–111). I simply do not understand what James is about in this passage. He seems to want to say that the "common people" believe in his finite god rather than in Hegel's absolute. It may be true that common people, if they had to choose between the God of David and Hegel's absolute, would choose David's God, but it is hard to see how that creator-God could be "finite."

In the conclusion to *A Pluralist Universe*, James says that the alternative to monism is to accept the notion that "it," by which I assume he means "the absolute," "is not all-embracing, the notion, in other words, that there is a God, but that he is finite, either in power or in knowledge, or in both at once. These, I need hardly tell you, are the terms in which common men have usually carried on their active commerce with God; and the monistic perfections that make the notion of him so paradoxical practically and morally are the colder addition of remote professorial minds operating *in distans* upon conceptual substitutes for him alone" (311–312). James clearly seems to assume that his "god" is what common people *really* worship whether they know it or not. Needless to say, he provides little evidence for such a claim.

words, it was not so much with Christianity that James was identifying when he referred to "us Christians" as with the "common man."[16]

My concern at this point, however, is not why James thought he was justified to call his over-belief "god."[17] Rather, my concern is to understand why James thought that what Christians believe about Christ, the Trinity, or the church are over-beliefs that can have no pragmatic justification. For example, in his chapter on "Conversion" in *Varieties,* James, using Luther as an example, discusses the Christian experience of forgiveness of sins. James notes that Luther no doubt thought that what Christ had done was part of his faith, but that is to conceive of faith intellectually. According to James, the intellectual side of faith is not its most vital aspect. The other part of faith

> is something not intellectual but immediate and intuitive, the assurance, namely, that I, this individual I, just as I stand, without one plea, etc., am saved now and forever. Professor Leuba is undoubtedly right in contending that the conceptual belief about Christ's work, although so often efficacious and antecedent, is really accessory and non-essential, and that the "joyous conviction" can also come by far other channels than this conception. It is to the joyous conviction itself, the assurance that all is well with one, that he would give the name of faith *par excellence.*[18]

16. The importance of James's discovery of the common man is wonderfully analyzed in James Livingston, *Pragmatism and the Political Economy of Cultural Revolution, 1850–1940* (Chapel Hill: University of North Carolina Press, 1994), 158–180. Livingston quotes the Whitmanesque hymn of James to the common man in his 1899 *Talks to Teachers on Psychology* (Cambridge: Harvard University Press, 1983), in which James describes a "revelation" he had on a train trip returning from a Chautauqua event. James was relieved to escape the suffocating routine of this "middle-class" utopia, realizing that he looked forward to returning to "the world," which for all its threatening character was at least interesting. Livingston suggests that this "trip" prepared James for the epiphany he describes in his talk: "Wishing for heroism and the spectacle of human nature on the rack, I had never noticed the great fields of heroism lying around me, I had failed to see it present and alive. I could only think of it dead and embalmed, labelled and costumed as it is in the pages of romance. And yet there it was before me in the daily lives of the laboring classes. Not in clanging fights and desperate marches only is heroism to be looked for, but on every railway bridge and fire-proof building going up today. On freight trains, on the decks of vessels, in cattle-yards and mines, on lumber-rafts, among the firemen and the policemen, the demand for courage is incessant; the supply never fails" (154–155). For a defense of James against those who would interpret such passages as patronizing, see Gerald Myers, *William James: His Life and Thought* (New Haven: Yale University press, 1986), 406–409. According to Myers, James's excited tone in such passages was the result of his having identified the decisive point that the inner lives of other people are hidden from our sensory observations, but their very resourcefulness serves to provide us with hope that life is worth living.

17. James seems never quite to have made up his mind whether to capitalize "god" or not. Sometimes he does, and sometimes he does not, but I can discern no reason for his practice one way or the other.

18. James, *Varieties,* 214.

Yet given James's own pragmatic method, how does Christ become a nonessential belief in contrast to James's vague faith that there is "more"? For example, in *The Meaning of Truth,* James, seeking to counter misunderstandings of pragmatism, suggests that pragmatism maintains a close connection between what is believed and what is required to make true such a belief. "The reasons why I find it satisfactory to believe that any idea is true, the *how* of my arriving at that belief, may be among the very reasons why the idea *is* true in reality."[19] It does not seem to occur to James that attending to the how of what it might mean to be forgiven is not separable from what Christians think God has done for the world in Christ.

The reason James never felt it necessary to explore the relation between the how and the what in Christianity is quite simple. James had an understanding of Christianity, of what he considered its truths and falsehoods, quite independent of his pragmatism.[20] Both defenders and critics of James too often have their attention so focused on his positive and constructive account of religious experience that they fail to attend to what James took Christianity to be. To that task I now turn, intending to show that James arbitrarily—at least within his own pragmatic method—relegates Christian beliefs to a world of unreality.

James on Christianity

One can object that it is unfair to criticize James for failing to understand Christianity. After all, he never pretended to be a Christian or a theologian. Yet James was far too serious a thinker to try to escape criticism of his account of Christianity through the disclaimer that he was not a theologian. Moreover, James saw clearly that unbelievers, if they are to be serious critics of religious belief, must be theologians: "To the extent of disbelieving peremptorily in certain types of deity, I frankly confess that we must be theologians. If disbeliefs can be said to constitute a theology then the prejudices, instincts, and common sense which I chose as our guides make theological partisans of us whenever they make certain beliefs abhorrent."[21]

James did indeed find certain Christian beliefs abhorrent, yet it is by no means clear that James's knowledge of Christianity ever extended

19. James, *The Meaning of Truth,* 275.

20. In *William James,* Myers supports this judgment, observing that James's "declaration at the beginning of *Varieties* that his approach was pragmatic, his focus on consequences, succeeded only in putting aside the question of how science might outdo philosophy in clarifying the sources of religious feeling. His own mystical interpretation was hardly pragmatic, for it ran not from phenomenon to consequences but from phenomenon to inferred origins such that there was no way for such an interpretation to be tested. His philosophy of religion is indeed intriguing, but it is certainly not pragmatic" (466).

21. James, *Varieties,* 279.

much beyond the limits of New England. James was obviously a cosmopolitan, benefiting as well as suffering from his father's eccentric views about how he and his brother should be educated.[22] Accordingly, he was not only exposed to the desiccated Calvinism of New England but surely would have gained some knowledge of Lutheran and Catholic Christianity from his many trips to Europe. Still, the more orthodox forms of Christian practice never seem to have made an impression on him.[23] At least they never seem to have made him rethink what I can describe only as a rather crude understanding of the God Christians worship.

In *A Pluralist Universe,* James attacks the presumption that God created the universe. Such a view, according to James, leaves the human subject outside the deepest reality of the universe. A creator God is assumed to be complete and sufficient unto God's self from eternity, and creation is the free act by which God throws off the world as if it is an extraneous substance. Between God and the world, humans are assumed to be a third substance, which creates a metaphysic in which God says "one," the world says "two," and humans say, "three,"—that, according to James, "is the orthodox theistic view."[24]

22. Much has been made of the significance for William James's own religious views of his father's conversion to Swedenborg, after his breakdown in England in 1844. Yet Swedenborg's influence on the elder James has been overblown. The father was certainly not, as is sometimes suggested, a scholar of Swedenborg's thought. Rather, he followed Swedenborg to the extent that Swedenborg's thought reinforced his own views. There can be no doubt that the senior Henry James was obsessed by philosophical questions about religion, and certainly James was very much his father's son in that respect. However, it is extremely unclear how William James was or was not influenced by his father's explicit views about religion. Insofar as their views are similar, I suspect that they simply shared the generalized assumptions about religion represented by the intellectual classes of their day.

23. Henry Levinson, surely one of the most insightful and sympathetic interpreters of James, observes that in spite of James's general attempt to receive new religions empathetically, he failed in his encounter with old and alien ones: "He treated Roman Catholics the way he treated European monarchies, and in the same breath. Roman Catholicism represented a spirit that had fallen below the secular or civilized level of humanity. During a period when the American Jewish population quadrupled, James failed to interact with Judaism at all. He followed Harvard's official, if informal, policy of taking bright Jews and making them American. It never occurred to him to visit the active Young Men's Buddhist Association in San Francisco when he visited there on several occasions, and the religions of Africa and Oceana were simply savage 'mumbo-jumbo.' It is not insignificant that the philosopher who begged his readers not to miss the joy of being other and different continually pictured 'the asian spirit' as threatening to the West. Being other and different did have its limits." *The Religious Investigations of William James* (Chapel Hill: University of North Carolina Press, 1981), 23–24. James's attitude toward Catholicism stands in marked contrast with that of Henry Adams. For an effective contrast between Adams and James in this respect, see John Patrick Diggins, *The Promise of Pragmatism: Modernism and the Crisis of Knowledge and Authority* (Chicago: University of Chicago Press, 1994), 108–113, 149–157. Robert Richardson, however, in a letter to me suggests that James did read Hindu and Buddist texts.

24. James, *A Pluralistic Universe*, 25.

Orthodox theism, according to James, has been

> so jealous of God's glory that it has taken pains to exaggerate everything in the notion of him that could make for isolation and separateness. Page upon page in scholastic books go to prove that God is in no sense implicated by his creative act, or involved in his creation. . . . God and his creatures are *toto genere* distinct in the scholastic theology, they have absolutely *nothing* in common; nay, it degrades God to attribute to him any generic nature whatever; he can be classed with nothing. There is a sense, then, in which philosophic theism makes us outsiders and keeps us foreigners in relation to God, in which, at any rate, his connexion with us appears as unilateral and not reciprocal.[25]

For James, the dualism intrinsic to the theistic view carries with it consequences for understanding our relationship to God. Humans cannot help but be mere subjects to God, outsiders with no standing. God cannot be the heart of our heart and reason of our reason; rather, God becomes the magistrate who requires that we mechanically obey God's arbitrary commands. Our relationship to such a God is largely determined by analogy to criminal law, which means that we can never hope to achieve intimacy with God. Orthodox theology has had to wage a fight against mystics who have sought such intimacy. James says that he has been told by "Hindoos" that the reason Christianity has not spread in their country is due to the "puerility of our dogma of creation. It has not sweep and infinity enough to meet the requirements of even the illiterate natives of India."[26]

James's account of the Christian doctrine of creation betrays his confusion of Christianity with theism, if not deism. Such confusion is, perhaps, forgivable, given that the Christianity with which James was most intimate was Calvinism shorn of Calvin's Christ. James, however, seems to have read Augustine's *Confessions.* At least in *Varieties,* he uses Augustine to exemplify what he takes to be the classic example of the divided will that achieves unity through conversion. Yet reading Augustine's account of desire, how his heart was restless until it found its rest in God, does not seem to have made James rethink his presumption that the God of Christian orthodoxy cannot be intimate with God's own creatures.[27]

In *Varieties,* James quotes a long passage from Newman that begins with a discussion of God's aseity, from which it is claimed all of God's perfections follow—that is, since God is one and only, his *essentia* and

25. Ibid., 25–26.
26. Ibid., 27–29.
27. James's discussion of Augustine's *Confessions* appears in the chapter in *Varieties* titled "The Divided Self, and the Process of Unification," 156–157.

his *esse* must be given at one stroke—which means that the absence of all potentiality in God obliges him to be immutable, omniscient, and omnipotent. James assumes that Newman's account only confirms his view of orthodox theism, so he breaks off his account of Newman, not wishing to "weary" his reader by pursuing such metaphysical determinations into, for example, the mystery of the Trinity.[28] It simply never seems to occur to James that the doctrine of the Trinity might have a bearing on how one understands creation or on why our knowledge of God's predications rests on analogy.

James thinks such considerations are simply beside the point. No matter how God's attributes are deduced, James thinks the whole exercise pointless. "I cannot conceive," he claims, "of its being of the smallest consequence to us religiously that any one of them should be true. Pray, what specific act can I perform in order to adapt myself the better to God's simplicity? Or how does it assist me to plan my behavior, to know that his happiness is absolutely complete?"[29] From the point of view of practical religion, "the metaphysical monster which [the metaphysical attributes of God] offer to our worship is an absolutely worthless invention of the scholarly mind."[30]

Unlike the metaphysical attributes, James thinks that the moral attributes ascribed to God clearly have pragmatic significance. To speak of God's holiness is to occupy a world in which God can will nothing but good; God's omnipotence secures the triumph of God's intentions; God's justice opens us to divine punishment,[31] even as God's love holds out the promise of pardon. In short, God's moral attributes determine fear and hope and provide a foundation for the saintly life. Nonetheless, James declares not only that "post-Kantian idealists" reject all arguments for God's moral attributes, but also that "it is a plain historic fact that [such arguments] never have converted any one who has found in the moral complexion of the world, as he has experienced it, reasons for doubting

28. James, *Varieties*, 365–367. In *Essays in Radical Empiricism*, James, in support of his account of the relation of agency and act, footnotes Thomas Aquinas on the distinction between *actus primus* and *actus secundus*, but James fails to see how Aquinas's understanding of activity is integral to his understanding of God and God's relation to his creation.

29. James, *Varieties*, 370.

30. Ibid., 371.

31. James had a particular animus against any view of God as judge. In a footnote in *Varieties*, James says that pragmatically the most important attribute of God is his punitive justice, but almost no theologian today would maintain the existence of hell on the basis of logic. Theologians, he claims, have had to draw on conventional ideas of criminal law to develop what it means for God to be a judge, but "the very notion that this glorious universe, with planets and winds, and laughing sky and ocean, should have been conceived and had its beams and rafters laid in technicalities of criminality, is incredible to our modern imagination. It weakens a religion to hear it argued upon such a basis" (372). As we shall see, James even has an account for how humankind has managed to free itself from such a view.

that a good God can have framed it."[32] The book of Job, James says, has forever made "silly" attempts to prove God's goodness by the scholastic argument that there is nonbeing in God's essence.

Just as assertions about God's metaphysical predications make no pragmatic difference, claims about creation are also without practical effect—which explains, according to James, why neither materialism nor theism is an important alternative for the pragmatist. The pragmatist cannot choose between the view that God created everything and the view that the universe is a result of blind physical forces. Pragmatically, such alternatives make no difference, since the world is already completed. For James, the actually experienced world is the same in its details by either hypothesis, namely, it stands there indefeasibly, "a gift which can't be taken back."[33] This is an extraordinary choice of words that should temper how we take James's assertion that a belief in creation has no pragmatic significance. James can hold this view only because he continues to trade parasitically on Christian speech.[34] I cannot imagine a materialist presuming to call the world "a gift."

James, to his credit, asks how humans who once believed in a God who created and judged could have come increasingly to leave such a God behind. Such a transition, he thinks, was simply the result of an empirical evolution.[35] After a few generations, secular alterations occurred that made it impossible to accept once widely accepted notions of the deity. Today, for example, a deity that required bleeding sacrifices to

32. Ibid., 371.

33. James, *Pragmatism,* 50–51.

34. I am not suggesting that the language of gift is without its own problems. For example, I am sympathetic with John Milbank's critique of accounts of God's grace that try to account for the gift in a manner that make the reception of what is given a matter of indifference. Milbank observes in criticism of Jean-Luc Marion that Marion does not see "that exchange equally *constitutes* distance and especially that the distance of Father from Son is a distance established in exchange, as much as an exchange established in stance. Of course, there is an absolute priority of the distance of the Trinity *from us* over our 'exchange' with the Trinity, yet we participate in the trinitarian exchange such that the divine gift only begins to be as gift to us at all (since in this case there is no neutral 'desert') *after* it has been received—which is to say returned with the return of gratitude and charitable giving-in-turn—by us." "Can a Gift Be Given? Prolegomena to a Future Trinitarian Metaphysic," *Modern Theology* 11, no. 1 (January, 1995): 136. James might well find Milbank's analysis lacking in "pragmatic significance," but such a reading can only be the result of a studied blindness.

35. It is not clear to me whom James was reading to shape his account of the development of religion. Levinson, *The Religious Investigations of William James,* reports that James had read historical criticism and in particular Strauss (17). In *Varieties* (100), James footnotes Harnack's *Das Wesen des Christentums,* but, as I suggested in the previous lecture, he never seems to have relied on the work produced by the Protestant liberals. On the whole, James did not seem particularly impressed by those who attempted to save some core of Christianity from its historical accidents—which seems odd, since much of his work can be interpreted as attempting just that.

placate him would be too sanguinary to be taken seriously.[36] Likewise, although a dose of cruelty (deemed retributive justice) and arbitrariness was required as a characteristic of the deity during times of monarchical sovereignty, today we rightly abhor such cruelty. In like manner, ritual worship appears to the modern transcendentalist as addressed to a deity of almost absurdly childish character.[37]

James's account of religious change clearly draws on a progressive account of history that assumes that the current state of consciousness is superior to what has gone before, but he gives us no basis for why we should share such a presumption.[38] James may have assumed that he was providing an argument for this view of history when he explained why all attempts to develop a natural theology are no longer persuasive. For James, the attempt to do natural theology is a response to the contradiction between the phenomenon of nature and the craving to believe that standing behind nature there is a spirit whose expression nature is.[39] Such a craving made arguments for God's existence persuasive for hundreds of years, but slowly counterarguments have washed out the mortar from between the joints of all arguments for God's existence.[40]

According to James, arguments for God's existence now only work for those who already believe in God. And the "bare fact" that all idealists since Kant have felt entitled to ignore such arguments show that they are not sufficient to serve as a foundation for religion. Furthermore, the argument from design has become impossible since Darwin. Darwin opened our minds to the power of chance happenings and showed the

36. James was not so naive as to believe that sacrifice had been eliminated from religious practices. He observes in *Varieties* that though sacrifices to the gods were omnipresent in primeval worship, as cults grew more refined, burnt offerings were superseded by sacrifices more spiritual in nature; for example, Christianity transfigured the notion of sacrifice in the form of the mystery of Christ's atonement (383).

37. Ibid., 279–280.

38. In "The Sentiment of Rationality," in *The Will to Believe,* James gives what can be described only as a "potted history" of what he calls the expansion of the human mind. For example, he suggests that primitive Christianity was an advance to the extent that it was an announcement that God recognized the weak and tender impulses that paganism overlooked. In particular, Christianity took repentance and made it one power within each of us that appealed to the heart of God. After the night of the middle ages, the platonizing renaissance proclaimed the archetype of verity lay in our whole aesthetic being. And what were Luther and Wesley but appeals to powers, faith, and self-despair, which the meanest of men could carry with them without priestly intermediation? The climax of James's account of increasing human creativity was Emerson, whose creed, according to James, was that everything that ever was or will be is here in the enveloping now. So the whole history of the human project is the working out of the principle "stand upon thy feet" (87–88).

39. James, "Is Life Worth Living?" 40.

40. James, *Varieties*, 363.

enormous waste of nature in producing results that get destroyed because of their unfitness. He also emphasized the number of adaptations which, if designed, would argue an evil rather than a good designer. To the grub under the bark the exquisite fitness of the woodpecker's organism to extract him would certainly argue a diabolical designer.[41]

For James, it was finally Darwin and the social arrangements that made Darwin possible that rendered the Christian belief in God unintelligible.

James's arguments against natural theology only confirm the suggestions I made in my first lecture concerning the disastrous results of separating such arguments from their theological home. Neither James's account of the arguments for God's existence nor his criticism of them are philosophically rigorous, but it is significant, for example, that he understood how Aquinas's arguments concerning God's existence work in the *Summa.* Nonetheless, it never occurred to James that the identity of the God one is arguing about matters theologically. James simply assumed, not without reason, that the arguments for God's existence confirmed his assumption that, metaphysically, Christianity entails some variant of theism.

James could not imagine that his rejection of the doctrine of creation might have some connection to his faith in the Darwinian dogma that human existence is an accident, that we have no reason to exist other than our ability to force meaning on the world of brute fact and chaos. James did not need Darwin to discover that we are animals; he could have learned that from Aquinas.[42] Aquinas would have simply found Darwin's views (which he would have no doubt subjected to rigorous critique) to be a confirmation of our status as creatures. What James could have also learned from Aquinas, and this he could not have learned from Darwin, is that it is hard to sustain the human project if we deny our created status. Humanism, even the eloquent humanism to which James gave voice, when separated from the source that makes it intelligible, cannot help but make of humans more or less than what we in fact are.

Just to the extent that James denied the creaturely status of human beings, I suspect it is a mistake to take too seriously his arguments against natural theology as the primary objections he had to Christianity. Those arguments were primarily an expression of James's deep moral objection to Christianity. What really bothered James was not that Christianity seemed to entail false views about the world, but that

41. James, *Pragmatism,* 57.

42. In *Dependent Rational Animals: Why Human Beings Need the Virtues* (Chicago: Open Court, 1999), Alasdair MacIntyre, for example, has provided a wonderful account of the relation of humans to other animals. MacIntyre, rightly I think, regards the account he gives to be one with which Aquinas might well have been sympathetic.

Christianity challenged the moral and political arrangements necessary to sustain the human project without God. James was profoundly right to see Christianity as the enemy of the world he hoped was being born. That James's world has come into being, a world about which he had some misgivings, makes it all the more important to attend to this aspect of his thought. Many Christians today want the world James wanted, while assuming that they can continue to have the Christian God. But James was right to think that you cannot have both.

James's Democratic Critique of Christianity

In the conclusion to *The Varieties of Religious Experience,* James observes:

> It would never do for us to place ourselves offhand at the position of a particular theology, the Christian theology, for example, and proceed immediately to define the "more" as Jehovah, and the "union" as his imputation to us of the righteousness of Christ. That would be unfair to other religions, and, from our present standpoint at least, would be an over-belief.[43]

Why is "unfairness" a concern for a pragmatist? In the next paragraph, James tries to justify his use of "less particularized terms" by arguing that he is working as a scientist of religions who must seek, in connection with the rest of science, to describe religion in terms psychologists may recognize as real. Yet why should "the science of religion" assume the task of being "fair"? Surely truth, not fairness, is the object, even of the science of religion. On the other hand, "fairness" is a crucial value for democracy.

In *A Pluralistic Universe,* James is even more candid about the incompatibility of Christianity with the way of life necessary to sustain democracy:

> The theological machinery that spoke so livingly to our ancestors, with its finite age of the world, its creation out of nothing, its juridical morality and eschatology, its relish for reward and punishments, its treatment of God as an external contriver, an "intelligent and moral governor," sounds as odd to most of us as if it were some outlandish savage religion. The vaster vistas which scientific evolutionism has opened, and the rising tide of social democratic ideals, have changed the type of our imagination, and the older monarchical theism is obsolete or obsolescent. The place of the divine in the world must be more organic and intimate. An external creator and his institutions may still be verbally confessed at Church in for-

43. James, *Varieties,* 421.

mulas that linger by their mere inertia, but the life is out of them, we avoid dwelling on them, the sincere heart of us is elsewhere.[44]

I have no reason to dispute James's description of the waning cultural power of Christian convictions in the face of more democratic social arrangements. But James clearly is not making just a descriptive case. He thinks the displacement of Christianity by democracy is a good thing. Moreover, he thinks democracy is not just a social and political arrangement but the very character of the emerging universe.

But on what grounds does James make such universal claims? Why, given his pragmatic account of truth, are the "particularistic claims" of Christianity to be discounted simply because they are assumed to be "unfair"? At work in such a judgment, I think, are not James's own philosophical reflections but the continuing influence of Emerson and, in particular, his famous 1838 Divinity School address at Harvard.[45] In that address Emerson declared:

44. James, *A Pluralistic Universe*, 29–30. James's appeal to "intimacy" to name the relationship between the self and the world is anything but accidental. The metaphysics James develops in *A Pluralistic Universe* is an attempt to recover intimacy as the mode of relation not only between humans but between all "eaches." Thus he says in a passage immediately after the one just quoted: "The inner life of things must be substantially akin anyhow to the tenderer parts of man's nature in any spiritualistic philosophy. The word 'intimacy' probably covers the essential difference" (31). David C. Lamberth provides an extremely helpful analysis of the importance of the concept of intimacy in James's work; see "Interpreting the Universe after a Social Analogy: Intimacy, Panpsychism, and a Finite God in a Pluralistic Universe," in *The Cambridge Companion to William James*, 237–259. Lamberth's article, as well as his book *William James and the Metaphysics of Experience* (Cambridge: Cambridge University Press, 1999), make clear that the oft made criticism of James's "individualism" is not wrong, but attention to his notion of intimacy would at least suggest that his account of the self was, like Peirce's, triadic. I am sure, moreover, that Lamberth is right to show that James's radical empiricism, and his correlative understanding of "eaches," was part of his resistance to all monism and all totalizing systems, which he associated with Hegel. Lamberth's book is particularly helpful to the extent that he shows how *A Pluralistic Universe* should be understood as part of James's overall agenda.

45. James's admiration for Emerson was constant throughout his life, even though he found himself in some disagreement with Emerson's philosophical views. In *Varieties*, James quotes at length from Emerson's Divinity College address in defense of the view that even though Emerson's views are "godless or quasi-godless creeds" they correspond to James's account of religion (46–48). In the chapter on saintliness in *Varieties* James takes delight in Emerson's remark that Luther would have cut off his right hand rather than nail his theses to the Wittenberg door, if he had supposed that "they were destined to lead to the pale negations of Boston Unitarianism" (281). Though this is an offhand remark, it nonetheless reveals James's general presumption that Protestantism began a progressive movement of the human spirit. For the most thorough as well as persuasive account of Emerson's influence on James, see Charles Mitchell, *Individualism and Its Discontents: Appropriations of Emerson, 1880–1950* (Amherst: University of Massachusetts Press, 1997), 73–114. For his 1903 Centenary Address on Emerson, James reread almost all of Emerson's work, which, according to Mitchell, resulted in the portrait of Emerson becoming for James a de-

Historical Christianity has fallen into the error that corrupts all attempts to communicate religion. It has dwelt, it dwells, with noxious exaggeration about the *person* of Jesus. Men have come to speak of revelation as somewhat long ago given and done, as if God were dead. The Church seems to totter to its fall making almost all life extinct. Historical Christianity destroys the power of preaching, by withdrawing it from the moral nature of man, where the sublime is, where are the resources of astonishment and power. . . . In how many churches, by how many prophets, tell me, is man made sensible that he is an infinite Soul; that the earth and the heavens are passing into his mind; that he is drinking forever the soul of God?[46]

Cornel West, drawing on Sydney Ahlstrom, suggests that Emerson is the creator of what might be called "the American religion."[47] West identifies the main tenets of Emerson's religion with the views that the only sin is limitation, that as such sin can be overcome, and that it is a beautiful and good thing for sin to exist and to be overcome. From this perspective, the emphasis on the "person" of Jesus is perverse because such an emphasis impedes the growth of the new universal religion of

---

scription of his own views. James discovered rereading Emerson that there was a remarkable convergence between Emerson's essays and his own work.

Lord Gifford was also a great admirer of Emerson, whom he describes as one who "does not profess to teach or to enforce religion, but his tone is eminently religious." Gifford observes that even though Emerson is claimed as a Unitarian, he is more a philosophical theist who inclines to "higher or subjective pantheism." "Ralph Waldo Emerson," in *Lord Gifford and His Lectures: A Centenary Retrospective,* ed. Stanley Jaki (Macon, Ga.: Mercer University Press, 1986), 104–105.

46. Ralph Waldo Emerson, "Divinity School Address," in *The Portable Emerson,* new ed., ed. Carl Bode (New York: Penguin Books, 1981), 78–85. I have used Sydney Ahlstrom's compilation of quotations from Emerson's address, in his *A Religious History of the American People* (New Haven: Yale University Press, 1972), 602–603. Given Emerson's views about the particularity of Jesus, it is not surprising that one of the reasons he gives for resigning from the ministry is his conviction that presiding at "the Lord's Supper" should not be one of the essential duties of the clergy. See his "The Lord's Supper," in *The Complete Writings of Ralph Waldo Emerson,* vol. 2 (New York: Wise and Co., 1929), 1099–1105.

47. Cornel West, *The American Evasion of Philosophy: A Genealogy of Pragmatism* (Madison: University of Wisconsin Press, 1989), 17. In *The Real American Dream: A Meditation on Hope* (Cambridge: Harvard University Press, 1999), Andrew Delbanco provides a fascinating account of the development of American religion in which Emerson and James are central actors. Delbanco notes that in the first phase of American civilization, hope was expressed through the Christian story. That story lasted almost two hundred years, but as Christianity came under the pressure of Enlightenment rationality, the Puritan concern for self-realization before God was transformed by Emerson and James into the idea of citizenship in a sacred union. That phase, which lasted until the 1960s, has finally resulted in a third phase in which "the idea of transcendence has detached itself from any coherent symbology" (4–5). According to Delbanco, this is a history of diminution. "At first, the self expanded toward (and was sometimes overwhelmed by) the vastness of God. From the early republic to the Great Society, it remained implicated in a national ideal lesser than God but larger and more enduring than any individual citizen. Today, hope has narrowed to the vanishing point of the self alone" (103).

the human spirit. According to West, Emerson founded this new American religion, but James, in rising to its defense, became its first theologian. In itself, there is nothing odd about the fact that James took on this role, but it is odd that he thought he could so easily dismiss Christian orthodoxy in the name of the practice of this new religion.

Odder still is James's failure to recognize that this religion of democracy could not help but lead to the very form of life he hated—that is, to the loss of the individual amid the collective. West quotes a letter James wrote to Mrs. Henry Whitman in 1899, in which he expresses his disdain for the developments he was beginning to see around him:

> I am against bigness and greatness in all their forms, and with the invisible molecular moral forces that work from individual to individual, stealing in through the crannies of the world like so many soft rootlets, or like the capillary oozing of water, and yet rending the hardest monuments of man's pride, if you give them time; the bigger the unit you deal with, the hollower, the more brutal, the more mendacious is the life displayed. So I am against all big organizations as such, national ones first and foremost; against all big successes and big results; and in favor of the eternal forces of truth which always work in the individual and immediately unsuccessful way, under-dogs always, till history comes, after they are long dead, and puts them on top.[48]

James's distaste for "bigness" is but the expression of the individualism he inherited from Emerson.[49] That individualism, West observes, created in James a genuine empathy for those undergoing hardship but also a naive view about what political means are needed for effective change. Politically, James was a man of neither the left nor the right. He was a libertarian with circumscribed democratic sentiments, an international outlook, and deep moral sensitivity, all of which combined to make him politically impotent, but nonetheless secure in his own sense of integrity.[50] James's criticism of Christianity was an expression of his

48. West, *The American Evasion of Philosophy*, 59.

49. In *Individualism and Its Discontents*, Mitchell criticizes West's interpretation of James's use of Emerson just to the extent that James, in contrast to West's suggestion, moved the "focus of Emersonian theodicy" in the direction of community rather than toward the individual. According to Mitchell, James rejected West's alternative insofar as James refused to consider the individual and society as contending forces. Indeed, James's "gradualism" grew out of his appreciation for the interdependence of social relations and personal experience; it was not, as West suggests, a screen for sacrificing the needs of the community to the desires of the individual (106–107).

50. West, *The American Evasion of Philosophy*, 60. In *Pragmatism and the Political Economy of Cultural Revolution*, Livingstone observes, in a manner similar to West's, that James's fascination with Walt Whitman is perfectly intelligible just to the extent that Whitman represents the kind of unproductive labor legitimated by capitalist developments (169–172). James identifies his general stance toward social change as "meliorism," which he un-

commitment to a social order that he found increasingly hard to justify on his own terms. Nowhere are James's misgivings about the developing social world better revealed than in his attitude toward wealth.

In his chapters on saintliness in *The Varieties of Religious Experience*, James observes that the Christian love of poverty has become unintelligible to English-speaking people:

> We have grown literally afraid to be poor. We despise anyone who elects to be poor in order to simplify and save his inner life. When we of the so-called better classes are scared as men were never scared in history at material ugliness and hardship; when we put off marriage until our house can be artistic, and quake at the thought of having a child without a bank-account and doomed to manual labor, it is time for thinking men to protest against so unmanly and irreligious a state of affairs.[51]

James recommends to his readers that they seriously ponder the development of this attitude toward poverty, judgmentally observing "that the prevalent fear of poverty among the educated classes is the worst moral disease from which our civilization suffers."[52]

---

derstands as an alternative to optimism and pessimism. Meliorism assumes that "salvation" is neither inevitable nor impossible; rather, it is a possibility that becomes a probability the more numerous the actual conditions of salvation become. James thinks that such a position is consistent with pragmatism, which assumes that "some conditions of the world's salvation are actually extant, and she cannot possibly close her eyes to this fact: and should the residual conditions come, salvation would become an accomplished reality" (*Pragmatism*, 137). It is difficult not to think that James's meliorism became the incrementalism of interest-group liberalism. Reinhold Niebuhr's social strategy, which does not seem to have been directly influenced by James, in many ways seems quite similar to what James understood by meliorism.

51. James, *Varieties*, 309. Earlier in his chapter on saintliness, James had sounded this theme more generally, observing that "a strange moral transformation has within the past century swept over our Western world. We no longer think that we are called on to face physical pain with equanimity. . . . The result of this historic alternation is that even in the Mother church herself, where ascetic discipline has such a fixed traditional prestige as a factor of merit, it has largely come into desuetude, if not discredit" (255).

52. Ibid., 310. James's views on the relation of poverty and religion can be interestingly compared to Richard Rorty's celebration of how being well-off has now freed us from the sources that once made religious practices seem intelligible. According to Rorty: "In past ages of the world, things were so bad that 'a reason to believe, a way to take the world by the throat' was hard to get except by looking to a power not ourselves. In those days, there was little choice but to sacrifice the intellect in order to grasp hold of the premises of practical syllogisms—premises concerning the after-death consequences of baptism, pilgrimage, or participation in holy wars. To be imaginative and to be religious, in those dark times, came to almost the same thing—for this world was too wretched to lift up the heart. But things are different now, because of human beings' gradual success in making their lives, and their world, less wretched. Nonreligious forms of romance have flourished—if only in those lucky parts of the world where wealth, leisure, literacy, and democracy have worked together to prolong our lives and fill our libraries. Now the things

Yet James failed to see that the fear of poverty that he thought was undermining the virtues necessary to sustain "a manly and religious way of life" was the result of the creation of an Emersonian world in which Christianity could not help but become what James wanted it to be—namely, a "religion" that had been privatized. For example, James "cordially" paraphrases an insight from Herbert Spencer to the effect that saintly conduct is the most perfect conduct possible in an environment in which all are saints, but in an environment where few are saints, the exact opposite is the case. According to James,

> the whole modern scientific organization of charity is a consequence of the failure of simply giving alms. The whole history of constitutional government is a commentary on the excellence of resisting evil, and when one cheek is smitten, of smiting back and not turning the other cheek also. You will agree to this in general, for in spite of the gospel, in spite of Quakerism, in spite of Tolstoy, you believe in fighting fire with fire, in shooting down usurpers, locking up thieves, and freezing out vagabonds and swindlers.[53]

In short, James wanted what Emerson wanted. But he recognized that in a democratic world some coercion would be necessary, even if such coercion could not be accounted for, much less justified, on Emersonian terms. James thought, however, that such violence would be necessary only on the "edges" of society. What he could not imagine or acknowledge is that violence exists in the very heart of the order he called "democratic."

If James's critique of Christianity in the name of democracy seems confused, it is because James himself was not just of two but of many minds morally about the world he found developing around him.[54] His formulary criticisms of ancient Christianity were but the mirror image

---

of this world are, for some lucky people, so welcome that they do not have to look beyond nature to the supernatural and beyond life to an afterlife, but only beyond the human past to the human future." "Religious Faith, Intellectual Responsibility, and Romance," in *The Cambridge Companion to William James,* 97.

53. James, *Varieties,* 300. James's admiration for utilitarianism seems odd in light of his concern with "bigness"; for surely utilitarianism was and remains the justification for the "scientific organization of charity," insofar as such an organization is but another name for capitalism. Perhaps because he wanted the benefits without the costs, James's views about such an "organization" were ambiguous. In *The Divided Self of William James,* Richard Gale provides a running commentary on the tension between James's utilitarian and deontological commitments.

54. James's understanding of democracy was much less developed than John Dewey's attempt to understand democracy as the working out of the experimental method. For James, "democracy" named the vague Emersonian intuition that a democratic social order was necessary for the production of self-actualizing individuals.

of his romantic celebration of the individual and democracy. What was wrong with Christianity for James was not that it failed to be pragmatic but that it failed to be democratic. In his essay "The Social Value of the College-Bred," James is, as usual, admirably candid, acknowledging that "democracy is a kind of religion" in which the nobility of the future will form a sort of "invisible church."[55] Such a social order is possible only through the creation of an elite formed in the developing university.[56]

The university, therefore, becomes for James—as well as many others who think it best to leave Christianity behind—an alternative to the church. At the very least, the university becomes the institution in modern societies that convinces even those who would remain Christian that their Christian convictions are but "over-beliefs" that can be used to sustain privatized fantasies but that have no purchase as knowledge. This marginalizing of Christianity is necessary to sustain democratic social orders in which the things we most care about must be privatized exactly because they are the things we most care about. In James's democratic world, were such things to be given a purchase in public, they would, at best, lead to what James could regard only as unfairness and, at worst, to escalating conflict.

The challenge facing Christians today is that James's world has so thoroughly become "our" world that we can imagine nothing else. MacIntyre ended his Gifford Lectures by trying to imagine a different kind of university and, by extension, a different world, and I think he was surely on the right track.[57] Any suggestions I might have about such matters must wait, as MacIntyre did, until the end of these lectures. Yet I think it is appropriate before leaving William James to observe that his account of the world he hoped for, as well as of the university that would make such a world feel inevitable, could not, on its own terms, acknowledge the extent to which the university is complicit

---

55. William James, "The Social Value of the College-Bred," in *The Moral Equivalent of War and Other Essays*, ed., with an intro., John Roth (New York: Harper Torchbooks, 1971), 20–21.

56. Frank Lentricchia observes that James underrated, but did not ignore, the corruptive power of capital in fluid democratic contexts. Yet James, according to Lentricchia, did not think that capital could prevent American intellectuals from being, as he thought he was, antiwar and anti-imperialist. "James *did* imagine the American intellectual as defender of a self that is, or should be, inaccessibly private property; a self that is, or should be, the motor principle of American anti-imperialism. . . . The elaborate but symptomatic difficulty in making sense of James is coming to see that his overt commitment to the inalienable private property of selfhood, the original feeling of spontaneous action, the freedom felt within, is an inscription of a contradiction at the very heart of capitalism (and theorists of capital like Adam Smith) because property under capitalism can be property only if it *is* alienable—only if it can be bought, sold, stolen, and when necessary, appropriated." *Ariel and the Police: Michel Foucault, William James, Wallace Stevens* (Madison: University of Wisconsin Press, 1988), 121.

57. Alasdair MacIntyre, *Three Rival Versions of Moral Enquiry: Encyclopaedia, Genealogy, and Tradition* (Notre Dame: University of Notre Dame, 1990), 216–236.

in legitimating the forms of life made possible by violence and sustained by coercion.

James thought pragmatism was an alternative to violence just to the extent that it avoided rationalism and monism. Pragmatism is fully armed and militant against the pretensions of those who would determine the world by theory. Pragmatism stands for no particular results or dogmas; rather pragmatism

> lies in the midst of our theories, like a corridor in a hotel. Innumerable chambers open out of it. In one you may find a man writing an atheistic volume; in the next someone on his knees praying for faith and strength; in a third a chemist investigating a body's properties. In a fourth a system of idealistic metaphysics is being excogitated; in a fifth the impossibility of metaphysics is being shown. But they all own the corridor, and all must pass through it if they want a practicable way of getting into or out of their respective rooms. No particular results then, so far, but only an attitude of orientation, is what the pragmatic method means. *The attitude of looking away from first things, principles, "categories," supposed necessities; and of looking towards last things, fruits, consequences, facts.*[58]

James assumed that the hotel corridor he imagined could be maintained nonviolently. Yet we have learned that no such corridor exists, even in universities. All corridors require patrols. Such patrols, particularly in universities, often claim to be nonviolent, and those who have been victors in the last war often claim to be on the side of "peace." To expose the arbitrary power that pretends to be nonviolent is no easy task. Yet in the name of Christian truth, Reinhold Niebuhr took this task as his life work. Niebuhr is, therefore, often interpreted as the Christian alternative to William James. But unfortunately, at least from my perspective, Reinhold Niebuhr agreed with James far more than he disagreed with him, or so I will argue in the next two lectures.

58. James, *Pragmatism,* 32.

4

The Liberalism
of Reinhold Niebuhr

Reinhold Niebuhr on Reinhold Niebuhr

William James and Reinhold Niebuhr make an odd pair. At the very least, they appear to be a study in contrasts. James was the product of a cosmopolitan and sophisticated world. Niebuhr's world was Midwest provincialism. James went to Harvard. Niebuhr went to Elmhurst College. James never doubted that he lived in a world absent the Christian God. Niebuhr could not imagine a world without Christianity. However, it will be the burden of my argument that these contrasting backgrounds should not distract us from recognizing that James and Niebuhr had far more in common than not. Indeed, I will argue that Niebuhr's Gifford Lectures are but a Christianized version of James's account of religious experience.

That Niebuhr was indebted to James helps explain why *The Nature and Destiny of Man*, at least in America, is second only to James's *Varieties of Religious Experience* as the defining text of the Gifford Lectures.[1] In spite of Niebuhr's early identification as a "neo-orthodox" theologian, he always worked within the "givens" of Protestant liberalism, which means, at the very least, that Niebuhr, like James, assumed that Christianity must be tested by standards generally accepted by the intellectual elites of the day. Niebuhr's emphasis on original sin and his attacks on what he regarded as liberalism's unwarranted confidence in human virtue led some to think that he was attempting an aggressive reassertion of Christian tradition. Yet from the be-

---

1. The same Modern Library selection of the one hundred best nonfiction books of the century that made James's *Varieties* second listed Niebuhr's *The Nature and Destiny of Man* as number eighteen.

ginning to the end of his life, Niebuhr understood that he was theologically a Protestant liberal, and he rightly objected to those who associated him with more orthodox versions of Christianity.[2] The animating center of Niebuhr's life and work was the crafting of an account of liberal Christianity acceptable to a liberal culture and politics. That he is still regarded by many as the last great public theologian of America testifies to his success.[3]

Nowhere is Niebuhr's liberalism more self-evident than in his description of how he understood his work. Defending himself in his "Intellectual Autobiography" against criticism by theologians he describes as representative of the "Barthian persuasion," Niebuhr denies that his apologetic interests compromise the Christian faith. Such criticism prompts him, he says, to expand and defend his

> conception of the circular relation between faith and experience. Since a guiding presupposition, held by faith, acts as a kind of filter for the evidence adduced by experience, it would seem that the theologians are right, and that the modern scientists are wrong in making "experience" a final arbiter of truth. But the matter is more complex. Guiding presuppositions do indeed color the evidence accumulated by experience; but they do not fully control experience. Presuppositions are like spectacles worn by a nearsighted or myopic man. He cannot see without the spectacles. But if evidence other than that gathered by his sight persuades him that his spectacles are inadequate to help him see what he ought to see, he will change his spectacles.[4]

2. In her 1961 biography of Niebuhr, Jane Bingham describes Niebuhr as the victim of inevitable misunderstandings. "There was no pre-existing group that fully agreed with him: if his ideas were too orthodox for the liberals, they were too liberal for the orthodox; and if too secular for the religious, they were too religious for the secular. The integral connection, moreover, between his dual ideas was not always visible to the casual eye. Instead it was like the stem of a tuning fork that has been buried in the ground with only the separate tines visible from the surface. Those people who wished to dig hard could find the underlying stem, but most people either had no wish to make the effort or were busy doing other things." *Courage to Change: An Introduction to the Life and Thought of Reinhold Niebuhr* (1961; reprint, New York: University Press of America, 1993), 44–45. Bingham's book is an invaluable resource for understanding Reinhold Niebuhr not only because she and Niebuhr were close friends, but because her book contains material not otherwise available. It would be stretching the evidence to say that Niebuhr thought his works were misunderstood; still, I think he would have largely agreed with Bingham's judgment. I do not think, however, that such a "misunderstanding" persisted to the end of Niebuhr's life because his work increasingly was accepted as the norm for thinking about Christian ethics.

3. Niebuhr's appearance on the cover of the March 8, 1948, edition of *Time* is often cited as evidence of his public significance. His friendships with people as diverse as Felix Frankfurter, Hubert Humphrey, Abraham Heschel, and W. H. Auden testifies not only to Niebuhr's gregarious and generous spirit, but to his ability to be valued by others because of his religious perspective.

4. Reinhold Niebuhr, "Intellectual Autobiography," in *Reinhold Niebuhr: His Religious, Social, and Political Thought,* ed. Charles Kegley and Robert Bretall (New York: The Macmillan Company, 1956), 15–16.

In 1956, the same year his "Intellectual Autobiography" was published, Niebuhr wrote to Professor Morton White, who had written an article critical of Niebuhr's appeal to original sin. In his letter to White, Niebuhr acknowledges that he may have been foolish for calling the inevitability of self-regard original sin. But he denies that he did so, as White suggests, on *a priori* grounds. Rather, Niebuhr makes the "rueful confession" that the chronology of his thought runs in the opposite direction. He explains that he first learned about "the mystery of the universality of inordinate self-regard and the paradox of our feeling of responsibility for our selfishness." Only later did he find that the resources of the Christian tradition helped him describe what he had discovered.

Niebuhr notes that it was only when he became a theological professor that he really studied the history of thought and, in particular, Augustine. In the process, he became a critical student of Augustine "because his presuppositions seemed to throw light upon facts that had perplexed me." Through Augustine, Niebuhr discovered Paul, whom he had heard of in church, but, he says, "being a liberal Christian, I was rather ashamed of being associated." In response to White, then, Niebuhr says that he arrived at his account of original sin by beginning not with a theological *a priori* but with what he thought he had learned from John Dewey, namely, that the empirical method cannot dispense with presuppositions.[5]

Niebuhr concludes his letter to White by confessing: "An examination of the whole nature of man's historical freedom led me to an espousal of more of the Christian faith than I possessed in the beginning." He explains that by "more of the Christian faith" he means that range of realities comprehended in ideas such as responsibility, sin, and grace. However, he then observes:

> [I have recently been so] shocked by religious obscurantism on the one hand, and religious self-righteousness on the other hand, that I would like to be as polemical against various religious manifestations as I have been against the complacency of the rationalist in the past decades. But I hope I will be empirical in constructing my categories so that I will not condemn the charitable souls together with the self-righteous prigs.[6]

I will explore the theological implications of Niebuhr's understanding of the relationship between faith and experience later in this lecture. The point I would like to make here is that Niebuhr's desire to be empirical, his view that faith, like a pair of spectacles, is "validated" by experience,

---

5. Niebuhr's letter to White is in *Remembering Reinhold Niebuhr: Letters of Reinhold and Ursula Niebuhr*, ed. Ursula Niebuhr (San Francisco: Harper, 1991), 378–379. Niebuhr notes that Dewey rightly saw that any rigorous method must be able to reexamine its own presuppositions, but he failed to see that this is more difficult than he imagined.

6. Ibid., 380.

makes it difficult to separate his theology from his life. With James, too, we confront ties between life and work, but with Niebuhr it is more difficult to separate the life from the work because the "experience" he used both to test and illumine theology was his own.

Of course, it was not just "his" experience because it was Niebuhr's genius to give voice to his experience in such a manner that others recognized their lives in his. That *Leaves from the Notebook of a Tamed Cynic* remains as compelling today as it was in 1929 is an indication not only of the eloquence of Niebuhr's prose, but also of the attraction of his gift for honesty of expression.[7] For example, near the end of this book reflecting on his years in the ministry in Detroit, Niebuhr writes:

> The way Mrs. __ bears her pains and awaits her ultimate and certain dissolution with child-like faith and inner serenity is an achievement which philosophers might well envy. I declare that there is a quality in the lives of unschooled people, if they have made good use of the school of life and pain, which wins my admiration much more than anything you can find in effete circles. There is less whining rebellion against life's fortunes, less morbid introspection and more faith in the goodness of God. And that faith is, whatever the little cynics may say, really ultimate wisdom.[8]

You want to believe anyone who can turn a phrase like "little cynics." Reading Niebuhr's sermons and prayers, as well as his more formal theology, cannot help but bring us pleasure, discovering as we do wisdom that was clearly the result of a life honestly and well lived. Moreover, the very fact that Niebuhr so confidently and successfully strode across the twentieth century seems to confirm his theological perspective. His life (1892–1971) has rightly been regarded as one that helps us understand what it might mean to say that the twentieth century was the American century.[9]

Niebuhr's confidence and success were hard won. He had no time for James-like angst about what he should do with his life. Niebuhr's back-

---

7. Reinhold Niebuhr, *Leaves from the Notebook of a Tamed Cynic* (New York: Living Age Books, 1957).

8. Ibid., 216.

9. There is no end to books and articles on Niebuhr and his family. The Niebuhrs are in their own way every bit as fascinating as the James family. Both families, moreover, can serve as prisms to illumine the cultural and political landscape they inhabited. I have already referenced Bingham's fine book on Niebuhr; equally important are Richard Fox, *Reinhold Niebuhr: A Biography* (New York: Pantheon Books, 1985), and Charles Brown, *Niebuhr and His Age: Reinhold Niebuhr's Prophetic Role in the Twentieth Century* (Philadelphia: Trinity Press International, 1992). In an appendix, Brown provides a useful overview of books on Niebuhr's life and work. The fact that Fox has the audacity to make negative judgments about Niebuhr and his work makes him the target of a vicious attack by Brown. Although I remain agnostic about Fox's psychological speculations concerning the relations between Reinhold and H. Richard, his book clearly remains the best book we have that helps us understand the complex relation between Niebuhr's life and thought.

ground required that, given his ambitions, his life would be one of constant work to "catch up." His mother and father were formidable figures, each contributing to his life in quite different but complementary ways. Niebuhr's father, Gustav, was a German emigrant who found his way into the ministry of the Evangelical Synod—a church that existed mainly in rural areas of the Midwest populated by Germans. German was Niebuhr's first language, which he thought put him at a disadvantage when he went to Yale Divinity School. As his career progressed, however, his ability to speak and read German turned out to be an advantage because the ability to read German was (and is) a crucial survival skill for American academics.[10]

Niebuhr offers this wonderful description of his father and his father's influence on him:

> He was a German-American pastor who combined the tradition of German pietism with devotion to the disciplines of liberal Protestantism as they were embodied in a very great theologian of that time, Adolph Harnack. So I had no sense of restriction, no yearning for any kind of alternative. I chose my profession as a clergyman, incidentally, for reasons my friends think are inadequate. I was thrilled by my father's sermons and regarded him as the most interesting man in our town. So what should I do but be a minister, in his image?[11]

10. Fox provides strong evidence that Niebuhr began to realize during his studies at Yale that he would have to choose between English and German. In a letter to Samuel Press, his most important teacher at Eden Seminary, he declared that he had made up his mind to "cast his lot with the English" (*Reinhold Niebuhr,* 28–29). This was a quite understandable decision, but it was not just a linguistic one. Niebuhr became one of the crucial figures in the Evangelical Synod for helping the church become "American." During World War I, he acted on behalf of the synod to reassure German-American soldiers of the synod that they were right to serve in the American army against Germany. That Niebuhr had to distance himself from his German background is not *the* reason for his Americanism or for the fact that he was such an Anglophile, but he certainly displayed many of the characteristics associated with second generation immigrants in America. In 1916, Niebuhr wrote an article for the *Atlantic* entitled "The Failure of German-Americanism," in which he argued that Germans in America had neither embraced American principles nor represented the best part of Germany, that is, liberal and progressive religion and politics. According to Fox, Niebuhr argued that German theologians had rightly taken the lead "in reinterpreting the old truths of the Christian faith in the light of modern scientific discoveries" (*Reinhold Niebuhr,* 44–45).

11. "An Interview with Reinhold Niebuhr," *McCall's* (February, 1966): 171. This is a remarkable interview conducted by John Cogley, who was the executive editor of *Commonweal.* Cogley was a Roman Catholic who knew Niebuhr and his work well. That the interview was published in *McCall's* is equally remarkable just to the extent that a middlebrow magazine with a wide readership would publish an interview with a theologian. Even in 1966, such an event was rare, and that it happened at all is a testimony to Niebuhr's general stature. Niebuhr responds to Cogley's closing question (whether or not he is glad he chose the ministry) by noting that he is on the whole glad, "insofar as I have adequately exploited the vision of my father. You can't ever be fully glad when you survey a long life in your old age and know how many inadequacies there were in it. I might

Very much his father's son, Niebuhr always regarded himself first and foremost a preacher, but a preacher whose congregation was constituted by a church called America.[12]

Due to his father's early death in 1913, Niebuhr had to miss the graduation exercises at Eden Seminary in St. Louis, even though he had been named the graduation speaker. He then assumed not only his father's ministry but, for the rest of his life, his father's familial responsibilities. These responsibilities included giving his older brother, Walter, financial help, as well as accepting (and benefiting from) his mother's constant presence in his life both in Detroit and New York. That Niebuhr learned to write and to write well was at least partly due to the necessity that he augment his income as a pastor in order to meet the needs of his family.[13]

Niebuhr enjoyed neither James's wealth nor his leisure and was, thus, spared that indecision about what to do with his life. Nonetheless, his different circumstances had an effect that made him quite similar to James in other respects. Niebuhr was, like James, essentially self-educated, and like many self-educated people, he not only possessed an extraordinarily independent mind but refused to allow his thinking to be determined by the increasing professionalization of disciplinary divisions in the universities of America. Even if it is true that the work he did in his denominational schools, Elmhurst and Eden, was not as deficient as he remembers, his highest degree remained the M.A. he received at Yale Divinity School in 1915.[14] Leaving Yale to begin his pastorate in Detroit, however, only

---

have been a historian, because I'm interested in history; but my critical daughter says, 'Daddy, you're not enough of an empiricist to be a good historian.'" Niebuhr often used self-effacement to gain sympathy, but his judgments about himself were usually genuine, honest, and accurate.

12. There are several collections of Niebuhr's sermons that, when published, he called "biblical or sermonic essays." *Beyond Tragedy: Essays on the Christian Interpretation of History* (New York: Charles Scribner's Sons, 1965) is probably his best known collection; but *Discerning the Signs of the Times: Sermons for Today and Tomorrow* (New York: Charles Scribner's, 1946) and *Justice and Mercy*, ed. Ursula Niebuhr (Louisville: Westminster/John Knox, 1974) are wonderful collections. The latter is particularly important as it contains many of Niebuhr's prayers that testify to his profound piety. Fox describes Niebuhr's father as "paradoxically" evangelical *and* liberal, which I think betrays Fox's failure to understand the close connection between pietism and liberalism.

13. Niebuhr's struggle to write as well as spell in English is amply illustrated in his 1914 B.D. thesis, "The Validity and Certainty of Religious Knowledge," which he wrote at Yale. He seems to have learned to write by doing it, but I wonder if he did not learn something from working as a reporter for Walter's newspaper. Whatever the explanation, there is simply no question that he became not only a mesmerizing speaker, but an extraordinary stylist.

14. Brown argues that the education Niebuhr received at Elmhurst and Eden was better than Niebuhr's later accounts suggest. Brown is certainly right that one of the great benefits of Niebuhr's work at Elmhurst was his proficiency in German, which later allowed him to read Troeltsch, Tillich, Brunner, and Kierkegaard (who had been translated into German) before they were translated into English (*Niebuhr and His Age*, 12–20).

meant that Niebuhr now had more time to read, not only theology and philosophy—which he confessed often bored him—but history, politics, and social theory.[15]

Niebuhr's reading habits did not change when in 1928 he went to Union Theological Seminary to teach social ethics. Perhaps nothing better describes Niebuhr's position at Union than the title he was ultimately given—Professor of Applied Christianity.[16] To be sure, as Niebuhr notes in his letter to White, going to Union provided him with the opportunity to school himself more thoroughly in the classics of Christian theology. But his life remained essentially one of constant activity, ranging from working on behalf of the socialist Norman Thomas to later seeking to shape the left wing of the Democratic party by establishing, with Hubert Humphrey, Americans for Democratic Action.

Niebuhr shared with James a passion to make a difference. Niebuhr was more the activist than James, but like James he wanted to do work that would make our lives better. Like James, Niebuhr was often criticized for writing too much, too carelessly, and for a popular audience. It is true that he never met a generalization he did not like. Of course, many of his generalizations—particularly about historical developments—are rightly criticized. For example, he may be wrong that such a thing as the "Classical View of Man" ever existed; or, if it did, he may not have rightly characterized such a view. Such criticisms, however, are beside the point, at least if they are used to dismiss Niebuhr and avoid coming to terms with the power of his central contentions.[17]

Niebuhr's work was his life, and his life was his work. His liberal optimism had been decisively tempered through his pastoral experience and the social realities of Detroit. His optimism thus gave way to a "realism" that required him to take seriously aspects of the Christian tradition he had originally thought outdated. When *Moral Man and Immoral Society* was published in 1932, it was taken by many at the time as a shot across the bow of the liberal optimism of the social gospel.[18] Niebuhr argued that the morality of groups requires calculations of self-interest, which often means

15. In his "Intellectual Autobiography," Niebuhr confesses that as much as he learned from and respected the philosophical theology of his Yale mentor, D. C. Macintosh, he was in time bored by Macintosh's "philosophical theories" (4).

16. There is a wonderful collection of Niebuhr's shorter essays called *Essays in Applied Christianity*, selected and edited by D. B. Robertson (New York: Living Age Books, 1959).

17. Reinhold Niebuhr, *The Nature and Destiny of Man*, intro. Robin Lovin (Louisville: Westminster John Knox Press, 1996), 4–12. Niebuhr characterizes the "classical view of man" as the identification of our rational faculties as the basis of human uniqueness.

18. Reinhold Niebuhr, *Moral Man and Immoral Society: A Study in Ethics and Society* (New York: Charles Scribner's Sons, 1960). That the book was seen by many of Niebuhr's benefactors and friends as a betrayal is some indication that Niebuhr's position appeared radical at the time. In *Reinhold Niebuhr*, Fox provides a useful account of the reception of the book (132–150). Though the early Niebuhr is often associated with the social gospel, it is

that the best that can be achieved in any social conflict is an equitable balance of power. Accordingly, any attempt to apply the self-sacrificial or disinterested love that may characterize relations between individuals to relations between groups is not only impossible but dangerous.[19]

Niebuhr's argument in *Moral Man and Immoral Society* is a departure from the pacifism he espoused for a time after World War I. It is by no means clear what Niebuhr's commitment to pacifism meant, but it is clear that he became disillusioned with the liberal pacifism spawned by the failure of the idealism used to justify the entry of the United States into World War I. This disillusionment, coupled with his increasing appreciation of the necessity of coercion for any reasonable social harmony, put him in search of a more adequate theology for his political "realism."[20] It may be that Niebuhr's attacks on liberal pacifism are so devastating because he is criticizing a position he once held. More interesting, however, than Niebuhr's critique of pacifism as an invitation to self-righteousness or as a naive social policy is his view that pacifism involves a denial of the Protestant doctrine of justification. In 1940, in "An Open Letter (to Richard Roberts)," Niebuhr said:

---

unclear what that means. Niebuhr assumed that Christian salvation involved more than the individual and, therefore, that the gospel must be applied to economic and political relations. That such views were simply assumed by Niebuhr surely is the result of the development of the social gospel. Yet there is little indication that Niebuhr read deeply in the works of the social gospelers. His 1957 article "Walter Rauschenbusch in Historical Perspective" credits Rauschenbusch with a rediscovery of the prophets but criticizes the social ethic of the social gospel for failing to understand that love is more imprudent and uncalculating than mutual love and contains more universalistic demands that will challenge any particular community. Moreover, Niebuhr argues, Rauschenbusch's legitimation of the regnant idea of progress in his time but proves how vulnerable we all are to the illusions of our generation. Niebuhr's essay on Rauschenbusch can be found in the collection of Niebuhr's essays entitled *Faith and Politics: A Commentary on Religious, Social, and Political Thought in a Technological Age*, ed. Ronald Stone (New York: George Braziller, 1968), 33–45. Needless to say, Niebuhr's account of Rauschenbusch fails to appreciate Rauschenbusch's quite sophisticated understanding of the complexities of social reform.

19. Niebuhr once said that the title of *Moral Man and Immoral Society* should have been *The Not So Moral Man in His Less Moral Communities;* the remark appears in his helpful 1965 overview of his work, *Man's Nature and His Communities: Essays on the Dynamics and Enigmas of Man's Personal and Social Existence* (New York: Charles Scribner's Sons, 1965), 22.

20. Niebuhr's renewed appreciation of "orthodoxy" found its first expression in the Rauschenbusch Memorial Lectures at Colgate-Rochester Divinity School in 1934. These lectures were published as *An Interpretation of Christian Ethics* (1934; reprint, New York: Living Age Books, 1956). Niebuhr's strategy to play liberalism and orthodoxy against one another, a strategy he used for the rest of his life, is fully on display in this book. According to Niebuhr, liberalism always runs the danger of capitulating to the prejudices of the contemporary age with its overly optimistic view of humanity. Orthodoxy's danger is to identify prematurely the transcendent will of God with canonical moral codes or an authoritarian church. In *An Interpretation*, Niebuhr is clear that the ethics of Jesus requires nonresistance, but that is why Jesus' ethic cannot be relevant to modern social ethics other than as an "impossible ideal" that judges all human accomplishments.

I do not believe that war is merely an "incident" in history but is a final revelation of the very character of human history. I do not believe that we ought to "soft-pedal the incarnation at every international crisis." I believe that an international crisis merely reveals in its most vivid form what human history is like, and I accuse pacifists of not being aware of its character until it is thus vividly revealed. At that moment they seek to escape history and its relative responsibilities by a supreme act of renunciation. I do not believe that the incarnation is "redemption" from history as conflict. Since I believe that sinful egoism expresses itself on every level of moral and spiritual achievement and is not absent from the highest levels of Christian life, I cannot regard redemption as freedom from sin. The redemption in Christ is rather the revelation of a divine mercy that alone is able to overcome the contradictions of human history from which even the best of us cannot extricate ourselves. I believe, with the Protestant Reformation, that any claim that we have overcome this contradiction and that Christ has become our possession merely leads to a new form of egoism, namely, pharisaic pride. In other words I take the Reformation doctrine of "justification by faith" seriously and I observe that the spiritual ground upon which our modern pacifism has grown is a sectarian perfectionism that hasn't the slightest idea of what the Reformation meant by its doctrine of "justification by faith."[21]

From 1940 on, Niebuhr devoted his life and work to the development of these ideas. Once he had made the decisive turn away from liberal optimism and pacifism (as he understood them), Niebuhr worked to provide a theological account that could justify what he had learned. In the process, he became for many people, both Christians and non-Christians, *the* theologian of his time, which is to say of the twentieth century. No doubt Niebuhr's reputation was partly due to his location in New York, but his influence is also a testimony to his remarkable energy and intelligence, his gregarious love of other people, and his rootedness in the culture produced by mainstream Christianity.

21. Reinhold Niebuhr, "An Open Letter (to Richard Roberts)," in *Love and Justice: Selections from the Shorter Writings of Reinhold Niebuhr,* ed. D. B. Robertson (New York: Meridian Books, 1967), 268–269. Because, allegedly, they knew they had to withdraw from political involvement, Niebuhr expresses respect for the pacifism of the groups that constituted what is called the left-wing of the Reformation, but he also thought his theological critique applied to them. John Howard Yoder responded decisively to Niebuhr's critique, but because Niebuhr had so effectively established the terms of the debate, Yoder's criticism had, at least until recently, little effect. See John Howard Yoder, "Reinhold Niebuhr and Christian Pacifism," *Mennonite Quarterly Review* 29 (April 1955), 101–117. This essay was later published as Christian Peace Mission Pamphlet 6 (Scottdale, Pa.: Herald Press, 1968). For a critique of Niebuhr that draws on Yoder in this respect, see Michael Cartwright, "Sorting the Wheat from the Tares: Reinterpreting Reinhold Niebuhr's *Interpretation of Christian Ethics,* in *The Wisdom of the Cross: Essays in Honor of John Howard Yoder,* ed. Stanley Hauerwas, Chris Huebner, Harry Huebner, and Mark Nation (Grand Rapids: Eerdmans, 1999), 349–372.

That Niebuhr's account of Christianity was so persuasive to so many is but a display of the vitality of the Protestant culture that produced and sustained him. That we can now see (or so I will argue) that his theology is no more persuasive than James's defense of religious experience is an indication that the Protestant culture Niebuhr required to make his work intelligible no longer exists. If I am right that Niebuhr was the theologian of a culture that has now passed, and if, as I suggested in the last lecture, the challenge facing Christians today is to be theologically imaginative in the Jamesian world that stands in its stead, then it is imperative that we understand why Niebuhr's attempt to validate the "biblical faith" not only failed but had to fail.

In one sense, Niebuhr's failure is James's success, just to the extent that James understood that a truly democratic social order could not hold on to the Christian God, not even the God of Protestant liberals. But, ironically perhaps, in another sense, Niebuhr failed precisely because he himself was a Jamesian. Indeed, by the time Niebuhr had finished at Yale, he had developed a theory to test the meaning and truth of religious claims by considering primarily their ethical implications. In effect, Niebuhr's life became one of the sites in which his theory was tested.

Niebuhr called this theory "pragmatism," and by his own account, he had learned of it from reading William James. To understand why Niebuhr's attempt to validate "biblical faith" had to fail is, first, to understand the relationship between James's pragmatism and Niebuhr's theory concerning the validation of theological claims. Niebuhr's theory is largely implicit in his Gifford Lectures, and it is one of the reasons they were so persuasive. To understand Niebuhr's theory and how it shaped his Gifford Lectures requires close attention to his earliest works and to the impact James had upon them.

The Validity and Certainty of Religious Knowledge: Niebuhr Applying James

As I have indicated, Niebuhr was often misunderstood as representing a return to Christian orthodoxy, particularly after the publication of *The Nature and Destiny of Man*. Moreover, throughout his work, Niebuhr engaged in a relentless critique of John Dewey, who for Niebuhr represented the typical liberal and optimistic view that social problems could be solved by more education coupled with scientific management.[22] Niebuhr's sup-

22. Niebuhr's attack on Dewey began in *Moral Man and Immoral Society*, which was originally published in 1932. Niebuhr accused Dewey of failing to see, "in spite of his great interest and understanding of the modern social problem," that the real cause of social inertia is "our predatory self-interest" (xiii–xiv). In *Reinhold Niebuhr and John Dewey: An American Odyssey* (Albany: State University Press of New York, 1993), Daniel Rice documents a conversation

posed orthodoxy together with his criticism of Dewey might give the impression that he had no use for pragmatism or for anyone in the pragmatic tradition. Yet in a letter to a friend, Niebuhr says: "I stand in the William James tradition. He was both an empiricist and a religious man, and his faith was both the consequence and the presupposition of his pragmatism."[23] And in 1961, Niebuhr wrote an introduction to a new edition of *The Varieties of Religious Experience,* which he praised as a "milestone" in religious thought: "For James combines a positive approach to religion with a nondogmatic and thoroughly empirical approach to the religious life and various types of religious experience."[24]

The influence of James on Niebuhr is nowhere more apparent than in his 1914 Yale Divinity School thesis, "The Validity and Certainty of Religious Knowledge." It may seem remarkably unfair to call attention to such an early and never published work, but the methodological convictions that determined all of Niebuhr's subsequent work are stated in his thesis.[25] Of course, over the years his argument became increasingly so-

---

late in Niebuhr's life in which he acknowledged that he and Dewey shared more than he had originally thought, which is certainly true (xvii–xix). Rice rightly contends that Niebuhr should be understood as "a second-generation pragmatist who, having learned well from both James and Dewey, was in the process of forging his own unique species of theological pragmatism" (xxii). In *Faith and Knowledge: Mainline Protestantism and American Higher Education* (Louisville: Westminster/John Knox, 1994), Douglas Sloan observes that Dewey and Niebuhr were very close: Dewey was pursuing an ethics of pragmatism in the context of his natural piety; Niebuhr was pursuing a similar path in the context of his biblical piety. Sloan notes that it would be relatively easy for critics to take the next step and say, "Let us just be pragmatic in whatever context we find ourselves" (123).

I suspect that Dewey was right, however, to distrust Niebuhr as a philosophical ally. Rice quotes a devastating letter Dewey wrote in 1947 in which he says that he has the impression that Niebuhr and Kierkegaard "have completely lost faith in traditional statements of Christianity, haven't got any modern substitute and so are making up, off the bat, something which supplies to them the gist of Christianity—what they find significant in it and what they approve of in modern thought—as when two newspapers are joined. The new organ says 'retaining the best features of both'" (86–87). Though Dewey is clearly wrong about Kierkegaard, his judgment about Niebuhr is very perceptive.

23. Quoted in Bingham, *Courage to Change,* 224.

24. Reinhold Niebuhr, introduction to William James, *The Varieties of Religious Experience* (New York: Collier Books, 1961), 5. Niebuhr's only critical remark about James is that his account of mysticism does not come to terms with "its tendency to flee the responsibilities of history and engage in premature adventures into eternity" (7). Fox describes Niebuhr as a "thoroughgoing Jamesian pragmatist," who believed that "truth in the moral realm was personal, vital, a product of will as much as mind, confirmed not in logic but in experience. Truth was what 'worked'—as long as it contravened no known facts—in the furtherance of desired ends. Christians could spark human brotherhood only by liberating the hidden resources contained in liberal Protestantism itself: Jesus' prophetic, paradoxical Gospel, a message not of propositional truths, but of poetic, dramatic, 'irrational' truths" (*Reinhold Niebuhr,* 84).

25. A copy of "The Validity and Certainty of Religious Knowledge" can be attained from the Library of Congress, which houses the Reinhold Niebuhr Papers in its manu-

phisticated and enriched by other sources, but his position remained basically the argument he developed in 1914. Richard Fox rightly observes, for example, that the fundamental structure of the first volume of *The Nature and Destiny of Man* was "already laid out in Niebuhr's B.D. thesis written at Yale almost three decades before."[26]

Niebuhr begins his thesis with a section entitled "The Decadence of Authority Religion." He observes that originally humans believed that it was impossible to know about God except from God, but as they came to realize the relativity of all knowledge, as well as the "special difficulties" of religious knowledge, they sought more certainty. The search for certainty resulted in the standardization of revelation through canonization. But as humans grew more rational and bolder in their use of reason, they looked for rational grounds for their faith as an alternative to appeals to authority. This revolt against authority became particularly acute with the development of the historical sciences applied to the canon and with the birth of natural science, which resulted in positivist philosophy. The historical sciences undermined certainty in the content of revelation, and natural science called into question the very possibility of revelation.

Niebuhr notes that in response to the application of the historical sciences to the canon, some people have tried to reassert the absolute authority of Christ by accepting the metaphysical doctrines of the ancient creeds. Niebuhr argues, however, that this response results in the falsification of Jesus' true authority, which is to be found in his personality. In *Does Civilization Need Religion?* which is in many ways but an updating of the argument he began in his B.D. thesis, Niebuhr says: "Jesus is valuable to the modern Christian because he offers an escape from the theological absurdities of the ancient creeds; meanwhile his ethical and religious idealism will not leave unaffected the lives of those who profess him. In time it may become the instrument of regeneration of Western society."[27] In his later work, Niebuhr was more appreciative of the "absurdity" of some of the church's creedal attempts, but he never abandoned the presumption that the Jesus who is the result of historical criticism is the only Jesus whom we can "follow."[28]

---

script division. Niebuhr wrote his thesis under the direction of D. C. Macintosh, a Protestant liberal theologian who was attempting to develop theology as an "empirical science" in which, in the words of Mark Heim, "experiential religious adjustment was believed to provide valid knowledge of God." "Prodigal Sons: D. C. Macintosh and the Brothers Niebuhr," *Journal of Religion* 65, no. 3 (July, 1985): 337. It was surely Macintosh who introduced Niebuhr to James.

26. Fox, *Reinhold Niebuhr,* 202.

27. Reinhold Niebuhr, *Does Civilization Need Religion?* (New York: The Macmillan Co., 1927), 68.

28. In a wonderful, short essay that Niebuhr wrote in 1914 for the Eden Seminary magazine, *The Keryx,* he defends Yale Divinity School from the charge of Unitarianism. He observes that the charge derives from the practice of the Yale scholars who hold the Bible to the same historical tests as any other text. This means that the Bible vanishes as a super-

Speaking of the birth of natural science, Niebuhr notes that religion has always had to deal with naturalism as a perennial foe; but natural science has made the challenge more formidable. Indeed, the discovery of the law of evolution seems to prove that naturalism is true and, as a result, makes all forms of supernaturalism incredible.[29] Niebuhr says that Bergson's work challenges the materialism that some presuppose is a correlate of evolutionary views; still, the more we discover about individual causes, the less need there is for a first cause. Moreover, the psychological sciences, which are not as developed as evolutionary science, tend to confirm naturalistic accounts of our existence.

In short, this newfound naturalism seems to have won the day; however, Niebuhr argues in his thesis that the inadequacy of naturalism is revealed by

> the generally recognized need of humanity for religion and religious truth. To put it as briefly as possible we may say that the demand for religion is the demand for personality. We find ourselves in an impersonal universe. Its laws do not respect those things which are dear to us and, as we think, necessary for our happiness. We cannot understand ourself

---

natural authority and that its truth, as Spinoza contended long ago, must, like any other position, appeal to the best reason and the highest spiritual interests of humanity. Yet according to Niebuhr, after this process has done its work, systematic theologians are left to formulate their own Christologies in light of the facts at hand, so conceptions of Christ may be as high as even the most conservative could wish. "Yale-Eden," in *Young Reinhold Niebuhr: His Early Writings, 1911–1931*, ed. William Crystal, foreword John Bennett (New York: Pilgrim Press, 1977), 53–58.

Niebuhr, however, was never tempted to defend a "high Christology." For example, he assumed throughout his work that it made sense to talk about "the ethics of Jesus" without the need to engage in any further christological claims. Of course, "Jesus' ethic" was primarily construed as disinterested love, for which the cross is the ultimate example. See, for example, Niebuhr's account of the ethic of Jesus in *An Interpretation of Christian Ethics*, 43–62. That Niebuhr never reconsidered his contention that the only Jesus we can follow is the Jesus of "history," and that, therefore, Christian ethics is reducible to what we can abstract from the life of Jesus is clear from his course on the history of Christian social ethics, which he taught every year until he retired. The second lecture in the course was entitled "The Ethics of the New Testament: Jesus in the Synoptics," and it was followed by the lecture "The Ethics of Jesus." Recordings of all of Niebuhr's lectures for this course are available from the Reinhold Niebuhr Audio Tape Collection of Union Theological Seminary in Richmond, Virginia. I have listened to Niebuhr's lectures several times, but I am also using a transcript of the lectures prepared by James Fodor. The audio collection also contains sermons and random lectures by Niebuhr and, in particular, his memorable retirement lecture.

29. In *Does Civilization Need Religion?* Niebuhr observes that there can be no question that the development of the physical sciences has increased the difficulty of justifying the personalization of the universe upon which all religious affirmations are based. Yet he maintains that "no total view of reality can ever be permanently mechanistic, for new types of reality do emerge and science is able to explain only the process and not the cause of their emergence" (11).

except in the light of the moral law. We find our life without purpose if it has not the purpose of striving for the right and the just. But the universe does not appreciate the moral order. It has no place for moral values. The laws of the external, of nature, totally disregard the peculiar spiritual realities of man. It destroys them. And yet we know that there can be no morality if it be not eternal. Man could not be brought to make a single moral struggle if he were forced to believe the results he achieves to be without permanence. It does not matter now whether or not man finds permanence and eternity of the values in himself necessary or whether he can be satisfied to know that the fruits of his struggle will be conserved in the universe. But the fact does matter that man cannot understand himself without the moral order nor the moral order without some warrant of permanence. This is the demand for an efficient God, for a God who insures the moral order and the permanence of moral values and personal realities. This need of the soul may as we shall see not be its only one, nor even its most important one, but it is certainly the one most widely recognized by thinkers outside of religion or those who study it from without. It is the religious problem of most philosophers. Fichte called it the faith in a moral order of the universe. For Jacobi it was the reality of the ideal. It is the need James assumes when he calls religion a consciousness of the highest social values.[30]

Niebuhr observes that the typical answer to this demand for personality is humanism; more specifically, the answer comes as a Comteian call for the preservation of moral values in the interest of the race. Yet society and humanity are but abstractions of the individual, which places naturalism in a dilemma because it has undermined the possibility of such a high evaluation of the personality. Personality simply cannot make sense in an impersonal universe. So humanism is an inadequate response to naturalism. In the face of this inadequacy, some people long for a God who can insure success in the struggle of life. Those desiring such a God

---

30. Niebuhr, "The Validity and Certainty of Religious Knowledge," 11–12 (with some corrections to Niebuhr's spelling). I find it impossible to read this passage without thinking that Niebuhr wrote it having just read the James's "Conclusions" in *The Varieties of Religious Experience*. In *Does Civilization Need Religion?* Niebuhr writes: "Even the refinements and artificialities of urban life will not save man from facing nature's last and most implacable servant—death, nor free him of the necessity of making some kind of appeal against the obvious victory which nature claims at the grave. The fight of personality against nature is religion's first battle, and that is one reason why there is always a possibility that other struggles will be neglected by it. Traditional religion fails in its social tasks partly because men have suffered longer from the sins of nature than from the sins of man; and religious forms and traditions are therefore better adjusted to offer them comfort for these distresses than any other from which they suffer. Religion is not yet fully oriented to the new perils to personality which are developed in civilization. At its best religion is both a sublimation and a qualification of the will to live" (25–26). Niebuhr does not support his contention that human beings have suffered longer from the "sins" of nature than from the sins of other human beings. It is surely a curious judgment.

are called "tender-minded" by some naturalistic thinkers. Yet the quest for purpose is a justified demand because otherwise we could not understand life with its moral struggle.

But, Niebuhr asks, can we believe that such a God exists? In reply to this rhetorical question, Niebuhr says that if we need such a God, then we should assume that this God exists, and we should act accordingly. Niebuhr says that this reply has been made possible by the recent development of pragmatic thought, which "is here fully appropriated."[31]

According to Niebuhr, Kant's distinction between pure and practical reason, which is essentially a distinction between reason and faith, made pragmatic justification possible. This distinction has culminated in pragmatism on the one hand and value judgment theory on the other.[32] Pragmatism is not, Niebuhr says, the extreme agnostic view that assumes that whatever works is true; rather, it is the view that we test the truth of ideas by the manner in which they "work." Accordingly, pragmatism "does not give us a conception of truth. It presents us only with a new method of obtaining it or, more correctly, explains a very old method."[33] "We see," Niebuhr says, concluding the second section of his argument, "that once the needs for religion are justified, the need for an efficient and intimate God, that positivism proves its own inadequacy."[34]

In the third section of his thesis, "Metaphysics and Supernaturalism," Niebuhr distinguishes his defense of theism from idealistic and monistic metaphysics. Religion needs a transcendent God, he says, but one whose separation from the world and from humanity does not preclude social

31. Niebuhr, "The Validity and Certainty of Religious Knowledge," 15. Whether Niebuhr "fully appropriated" James is open to question. For example, Niebuhr seems to have a much less sophisticated account of Darwin's significance than James does. For Niebuhr, Darwin seemed to confirm a mechanistic account of the universe. James rightly saw that Darwin's challenge was to raise the question of the chance character of our existence. It also appears that Niebuhr failed to appreciate how *The Principles of Psychology* serve as the necessary background to James's account of "will" in "The Will to Believe." Niebuhr never seemed to appreciate the relationship between James's account of habit and his account of "belief." I am indebted to Mr. Roger Owens for helping me see the importance of Niebuhr's failure fully to appropriate James.

32. Niebuhr, "The Validity and Certainty of Religious Knowledge," 31. Niebuhr associated theories of "value judgment" with the work of Albrecht Ritschl, whom he also appropriated. Whether the influence of Troeltsch later modified Ritschl's influence on Niebuhr is not clear, but certainly Niebuhr's later work indicates that Ritschl's work was but background for him.

33. Ibid., 15.

34. Ibid., 16. The full conclusion to Niebuhr's argument is as follows: "If God and his activity is necessary to understand personal existence and if a certain knowledge of Him and His activity is necessary to make life bearable and if furthermore the old certainty of this knowledge has been taken from us, it becomes then our task to find, if possible, a new rational ground of certainty regarding the supernatural world and its existence. We have seen that this certainty has centered around the experience of religion in the heart of men" (16).

intercourse between humans and God. According to Niebuhr, idealism does not support this kind of God because, as James rightly observes, you can never be intimate with the God of Spinoza or Hegel. Even more problematic is the fact that the world of absolute idealism is a world of necessity in which there is no room for freedom. Such a world, Niebuhr suggests, quoting James, gives humans a moral holiday that turns out to be a counsel of despair because individuals will never do their best if they do not feel that things depend on them. James's revolt against such a world is not only the revolt of philosophers against a system of thought, but "the revolt of a growing moral consciousness in men, that is becoming increasingly impatient with a universe in which its struggles are without effect and its powers not its own. Man wants to know that the battle of life is not a sham battle before he can be persuaded to take a real interest."[35]

If idealism is rejected, however, then, says Niebuhr, realism seems to be the only alternative; but realists are "tough-minded" because they do not desire to be friends of religion. Yet according to Niebuhr, realism is comparatively young, and in its youth it says nothing of the supernatural; it thus leaves room for what James calls "over-beliefs," which are just what we need for religious certainty. What matters is not that metaphysical realism supports religion, but that it is not against it. "In this task realism promises to become a real friend of religious supernaturalism. The work of such men as James and Bergson shows us how favorable to religion the verdict of realistic thought may be."[36] Moreover, realism uses the empirical method, which means that it has no preconceived metaphysics but is willing to alter its views if the facts warrant such alteration. Realism is even willing to accept facts even if it has difficulty bringing them into perfect consistency with other facts.[37]

To expand his account of the friendly relationship between realism and religion, Niebuhr draws on Bergson and distinguishes three "lines" of

35. Ibid., 21. Brown says that in preparation for writing his thesis, Niebuhr read some fifty books, which included *The Varieties of Religious Experience, The Will to Believe,* and *Pragmatism: A New Name for Some Old Ways of Thinking* (*Niebuhr and His Age,* 17–18). Brown notes that Niebuhr kept James's volumes for the rest of his life, which I am sure must be true, but I suspect he seldom returned to them. Niebuhr was not one to dwell over positions he thought he had mastered, nor did he read with the attitude that he really wanted to understand what this or that author was saying. He read to learn and to use, which, when everything is said and done, meant he often read well indeed.

36. Niebuhr, "The Validity and Certainty of Religious Knowledge," 22.

37. Robin Lovin has provided the best analysis and defense we have of Niebuhr's "realism"; see *Reinhold Niebuhr and Christian Realism* (Cambridge: Cambridge University Press, 1995.) Lovin maintains that Niebuhr was not only a political realist, but also a moral and theological realist. According to Lovin, a moral realist "holds that whether a moral statement is true or false depends on a state of affairs that exists independently of the ideas that the speaker or the speaker's community holds about the appropriate use of moral terms" (13). If that is what realism entails, then I am sure Niebuhr was a realist, but I suspect that he is more properly understood as an empiricist.

reality: matter, life, and consciousness. In matter, necessity reigns, but as soon as we find organized life we can observe a certain freedom. Such freedom increases in higher animals and reaches its culmination in the consciousness of humans. Consciousness, according to Bergson, enters matter and overcomes its inertia, but consciousness is also overcome by matter. "Therefore," Niebuhr says "that which we call unconscious life is a curious compromise between consciousness and matter. But it is natural that if this is the nature of life it cannot be understood without complete consciousness somewhere and so we have a superconsciousness, God. Thus supernaturalism is the result of the strictly empirical method."[38] On these grounds, Niebuhr suggests that the recent history of thought gives us hope that the necessity of supernaturalism and the primacy of consciousness can be arrived at empirically. And he suggests that this empirical exercise points us toward a conception of God that comes close to traditional theism, or at least to a theism that is more serviceable to modernity than is a religion based on miracles.

Niebuhr says that such a conception of God can be neither completely transcendent (as in absolute idealism) nor completely immanent (as in absolutistic theology). As long as God is thought to be in all the processes of time and also free in willing them, we can find no place for human freedom or for a conscious relationship with God. Again, Niebuhr declares, Bergson's distinction between consciousness and life makes it possible to understand how God could be immanent in the activities of the universe and of human beings, but in a manner that leaves a place for human freedom:

> God becomes limited by finite powers as he enters them. . . . He is limited by the determinism and necessity of fields which he enters. Here in human consciousness determinism is at its minimum. In other words, whatever other miracles may be possible (we can never establish the exact limits of this transcendence) the miracle of revelation, of conscious communion with God, is the most certainly possible. And while miracles have been called the dearest children of faith I think we can readily see that of all miracles of revelation, God's conscious relation to man is the only one absolutely necessary.[39]

Niebuhr observes that the principle objection to such a theism is that God is not in sufficient control of the universe to insure God's purposes. Niebuhr responds that this insufficiency of divine power may be a weakness of the "new theism," but we must not consider it a necessary weakness because then we would be plunged back into the old absolutism. Faith as a means

---

38. Niebuhr, "The Validity and Certainty of Religious Knowledge," 23–24.

39. Ibid., 26. Niebuhr observes that James's philosophy in this respect is similar to Bergson's, but James does not make the same exhaustive investigation of consciousness. "James's reason for believing in the transcendent God of religion is rather his belief that religious experience establishes the reality of such a God" (26–27).

of securing truth can be justified only by being proven to be in harmony with reason and knowledge. But as Kant pointed out, Niebuhr says, one of the peculiarities of the truths of faith is they cannot be completely verified. And the less we can verify a judgment, the more we must enter into it with all of our previous conceptions and ways of thinking. According to Niebuhr, that is why we call religious knowledge "faith" and say that it comes from the heart rather than the head. Such knowledge may be beyond complete verification, but it is not without justification. Rather, this new theism, Niebuhr declares, is congruent with James's brilliant defense of the "will to believe"—which points out not only that almost all our judgments are made on the basis of such subjective factors, but that our personal values are more certainly true than anything in the scheme of existence.[40]

James would not have been entirely happy with Niebuhr's "use" of his work. At the least, Niebuhr's theism appears more robust than any theism with which James, even in his most expansive mood, would have felt comfortable. What is crucial about Niebuhr's account, however, is not whether he got James right, but that in this B.D. thesis we see the influence of James upon the fundamental methodological moves that would shape all of Niebuhr's subsequent work.

By his own description, as well as the description of others, Niebuhr's subsequent work was the work of Christian ethics; however, his ethics was but a part of his ongoing attempt to validate his religious convictions. An early example of this intertwining of ethics and the validation of religion can be found in *Does Civilization Need Religion?* where Niebuhr observes: "The fact is more men in our modern era are irreligious because religion has failed to make civilization ethical than because it has failed to maintain its intellectual respectability."[41] Another example can be found in a collection of his essays called *Faith and Politics*, which appeared forty years later. In the preface to this collection, Niebuhr describes his work in terms reminiscent of his B.D. thesis. He observes that the essays collected in this volume exhibit what some may take to be two contrasting themes. The first theme is evident in his attempt

to validate the resources of biblical faith by applying its moral imperatives and its law of love, enjoining responsibility for the neighbor's welfare in a technical age. Today, social responsibilities must be guided by norms derived from all moral and empirical disciplines. A sacred text or a religiously sanctified tradition of past ages are inadequate guides to the ever-changing human relations of a secular culture. The second theme is an explanation of the vitality of religious life in an age which expected the death of religion, after historical scholarship had discredited the legends in which the early life of religion abounds. The reason for this vitality is that religious faith is

40. Ibid., 34.
41. Niebuhr, *Does Civilization Need Religion?* 12.

an expression of trust in the meaning of human existence, despite all the cross purposes, incongruities, and ills in nature and history. It is one of the misunderstandings of modern culture that these ills make faith in God impossible. In fact they make it necessary. Faith in an ultimate and mysterious source and end of existence gives men the possibility of affirming life.[42]

This is a quintessential Niebuhrian passage, but the sentiment is surely pure James. Of course, one might argue that although the sentiment is James, the content is not, given that Niebuhr's pragmatic validation of religion involved theological commitments that James did not share. In fact, however, Niebuhr was a Jamesian in both sentiment and substance, which will become evident if I analyze what can be called, for lack of a better description, Niebuhr's theological method—a method he learned from Ernst Troeltsch.

Niebuhr's Theological "Method"

Troeltsch admired James's work almost as much as Reinhold Niebuhr did. Indeed, Troeltsch thought that James was the first American to have made a decisive contribution to the philosophy of religion.[43] One of the reasons Troeltsch was sympathetic to James was that, like James, he had admired, learned from, and was critical of Wilhelm Wundt's psychological research.[44] Both Troeltsch and James were critical of what they took to be Wundt's reductionist account of religion. Troeltsch attributed Wundt's reductionism to his positivism, and he thought that James's attempt to provide an empirical and nonreductionist account of religious experience was "saturated with reality" and a great step forward. Yet Troeltsch also thought that James's empiricism was foreign to European empiricism, which, according to Troeltsch, rightly remained committed to Platonism.

Troeltsch argued that Platonism maintains a necessary relationship between the noumenal spirit and phenomenal experience. He thought James failed to understand that the purport of the science produced by Kepler,

---

42. Niebuhr, *Faith and Politics*, vii–viii. This is the best anthology of Niebuhr's work that has ever been put together not only because it contains essays that are otherwise relatively inaccessible, but because the essays chosen make so clear the interconnections in Niebuhr's work. Stone's volume is far superior to *The Essential Reinhold Niebuhr: Selected Essays and Addresses*, ed., with an intro., Robert McAfee Brown (New Haven: Yale University Press, 1986), as well as to *Reinhold Niebuhr: Theologian of Public Life*, ed. Larry Rasmussen (Minneapolis: Fortress Press, 1991). That Niebuhr's work requires such collections is due not only to his voluminous corpus, but also to the way he wrote, which makes it difficult to "capture" in one book or essay what he was about.

43. Ernst Troeltsch, "Empiricism and Platonism in the Philosophy of Religion: To the Memory of William James," *Harvard Theological Review* 5, no. 4 (October 1912): 401–422.

44. Martha Gail Hamner provides a good overview not only of Wundt's work but of James's reaction to Wundt; see "Habits of a Christian Nation: An Alternative Genealogy of American Pragmatism" (Ph.D. diss., Duke University, 1997).

Galileo, Descartes, and Newton was the "discovery of a rational necessity in the processes of nature." According to Troeltsch, this discovery was but the recognition of rationally necessary laws derived from Platonism. Even Kant, therefore, was a Platonist to the extent that he construed these natural laws as a rational necessity of the mind against pure relativism and the materialism that annuls necessity and mind together.[45]

In spite of Troeltsch's criticism of James's empiricism, he thought that he and James agreed more often than they differed and thus arrived at similar results:

> In both cases the result is a complete reaction from dogmatic theology, church, ecclesiastical worship, ritual, sacrament, and canonical law to the element of purely personal religious attitude. . . . In both cases the theory emphasizes the immediateness of the religious life, in contrast to historical authorities and traditions and to sociological constructions. The historical sinks to an inciting occasion, and redemption lies in the elevation of the subject into immediate unity with the divine power. In neither case does the philosophy of religion substitute a "pure religion" for the dominant religions; it simply furnishes a solid foundation and justification for the religious life in general, leaving free its living course, which it essays to regulate only for those to whom reflective thought is a necessity. This means

45. Troeltsch, "Empiricism and Platonism in the Philosophy of Religion," 405. For a useful account of Troeltsch's evaluation of James, see Henry Levinson, *The Religious Investigations of William James* (Chapel Hill: University of North Carolina Press, 1981), 277–281; and Roger Johnson, "Looking for Lost Absolutes: Troeltsch's Reading of William James," in *Studies in the Theological Ethics of Ernst Troeltsch*, ed. Max Myers and Michael LaChat (Lampeter, Wales: Edwin Mellen Press, 1991), 119–147. Troeltsch developed his account of the unavoidability of "Platonism" for a defense of religion in an article that appeared in 1913 entitled "*Logos* and *Mythos* in Theology and Philosophy of Religion"; the article now appears in the collection of his essays titled *Religion in History*, trans. James Luther Adams and Walter Bense (Minneapolis: Fortress Press, 1991), 46–72. In this essay, Troeltsch characterizes the development of an anti-intellectual religiosity that accepts the findings of science but assumes that such findings have no effect on religion. Such a view, Troeltsch observes, if "it takes note of philosophy at all, is less adverse to the pragmatism of a William James or the biologism of a Bergson than to systems of all-encompassing logical necessity. It happily seized upon Kant's famed distinction between theoretical and practical reason, but only to reinterpret the distinction completely: theoretical reason is identified with the organization of experience, which is important solely for practical purposes, while practical reason is identified with the sovereign unfolding of the will-to-live" (55). It would be hard to find a better description of Niebuhr's basic views.

In a fascinating manner, James Gustafson appeals to Troeltsch in support of his version of a "theocentric ethic." Gustafson credits Troeltsch for "laying down the gauntlet" against anthropocentric theology, which ignores what we have learned from science about the creation of the universe, the evolution of the species, and the likely end of the planet. Acknowledging that Troeltsch's views are not "accurate in terms of recent science," Gustafson nonetheless thinks that Troeltsch was right when he said:

> We obviously cannot lock out the consequences of a Copernican system. We may not shrink from the immensity of the All, in which we together with our whole solar sys-

that in the end both views see on the whole the highest, or most valuable, evolutionary form in an individualized and spiritualized Protestantism, such as has resulted from a great part of Protestant history, and itself, indeed, stands under the influence of such theories.[46]

Troeltsch's account of the commonalities between himself and James may not accurately describe James, but it certainly describes Niebuhr's central theological presumptions. I am not suggesting that Niebuhr's most basic theological presumptions were shaped by Troeltsch. His liberalism had been well formed before he ever read Troeltsch. But I think it is surely the case that Troeltsch became for Niebuhr the theologian who, so to speak, brought it all together. H. Richard Niebuhr wrote his dissertation, "Ernst Troeltsch's Philosophy of Religion," at Yale in 1924.[47] It is hard to imagine that Reinhold did not read his brother's book as well as Troeltsch's *Die Soziallehren der christlichen Kirchen und Gruppen.*[48] Richard Fox is surely right when he says that Niebuhr was always

---

tem, are swept upon paths which defy thought. In view of the uniformity of the entire universe opened up by spectral analysis, the geocentric and anthropocentric view of things may vanish. Man has to adapt himself to no longer being able to establish a physical centre of the universe. . . . We know that the formation of our earth arose by detachment from another heavenly body, and our entire organic life on this earth seems in comparison to the duration of the world, like breath on cold window panes which disappears the next moment. But what the world is without organic life, we do not know. At a certain point we emerged from the development, at a certain point we will disappear again. More science does not say. As the beginning was without us, so will the end also be without us. Transferred to religion, this insight means: the end is not that of the Apocalypse.

By affirming these words from Troeltsch, Gustafson seems to align himself with James's view that we are but "bubbles—epiphenomena" and with Niebuhr's view that we live in an "impersonal universe." Troeltsch, James, Niebuhr, and Gustafson, therefore, share the view that there is no purpose other than the purpose that humans are able to impose on purposeless "nature." As a result, I think it fair to say that each of them is far closer to Stoicism than to Christianity. For Gustafson's use of Troeltsch, see *Ethics from a Theocentric Perspective,* vol. 1 (Chicago: University of Chicago Press, 1981), 97–98.

46. Troeltsch, "Empiricism and Platonism in the Philosophy of Religion," 417–418.

47. H. Richard Niebuhr, "Ernst Troeltsch's Philosophy of Religion" (Ph.D. diss., Yale University, 1924). Niebuhr's work is still one of the best accounts of Troeltsch's philosophical theology. Given what it tells us not only about Troeltsch but about H. Richard Niebuhr, it is a shame that it has never been published. Niebuhr observes that "Troeltsch's philosophy reveals itself as an attempt to combine social, traditional religion with personal, more or less mystical, religion not only to carry the assurance of mysticism and Kantian rationalism into the realm of immediate and non-rational, empirical religion, but to do justice to the social necessity of cult and the historical character of religious thought" (116). A better summary of Troeltsch would be hard to find.

48. Brown says that Niebuhr certainly read Troeltsch's *Social Teachings* before they were translated, but he does not say if Reinhold read H. Richard's dissertation (*Niebuhr and His Age,* 32). Niebuhr's course on the history of Christian social ethics at Union year in and year out was essentially a rehearsal of Troeltsch's *Social Teachings,* with Niebuhrian emphases.

a liberal modernist Christian, true heir to the German liberal theologians Harnack and Troeltsch. He [Niebuhr] was right when he singled out Troeltsch to John Bennett in 1929 as one of the major formative influences on his intellectual outlook. Like Troeltsch his starting point was always human needs, human powers, human responsibilities. Christianity was a resource for man in the world, not a call for man to transcend the world. The progression of his thought went from humanity to God, not—as with Barth and to some extent Richard Niebuhr—from God to humanity.[49]

Ronald Stone suggests that Troeltsch's influence on Niebuhr is apparent in *Does Civilization Need Religion?* which was published in 1927. Stone observes that it was under Troeltsch's influence that Niebuhr acquired the confidence to address social questions.[50] I have no doubt that Stone is right if by "social questions" he means that Niebuhr had learned from Troeltsch that the future of Western civilization depends on the ability of liberal Christianity to champion the cause of personality. This is certainly the lesson Niebuhr gestured toward with the title of his 1927 book, and in the book itself he recited the lesson flawlessly:

There are resources in the Christian religion which make it the inevitable basis of any spiritual regeneration of Western civilization. Christianity, as Dr. Ernst Troeltsch has observed, is the fate of Western society. Spiritual idealisms of other cultures and societies may aid it in reclaiming its own highest resources; and any universal religion capable of inspiring an ultimately unified world culture may borrow from other religions. But the task of redeeming Western society rests in a peculiar sense upon Christianity. It is congenial to the energy and activism of Western peoples and is yet capable of setting bounds to their expansive desires. It has reduced the eternal conflict between self-assertion and self-denial to the paradox of self-assertion through self-denial and made the cross the symbol of life's highest achievement. Its optimism is rooted in pessimism and it is therefore able to preach both repentance and hope. It is able to condemn the world without enervating life and to create faith without breeding illusions. Its adoration of Jesus sometimes obscures the real genius of his life but cannot permanently destroy the fruitfulness of his inspiration. If there is any lack of identity between the Jesus of history and the Christ of religious experience, the Jesus of history is nevertheless more capable of giving historical reality to the necessary Christ idea than any character of history. . . . When dealing with life's ultimates, symbolism is indispensable, and a symbolism which has a basis in historic incident is most effec-

49. Fox, *Reinhold Niebuhr,* 146. I simply cannot attempt to describe the complex relation between the work of Reinhold and H. Richard. Suffice it to say that I think accounts of their difference have been exaggerated.

50. Stone, *Professor Reinhold Niebuhr: A Mentor to the Twentieth Century* (Louisville: Westminster/John Knox Press, 1992), 1. Stone notes that Niebuhr also, through the influence of Troeltsch, had begun to read Max Weber.

tive. The idea of a potent but yet suffering divine ideal which is defeated by the world but gains its victory in the defeat must remain basic in any morally creative world view.[51]

What Troeltsch provided Niebuhr was the ability to appropriate the "absurdities" of the Christian faith while avoiding literalist errors. Niebuhr's appropriation of Christianity on these terms involved recourse to the notion of "myth," and here again Troeltsch was influential. In his dissertation, H. Richard Niebuhr provides an extensive discussion of Troeltsch's understanding of myth. According to H. Richard, Troeltsch thought that myth was one of the necessary features of religion through which men's naive imagination articulates intuitions that otherwise cannot be expressed.[52] On such a view, myths are indispensable for the expression of religious truth, but they are also misleading, if we understand them or try to apply them as if they are literally true. There is no way to know if Reinhold drew on his brother's dissertation for this understanding of myth, but there is no question that this became his way to express how he thought religious language works.[53]

In an extraordinary sermon on 2 Corinthians 6:4–10, entitled "As Deceivers, Yet True," Niebuhr explains why such an understanding of myth has always been at the heart of what Christians believe. The Christian religion, Niebuhr observes, has been characterized by the manner it has transmuted primitive religious and artistic myths and symbols without fully rationalizing them. It is the heart of every Christian myth to express at once the meaningfulness and incompleteness of the world. That this is the mode of Christian expression is but an indication that it truthfully reflects that we cannot give a fully rational account of our existence. That is why "we are deceivers yet true, when we say that God created the world."[54]

By invoking the language of myth, however, Niebuhr intended to do more than mark the limits of our ability to account for our existence with reason alone. Niebuhr also meant to call attention to the fact that in our

51. Niebuhr, *Does Civilization Need Religion?* 235–237. In *An Interpretation of Christian Ethics,* Niebuhr suggests "that the Jesus of history actually created the Christ of faith in the life of the early church, and his historic life is related to the transcendent Christ as a final and ultimate symbol of a relation which prophetic religion sees between all life and history and the transcendent" (111–112). Though Niebuhr is hesitant to leave the "Jesus of history" behind, he never successfully explained why the Christ idea requires the "Jesus of history."

52. H. Richard Niebuhr, "Ernst Troeltsch's Philosophy of Religion," 154–156.

53. In a 1920 entry in *Leaves from the Notebook of a Tamed Cynic,* Niebuhr writes: "Religion is poetry. The truth in the poetry is vivified by adequate poetic symbols and is therefore more convincing than the poor prose with which the average preacher must attempt to grasp the ineffable" (50). This way of putting the matter seems to be a forerunner of his more developed view.

54. Niebuhr, *Beyond Tragedy,* 7.

times the Christian belief that God created the world must be mythical for no other reason than that modern science has seemed to make such a claim irrelevant and implausible. Modern empirical sciences, Darwinian theories of causal sequences, and theories of evolving forms and structures have made the temporal order seem self-explanatory. According to Niebuhr, such developments have made "obscurantist views" of special acts and events in creation implausible. Moreover, orthodox conceptions of "special providence, which presuppose an arbitrary monarch whose caprice accounts for specific events in the whole variegated drama of human history," are simply not believable.[55]

According to Niebuhr, stories of God the creator are mythical, yet there is a penumbra of mystery even in the most empirically analyzed stream of natural and historical events. These events always reveal previous causes and sequences and novelties for which there is no adequate explanation. So even if the creation myths of the great religions seem primitive in the light of modern science, "the myth of creation," Niebuhr says, "while prescientific, has elements of permanent validity in the sense that the mystery of creation hovers over any evolutionary chain of causes."[56] In short, for Niebuhr the myth of creation is necessary because it alone is capable of picturing the coherence of the world without denying its incoherence. Primitive myths, to be sure, must be left behind, but liberal Christians make a grave error if in denying primitive myths they also disavow the need for permanent myths.[57]

Niebuhr did not explicitly make the connection, but what James called "over-beliefs," Niebuhr called "permanent myths." Niebuhr assumed that he was a pragmatist opposing the Barthians, who asserted dogmatically the total truth of the biblical myth with no effort to validate Christianity in experience against the competition of other reli-

55. Niebuhr, "Faith as the Sense of Meaning in Human Existence," in *Faith and Politics,* 3–13, esp. 6. This essay was written in 1966.

56. Ibid., 6. In *An Interpretation of Christian Ethics,* Niebuhr puts the matter this way: "It is the genius of true myth to suggest the dimension of depth in reality and to point to a realm of essence which transcends the surface of history, on which the cause-effect sequences, discovered and analyzed by science, occur" (21). Douglas Sloan, with much justification, describes this general strategy, which characterized not only Reinhold Niebuhr's work but also that of H. Richard Niebuhr and Paul Tillich, as attempts to develop a "two-realm theory of truth." Sloan judges such an enterprise to be a noble but failed attempt to say in what way religious claims should be considered cognitive.

57. Niebuhr makes the distinction between primitive and permanent myths in his important essay "The Truth in Myths," which appeared originally in *The Nature of Religious Experience,* ed. J. S. Bixler, R. L. Calhoun, and H. Richard Niebuhr (New York: Harper and Row, 1937), a book of essays designed to honor D. C. Macintosh. The essay now appears in *Faith and Politics.* Niebuhr observes that religion had no right to insist on the scientific accuracy of its mythical heritage and rightly retreated once the causal relations that constitute our natural and historical world were established. Yet permanent myth remains necessary to deal with those aspects of reality that are suprascientific (16).

gions. It was Niebuhr's contention that such dogmatism could be overcome with the realization that

> though human knowledge and experience always point to a source of meaning in life which transcends knowledge and experience, there are nevertheless suggestions of the character of this transcendence in experience. Great myths have actually been born out of profound experience and are constantly subject to verification by experience.[58]

Niebuhr's theological method was an interesting blend of Troeltsch and James. Like Troeltsch, he presumed that modern intellectual developments had rendered Christian beliefs unintelligible. Such beliefs, however, could be revived by plumbing them for their insights into the human condition. The truth of permanent myths, moreover, could be validated through a James-like empirical testing. Niebuhr's Gifford Lectures were his most sustained attempt to verify the Christian myth, which requires that we at once affirm the meaningfulness of life and accept the fact of evil. According to Niebuhr, this affirmation and acceptance require the recognition that God, who is love, can be found in this life only as the crucified. It is the task of the next lecture to consider Niebuhr's Gifford Lectures and to unfold in some detail his account of the Christian myth.

---

58. Niebuhr, "Truth in Myths," 30.

Reinhold Niebuhr's Natural Theology

Anthropology as Natural Theology

Sin! Not just sin, but original sin, is taken to be what distinguishes Niebuhr from Protestant liberalism. Thus Niebuhr's Gifford Lectures, which he titled *The Nature and Destiny of Man,* are assumed to represent Niebuhr's break from the liberalism that characterized his earlier work. Niebuhr is partly responsible for those who would read *The Nature and Destiny of Man* in discontinuity with his previous work, because he often expressed his surprise that the reading he did in preparation for the Gifford Lectures led him to discover that he had deeper sympathy with aspects of Christian orthodoxy, and in particular with Augustine, than he had anticipated. In his "Intellectual Autobiography," Niebuhr expresses surprise at how late he came to study Augustine with care, because Augustine not only answered many of his unanswered questions but emancipated him "from the notion that the Christian faith was in some way identical to the moral idealism of the past century."[1]

---

1. Reinhold Niebuhr, "Intellectual Biography," in *Reinhold Niebuhr: His Religious, Social, and Political Thought,* ed. Charles Kegley and Robert Bretall (New York: The Macmillan Co., 1956), 9. Niebuhr's reading of Augustine, particularly his account of the "two cities," continues to be persuasive for many. But Niebuhr was aware that Augustine's account of the church was quite different from his own. See, for example, his essay "Augustine's Political Realism," in *Christian Realism and Political Problems* (New York: Charles Scribner's Sons, 1953), 119–146. In this essay, he accepts Anders Nygren's argument that Augustine was too influenced by Plotinus, which leads Niebuhr to conclude that Augustine's account of agape is too "mystical." This interpretation suggests that Niebuhr read Nygren better than he read Augustine. Equally problematic is his interpretation in *The Nature and Destiny of Man*

No doubt Niebuhr thought his Gifford Lectures represented a decisive break with some aspects of his previous work; nonetheless, he continued—as he well knew—to work within the presuppositions of Protestant liberalism. With his usual candor, he notes that when he was invited to give the Gifford Lectures, he focused on "the nature and destiny of man" because "the other fields of Christian thought" were beyond his competence.[2] Niebuhr gives no indication that his attempt to characterize the "human condition" was but a continuation of James's project. But like James, who had subtitled his Gifford Lectures *A Study in Human Nature,* Niebuhr assumed with his liberal forebears that theology was first and foremost an account of human existence.[3] Niebuhr's

---

of Augustine's understanding of the self as a discovery of self-consciousness. For a recent account of Augustine that runs almost exactly counter to Niebuhr's interpretation, see Denys Turner, *The Darkness of God: Negativity in Christian Mysticism* (Cambridge: Cambridge University Press, 1995), 74–101. My citations of *The Nature and Destiny of Man* refer to a reprint of the 1964 edition, intro. Robin Lovin (Louisville: Westminster John Knox Press, 1996). I will cite the page numbers parenthetically in the text. Furthermore, all such parenthetical citations in this lecture will refer to *Nature and Destiny* unless otherwise noted. The pagination of the 1964 edition remain the same as the original, two-volume edition published in 1941 and 1943. Because the page numbering of the second volume begins anew, page numbers in that volume will be preceded by "2."

2. Niebuhr, "Intellectual Biography," 9. Niebuhr did not and would not have claimed that his work should be regarded as having the significance I attribute to it. He always denied that he should be considered a theologian. For example, Niebuhr begins his "Intellectual Autobiography" by confessing: "It is somewhat embarrassing to be made the subject of a study which assumes theology as the primary interest. I cannot and do not claim to be a theologian. I have taught Christian Social Ethics for a quarter of a century and have also dealt in the ancillary field of 'apologetics.' My avocational interest as a kind of circuit rider in the colleges and universities has prompted an interest in the defense and justification of the Christian faith in a secular age, particularly among what Schleiermacher called Christianity's 'intellectual despisers.' I have never been very competent in the nice points of pure theology; and I must confess that I have not been sufficiently interested heretofore to acquire the competence. De Tocqueville long since observed the strong pragmatic interest of American Christianity in comparison with European Christianity; and that distinction is still valid. I have been frequently challenged by the stricter sects of theologians in Europe to prove that my interests were theological rather than practical or 'apologetic,' but I have always refused to enter a defense, partly because I thought the point was well taken and partly because the distinction did not interest me" (3). As usual, Niebuhr's self-assessment is correct, but also misleading. His declaration that he is not competent in the "nice points of pure theology" is but an indication that he assumes "the nice points of pure theology" are Jamesian over-beliefs that cannot be true or false.

3. Niebuhr mentions James only once in *Nature and Destiny,* and that is in reference to James's denial of the unity of consciousness and the transcendental ego as necessary for psychology as an empirical science. Niebuhr observes that this is but an indication of the limits of science, noting that a "science which is only science cannot be scientifically accurate" (73). Given Niebuhr's account of sin, it is particularly puzzling that he says nothing of James's contrast between the once-born and the twice-born. James's characterization of the latter would have offered Niebuhr a rich resource to explore the similarities and differences between his own views and those of James. In particular, such a contrast would

project was not natural theology, if by that you mean the attempt to "prove" God; rather, he sought to naturalize theological claims in a manner that would make them acceptable to the scientific and political presuppositions of his day. Thus, that he was asked to give the 1939 Gifford Lectures was not only appropriate but inspired.[4] Niebuhr did not pretend to be a philosopher or a theologian capable of proving the existence of God; nonetheless, he took it as his task to provide evidence for religious experience within the constraints of Lord Gifford's will.

For Niebuhr, theology was tested—or, to use his language, validated—by its ability to provide provocative accounts of the human condition. Accordingly, Niebuhr's theology seems to be a perfect exemplification of Ludwig Feuerbach's argument that theology, in spite of its pretentious presumption that its subject matter is God, is in fact but a disguised way to talk about humanity.[5] For example, Van Harvey concludes his detailed and careful account of Feuerbach with an illuminating comparison of Feuerbach and Ernest Becker. According to Harvey, Becker's account of the human condition—an account he borrowed from Kierkegaard—is familiar to any reader of the theology that flourished in the period after the World War II, a theology exemplified in the work of such figures as Bultmann, Buri, Brunner, Tillich, Rahner, and the Niebuhr brothers.[6]

---

have allowed Niebuhr to make clear how his account of sin required theological claims unavailable to James.

4. John Baillie and Reinhold Niebuhr had become friends in the early 1930s when Baillie had taught at Union. In *Reinhold Niebuhr: A Biography* (New York: Pantheon Books, 1985), Richard Fox reports that Baillie took a rapid liking to Niebuhr and helped him come to appreciate theology "as such." "Baillie vindicated theology in Niebuhr's eyes because he preserved the standard liberal starting point of man's own natural potential for knowledge of God" (125). No doubt Baillie's return to Scotland to teach at Edinburgh had much to do with Niebuhr's invitation to deliver the Gifford Lectures.

5. As far as I can tell, Niebuhr never mentions (much less discusses) Feuerbach anywhere in his vast corpus. Moreover, I have found no one who discusses why he failed to take up Feuerbach's challenge. Niebuhr may have assumed that Freud's account of religion as illusion represented a much more important counter to Christianity than did Feuerbach. If this was the case, Niebuhr was mistaken.

6. Van Harvey, *Feuerbach and the Interpretation of Religion* (Cambridge: Cambridge University Press, 1995), 295. Harvey is certainly right that many theologians at this time shared, in broad outline, quite similar accounts of the human condition. This fact helps explain what many take to be an embarrassing exchange between Brunner and Niebuhr in the Kegley and Bretall collection. In his contribution to the volume "Reinhold Niebuhr's Work as a Christian Thinker," Brunner expresses his "astonishment" that even though in *Nature and Destiny* Niebuhr was preoccupied with ideas Brunner himself had put forward in his 1937 book *Man in Revolt,* he does not think Niebuhr appropriately acknowledged his dependence on him. Brunner says that he knows Niebuhr had read his book because Niebuhr told him as much in 1938 (32–33). In his "Reply," Niebuhr acknowledges his debt to Brunner, from whom he had learned much, but in the process of tracing the doctrine of sin "through as much of history as I could encompass" he lost sight of how much he had

In this account, the human being differs from other organisms by virtue of being an embodied consciousness. This defining characteristic creates what Becker considered the human dilemma: we are creatures destined to die, but we are cursed, as no other animal is, with the awareness that we will die. As conscious beings we possess a freedom that creates possibilities, but these possibilities cannot help but be frustrated by our knowledge that we will die. The roots of religion lie in this ontological structure. We are caught between the Promethean desire to flourish and the anxiety of the psyche in the face of necessity and death.

According to Harvey, the only difference between Feuerbach and Becker is that for Feuerbach religion is simply an illusion, whereas for Becker religious illusion is justified to the extent that it enables us to live with the terror of creatureliness.[7] Drawing on what he thought he had learned from James, Niebuhr certainly sought to defend Christianity as more than a "necessary illusion." But the continuing influence of James makes it unclear if Niebuhr can really mount such a defense, given that James, as we saw, was probably trying to say no more than Becker: Christianity is nothing more than a disguised humanism, and theology is really anthropology.

Niebuhr developed his anthropology as part of a project that transcended his Gifford Lectures. In the preface to the 1964 edition of *The Nature and Destiny of Man,* Niebuhr says that the thesis of his work was an attempt to characterize the two main emphases of Western culture, "namely the sense of individuality and the sense of meaningful history, [both] were rooted in the faith of the Bible and had primarily Hebraic roots. It was my purpose to trace the growth, corruption and purification of these two concepts in the ages of Western history in order to create a better understanding between the historic roots and the several disciplines of our modern culture which were concerned with the human situation."[8] Such a project could not help but result in a sprawling argument not easily summarized, much less criticized.

My account of Niebuhr's position will ignore for the most part his characterizations of the classical and modern views of the human, as well as his understanding of rationalism, naturalism, romanticism, and his call for a synthesis of the Reformation and the Renaissance. His

---

learned from Brunner. He acknowledges that he is more indebted to Brunner than to any other contemporary theologian and that Brunner's position is close to his own. That Niebuhr "forgot" his indebtedness to Brunner is not so surprising given the fact that Brunner's theological account was not peculiar to Brunner.

7. Harvey, *Feuerbach,* 300.

8. Reinhold Niebuhr, preface to the 1964 edition of *Nature and Destiny,* xxv. Troeltsch's influence on Niebuhr is unmistakable. Like Troeltsch, he simply assumes that Christianity's intelligibility depends on its ability to respond to the challenge "of reorienting the culture of our day" (2:205).

views on these broad historical developments are extremely interesting and not irrelevant to his overall argument. Yet I think it is clear that Niebuhr employs these historical movements as tropes to illustrate his understanding of the human condition and to explain why, as he sees it, his account is inextricably theological.[9] In other words, Niebuhr's historical generalizations are his way of making concrete what is essentially, in spite of his claims about the importance of history, a timeless view of the human relationship to God.[10]

Niebuhr on Sin, God, and Revelation

The first hint in Niebuhr's Gifford Lectures that his theology is in fact anthropology is that he does not begin *The Nature and Destiny of Man* with an account of our sinfulness but with the generalized anthropological observation that "man has always been his own most vexing problem." Every affirmation human beings make about their status, Niebuhr says, becomes a contradiction when fully analyzed (1). That humanity's

9. My characterization of Niebuhr's attempt to illumine broad historical developments is not meant as a criticism, even though I am critical of the fundamental theological presupposition from which Niebuhr worked. I assume that Christian theological claims require the kind of work Niebuhr undertook. We find it, for example, in Augustine's *City of God* and, more recently, in John Milbank's *Theology and Social Theory: Beyond Secular Reason* (Oxford: Basil Blackwell, 1990). There is, however, a great difference between how Niebuhr conceives of his task and how Augustine and Milbank conceive of theirs. Augustine and Milbank assume that the church is the true bearer of history, whereas Niebuhr assumes that the church, at best, may have a role in a history that is but the unfolding of the human condition, as Niebuhr understands it.

10. Niebuhr assumed that his work presupposed the "historical character" of Christianity required by the "scandal of particularity." However, his way of expressing the "scandal" is anything but "particularistic." For example, in *Justice and Mercy,* ed. Ursula Niebuhr (Louisville: Westminster/John Knox, 1974), Niebuhr says: "We affirm that a timeless truth was spoken by the prophets or by Christ at a particular moment in time" (135). Obviously for Niebuhr the particular does not effect the timeless character of the truth. His only sustained theological reflections after *Nature and Destiny* continued to deal with "the problem of history": *Faith and History: A Comparison of Christian and Modern Views of History* (New York: Charles Scribner's Sons, 1951) and *The Self and the Dramas of History* (New York: Charles Scribner's Sons, 1955). In his "Intellectual Autobiography," he describes *Faith and History* as an elaboration of the second part of his Gifford Lectures, thereby alerting readers that in the years after the Gifford Lectures his theological interests remained ethical and apologetic (9). Niebuhr rightly judged that his work after *Nature and Destiny* was not theological; it was, rather, an attempt to "apply" the position of the Giffords. One of the striking aspects of Niebuhr's work is the absence of theological curiosity, which gives his later work a repetitive quality that borders on boredom. For an analysis and critique of Niebuhr's understanding of "history," see my "History as Fate: How Justification by Faith Became Anthropology (and History) in America," in *Wilderness Wanderings: Probing Twentieth-Century Theology and Philosophy* (Boulder, Colo.: Westview Press, 1997), 32–47.

Niebuhr's timeless view creates a theological problem for Christians, because we believe that the God found in Jesus Christ is not timeless—a belief that, at the least, requires

knowledge of itself results in such paradoxes points to two facts, one of which is obvious, the other less so:

> The obvious fact is that man is a child of nature, subject to its vicissitudes, compelled by its necessities, driven by its impulses, and confined within the brevity of the years which nature permits its varied organic form, allowing them some, but not too much, latitude. The other less obvious fact is that man is a spirit who stands outside nature, life, himself, his reason and the world. (3)[11]

Though Niebuhr no longer uses the language of personality to name our capacity to rise above our nature, this account of the human condition is no different from the one he developed under the influence of Bergson and James in 1914 in his B.D. thesis; nor is it different from the account he offered in 1927 in *Does Civilization Need Religion?*[12] Moreover, the understanding of the moral capacities of individuals and groups that he developed in *Moral Man and Immoral Society* (1932) is but a correlate of this anthropology. According to Niebuhr, individuals may be able, because of a rational faculty that prompts them to a sense of justice, to rise above their self-interested desire for survival and achieve a

---

a transformation of our understanding of time. The most sustained analysis of God's time-fulness is to be found in Robert Jenson, *Systematic Theology: The Triune God*, vol. 1 (New York: Oxford University Press, 1997). Discussing in what manner Christ is "preexistent," Jenson observes that Christian theologians rejected Aristotle's view of time as the measure of physical events because they realized that the doctrine of creation requires "this time to be the measure only of *created* events, so that the notion of a stretch of linear time preceding creation must be oxymoronic. Augustine's formulas are classic: 'The world was not made in time but with time'; 'In time was there not time'" (138–139).

11. The significance of this formula for Niebuhr is at least partly indicated by the fact that he never seemed to tire of repeating it in almost everything he wrote.

12. From my perspective, Niebuhr's account of the human condition in *Nature and Destiny* represents a loss of the more critical perspective of *Does Civilization Need Religion?* (New York: Macmillan Co., 1927). In 1927 Niebuhr could write: "The kind of liberal religion which thrives among the privileged classes of the city gives them some guarantee of the worth of their personalities against the threats of a seemingly impersonal universe which science has revealed, but it does not help to make them aware of the perils to personality in society itself. The final test of any religion must be its ability to prompt ethical action upon the basis of reverence for personality. To create a world view which justifies a high appreciation of personality and fails to develop an ethic which guarantees the worth of personality in society is the great hypocrisy. It is the hypocrisy which is corrupting almost all modern religion. In a sense hypocrisy is the inevitable by-product of every religion. Men are never as good as their ideals and never as conscious as the impartial observer of their divergence from them" (31). Niebuhr was still enough of a Marxist in 1927 to see that his account of the human condition could easily be the ideology of class interest. In *Nature and Destiny*, Niebuhr gives no indication that his account of "the nature of man" might reflect a class bias.

fair measure of objectivity. But all these achievements are more difficult, if not impossible, for human societies and social groups. In every human group there is less reason to guide and to check impulse, less capacity for self-transcendence, less ability to comprehend the needs of others and therefore more unrestrained egoism than the individuals, who compose the group, reveal in their personal relations.[13]

Though the correspondence is not exact, it is not difficult to see that for Niebuhr the individual is to the group as spirit is to nature.[14]

Like Feuerbach and Becker, then, Niebuhr identifies the contradiction between our finiteness and our freedom as the problem that underlies all religion (178).[15] Yet from a biblical point of view, our problem is not our finiteness but sin, which is occasioned but not caused by the contradiction in which we stand. Because we are both free and bound, limited and limitless, we are anxious. "Anxiety," Niebuhr says, "is the inevitable concomitant of the paradox of freedom and finiteness in which man is involved. Anxiety is the internal precondition of sin" (182).[16] Anxiety itself is not sin, however, because sin is known only in its actualizations and, more importantly, because anxiety is the source of our creativity.[17] According to Niebuhr, we are anxious not only because our life is limited, but because we do not know the limits of our possibilities. Every achievement beckons beyond what we have accomplished to further possibilities. This beckoning is the source both of human creativity

13. Reinhold Niebuhr, *Moral Man and Immoral Society* (New York: Charles Scribner's Sons, 1932), xi–xii.

14. Niebuhr's reputation as a *social* ethicist has meant that his emphasis on the individual has often been overlooked. Those who would accuse James of individualism would have to make the same accusation against Niebuhr.

15. Niebuhr begins chapter 7 of *Nature and Destiny* with a quotation from Albrecht Ritschl that describes the human contradiction by saying that we are a part of nature but also claim to have the ability to dominate nature. Niebuhr thinks Ritschl is right in his analysis but fails to see that the biblical view subordinates the problem of finiteness to the problem of sin. It is doubtful that Niebuhr's account of Ritschl is correct, but the contrast Niebuhr draws is one of the reasons he was often thought to have distanced himself from Protestant liberalism.

16. Niebuhr describes Kierkegaard's analysis of the relation of anxiety to sin in *Die Begriffder Angst* as "the profoundest in Christian thought."

17. Niebuhr is obviously struggling to avoid identifying sin with the human condition. According to Niebuhr, sin is not necessary, but it is inevitable (251–260). As with many of Niebuhr's formulas, one would like to think such a way of putting the matter is so clever that it must be true; but on analysis, Niebuhr's verbal agility is not sufficient to save his position from the error he is trying to avoid. Another example of his attempt to avoid an unsolvable problem by verbal sleight of hand is his claim that even though we are all sinful we are not equally guilty. One can appreciate Niebuhr's attempt to make discriminating judgments about different kinds of sins, but his distinction cannot finally avoid underwriting utilitarian calculations for determining guilt in terms of the effects of our actions.

and of our temptation to overreach our powers in the hope that we can secure what we have accomplished (183).[18]

Thus, according to Niebuhr, temptation "resides in the inclination of man, either to deny the contingent character of his existence (in pride and self-love) or to escape from his freedom (in sensuality)" (185). Niebuhr's account of pride often draws the attention of his interpreters, no doubt because of his illuminating account of the pride of groups (208–227). However, his understanding of sensuality not only as inordinate desire but also as the attempt to avoid the agony of our self-knowledge by "a plunge into unconsciousness" remains one of Niebuhr's most compelling descriptions of the work of sin (228-240, esp. 239).

According to Niebuhr, the complexity of the psychological facts associated with pride and sensuality validates the doctrine of original sin (251). Given that the fact or actuality of our sin does not flow from our anxiety even though our anxiety is the precondition of sin, Niebuhr says that "the bias toward sin from which actual sin flows is anxiety plus sin. Or, in the words of Kierkegaard, sin presupposes itself. Man could not be tempted if he had not already sinned" (250-251). Original sin is, therefore, a correlate of a Christian view of the self that "is only possible from the standpoint of Christian theism in which God is not merely the x of the unconditioned or the undifferentiated eternal. God is revealed as loving will; and His will is active in creation, judgment, and redemption" (252). In other words, as Niebuhr sees it, the human condition makes sense only in the light of sin, but sin makes sense only in a world created judged, and redeemed by God. If God is simply the "undifferentiated eternal," then God does not care, and sin does not exist, and the human condition defies explanation.

Thus Niebuhr's account of original sin is his attempt to do natural theology. Christians may not be able to convince agnostics and nonbelievers that God exists, but Christians can convince nonbelievers that sin exists. Moreover, if sin exists, it makes some sense to think that God exists. Niebuhr's project is to provide an account of the human condition that is so compelling that the more "absurd" aspects of "orthodox Christianity"—such as the beliefs that God exists and that God is love—might also receive a hearing.

Yet for Niebuhr "orthodox Christianity" turns out to be the name of the "permanent myths" or symbols necessary to describe the paradoxical aspects of our experience. For example, in his preface to the 1964 edition of *The Nature and Destiny of Man,* Niebuhr reaffirms his analysis of sin, noting that he still believes that human evil, which is primarily ex-

---

18. One of Niebuhr's great insights is that sin finds its most natural home not in our evil desires but in the good that we would do. He knows, for example, that our very ability to transcend our self-interest as well as the self-interest of our communities depends on wider sets of loyalties that are no less corrupted by sin.

pressed in undue self-concern, is a corruption of humanity's essential freedom and grows with that freedom. Accordingly, sin may be reflected in ignorance or the disordered passions of the body; but neither ignorance nor the passions are the source of sin. Niebuhr explains that his use of traditional religious symbols of the "Fall" and of "original sin," which he now regrets, was the attempt to counter these superficial accounts of sin. "I did not realize that the legendary character of the one and the dubious connotations of the other would prove so offensive to the modern mind, that my use of them obscured my essential thesis and my 'realistic' rather than 'idealistic' interpretations of human nature."[19] But if original sin is but a name for a reality that can be known separate from the Christian view of the self and God, then how are we to understand the status of Niebuhr's theological claims?

In the first chapter of *The Nature and Destiny of Man*, Niebuhr seems to lay his theological cards on the table, so to speak. Just as the classical view of the human was determined by Greek metaphysical views, so the Christian view is determined by the "ultimate presuppositions of the Christian faith." Niebuhr, therefore, appears to assert unapologetically that the Christian faith in God as creator of the world matters. Moreover, the Christian God is no mere demiurge who forms previously formless stuff; rather this God transcends the antinomies of mind and matter: "God is both vitality and form and the source of all existence. He creates the world. This world is not God; but it is not evil because it is not God. Being God's creation, it is good" (12).

According to Niebuhr, one aspect of God's good creation is human uniqueness, which cannot be found in our rational capacity or in our relation to nature but is constituted by God's relation to us (12–13). For Niebuhr,

---

19. Niebuhr, preface to the 1964 edition of *Nature and Destiny*, xxv. Niebuhr makes a similar set of remarks in *Man's Nature and His Communities* (New York: Charles Scribner's Sons, 1965), adding that the use of "original sin" was historically and symbolically correct but pedagogically an error. Even though he had taken pains to deny the historicity of the primitive myth of the Fall and had disavowed Augustine's "horrendous conception" that sin was generated across generations by lust, political philosophers who were otherwise convinced by his realism distanced themselves from his "theological presuppositions." Accordingly, Niebuhr says, in the "present volume," which deals with the same human nature, he will use "more sober symbols" when describing "well-known facts." Yet he observes: "I still think the *London Times Literary Supplement* was substantially correct when it wrote some years ago: 'The doctrine of original sin is the only empirically verifiable doctrine of the Christian faith'" (23–24).

It is certainly unfair to hold a thinker to a clever throw-away line; yet I cannot help but think the quotation from the *TLS* is Niebuhr's most considered view. But if that is the case, then what are we to make of his claim that the Christian doctrine of original sin, which he wrongly describes as a "doctrine," is a correlative of Christian theism? For my critique of Niebuhr-like accounts of sin, see "'Salvation Even in Sin': Learning to Speak Truthfully about Ourselves," in *Sanctify Them in the Truth: Holiness Exemplified* (Nashville: Abingdon Press, 1998), 61–74.

our "real individuality" is grounded in God, who is both will and personality. Niebuhr puts it this way: "Faith in God as will and personality depends upon faith in His power to reveal Himself. The Christian faith in God's self-disclosure, culminating in the revelation of Christ, is thus the basis of the Christian concept of personality and individuality" (15).

With his account of the "ultimate presuppositions of the Christian faith," Niebuhr seems to begin with an uncompromising declaration not only that God exists, but that the God who exists must be the God Christians worship. This declaration is not surprising. Niebuhr was, as I indicated in the last lecture, a child of the church. He spoke and preached about and prayed to God in a manner that leaves no doubt of his profound faith in the God of Jesus Christ. Yet exactly because he was such a vital Christian believer, Niebuhr felt free to provide an account of our knowledge of God that seems little more than a pale theism. In short, Niebuhr's practice, his use of Christian speech, prevented him, as well as those influenced by him, from seeing that metaphysically his "god" was nothing other than a Jamesian sense that "there must be more." Indeed, it is by no means clear why we ought to call "the vitality and form and the source of all existence" "God"—much less why we ought to identify such a god with the Christian God. As it turns out, the revelation that is required for us to know Niebuhr's god is but a reflection of ourselves. This is a harsh judgment, but one that I think I can sustain.

For Niebuhr, what it is about God that is revealed is less important than the simple fact that God is revealed. Another way to put the matter is to say that Niebuhr makes his understanding of God correlative to his understanding of the human need for revelation. Unable to stand outside or beyond our world, we are tempted to regard ourselves as gods around which the universe revolves. Yet we are too captured by the flux and finiteness of nature to make our pretensions plausible. The very principle of comprehension—namely, the presumption that in our freedom we are bounded by eternity—is beyond our comprehension. "Man is thus in the position of being unable to comprehend himself in his full stature of freedom without a principle of comprehension which is beyond his comprehension" (125). Our condition, therefore, requires that we receive revelation, and fortunately Christianity is a religion of revelation that does justice to both the freedom and finiteness of humanity.

The revelation of God, however, is twofold, requiring both

a personal-individual revelation, and a revelation in the context of social-historical experience. Without the public and historical revelation, the private experience of God would remain poorly defined and subject to caprice. Without the private revelation of God, the public and historical revelation would not gain credence. Since all men have in some fashion the experience of a reality beyond themselves, they are able to entertain the more precise revelations of the character and purpose of God as they come to them in the most significant experiences of prophetic history. Private revelation is, in a sense, synonymous with "general" revelation, without the presuppositions of which there could be no "special" revelation. It is no less universal for being private. Private revelation is the testimony in the consciousness of every person that his life touches a reality beyond himself, a reality deeper and higher than the system of nature in which he stands. . . . The experience of God is not so much a separate experience, as an overtone implied in all experience. (127)[20]

Private or general revelation, according to Niebuhr, comprises three types of experience: (1) a sense of reverence for the majesty of, as well as a dependence upon, an ultimate source of being; (2) a sense of moral obligation that seems to come from a source beyond us, and before which we feel unworthy; and (3) a longing for forgiveness (131).[21] Correlative to these types of experience are three types of revelation, in which God becomes defined specifically as creator, judge, and redeemer. To regard God as creator does not mean that we believe that at one time the world did not exist; rather, it is to regard the "world in its totality as a revelation of His majesty and self-sufficient power" (132).[22]

It "might be argued," Niebuhr observes, that the content of our experience of general revelation must be defined with the aid of historical or "special" revelation. However, such an argument does not take into account the "point of contact" between grace and the natural endowments of the soul, without which we could have no basis for believing that God is gracious (2:117).[23] It is certainly true, Niebuhr says, that without the principle of interpretation furnished by "special revelation," the general experience of revelation in conscience can become falsified. Nonetheless, on its own terms, general revelation defines the content of our

20. In support of this view, Niebuhr appeals to Romans 1:20, asserting that Paul is speaking of humanity's "experience" of God. Niebuhr, as usual, is not the least embarrassed by the fact that Paul makes no reference to experience as the mode through which humans are judged.

21. H. Richard Niebuhr's account of the self in time and history, in absolute dependence, and in sin and salvation mirrors Reinhold's account in *Nature and Destiny* in fascinating ways. See H. Richard Niebuhr, *The Responsible Self: An Essay in Christian Moral Philosophy* (New York: Harper and Row, 1963).

22. Niebuhr observes, and I confess I have never understood what he means, that the biblical doctrine of creation is itself not a doctrine of revelation but the *basis* for the doctrine of revelation. He attempts to explain this claim by observing that the doctrine of creation perfectly expresses the basic biblical idea that God is at once transcendent and in an intimate relation to the world (133). But why do you need the doctrine of creation to express the transcendence and immanence of God? All you need is James's account of the "more."

23. Niebuhr's use of "point of contact" is an explicit reference to the Barth-Brunner debate about natural theology. Niebuhr had observed earlier in *Nature and Destiny* that Brunner is right and Barth wrong, but that Barth had won the debate because Brunner accepted too many of Barth's basic premises (2:64).

experience. Moreover, without the point of contact between grace and our soul that exists outside of special revelation, Christians could not undertake the positive apologetic task in which the "special" truths apprehended by faith are correlated to general truths about life and history. In other words, for Niebuhr, general revelation not only lends defining content to our experience but also makes it possible for Christians to articulate special revelation in a manner that illuminates the paradoxes of human existence.[24]

Niebuhr on Christ, the Cross, and the Validation of Christian Truth

Niebuhr's understanding of the relationship between general and special revelation is displayed clearly in his account of the revelation of God's mercy at the cross. Whereas we may know God as creator and judge from general revelation, the assurance of faith that God has resources of love that transcend his judgment is not something that can be known by general revelation. The Christian faith, according to Niebuhr, rightly regards the revelation in Christ as final because in Christ the unresolved question of how God's mercy is to triumph over his wrath is resolved. As creatures we are under judgment because our effort to make our lives independent and secure results in our willful refusal to acknowledge our creatureliness and dependence on God. The wrath through which God punishes our pride is revealed through the catastrophes of history and the sheer indifference of nature to human projects (138–139).[25] The good and revelatory news of the gospel, however, is "that God takes the sinfulness of man into Himself; and overcomes in His own heart what cannot be overcome in human life, since

24. Niebuhr, *Faith and History*, 165. By Niebuhr's own admission, Tillich exercised a profound influence on him. He thought that Tillich was finally too "Platonic" and romantic, but Tillich's "method" of correlation at the very least named for Niebuhr some of his most fundamental methodological assumptions.

25. I am not suggesting that Niebuhr thought that God, or at least the God of judgment and wrath, is just another name for the blind forces of history and nature. I think it is fair to say, however, that given Niebuhr's general views concerning God's presence, he provided little grounds to guard against those who might think that he is closer to Stoicism than Christianity in terms of his account of God's wrath. For example, in a sermon he preached in 1952 based on Matthew 5:43–48, Niebuhr observed that in history there are no simple correlations of reward for good and punishment for evil. "God is like nature, says Jesus, like the impartial nature which you could accuse of not being moral at all, because the sun shines upon both the evil and the good, and the rain descends upon the just and the unjust. A nonmoral nature is made into the symbol of the transmoral mercy." "The Providence of God," in *Justice and Mercy*, 15.

Later in the same sermon Niebuhr confesses that "the nuclear dilemma," which makes clear that life cannot be correlated easily into simple moral meanings, creates a certain emhuman life remains within the vicious circle of sinful self-glorification on every level of moral advance" (142). Thus for Niebuhr the revelation of God's love revealed at the cross is final because it serves not only as the category necessary for "interpreting the total meaning of history but also as a solution for the problem of the uneasy conscience in each individual" (143). Niebuhr understands God's forgiveness as the most distinctive content of special revelation; even here, however, general revelation comes into play: because we have a longing for forgiveness, once this character of God is apprehended in terms of special revelation, "common human experience can validate it" (143).

To say that common human experience validates the special revelation of God's mercy is not to say that Christian accounts of the cross are rational; indeed, according to Niebuhr, they are absurd. Nonetheless, Niebuhr criticizes Protestant liberals for rejecting the "rationally absurd orthodox doctrine of the two natures of Christ." What liberals fail to see is that this absurd doctrine contains the Christian understanding of the relation of time to eternity. Contained in this understanding are answers to questions concerning whether anything in the flux of history is worthy of our highest devotion, and, if so, by what criterion we might determine what it is that has this special eminence. Christians believe that the only adequate norm of such devotion is the "historic incarnation of a perfect love which actually transcends history, and can appear in it only to be crucified" (147). The doctrine of the incarnation is absurd because it was stated in terms of the absolute gulf in Greek metaphysics between the passible and impassible. Yet the incarnation remains useful, Niebuhr argues, as a way to express the necessary paradox that the perfect love exemplified in the life of Christ was in history yet remains suprahistorical.

---

barrassment for him concerning the great debate between Christianity and secularism. "I am convinced of the Christian faith in the God revealed in Christ and whom Christ says is partially revealed in the impartialities of nature. Yet it seems to me also true that a certain type of secularism has advantages over us on any point where, to quote William James, Christianity becomes 'an effort to lobby in the courts of the almighty for special favors.' Against this lobbying for special favors, one must admit that there is an element of nobility either in modern or ancient Stoicism. . . . There is a certain nobility in Stoic courage. It has no sense of an ultimate relationship to God as a final expression of the Christian faith, but as far as it goes, is it not true? Modern man, under the influence of natural science, sees the problem more critically that it was seen before. We see that nature, whatever may be God's ultimate sovereignty over it, moves by its own laws" (19). In *The Character of God: Recovering the Lost Literary Power of American Protestantism* (New York: Oxford University Press, 1997), Thomas Jenkins observes that Niebuhr, like many nineteenth-century theologians before him, tried to save God by exteriorizing God's wrath, by making wrath a largely automatic expression of law, history, or the order of the world. They distanced God from God's wrath, but in so doing produced a sentimental God. Sentimentality is not usually a word associated with Niebuhr, but Jenkins argues that sentimentality almost perfectly describes Niebuhr's understanding of God (166–171).

Niebuhr's "Christology" begins and ends with his understanding of the cross as the historical revelation of God's love, which always transcends history. In Jesus we see a "remarkable coincidence of purpose and act" because of his uncompromising conformity to God's will without reference to the relativities of the human situation. The animating purpose of his life was to conform to the *agape* of God. Accordingly, his life symbolizes the perfection of love as self-sacrifice, but for Niebuhr the cross as symbol is more than any culmination of individual acts—even the actions in that life identified with Jesus:[26]

> The Cross symbolizes the perfection of *agape* which transcends all particular norms of justice and mutuality in history. It rises above history and seeks conformity to the Divine love rather than harmony with other human interests and vitalities. This harmony is a desirable end of historical striving; but it can never be a final norm. For sinful egoism makes all historical harmonies of interest partial and incomplete; and a life which accepts these harmonies as final is bound to introduce sinful self-assertion into the ethical norm (2:74).

According to Niebuhr, the cross cannot be reduced to the limits of history nor dismissed as irrelevant because it transcends history. Rather, the cross transcends history as history transcends itself. The Christian faith, which is "beyond all canons of common sense and all metaphysical speculations," has rightly maintained that "the perfection of the Cross represents the fulfillment—and the end—of historical ethics" (2:75).[27] In other words, the self-sacrificial love of the cross challenges all other ethical systems and justifies Christian claims for the truth of Christian belief. "Christianity can validate its truth about life and history only when it is possible, from the standpoint of that truth,

26. Niebuhr says Christians rightly believe that it is through Christ that the vague sense of the divine, "which humans never lose," is crystallized into a revelation of divine mercy and judgment. But Christians must guard against the assumption that only those who know Christ in the actual historical revelation are capable of such a conversion. "A 'hidden Christ' operates in history. And there is always the possibility that those who do not know the historical revelation may achieve a more genuine repentance and humility than those who do" (2:109–110).

27. Niebuhr discusses the relation of eternity and time as part of his attempt to "save" the "truth" that the church was trying to articulate in the doctrine of the incarnation. However, his presumption is against all such metaphysical expressions. For example, he later observes that "the realization within the post-apostolic church that the primary issue of life and history is the relation of grace to sin, rather than the subordination of eternity to time, comes to its first clear and explicit expression in the thought of Augustine" (2:134). Niebuhr thinks Augustine was right to subordinate metaphysics to salvation. Oddly enough, I think Niebuhr is right, to the extent that Christian theology is first and foremost eschatological. Unfortunately, Niebuhr's account of grace lacks the eschatological displays that might make his theological claims coherent.

to comprehend the rise of the false truths which use Christianity as their vehicle" (2:129). That the cross is the name of Christian truth is a reminder that the "final truth about life is always an absurdity but it cannot be an absolute absurdity" (2:38).

Niebuhr is well aware that such claims cannot help but drive rationalists to despair, but the cross for him names the basic character of our existence, as well as the kind of God required to sustain our ability to act in the world as we find it.[28] For Niebuhr, Christ and the cross are not realities limited to the specific revelation found in Christianity; rather they are symbols of the tensions we must endure as people who expect history to be fulfilled, who expect "a Christ."[29] Just as sin describes our nature, so Christ and the cross describe our destiny. And, as Niebuhr sees it, in both cases the descriptions, though absurd, are open to validation.

The claims about God that Niebuhr makes in *The Nature and Destiny of Man* are consonant with the position he developed in 1914 in "The Validity and Certainty of Religious Knowledge." In an extremely important 1951 article, "Coherence, Incoherence, and Christian Faith," Niebuhr defends the position he developed in *The Nature and Destiny of Man* in a manner similar to his B.D. thesis.[30] He argues that for a full understanding of the possibilities of both the good and evil of human freedom, a definition of God is required that stands beyond the limits of rationality. Thus Christians rightly understand God in trinitarian terms in an attempt to appreciate how God is at once the almighty creator who transcends history and the redeemer who suffers in history.[31] The Christian attempt to make the doctrine of atonement and

28. Niebuhr says that "the *wisdom* apprehended in Christ finally clarifies the character of God. He has a resource of mercy beyond His law and judgment but He can make it effective only as He takes the consequences of His wrath and judgment, upon himself" (2:55). Niebuhr was an impressive critic of anti-Semitism as well as a supporter of Israel, but structurally his position, like that of most Protestant liberals, committed him to a progressive view of our knowledge of God that renders the God of Israel less than God.

29. According to Niebuhr, the basic distinction between historical and nonhistorical religions and cultures is the difference between those who regard history as potentially meaningful, and who await full disclosure and fulfillment of its meaning, and those who do not. "A Christ" is not expected wherever the meaning of life is subordinated to nature or supernature in such a manner that it is assumed either that history is meaningless or that history's meaning is inaccessible to us. Niebuhr says that the latter view of life is best exemplified religiously by Buddhism and philosophically by naturalism and rationalism. Needless to say, Niebuhr's account of Buddhism was not informed by any close study of Buddhist texts (2:4–5).

Niebuhr never takes the Buddhist option as a possibility for "the West." Like Troeltsch, he simply assumed the superiority of the West to the East because the West had a sense of history and creativity.

30. Reinhold Niebuhr, "Coherence, Incoherence, and Christian Faith," in *Christian Realism and Political Problems* (New York: Charles Scribner's Sons, 1953), 175–203. This essay was first published in *The Journal of Religion* 31, no. 3 (July, 1951).

the Trinity rationally explicable can never be successful, except in the sense that alternative propositions can be proved to be too simple. Niebuhr argues that the "ultrarational pinnacles of Christian truth" are plausible as keys that make the drama of human life comprehensible but that, nonetheless, avoid oversimplification.[32]

In his 1951 article, Niebuhr contrasts this account of how Christian truths may be validated with Barth's account, which, according to Niebuhr, results in relativism, positivism, and literalism.[33] That Barth's position has these results is due to his attempt to fashion a theology for the catacombs and, thereby, to abandon the task of transfiguring the natu-

---

31. Niebuhr seldom developed at length his views on the Trinity. It was for him but another symbol for holding together God's transcendence and immanence. In his "Reply to Interpretation and Criticism," in Kegley and Bretall, *Reinhold Niebuhr: His Religious, Social, and Political Thought*, he objects to the Jesuit Gustave Weigel's suggestion that he believes in the Trinity or the divinity of Christ only "symbolically but not literally" by observing that he does not know how it would be possible to believe in anything pertaining to God and eternity "literally." He notes that he does not equate symbolic with subjective and that his position is, therefore, wrongly confused with the view of Bultmann, who fails to adequately distinguish prescientific myths and permanently valid symbols (446). Niebuhr is quite right to object to "literal," but his reply fails to do justice to Weigel's concern to the extent that Niebuhr continues to think of the Trinity as no more than a theological idea that describes our "experience" of God. In more pastoral contexts, however, Niebuhr sometimes uses trinitarian language without apology. See "The Hazards and the Difficulties of the Christian Ministry," in *Justice and Mercy*, 129–130.

32. Niebuhr, "Coherence, Incoherence, and Christian Faith," 185. In *Faith and History*, Niebuhr provides one of the most concise accounts of his understanding of what he calls a limited rational validation of the gospel: "It consists of a negative and a positive approach to the relation of the truth of the Gospel to other forms of truth, and of the goodness of perfect love to historical forms of virtue. Negatively the Gospel must and can be validated by exploring the limits of historic forms of wisdom and virtue. Positively it is validated when the truth of faith is correlated with all truths which may be known by scientific and philosophical disciplines and proves itself a resource for coordinating them into a deeper and wider system of coherence" (152).

33. Niebuhr seems to have had an almost unlimited animus against Barth. His essays against Barth have been collected in Reinhold Niebuhr, *Essays in Applied Christianity*, ed. D. B. Robertson (New York: Living Age Books, 1959), 141–196. Niebuhr's criticisms of Barth are not always consistent. For example, he accuses Barth of "relativism" but also thinks that he is a Platonist because he makes an unqualified distinction between the finite and the infinite. According to Niebuhr, by making this distinction Barth abandons the prophetic tradition that insisted on the unity of body and soul and thereby made history possible (160). Even though Platonism and relativism are often understood to be in tension, it may be possible to be both a Platonist and a relativist, but Niebuhr at least owes us an account of how he understood Barth to be both. In *Nature and Destiny*, Niebuhr briefly criticizes Barth's rejection of all forms of analogical reasoning, observing that Barth cannot avoid analogy just to the extent that he inverts analogical logic by attributing personality to humans on the basis of God's personality. Niebuhr observes that Barth cannot hide the fact that he has taken the concept of personality from human life and applied it to the divine (2:6–67). What makes this criticism fascinating is that Niebuhr, as far as I know, never considered why knowledge of God must be analogical. I will revisit Niebuhr's criticism of Barth on these grounds in the next lecture.

ral stuff of politics with the grace and wisdom of the gospel. Moreover, by Niebuhr's account, Barth fails to see that there is no possibility of fully validating the truth in the foolishness of the gospel without taking every cultural discipline seriously, to the point that such disciplines become conscious of their own limits and, in the process, signify how reality in its totality is more complex than any scheme of rational meaning. But to take every cultural discipline this seriously is to depart from the biblical picture. For example, Niebuhr says, it is clear that the "accumulated evidence of the natural sciences convinces us that the realm of natural causation is more closed, and less subject to divine intervention than the biblical world view assumes."[34]

According to Niebuhr, that God cannot act in the natural world—as we now understand because of what we have learned from science—does not mean that we cannot interpret the drama of human history as an engagement between humanity and God. Even more, we can recognize that particular events in history help us penetrate to the meaning of the whole. But we can no longer believe in miracles, which means that we cannot "believe in the virgin birth, and we have difficulty with the physical resurrection of Christ."[35] Therefore, the truth of revelation cannot be accepted as historical fact, nor miraculously validated; rather, we must understand the deeper truth of revelation as "the key which unlocks the mystery of what man is and should be and of what God is in relations with men."[36]

34. Niebuhr, "Coherence, Incoherence, and Christian Faith," 197. Niebuhr assumes that the truths of the social sciences cannot attain the status of those of the natural sciences because when social scientists record data, they act as agents as well as observers. Even though Niebuhr held that all knowledge is characterized by interest and power, he privileged the knowledge of the physical sciences. Just to the extent that history involves a realm of unique events, it is to be distinguished from occurrences in the physical world. See "Ideology and the Scientific Method," in *Christian Realism and Political Problems*, 75–94. Niebuhr sometimes even suggests that the "conceptual schemes" the physical sciences use are "hidden dogmas," but in contrast to the social sciences they have proved "themselves powerful enough to determine the evidence by which they were supposed to be tested." *Reinhold Niebuhr on Politics*, ed. Harry Davis and Robert Good (New York: Charles Scribner's Sons, 1960), 49–50.

35. Niebuhr, "Coherence, Incoherence, and Christian Faith," 198. Niebuhr condemned as obscurantist all attempts to maintain the resurrection of the body. In his "Reply to Interpretation and Criticism," he responds to Richardson's suggestion that historical scholarship does not call this "miracle" into question in classical Bultmannian fashion. "My impression was that historical scholarship seemed to indicate that the story of the empty tomb was an afterthought and that the really attested historical fact was the experience of the risen Christ among his various disciples" (438). As usual, such comments do not mean that Niebuhr thought that Christians should quit talking about the resurrection, because "by the symbol of the Resurrection the Christian faith hopes for an eternity which transfigures, but does not annul, the temporal process" (*Faith and History*, 237).

36. Niebuhr, "Coherence, Incoherence, and Christian Faith," 198.

Niebuhr acknowledges that this way of interpreting the truth of the gospel runs the danger of reducing Christianity to just another philosophy. In response, he claims that he takes "historical facts seriously but not literally," which, he admits, may be a way not to take them as historical facts at all.[37] Niebuhr says that there is no simple solution to this problem, but any solution will rest on two primary propositions. First, because of the unique character of human freedom, a radical distinction, though not division, must be maintained between the natural world and the world of human history. Second, "human history must be understood as containing within it the encounters between man and God in which God intervenes to reconstruct the rational concepts of meaning which men and cultures construct under the false assumption that they have a mind which completely transcends the flux of history, when actually it can only construct a realm of meaning from a particular standpoint within the flux."[38]

At this point, even the most sympathetic reader of Niebuhr cannot help but wonder whether we have not returned to where we began, that is, to our experience. What does it mean for God to "intervene to reconstruct rational concepts of meaning"?[39] Whatever such a claim might mean, it is hard to think that Niebuhr's God is anything more or less than an unavoidable aspect of our consciousness. Of course, "our consciousness" may, and according to Niebuhr must, include the recognition that human consciousness cannot account for itself and, therefore, that there must be more to human existence than human consciousness. But is that finally saying anything more than James said in the conclusion of *The Va-*

---

37. Ibid. This comment is but a paraphrase of Niebuhr's claim in *Nature and Destiny* that "it is important to take Biblical symbols seriously but not literally" (2:50). According to Niebuhr, theologies that do not take the eschatological symbols of the Christian faith seriously end up not taking history seriously either. "They presuppose an eternity which annuls rather than fulfills the historical process. The Biblical symbols cannot be taken literally because it is not possible for finite minds to comprehend that which transcends and fulfills history" (2:289). For criticism of Niebuhr's use of the Bible, see Richard Hays, *The Moral Vision of the New Testament: Community, Cross, New Creation* (San Francisco: Harper San Francisco, 1996), 215–224.

38. Niebuhr, "Coherence, Incoherence, and Christian Faith," 199–200.

39. In *Reinhold Niebuhr,* Richard Fox relates an exchange between Niebuhr and Joseph Haroutunian, a former student and friend who in a review of *Beyond Tragedy* had criticized Niebuhr for being a Platonist. Niebuhr wrote to object to such a characterization, but the unrepentant Haroutunian replied: "I called you a Platonist because your God is primarily the ethical ideal which passes judgment upon us by its sheer unattainable excellence. The 'tension' between the ideal and the real seems to me to be the essence of your religion. Your God does not perform miracles; never has and never will; hence to you the Incarnation and the Resurrection of the dead are myths, not fantasies indeed (I never said so, nor made an 'effort' to say so), and yet 'trans-historical'—shall we say, unhistorical? . . . Reiny, for truth's sake, tell me, just what do you do with Paul, Augustine, and Luther, for whom sin and death, *together,* were what Christ saved us from? . . . Yours is a truncated Christianity, one that pushes aside the cry of the human heart for life with God in eternity" (183).

rieties of Religious Experience? It appears that for Niebuhr God is nothing more than the name of our need to believe that life has an ultimate unity that transcends the world's chaos and makes possible what order we can achieve in this life. Niebuhr does not explain why he thinks anyone would feel compelled to worship or pray to a god so conceived.

Robert Song observes that Niebuhr's language often promises more than his theological system can deliver. He uses trinitarian language, but operatively the God of *The Nature and Destiny of Man* remains unitarian.[40] Contrary to Niebuhr's claim, the Christian doctrine of the Trinity does not begin as an attempt to understand the relation of time to eternity but is a way to insist that the God found in the life, death, and resurrection of Jesus is not different from the God of Israel. Song argues that it may even be far too generous to think that Niebuhr's theology is ultimately focused on God at all, even a unitarian God. Rather, from beginning to end Niebuhr's primary aim was to give "significance to human finitude, and in particular to prompting people 'to accept their historical responsibilities gladly.'"[41]

Do we have anything more in Niebuhr than a complex humanism disguised in the language of the Christian faith? Probably not, but before pronouncing such judgment, a brief analysis of how Niebuhr understood the relation between his theology and his ethics is required. James thought that pragmatism named those aspects of our lives that require the existence of habits acquired through training. In contrast, Niebuhr's ethic names a change in attitude, such that we learn to accept that the way things are is the way things have to be.

40. Robert Song, *Christianity and Liberal Society* (Oxford: Clarendon Press, 1997), 78. Song notes, for example, that Niebuhr asserts that "Father and Son are equally God" but is unwilling to give this claim its full *prima facie* weight. Furthermore, Niebuhr sounds orthodox when he asserts that the Holy Spirit is "the Spirit of God indwelling in man," but he evacuates such a claim of substance when it turns out that he is referring to the holiness of the *human* spirit (78). Nor can Song understand why Niebuhr says that God's supreme revelation is in Christ; if, as Niebuhr asserts, God has done nothing in history, it is unclear why the life, death, and resurrection of Christ should have significance (80). In 1964, Rachel King had developed criticism of Niebuhr similar to Song's; see *The Omission of the Holy Spirit from Reinhold Niebuhr's Theology* (New York: Philosophical Library, 1964). King's criticisms of Niebuhr are devastating but were ignored and, as far as I know, did not qualify his influence. Niebuhrians, if they paid any attention to King's work at all, dismissed her as a "fundamentalist." At the end of her book, King provides an instructive two-column list comparing "Beliefs to Which Reinhold Niebuhr Subscribes" to "Ideas Reinhold Niebuhr Loves but Does Not Believe to Be True" (216). That Niebuhr felt free, in an almost Alice-in-Wonderland fashion, to make words mean anything he wanted them to mean had everything to do with his assumption that Christianity was here to stay. Accordingly, he did not feel any burden to say again what the words, sentences, paragraphs, and books of the Christian tradition already say. His "creativity" in using words is a testimony to his homiletical gifts.

41. Song, *Christianity and Liberal Society*, 82. The internal quotation is from *Nature and Destiny*, 2:332.

Niebuhr on Ethics and the Church

After *The Nature and Destiny of Man,* Niebuhr's theological views were set. *Faith and History* (1951) and *The Self and the Dramas of History* (1955) were certainly theological essays, but they added little to what Niebuhr had done in *Nature and Destiny*. In effect, *The Nature and Destiny of Man* freed Niebuhr to turn to his first love—ethics and politics. Of course, his ethical reflection was shaped by his theological work, but he did not have to return, for example, to Christological questions to explore the relation of love and justice.

One might say that Niebuhr's work on ethics became less explicitly theological as his life, after the Gifford Lectures, became increasingly shaped by his role in the American political establishment. Fox notes that Niebuhr became "the man of the hour in the secular political realm."[42] But it would be a mistake to assume that becoming a player in American politics and foreign policy led Niebuhr to modify or compromise his theological and ethical convictions. Rather, his theological and ethical convictions proved to be consonant with, for example, his membership on the Council on Foreign Relations and his acceptance of an invitation from George Kennan to participate in the deliberations of the Policy Planning Staff of the State Department.[43] In other words, Niebuhr's "realism," his understanding of justice as the most equitable balance of power, seemed perfectly to match the world that was coming to be after World War II. It is, therefore, not surprising that Niebuhr's life confirmed his thought.

Many of Niebuhr's friends and enemies thought that his ethics, which they celebrated, was independent of his theology, which they did not celebrate.[44] Some of Niebuhr's enemies even became concerned

42. Fox, *Reinhold Niebuhr,* 234.

43. Ibid., 238. Fox notes that though he does not recall it, Kennan is reported to have described Niebuhr as "the father of us all." Niebuhr's anticommunism was important for his status with people like Allen Dulles and John Foster Dulles, but it was also heartfelt and consistent with his "realism." Eugene McCarraher argues that historians have misconstrued the debate over realism among liberal Protestants because the conflict did not pivot on the issues of socialism and violence but on the political nature of Christianity. According to McCarraher, though Niebuhr was identified with the left, he actually inhibited the creation of a democratic left to the extent that his position devalued the importance of religion. McCarraher argues that far from introducing a more religious sense of sin that invalidated the power of experts "Niebuhr's neo-orthodoxy—the most advanced modernist expression of liberal religious idealism—served to weaken religion as a distinctive political identity and to cede the terrain of social and cultural politics to professional and managerial elites. In his role as a Protestant socialist, Niebuhr rehearsed his part as *pontifex maximus* to Cold War liberals." *Christian Critics: Religion and the Impasse in Modern American Social Thought* (Ithaca: Cornell University Press, 2000), 64.

44. Fox reports that many of Niebuhr's liberal friends, in particular, Arthur Schlesinger, Jr., liked Niebuhr's somber tones and tempered hopes but wondered if the

that there was a growing movement of "atheists for Niebuhr."[45] I suspect that such a movement would have amused and secretly pleased Niebuhr because he did not think atheism was a problem. Indeed, it is not even clear, given Niebuhr's understanding of our lives, if atheism exists. For Niebuhr, atheism is difficult, if not impossible, because one cannot "live without presupposing some system of order and coherence which gives significance to one's life and actions."[46] Thus, according to Niebuhr, the problem is not atheism but an idolatrous worship of a false god.[47]

Niebuhr's views on atheism provide further evidence that his theology works within the constraints of a naturalistic view of the world. His ethics is designed to be an ethic for anyone. Of course, an ethic "for anyone" does not necessarily entail a naturalistic account of morality, but in fact Niebuhr was committed to developing a form of ethical naturalism that would be capable of providing a response to what he considered to be the challenges before our civilization. This ethical naturalism leads John Milbank to suggest rightly that Niebuhr's ethics is Stoicism restated in Christian terms.[48]

---

part about God and sin was necessary (*Reinhold Niebuhr,* 225). In his autobiography, *A Life in the Twentieth Century: Innocent Beginnings, 1917–1950* (Boston: Houghton Mifflin, 2000), Schlesinger confirms Fox's account, noting that "Niebuhr's interpretation of man and history came as a vast illumination. His arguments, for which Perry Miller's meditations on Puritanism has predisposed me, had the great merit of accounting both for Hitler and Stalin and for the necessity of standing up to them" (250). Schlesinger notes that he was predisposed toward Niebuhr just to the extent that he was more sympathetic with the pragmatism of William James than with that of the optimistic Dewey. Later in his autobiography, Schlesinger observes that he came to understand that original sin, a proposition that he was prepared to accept as a powerful metaphor though not as revealed truth, undermined "absolutist pretensions and set sharp limits on human wisdom and aspirations" (512). Such an understanding, as we have seen, is not far from Niebuhr's position. Schlesinger's book makes clear that it was not only Niebuhr's position that attracted him and other "atheists for Niebuhr," but also Niebuhr's (and Ursula's) personality and lack of "sanctimoniousness." Not all secular intellectuals were as enthralled with Niebuhr. Jane Bingham quotes Sidney Hook's observation that "logically not a single one of Reinhold Niebuhr's social, political, and ethical views can be derived from his theology. This is demonstrable: his theology and metaphysics are perfectly compatible with the opposite of his views." *Courage to Change: An Introduction to the Life and Thought of Reinhold Niebuhr* (1961; reprint, New York: University Press of America, 1993), 229.

45. Fox, *Reinhold Niebuhr,* 246.

46. Niebuhr, *Faith and History,* 153.

47. Niebuhr rarely discusses atheism, but his remarks about idolatry are found in *Faith and History,* 152–153. In *Christianity and Power Politics* (New York: Charles Scribner's Sons, 1940), he commends atheists, who often represent an implicit and higher theism against the profane worship of God by believers (217–218).

48. John Milbank, "The Poverty of Niebuhrianism," in *The Word Made Strange: Theology, Language, Culture* (Oxford: Blackwell, 1997), 233–251. Milbank notes: "In chapter 5 of *An Interpretation of Christian Ethics,* Niebuhr attributes to the Stoics the discovery of natural law as the view that life in its 'essence' ideally involves much more than is possible in our

Niebuhr often criticized ethics based on natural law for absolutizing the relative,[49] but formally his understanding of the law of love is an attempt to develop a natural law ethic.[50] Thus Niebuhr insists that the "law of love," that is, the disinterested regard we owe one another, is required by "the real structure of life" (275).[51] We are created in a manner that makes it impossible for us to realize ourselves without the other. We can be ourselves only in loving relations with our fellows. "The law of love is a requirement of human freedom; and the freedom of the self and the other both require it" (295). That love must take the form of law—"thou shalt"—is but an indication that the harmony of the soul with God and neighbor can never be fully realized in this life because of our selfishness. Furthermore, Niebuhr says, that love in practice is always betrayed into self-love is the reason that philosophy, which some-

---

concrete existence; our actual lives must be conformed to this essence as far as possible" (235). Milbank observes that what many readers of Niebuhr miss is that "it is this understanding of natural law to which Niebuhr *himself* adheres." Niebuhr had acquired his understanding of the Stoics from Troeltsch, who argued that without the Stoic conception of natural law Christianity would not have a "social ethic." The Stoics are obviously natural allies for those who think "social ethics" is the attempt to name the requirements necessary to run an empire.

49. Niebuhr seems to have seldom thought about matters such as divorce, abortion, suicide, or homosexuality. For the most part, he simply assumed the position of the consensus of most mainstream Protestants about the morality of such behavior. He does consider such questions in *Nature and Destiny* in connection with his discussion of natural law. He observes that it is not possible to escape the natural fact that the primary purpose of bisexuality in nature is that of procreation. But it is not easy, he notes, to establish a universally valid law of reason to set the bounds of sex in the historic development of the human personality. He does suggest that the natural bond between mothers and their children means that rationalistic feminism cannot but transgress the inexorable bounds set by nature. Moreover, "there are of course certain permanent norms, such as monogamy, which, contrary to the relativism of such Protestant skeptics as Karl Barth, are maintained not purely by Scriptural authority but by the cumulative experience of the race" (282–283). Niebuhr does not explain how those cultures in which monogamy is not a permanent norm, cultures like the modern West, have failed to embody the "cumulative experience of the race."

50. Niebuhr's criticism of natural law ethics appears throughout his work, but the fullest account is still in *Nature and Destiny*, 278–298. As far as I know, George Lindbeck was the first to show that Niebuhr's work, in spite of his denials, could be construed in natural law terms. See "Revelation, Natural Law, and the Thought of Reinhold Niebuhr," *Natural Law Forum* 4 (1959): 146–151.

51. Niebuhr oscillates in his description of *agape*. In the last chapter of *An Interpretation of Christian Ethics*, he treats love as forgiveness, but in *Nature and Destiny* he usually describes love as disinterested regard for the neighbor. He seems to have assumed that in some way the disinterested regard for the neighbor requires the sort of sacrifice of the self that is involved in forgiveness. For the most part, however, he simply never worked out the relationship between these two emphases. In spite of Niebuhr's criticism of Kant, the Kantian resonances in his account of love are unmistakable.

times sees the necessity of love but lacks a concept of sin, fails to understand love's law-like character (286).[52]

According to Niebuhr, the ultimate requirements of the Christian ethic—"love thy neighbor as thyself," "love the Lord thy God," and "be not anxious"—are not counsels of perfection that merely "top" natural goodness. Rather, they are basic requirements that are structured into our freedom (272). We see them as counsels of perfection only because as sinners we are incapable of achieving them. But exactly because we are sinners we cannot and should not try to make the law of love a realized possibility in our relations with one another. Niebuhr acknowledges that Jesus' ethics of sacrificial love may be a possibility for relations between two individuals, but as soon as a third person is introduced into the relation, even "the most perfect love requires a rational estimate of conflicting needs and interests" (2:248).[53] Accordingly, the cross—the symbol of sacrificial love—must stand on the edge of history acting as an indiscriminate norm that judges all our attempts to attain justice.[54]

In contrast to James, Niebuhr thought that the great enemies of the moral life are those who seek to be holy. He observes that the question of

52. Niebuhr's ethics shares more with Kant than he acknowledges. He criticizes Kant for exhibiting the complacency characteristic of most idealistic philosophies. He acknowledges, however, Kant's remarkable account of sin in *Religion within the Limits of Reason Alone* (which, according to Niebuhr, stands in complete contradiction to Kant's general system). He attributes Kant's recognition of "radical evil" to the influence of pietism, and, therefore, it is not integrated into Kant's general system. According to Niebuhr, if Kant had taken sin seriously, it would have "shattered" his system. Perhaps another way to see the matter is that if Niebuhr had taken Kant seriously, it would have "shattered" his easy dismissal of "rationalism."

53. Niebuhr observes that because the family avails itself of customs and stereotypes, *even* families may need to enter into fresh calculations of competing interest. What seems odd is that Niebuhr thought the qualifier "even" was required. Niebuhr, of course, thought mutual love was a possibility that somehow hovers between sacrificial love and justice, but even mutual love cannot be made the intention and goal of action. For his understanding of the relation of sacrificial and mutual love, see *Nature and Destiny*, 68–70.

54. The complexities of Niebuhr's understanding of justice are beyond the scope of my work in this lecture. He simply assumes rather than defends, for example, that "a higher justice always means a more equal justice" (254). His account of justice is obviously a part of his social and political theory, which presumes the necessity of a central organizing power that makes possible continuing negotiations concerning the balance of power between social groups. He assumes democracy, and in particular American democracy, is the political system that most perfectly exemplifies "justice" so understood. His assumption that the basic political issue is to negotiate between anarchy and tyranny no doubt seemed more persuasive immediately after World War II than it does today. Niebuhr does not think that his account of justice, which is the cornerstone of his political ethics, can be divorced from his theology, but such a presumption is not an unreasonable inference given his work after *Nature and Destiny*. For example, in *The Structure of Nations and Empires* (New York: Charles Scribner's Sons, 1959), he discusses "Western Christendom," but any theology in the book is but a restatement of his anthropological presumptions (which, to

whether Christians, who through their faith have apprehended the basic character of human history, can overcome that history seems to have one answer in logic and another in experience. It seems logical to think our awareness of self-love and its incompatibility with divine will could break the power of our self-regard. There is even some evidence that repentance does initiate a new life. But such an observation only provides the occasion for Niebuhr to unleash his attack on all moral presumption:

> The sorry annals of Christian fanaticism, of unholy religious hatreds, of sinful ambitions hiding behind the cloak of religious sanctity, of political power impulses compounded with pretensions of devotion to God, offer the most irrefutable proof of the error in every Christian doctrine and every interpretation of the Christian experience which claim that grace can remove the final contradiction between man and God. The sad experiences of Christian history show how human pride and spiritual arrogance rise to new heights precisely at the point where the claims of sanctity are made without due qualifications (2:122).

That is the heart of Niebuhr's ethics.[55] Justification by faith is loosed from its Christological context and made a truth to underwrite a generalized virtue of humility in order to make Christians trusted players in the liberal game of tolerance.[56] Catholicism, the Renaissance, Calvinism, and the sectarian Protestants: Niebuhr judges them all to be mistaken attempts to make an ethic of sanctification a reality.[57] These historical

---

be sure, he assumed were theological). For a more extensive critique of Niebuhr's social and political thought, see my *Dispatches from the Front: Theological Engagements with the Secular* (Durham: Duke University Press, 1994), 91–106; and *Wilderness Wanderings: Probing Twentieth-Century Theology and Philosophy* (Boulder, Colo.: Westview Press, 1997), 48–61.

55. Niebuhr's course on Christian ethics consisted in his account of the tension across history between those who represented "the impulse toward perfection" and those who represented "the impulse toward responsibility." The whole point of the course was to insure that the students "appreciated the former" but would embody the latter. For Niebuhr's specific avowal of the theme of the course, see his lecture "The Ethics of Sectarian Protestantism: The Pacifist Sects." Reinhold Niebuhr Audio Tape Collection, Union Theological Seminary, Richmond, Virginia. In the transcript of the lectures prepared by James Fodor, the reference in question is on page 203.

56. To be fair to Niebuhr, he quite rightly sees that tolerance can result, as he puts it, in "an irresponsible attitude towards the ultimate problem of truth, including particularly the problem of the relation of *the* truth to the fragmentary truths of history. In the same way tolerance in political struggles may merely reveal irresponsibility and indifference towards the problem of political justice" (2:238).

57. Niebuhr's animus toward Catholicism is particularly noteworthy. According to Niebuhr, Catholicism involves the mistaken identification of the church with the kingdom of God. For a good collection of Niebuhr's essays criticizing Catholicism, see *Essays in Applied Christianity*, 197–262. It is a mistake to think that Niebuhr is critical of Catholicism primarily because of its alleged failure to understand that all human institutions including the church are sinful. No doubt he assumed that that was the central issue, but more importantly, Niebuhr sensed that Catholicism rests on the claim that our knowledge of

options, to be sure in quite different ways, result in a false attempt to make history conform to perfect love, or, frustrated by the attempt, their adherents undertake an irresponsible withdrawal from the world. For Niebuhr, sanctification in the realm of social relations demands recognition of the impossibility of sanctification (247).[58]

In neither his ethics nor his theology did Niebuhr provide an account of the church. The standard explanation for the absence of the church from Niebuhr's work is that his focus on economic and political matters simply did not allow him to develop an ecclesiology. This explanation makes it appear that the absence of the church in Niebuhr's work is an accidental oversight, but in fact the absence is integral to Niebuhr's theology and his ethics.

Niebuhr, no doubt, regarded the church as a sociological necessity for Christianity to exist across time, but he did not regard it as an ethical or epistemological necessity. Given his theological perspective, he could not believe that "church" might name a people in service to a God who has set them off from the world. Nor could he see anything other than absurdity in the notion that the existence of such a people is necessary for any account of the truths of faith. Yet without an account of the church, Niebuhr has even less to offer Christians than James does.

So in a sense, "atheists for Niebuhr" were wrong. Niebuhr's ethics and his theology were of a piece. His theology sought to make Christian belief intelligible within the naturalistic presumptions that he thought were a prerequisite of modern science. His ethics sought to make Christian belief intelligible and even useful within the presuppositions of political liberalism. Theological liberals after Niebuhr often want his theology without his ethics; and political conservatives, like the "atheists for Niebuhr," often want his ethics without his theology. Yet Niebuhr, I think, rightly saw that you cannot have one without the other.

That Niebuhr's account of the human condition still seems persuasive to many is not surprising—for no matter how desiccated Niebuhr's

---

God must be mediated. Nowhere is the gnostic character of Niebuhr's position more apparent than in his reaction against Catholicism.

Completely missing in Niebuhr's ethics is any sense of the significance of habits and their importance for an account of the virtues. In this respect, Niebuhr fails to exploit a resource that James would have provided. Indeed, the matter can be put more strongly, for just to the extent that Niebuhr fails to appreciate James's understanding of habit, Niebuhr's "pragmatism" cannot help but be truncated. In theological terms, James is much more a "sanctificationist" than Niebuhr is, which means that Niebuhr's pragmatism—or perhaps better, his empiricism—cannot give a Jamesian account of how the kind of person we are makes a difference for our understanding of the way things are.

58. James and Niebuhr share a fear of attempts to engage in wide-ranging social programs. Niebuhr gives James's ameliorism theoretical justification through his account of democratic incrementalism. Accordingly, Niebuhr underwrites "issue politics" not only because it is safe but because such a politics is all that is needed once democracy is in place.

account of Christianity may be, people formed by a liberal social order cannot even begin to imagine that they might accept the Christian faith on any other terms. Niebuhr's account of "original sin" is a comforting doctrine for a people so formed, because Niebuhr makes sin intelligible, a given of the human condition, without requiring a transformation of the self through the formation provided by the church—an odd position for a thinker who claims to be a pragmatist.[59]

My account of Niebuhr may seem harsh. For many people, Niebuhr (and Tillich) provide a robust account of Christianity that make it possible for them to be Christians.[60] And "postliberal" theologians sometimes understandably and plausibly read Niebuhr as an exemplification of a theologian who was able to absorb ethics into the scriptural narrative. I do not mean to ignore this impact of Niebuhr's thought, nor to dismiss such people as mistaken. Indeed, as I have suggested, Niebuhr's theology and practice was often richer than his naturalistic convictions should have allowed. He was, despite his role in the American political establishment, embedded in the language and practices of the church. And though he gave this church little status in his theology, it nonetheless often allowed him to speak and act in a manner at odds with his theoretical commitments. Certainly his prayers sometimes witness to a God who is more than the god of *The Nature and Destiny of Man*.[61]

That said, I think anyone who would put Niebuhr on the side of the angels must come to terns with the extraordinary "thinness" of his theology. Niebuhr's god is not a god capable of offering salvation in any material sense. Changed self-understanding or attitude is no substitute for the existence of a church capable of offering an alternative to the world. Of course, Niebuhr did not seek to offer such an alternative, which is why he could not help but become the theologian of a domesticated god capable of doing no more than providing comfort to the anxious conscience of the bourgeoisie.

In his Gifford Lectures, MacIntyre followed his wonderful lecture on "Aquinas and the Rationality of Tradition" with a lecture entitled "In

---

59. See, for example, my "'Salvation Even in Sin,'" 61–76; and James Alison, *The Joy of Being Wrong: Original Sin through Easter Eyes* (New York: Crossroad Herder Books, 1998).

60. Tillich's influence on Niebuhr's work is obvious, though perhaps insufficiently acknowledged by Niebuhr. Indeed the role Tillich might be given in the story I am telling would be a fascinating subplot. Toward the end of his account of Tillich, Eugene McCarraher makes the fascinating and, I think, insightful remark that "if the religiosity of abstract expressionism was William James on canvas, the absolute faith of Tillich was William James in the pews" (*Christian Critics*, 144).

61. Consider, as one example among many, this prayer: "Grant us grace, our Father, to do our work this day as workmen who need not be ashamed. Give us the spirit of diligence and honest inquiry in our quest for the truth, the spirit of charity in all our dealings with our fellows, and the spirit of gaiety, courage, and a quiet mind in facing all tasks and responsibilities" (*Justice and Mercy*, 12).

the Aftermath of Defeated Tradition."[62] Were I to title my next lecture in a similar vein, I would have to call it "In the Aftermath of a Victorious Tradition," because where Aquinas failed, Niebuhr succeeded, or at least his life and work represent the success of the tradition of Protestant liberal theology. Under Niebuhr's influence, theology—particularly in America—became ethics, and ethics became the investigation of the conditions necessary to make a liberal social order work.[63] As I suggested in the last lecture, however, the Protestant culture that made Niebuhr intelligible no longer exists, which is not to say, exactly, that it has been defeated, but that we are no longer surrounded by the spoils of its victory.

If in our current cultural climate, James (or James-like positions) seems for many an attractive alternative to Niebuhr, it is simply because the Christian veneer that was once thought necessary for our societies is no longer needed. Why go through Niebuhr's verbal gymnastics to save the "symbols" of Christianity when James can give you everything Niebuhr wanted in a less confused way? Moreover, Niebuhr's acceptance of the basic outlines of James's position makes it difficult to criticize, from Niebuhr's perspective, those who find James more persuasive. However, as I have suggested, Jamesians and Niebuhrians alike remain haunted by thinkers such as Nietzsche and Foucault who refuse to look away from the empty blackness at the heart of modernity.[64]

To live in the aftermath of Protestant liberalism's victory is to live in a world haunted by what Nietzsche described as the abyss, but it is also to live in a world where we are now able to appreciate Karl Barth as an alternative to Niebuhr (and to Nietzsche). Barth's theology was unintelligible in a Niebuhrian world. That it has begun to make sense is surely an indication that, indeed, the world in and for which Niebuhr wrote is becoming unintelligible to itself. In an odd way, Niebuhr's work now represents the worst of two worlds: most secular people do not find his theological arguments convincing; yet his theology is not sufficient to provide the means for Christians to sustain their lives. If Niebuhr's account of Christian theology is no longer persuasive, it is surely bad news for those who believe that the future of Christianity depends on a concordat with liberal social and political arrangements. On the other

62. Alasdair MacIntyre, *Three Rival Versions of Moral Enquiry: Encyclopaedia, Genealogy, and Tradition* (Notre Dame: University of Notre Dame Press, 1990), 127–169.

63. For an extended account of this development, see my "Christian Ethics in America (and the JRE): A Report on a Book I Will Not Write," *Journal of Religious Ethics* 25, no. 3 (25th Anniversary Supplement): 57–76. A slightly revised version of this essay can be found in my book, *A Better Hope: Resources for a Church Confronting America, Capitalism, and Postmodernity* (Grand Rapids: Brazos Press, 2000).

64. For an account of the challenge of Nietzsche and Foucault, see David Toole, *Waiting for Godot in Sarajevo: Theological Reflections on Nihilism, Tragedy, and Apocalypse* (Boulder, Colo.: Westview Press, 1998).

hand, for those who believe, as I do, that the truth of Christian convictions requires a recovery of the confident use of Christian speech about God, speech that cannot help but put us at odds with Niebuhr-like accounts of ethics, then the newfound intelligibility of Barth's theology is surely good news. Niebuhr's theology reflects the loss of truthful Christian speech and, hence, of faithful Christian practice. In contrast, Barth's theology is an unfaltering display of truthful Christian speech and, as such, is a resource that we literally cannot live without, if we are to be faithful to the God we worship.

6

The Witness
That Was Karl Barth

Approaching Barth

Nein! was the title Barth gave to his 1934 response to Emil Brunner's defense of natural theology, namely, that there must be a point of contact between God and humanity for revelation to be intelligible. *Nein!* sums up for many people what they take to be the heart of Karl Barth's theology.[1] For example, the *Scotsman* reported that Brand Blanshard in his Gifford Lectures in 1952 characterized Barth's theology (and Brunner's) as the attempt "to save religious faith by making it irrational." According to Blanshard, "Barth and Brunner, like their master, Kierkegaard, revelled in paradoxes. Indeed they represented God as being so completely 'other' that He almost disappeared; we were supposed to believe things about Him that, by our standards, were self-contradictory, and ascribe actions to Him that our moral sense could only regard as evil." Blanshard thought the probable effect of this strategy would be the complete repudiation of faith by thoughtful people.[2]

---

1. *Natural Theology: Comprising "Nature and Grace" by Professor Dr. Emil Brunner and the Reply "No!" by Karl Barth*, trans. Peter Fraenkel, intro. John Baillie (London: Geoffrey Bles, 1946). Barth understood "natural theology" to be "every formulation of a system which claims to be theological, i.e., to interpret divine revelation, whose subject, however, differs fundamentally from the revelation in Jesus Christ and whose method therefore differs equally from the exposition of Holy Scripture" (74).

2. Blanshard's views are reported in "Theology of Crisis: Professor Blanshard Resumes Gifford Lectures," *The Scotsman* (April 9, 1952). I am indebted to Professor Iain Torrance of the University of Aberdeen for making this article and the subsequent exchange of letters between T. F. Torrance and Blanshard available to me.

The article in *The Scotsman* resulted in a fascinating exchange of letters between T. F. Torrance and Blanshard. Torrance was "astonished" that a philosopher as distinguished as Blanshard continued to perpetrate a view of Barth's work that, though it might mistakenly but understandably derive from an impression left by Barth's early work, failed to appreciate the later developments in Barth's theology. According to Torrance, Barth is the ultimate rationalist just to the extent that he holds

> to the basic point that reason is unconditionally bound to its object and determined by it and that the nature of the object must prescribe the specific mode of the activity of reason. Faith is this reason directed to the knowledge of God, and involves a rational apprehension which answers appropriately to the object given. Here the object is unique and incomparable. What is expected of theology, therefore, is that it should exhibit the kind of rationality which corresponds with the unique object of thought.[3]

From Torrance's perspective, Barth, rather than representing a sacrifice of the intellect, stands against the irrationalism so characteristic of European thought after World War II. In response, Blanshard expresses his astonishment that anyone would be astonished by his understanding of Barth's irrationalism.[4] Blanshard would be even more astonished, I think, that Barth, in spite of his disavowal of natural theology, provides the resources necessary for developing an adequate theological metaphysics, or, in other words, a natural theology. Of course, I assume that "natural theology" simply names how Christian convictions work to describe all that is as God's good creation.

The title of Barth's Gifford Lectures, *The Knowledge of God and the Service of God according to the Teaching of the Reformation,* given in Aberdeen in 1937 and 1938, indicates that Barth rightly refused to separate our knowledge of God from how we are to live if God is properly acknowledged.[5] Even though I have been critical of some aspects of Barth's "ethics," I believe that Barth's extraordinary achievement not only helps Christians recover

3. T. F. Torrance, "Theology of Karl Barth," *The Scotsman* (April 14, 1952): 4.

4. Brand Blanshard, "Theology of Karl Barth," *The Scotsman* (April 16, 1952): 6. In subsequent letters to *The Scotsman,* Torrance argued that Blanshard's views entailed a view of rationality that was no longer accepted by philosophers such as Donald Mackinnon, Gilbert Ryle, and John Macmurray. According to Torrance, Blanshard assumes that reason can be its own object in a manner that belies the way we have increasingly understood how reason functions in the sciences. Expressing due respect to such an able theologian, Blanshard withdrew from the battle, observing that Torrance was but "juggling with words." *The Scotsman* (April 22, 1952): 6.

5. Karl Barth, *The Knowledge of God and the Service of God according to the Teaching of the Reformation,* trans. J. L. M. Haire and Ian Henderson (London: Hodder and Stoughton Publishers, 1938); hereafter simply *Knowledge of God.* In *Truthful Action: Explorations in Practical Theology* (Edinburgh: T. & T. Clark, 2000), Duncan Forrester observes: "The fact that Barth chose to base his 1937–8 Gifford Lectures at Aberdeen on the *Scots Confession* of 1560, by

a confidence in Christian speech, but also exemplifies how Christian language works. For this reason, we will fail to appreciate the power of Barth's accomplishment if we ignore that, from beginning to end, Barth's theology is designed to make the reader a more adequate knower of God.

That I think Barth can be counted among those who were faithful to Gifford's will indicates that, given the terms of the debate, I am sympathetic with Torrance's defense of Barth against Blanshard.[6] Yet Blanshard's reaction to what he understood to be Barth's position remains instructive. Blanshard gives voice to the reaction of the world—particularly the educated world—to Barth's work. Consider that in the world as we know it, James and Niebuhr do not need to be "explained." You do not need to have your conceptual machinery, to say nothing of your life, turned upside down to understand James or Niebuhr. However, Barth turned his back on the world that seems to make James and Niebuhr so intellectually and morally persuasive. That he did so was, I think, necessary and right; but it makes any attempt to understand Barth particularly challenging.

With his usual candor, Reinhold Niebuhr wonderfully exemplifies how difficult it is for anyone formed by the world of James and Niebuhr to begin to appreciate what Barth is about. Niebuhr observes that though Barth protests against all forms of analogical reasoning, he nevertheless avails himself of the concept of personality when "defining the character of the divine." According to Niebuhr, Barth tries to hide his recourse to analogy by declaring in the first volume of *Church Dogmatics* that the concepts of human personality are derived from the concept of divine personality. Obviously seeking to expose the absurdity of Barth's position, Niebuhr quotes Barth's claim that "the problem is not whether God is a person but whether we are. Or shall we find among us one who in the full and real sense of this concept we can call a person. But God is really a person, really a free subject." Niebuhr observes that Barth cannot hide the fact that he has taken the very concept of personality

---

then largely forgotten in Scotland, came as a great surprise. It apparently had not occurred to many Scots theologians themselves that their Reformation heritage might have something to offer the crisis of the mid-twentieth century" (180).

6. At the beginning of his Gifford Lectures, Barth observes that natural theology is primarily a protest movement in theology proper. When, however, natural theology loses its adversary, it "becomes arid and listless" and interest in it begins to flag (6–7). Accordingly, Barth claims that he is being faithful to Gifford's will by giving natural theologians a position against which they can strike their blows. Toward the end of his lectures, Barth notes that no representative of natural theology can avoid what he has said, since any such representative will find Barth's tenets to be "the direct opposite of his own tenets and therefore of necessity extraordinarily interesting and profitable for his own particular undertaking. I feel therefore that I have fulfilled my obligations toward the Gifford lectures" (243).

from human life and applied it to the divine. "From what other source could he have derived it?"[7]

That Niebuhr seems completely ignorant of Barth's positive account of analogy, exemplified in his 1931 book on Anselm, is understandable. Almost no one at that time in America knew about (much less understood) Barth's increasingly sophisticated account of *analogia fidei*. What Niebuhr clearly cannot imagine is that Barth really thinks theology is about God. Yet for Barth theology can have no other subject. I call attention to Niebuhr's attempt to make Barth look absurd not because I have provided reasons why we should prefer Barth to Niebuhr, but to suggest that Barth and Niebuhr simply occupy different worlds, which is not to say they have nothing in common.

We cannot appreciate the significance of Barth's accomplishment if we read him only in discontinuity with either Niebuhr or James. Barth was a child of the same philosophical and theological sources that produced James and Niebuhr. For example, Kant remains in the background for all three thinkers, and perhaps most prominently so in Barth's work. It may well be that Barth's extraordinary endeavor to recover the integrity of Christian speech was often hampered by the philosophical resources he thought he had left behind. Yet one of Barth's great virtues was the courage to say what he knew needed to be said before he had figured out how to defend it.[8] Indeed, what Barth actually says is often better than his attempt to defend what he says.

Of course, even at his best, Barth is challenging, and not only for those whose Jamesian or Niebuhrian formation has predisposed them to find Barth unintelligible. Even more sympathetic readers struggle with Barth, and Joseph Mangina has, I think, identified the problem:

> Since Barth treats the cross as bringing history to a close, the Spirit's work is "short-circuited." The Spirit can only appear as a predicate of Christ's reconciling work, a *manifestation* of the latter rather than an *agency* of its own. Correspondingly, the church "shows" or signifies Christ but does not serve as the means through which believers begin to participate in the new life he brings. The result is an odd hiatus between the church (in a full theological sense) and the ordinary, empirical practices of the Christian community across time.[9]

---

7. Reinhold Niebuhr, *The Nature and Destiny of Man,* intro. Robin Lovin (Louisville: Westminster/John Knox Press, 1996), 2:66–67. The quotation from Barth comes from *Church Dogmatics,* 1/1, trans. G. T. Thomson (Edinburgh: T. & T. Clark, 1960), 157.

8. Barth approvingly quoted Franz Overbeck's comment, "Theology can no longer be based on anything but daring." Overbeck was a church historian, atheist, and a friend of Nietzsche whose work Barth admired. Barth's comment occurs in his essay "Liberal Theology: Some Alternatives," *Hibbert Journal* 59 (1961): 219. I am indebted to Professor William Buckley for calling my attention to this essay.

9. Joseph Mangina, "Bearing the Marks of Jesus: The Church in the Economy of Salvation in Barth and Hauerwas," *Scottish Journal of Theology* 52, no. 3 (1999): 270. I am indebted

Put simply, and no doubt too simply, the question is whether, when all is said and done, Barth is sufficiently catholic. By raising the question of Barth's catholicity I am not referring to his characterization and subsequent rejection of "natural theology." To make Barth's catholicity turn on the question of natural theology would mistakenly make catholic identity turn on that question. Rather, I will suggest that Barth is not sufficiently catholic just to the extent that his critique and rejection of Protestant liberalism make it difficult for him to acknowledge that, through the work of the Holy Spirit, we are made part of God's care of the world through the church.[10] Barth, of course, does not deny that the church is constituted by the proclamation of the gospel. What he cannot acknowledge is that the community called the church is constitutive of the gospel proclamation.

Such a criticism may seem strange, because I will also argue that Barth has a fairly developed account of Christian sanctification. Yet Barth never quite brings himself to explain how our human agency is involved in the Spirit's work. As a result, Barth's understanding of our faith in Jesus Christ made possible by the Spirit falls short. Again Mangina puts it well when he says that an adequate account of the role of the Spirit in faith not only involves "the glad acceptance of the church's preaching, but acceptance of the church itself as the binding medium in which faith takes place. The medium is, if not the message, the condition of possibility of grasping the message in its truth."[11]

Whatever its shortcomings, Barth's theology, as I hope to show, is not just another "position" to be categorized, evaluated, and put on the shelf of intellectual curiosities. Barth staged a frontal attack on some of the most cherished conceits of modernity, not the least being the conceit that humans are the measure of all that is. Barth's unrelenting attack on the humanistic presumptions that constitute our own self-understanding and that legitimate our social and political arrangements make cavalier dismissals of his work such as Blanshard's seem, for many, all too reasonable. But if I am right, Barth shows us the way that theology must be done if the subject of theology, that is, the God of Jesus Christ,

---

to Mangina for helping me not only see but understand the difference, but not necessarily disagreement, between my work and Barth's. Matters, however, are never simple with Barth. For example, he says explicitly: "The church is the historical form of the work of the Holy Spirit and therefore the historical form of the faith." *Church Dogmatics*, 2/2, trans. G. W. Bromiley, et al. (Edinburgh: T. & T. Clark, 1957), 160.

10. See, for example, Reinhard Hütter's "Karl Barth's 'Dialectical Catholicism': *Sic et Non*," *Modern Theology* 16, no. 2 (April 2000): 137–158. Hütter argues that Barth failed to give an account of how the church can exist in an embodied form. Nicholas Healy began this line of criticism in "The Logic of Karl Barth's Ecclesiology: Analysis, Assessment, and Proposed Modifications," *Modern Theology* 10, no. 1 (1994): 253–270.

11. Mangina, "Bearing the Marks of Jesus," 294–295.

is to be more than just another piece of the metaphysical furniture in the universe.

For Barth, theology is in service to the church's witness to God's reconciling and redeeming work in Jesus Christ. If natural theology is to be a necessary feature of theology, it cannot pretend to be more than a part of the witness that is the church. In his life and in his work, Barth sought nothing other than to be a witness to God's reconciling and redeeming work in Jesus Christ. He therefore did not try to "explain" the truth of what Christians believe about God and God's creation. He understood that such an explanation could not help but give the impression that the explanation is more important than the witness. Because Barth was nothing other than a witness, any attempt to understand him requires attention not only to what he says but to how he says it—a daunting observation in the light of Barth's long life (1886–1968) and even more massive work. Yet as I will show, particularly in the next lecture, the massive character of Barth's work is not incidental, given his understanding of the nature and task of theology.

Given the sheer size of Barth's corpus, my attempt to show why Barth is the alternative to James and Niebuhr cannot help but be less than adequate. It is impossible to summarize Barth, as Hans Frei observes:

> Whether one agrees with Barth or not, and despite the endless repetition of themes and the stylistic heaviness, much increased by the translation, which loses the almost colloquial vigor of the German original, there is an increasingly compelling, engrossing quality to the material. And it is much more accessible than much modern theology: Even the technical terms don't lose sight of ordinary language, and Barth possesses astonishing descriptive powers. But then, as one tries to restate it afterwards, the material dies on one's hands. It can be done, but there is nothing as wooden to read as one's own or others' restatements of Barth's terms, his technical themes and their development. It is as though he had preempted that particular language and its deployment. For that reason reading "Barthians," unlike Barth himself, can be painfully boring.[12]

---

12. Hans Frei, "Eberhard Busch's Biography of Karl Barth," in Hans Frei, *Types of Christian Theology*, ed. George Hunsinger and William Placher (New Haven: Yale University Press, 1992), 157. Katherine Sonderegger echoes Frei in her lovely article, "On Style in Karl Barth," *Scottish Journal of Theology* 45, no. 1 (1992): 65–83. Sonderegger notes that the lengthy and seemingly endless critiques of Barth's method, which may be more or less on target, march on, but they reveal so little "of the joyful delight and freedom of movement Barth shows at every turn. How lifeless these essays seem, held up to the light of Barth's remarkable, full-throated style. They are summaries of an exposition, and give off the condensed flavor that is so hard to mask. But it is more than that, as any critic knows. To read Barth carefully, at length, is to be caught up in a drama of light and shadow, of figures in chiaroscuro, of exposition inflamed with passion and twists of irony and compassion. The drama is drawn in master strokes, and no critic can encompass them or domesticate them" (65).

I confess that I would rather be wrong than "painfully boring." But given the argument I am trying to make, it will be even worse if Barth dies in my hands, for then all will be lost. Frei may be right; still, I must "restate" Barth in order to explain why his life and work provides those of us who have come after him a resource, a witness, that we literally cannot live without.

Barth's life was as dramatic as his theology; but he did not describe either his life or his work in terms of the risk both manifest. Barth thought that he was simply doing what he had to do. Yet most theologians in Germany did not think that they had to oppose Hitler or that they had to write the Barmen Declaration. Barth did both of these things, and that he did so cannot be incidental to any account of his theology.[13] Thus I cannot avoid providing an account of how Karl Barth was forced to leave behind the Protestant liberal world that had constituted his life and education and, in the process, become Karl Barth.

How Barth Learned to Be Karl Barth

"I am by nature a gentle being and entirely averse to all unnecessary disputes. If anyone, faced with the fact that he is here reading a controversial treatise, should suggest that it would be so much nicer if theologians dwelt together in unity, he may rest assured that I heartily agree with him."[14] So begins Barth's famous attack on Brunner's defense of natural theology. Given the vociferous character of his response to Brunner, as well as the controversies that constitute Barth's life, some people find it hard to take Barth's self-description seriously. Yet Barth really was a "gentle being" who avoided "unnecessary disputes." After all, he did not plan to be a theologian. He never acquired a Ph.D. and thought he was destined to be a pastor in the Swiss Reformed Church. From Barth's perspective, it was not his fault that his duties as a pastor led him to a rediscovery of the God of Scripture, and that this rediscovery required him to forsake his liberal theological forebears.

13. In his biography of Barth, Eberhard Busch observes "that just as Karl Barth's work was an essential part of his life, so too his life is an essential part of his work. It is significant that so many people did not really understand him until they had come to know him personally. Thus the reader will discover that Barth's 'doctrines' are not merely theoretical pieces of armchair wisdom, but explanations and discoveries which he came upon during the course of a life-long struggle and quest." *Karl Barth: His Life from Letters and Autobiographical Texts,* trans. John Bowden (Philadelphia: Fortress Press, 1976), xv. Busch's biography remains the indispensable source for understanding Barth's life and thought just to the extent that it is not really a biography. To his great credit, Busch does not try to interpret Barth's life; rather, by drawing on Barth's autobiographical reflections, his letters, and his work, he tries to let Barth tell us about Barth. All future attempts to write a biography of Barth will owe Busch a great debt.

14. Barth, "No!" 67.

If one allows for the difference that being raised in America and Switzerland must involve, Reinhold Niebuhr and Karl Barth have quite similar stories. Both were products of the Reformed parsonage (though Barth's father, Fritz, became a professor at the University of Bern). Fritz Barth was more theologically sophisticated than Gustav Niebuhr, but they were both on the "conservative" side of the options within Protestant liberalism. Both Niebuhr and Barth were the product of a church culture that made their decisions to go into the ministry seem inevitable. In the ministry, both engaged "social questions," developed socialist sympathies, and sided with labor. Both had younger brothers who were academics and with whom they had complex relations. Throughout their lives, both Barth and Niebuhr were passionately engaged in the political and cultural issues of their day. Both seemed to have more energy than most human beings, which meant that their writing was given added power through their teaching and lecturing. Both were essentially self-educated, being forced to acquaint themselves with the texts of the Christian tradition when they became teachers. The World Wars left quite different but no less indelible marks on their lives and work. Yet somehow Barth discovered that he must leave behind the Protestant liberalism that animated Niebuhr's life and work from the beginning to the end.

Barth's formal education was entirely shaped by Protestant liberalism. At the time, particularly within the German context, it would have been difficult to have found any alternative. After finishing his theological training at Bern in 1906, Barth wanted to go to Marburg. His father, however, thought Marburg too liberal, so Barth went to Berlin, where, as Barth puts it, he heard from Harnack's very lips that "the dogma of the early period was a self-expression of the Greek spirit in the sphere of the gospel."[15] In Berlin, Barth acquired a high regard not only for Harnack but also for Kant and Schleiermacher, who, he says, "took a clearer place in my thought than ever before."[16] In a lecture in 1925, however, Barth says that it was Wilhelm Herrmann who

> was *the* theological teacher of my student years. The day twenty years ago in Berlin when I first read his *Ethik* I remember as if it were today. If I had the temperament of Klaus Harms, I could speak of Herrmann in the way he spoke of Schleiermacher, or I could say as Stilling did of Herder, "From this book I received the push into perpetual motion." With more restraint,

---

15. Busch, *Karl Barth*, 39.

16. Ibid., 40. Barth's lifelong love affair with Schleiermacher is well known. In spite of his criticism of Schleiermacher, he admired as well as continued to learn from Schleiermacher's presentation of "a single, astonishingly coherent view of the separate parts *(disjecta membra)* of the historical Christian faith." *Theology and Church: Shorter Writings, 1920–1928,* trans. Louise Smith (New York: Harper and Row, 1962), 181.

but with no less gratitude, I can say that on that day I believe my own deep interest in theology began.[17]

Barth wanted to go to Marburg to study with Herrmann, but his attempt to please his father led to a detour back to Bern and then to Tübingen before finally arriving at Marburg in 1908. Barth heard Herrmann's lectures on dogmatics (in a course titled "Prolegomena to the Concept of 'Religion'") and ethics. He tells us that he "soaked Herrmann in through all my pores," and it was a soaking that left an indelible mark. According to Barth, Herrmann taught him one essential truth that later forced him "to say almost everything else quite differently and finally led me even to an interpretation of the fundamental truth itself which was entirely different from his."[18] That "truth," as Barth puts it, was that "although Herrmann was surrounded by so much Kant and Schleiermacher, the decisive thing for him was the christocentric impulse, and I learnt that from him."[19]

It may well be, however, that Herrmann's Kantianism was at least as enduring an influence on Barth as Herrmann's Christocentrism. Though Herrmann was critical of neo-Kantians such as Hermann Cohen and Paul Natorp, with whom Barth also studied at Marburg, Herrmann's basic theological stance was Kantian. Barth had certainly studied Kant before he arrived at Marburg,[20] but it was from Herrmann that Barth came to see that all "intellectualist conceptions of religion"— that is, attempts to prove God on the basis of science and/or metaphysics—could not help but betray, in Herrmann's terms, how the inner life of Jesus must become a reality in our own experience.[21] From Herrmann, Barth learned that "a proved God is world, and a God of the

17. Barth, *Theology and Church*, 238.
18. Ibid., 239.
19. Busch, *Karl Barth*, 45.
20. Busch quotes from a conversation with Barth in which Barth says he went to Marburg in the first place because Herrmann was a Kantian. Barth says: "I myself had worked through the whole of Kant before I made my pilgrimage to Marburg! That is really where I came from: first I studied Kant's *Critique of Practical Reason*, and then I went twice through the *Critique of Pure Reason* almost with a toothcomb. At the time we thought that it was the way one had to begin theology. And after Kant, I then hit upon Schleiermacher" (45). Bruce McCormack argues that to the extent Barth concerned himself with philosophical epistemology, he was a Kantian idealist. Yet he says all of Barth's efforts in theology may be considered, from one point of view, "as an attempt to overcome Kant by means of Kant; not retreating behind him and seeking to go around him, but going through him." It is from this point of view that McCormack characterizes Barth's theological epistemology as "critical realism." *Karl Barth's Critically Realistic Dialectical Theology: Its Genesis and Development, 1909–1936* (Oxford: Clarendon Press, 1995), 465–466.
21. Barth, *Theology and Church*, 249–250. Even before he studied with Herrmann, Barth seems to have had a negative reaction to Troeltsch's attempt to develop an account of Christianity as part of a general science of religion. From autobiographical notes Barth began late in life but later abandoned, Busch quotes Barth's observation that for awhile

world is an idol."[22] The extent to which Barth's later theology continued to presuppose a Kantian framework remains a matter of dispute among Barth's critics, as well as his advocates. I hope to show, however, that Barth's work cannot be understood by trying to pin down the intellectual influences in his background. When all is said and done, he simply did theology as if it mattered.

In 1909, Barth's life as a university student ended and his life as a pastor began. He was briefly an assistant pastor in Geneva before becoming the pastor of the Reformed church in Safenwil from 1911–1921. There is no question that Barth's theological perspective, as well as his life, changed while he was at Safenwil, but it is not clear that any one factor precipitated what Barth described as his discovery of the "strange new world within the Bible." According to Barth, that discovery entailed the

---

among fellow students "the name of Troeltsch stood in the center of our discussions; it denoted the point beyond which I felt that I had to refuse to follow the dominant theology of the time" (50). McCormack provides an extremely helpful account of Troeltsch's criticism of Herrmann and the effect it had on Barth once he realized he could no longer accept Herrmann's account of how the personality of Jesus becomes an experiential fact for the believer. See *Karl Barth's Critically Realistic Dialectical Theology,* 64–66, 73–77. McCormack also provides an indispensable account of Barth's relation to Herrmann. For Barth's own evaluation of Troeltsch, see *Church Dogmatics,* 4/1, trans. G. W. Bromiley (New York: Charles Scribner's Sons, 1956), 383–387. Barth observes that Troeltsch's doctrine "depends on the fact that he is conscious of corresponding to the present-day structure of the Christian world. Its understanding of itself is historicist. Schleiermacher had seen the task of dogmatics in the same light. It has to develop the doctrine which is current in the Church and which corresponds to the principle of the period" (383). Given this historicism, Troeltsch could not help but represent the position Barth thought must be overcome.

22. Barth, *Theology and Church,* 243. In his wonderful 1925 essay "The Principles of Dogmatics according to Wilhelm Herrmann," Barth comments on Herrmann's view that apologetics is a subordinate and temporary activity destined to vanish. He then quotes Herrmann's remark, "Knowledge of God is the expression of religious experience wholly without weapons" (*Theology and Church,* 248). Though Barth obviously abandoned Herrmann's understanding of religious experience, from the beginning to the end of his work, Barth shared Herrmann's view of the role of apologetics. For example, in his extremely important essay "Evangelical Theology in the 19th Century," Barth criticized liberal theologians for abandoning the positive tasks of theology in favor of the secondary tasks of relating to the various philosophies of the time. As a result, we "miss a certain carefree and joyful confidence in the self-validation of the basic concerns of theology, a trust that the most honest commerce with the world might best be assured when the theologians, unheeding the favors or disfavors of this world, confronted it with the results of theological research carried out for its own sake. It did not enter their minds that respectable dogmatics could be good apologetics. Man in the 19th century might have taken the theologians more seriously if they themselves had not taken him so seriously." *The Humanity of God,* trans. Thomas Wieser and John Thomas (Richmond: John Knox Press, 1963), 20. Gary Dorrien provides a particularly astute account of Barth's relation to Herrmann in *The Barthian Revolt in Modern Theology: Theology without Weapons* (Louisville: Westminster/John Knox Press, 1999). Dorrien's book is an essential guide to Barth's relation to other theologians; it also helps us understand Barth's theological development.

insight that it is not right human thought about God that forms the content of the Bible:

> The Bible tells us not how we should talk with God but what he says to us; not how we find the way to him, but how he has sought and found the way to us; not the right relation in which we must place ourselves to him, but the covenant which he has made with all who are Abraham's spiritual children and which he has sealed once and for all in Jesus Christ. It is this which is within the Bible. The word of God is within the Bible.[23]

Whether having to teach confirmation classes as well as preach every Sunday could occasion such a change is not clear, but it should not be discounted. There is no question that Barth's increasing involvement in the labor disputes in Safenwil and the influence of religious socialists such as Christoph Blumhardt, Hermann Kutter, and Leonhard Ragaz worked to change his theological agenda. It was not so much their theology that impressed Barth as it was their willingness to face questions that Barth began to think exposed the inadequacy of his Protestant liberal convictions.[24] Barth was able to explore his theological restlessness with Eduard Thurneysen, who was the pastor of the village across the mountain from Safenwil and who was destined to become Barth's lifelong friend; Thurneysen was clearly one of the most important resources that made Barth's theological transformation possible.[25]

23. Karl Barth, "The Strange New World within the Bible," in *The Word of God and the Word of Man*, trans. Douglas Horton (New York: Harper Torchbooks, 1957), 43. This was an address Barth delivered in the church at Lentwil in the autumn of 1916.

24. McCormack provides an extremely useful account of the tensions between Ragaz and Kütter and of why Barth felt that he finally must distance himself from them; see *Karl Barth's Critically Realistic Dialectical Theology*, 78–125. The significance of Barth's lifelong socialist convictions for shaping his theology is a hotly debated issue. Though Friedrich Wilhelm Marquardt may have overstated the significance of Barth's socialism for the shaping of his theology, I remain sympathetic to Marquardt's insistence that Barth's theological developments cannot be divorced from his ongoing concerns with "social questions." For example, Marquardt quite rightly calls attention to Barth's observation in the foreword to *Church Dogmatics* 1/1 that he was "firmly convinced that we cannot reach the clarifications, especially in the broad field of politics, which are necessary today and to which theology today might have a word to say (and indeed it ought to have a word to say to them!), without having previously reached those comprehensive clarifications, in theology and about theology itself, with which we should be concerned here." For an extremely useful collection of essays surrounding the Marquardt controversy, see *Karl Barth and Radical Politics*, ed. and trans. George Hunsinger (Philadelphia: Westminster Press, 1976). Hunsinger's collection includes Marquardt's "Socialism in the Theology of Karl Barth," 47–76, as well as Hunsinger's own helpful concluding essay. Dorrien also provides a helpful account of this aspect of Barth's life and work in *The Barthian Revolt in Modern Theology*, 32–34.

25. My account of Barth's years at Safenwil is completely dependent on Busch, *Karl Barth*, 60–125.

Barth's own account of his transformation focuses on the "fateful year of 1914":

One day in early August 1914 stands out in my personal memory as a black day. Ninety-three German intellectuals impressed public opinion by their proclamation in support of the war policy of Wilhelm II and his counselors. Among these intellectuals I discovered to my horror almost all of my theological teachers whom I had venerated. In despair over what this indicated about the signs of the time I suddenly realized that I could not any longer follow either their ethics and dogmatics or their understanding of the Bible and of history. For me at least, 19th-century theology no longer held any future.[26]

Amid everything that was happening in Barth's life in Safenwil, it matters little whether his later memory does justice to all the factors that led him to rebel against the liberalism of his teachers. It is more important that in 1918, four years after this "black day," he "dropped a bomb on to the playground of the theologians"[27] with his extraordinary commentary on Paul's Epistle to the Romans. That book not only changed Barth's life but changed the world of theology. That it did so seems quite remarkable, since its message is not so strange—given Paul's letter to the Romans. In his Romans commentary, Barth was doing no more than reminding us that what is wrong with the world is its failure to acknowledge that God is God. This news, of course, came as quite a surprise to Protestant liberals who had long regarded humans, not God, as the center of Christian faith.[28] The conceptual and moral implications of the claim that God is God and that we are not would occupy the rest of Barth's life and work.

Bruce McCormack notes that beginning with his Romans commentary, the fundamental problem Barth gave himself was "how can God

26. Barth, *The Humanity of God*, 14. Barth indicates that one of the other decisive events of 1914 was Troeltsch's move from a chair in systematic theology to one in philosophy. Such a move indicated that theology was intellectually in a perilous position.

27. This comment was made by the Roman Catholic theologian Karl Adam in the June, 1926 issue of the Roman Catholic monthly *Hochland*. It was later quoted by John McConnadine in his article "The Teachings of Karl Barth: A Positive Movement in German Theology," *The Hibbert Journal* 25 (April, 1927): 385–386. I am indebted to Joe Mangina for locating the source of this quotation.

28. McCormack observes that it is clear that in his commentary on Romans, Barth's analysis of sin had as its target the "'modern' (idealistic) conception of consciousness as structured by the autonomous generation (and realization of tasks). Where for the theologians of the Ritschlian school (as well as for neo-Kantian philosophy), the development of the 'free' (which is to say, autonomous) personality is synonymous with the creation of an ethical agent, for Barth the desire for autonomy is the ordinal sin. The quest for autonomy is the source of individualism, disorganization, and chaos in society" (*Karl Barth's Critically Realistic Dialectical Theology*, 167).

make Himself known to human beings without ceasing—at any point
in the process of Self-communication—to be the *Subject* of revelation."[29]
Barth did not make any resolution to that problem easy. The heated language of the second edition of the Romans commentary makes clear
that Barth was not interested in taking prisoners. Barth's characteristic
themes are sounded, for example, in the following passage from the introduction:

> God is the unknown God, and precisely because He is unknown, He be-
> stows life and breath on all things. Therefore the power of God can be de-
> tected neither in the world or nature nor in the souls of men. It must not
> be confounded with any high, exalted force, known or knowable. The
> power of God is not the most exalted of observable forces, nor is it either
> their sum or their fount. Being completely different, it is the *Krisis* of all
> power, that by which all power is measured, and by which it is pro-
> nounced to be both something and—nothing, nothing and—something.
> . . . The appointment of Jesus to be the Christ takes place in the Spirit and
> must be apprehended in the Spirit. It is self-sufficient, unlimited, and in it-
> self true. To the proclamation and receiving of this Gospel the whole activ-
> ity of the Christian community—its teaching, ethics, and worship—is
> strictly related. But the activity of the community is related to the Gospel
> only in so far as it is no more than a crater formed by the explosion of a
> shell and seeks to be no more than a void in which the Gospel reveals it-
> self. The people of Christ, His community, know that no sacred word or
> work or thing exists in its own right: they know only those words and
> works and things which by their negation are sign-posts to the Holy One.
> If anything Christian(!) be unrelated to the gospel, it is a human by-
> product, a dangerous religious survival, a regrettable misunderstanding.
> For in this case content would be substituted for a void, convex for con-
> cave, positive for negative, and the characteristic marks of Christianity
> would be possession and self-sufficiency rather than deprivation and
> hope. If this be persisted in, there emerges, instead of the community of
> Christ, Christendom, an ineffective peace-pact or compromise with that
> existence which, moving with its own momentum, lies on this side resur-
> rection. Christianity would then have lost all relation to the power of
> God.[30]

Such a passage, which is replicated on almost every page of the second edition of *The Epistle to the Romans,* is sufficient to fuel the fires of
Barth's defenders and critics. It is easy to see that Barth's work could not
help but make people assume (and it was the reaction Barth desired) that
you either had to be for him or against him. Not only what Barth said
but how he said it seemed to allow for no other alternative. Yet in the

29. Ibid., 207.
30. Karl Barth, *The Epistle to the Romans*, trans. Edwyn Hoskyns (London: Oxford University Press, 1960), 36–37.

light of Barth's later work, the Romans commentary is best read simply as the beginning of an exploration into the grammar of speech about God.

In other words, Barth's commentary on Romans does not represent anything like a "position"; rather, it was a discovery whose implications Barth investigated and explored for the rest of his life. For example, in the preface to the second edition, Barth responds to a reviewer's suggestion that his dialectical method represents a "system" that he has used to impose meaning upon the text:

> My reply is that, if I have a system, it is limited to a recognition of what Kierkegaard called the "infinite qualitative distinction" between time and eternity, and to my regarding this as possessing negative as well as positive significance: "God is in heaven, and thou art on earth." When I am faced by such a document as the Epistle of Paul to the Romans, I embark on its interpretation on the assumption that he is confronted with the same unmistakable and unmeasurable significance of that relation as I myself am confronted with, and that it is this situation which moulds his thought and its expression.[31]

What many of Barth's advocates and critics have ignored about this famous statement is the conditional, "if I have a system." That conditional is particularly important for questions concerning whether Barth abandoned the "dialectical method" in favor of the *analogia fidei*.[32] There is no question that Barth's call in 1921 to teach Reformed theology at Göttingen provided him with the opportunity to read works that en-

---

31. Ibid., 10. Barth's understanding of Kierkegaard would require a study in itself. He seems to have read him in any concentrated way only in the time between the first and second editions of the Romans commentary. In his later work, he became increasingly critical of Kierkegaard, but the Kierkegaard he was criticizing looked more like Bultmann than the Dane. In a lovely, late short essay on Kierkegaard, Barth observes that we can now see that Kierkegaard was bound more closely to the nineteenth century than we were once willing to believe. Yet Barth maintains that Kierkegaard is "a teacher whose school every theologian must enter once." Karl Barth, "A Thank-You and a Bow," in *Fragments Grave and Gay*, trans. Eric Mosbacher, with a forward and epilogue by Martin Rumscheidt (London: Collins, 1971), 95–101. "A Thank-You and a Bow" was Barth's speech accepting the Sonning Prize in Copenhagen, which is awarded to those who are judged to have made a great contribution to European culture. In his acceptance speech Barth's irony is at its best.

32. Of course, Barth is the source of the view that his thought went through a significant, if not radical, shift signaled by the publication in 1931 of his *Anselm: Fides Quaerens Intellectum* (New York: Meridian, 1960). In the preface to the second edition of that book, Barth commends Hans Urs von Balthasar for recognizing that his interest in Anselm was never a side issue for him. Barth complains that most commentators on his work have failed to see that his book on Anselm contains "a vital key, if not the key, to an understanding of that whole process of thought that has impressed me more and more in my *Church Dogmatics* as the only one proper to theology" (11). Later in his famous essay on "The

riched his theological and conceptual repertoire. Indeed, as I will suggest, I think McCormack is right to argue that the "Dogmatics" Barth wrote in Göttingen but never published in his lifetime represent the fundamental Christological developments that are crucial for understanding the *Church Dogmatics*.[33] However, focusing on questions of

---

Humanity of God," Barth again acknowledged von Balthasar's point that the concept of diastasis (dialectic) dominated his early work and that the complementary concept of analogy was only seldom and incidentally used. Barth admits that this may have been the case but thinks that not much hangs on it. Rather, Barth says that the "essential infirmity" in his thinking at that time was "that we were wrong exactly where we were right, that at first we did not know how to carry through with sufficient care and thoroughness the new knowledge of the *deity* of God which was so exciting to both ourselves and others." Barth denies that in his commentary on Romans he was teaching that God is everything and man is nothing, noting that certain hymns of praise to humanism were occasionally raised in his early work. Yet he acknowledges that the image and the concept of a "wholly other" had captured his imagination, which resulted in the identification of the deity of the One who is called in the Bible *Yahweh-Kyrios* with the God of the philosophers (*The Humanity of God*, 44–45). Barth's references to von Balthasar are to his great book, *The Theology of Karl Barth*, trans. Edward Oakes, S.J. (San Francisco: Ignatius Press, 1992). Barth's most important exploration of his relation to philosophy is in his 1929 essay "Fate and Idea in Theology," which now appears in *The Way of Theology in Karl Barth: Essays and Comments*, ed. Martin Rumscheidt, intro. Stephen Sykes (Allison Park, Pa.: Pickwick Publications, 1986), 25–61. Dorrien provides a useful discussion of the significance of this essay in *The Barthian Revolt in Modern Theology*, 92–96.

33. For my purposes, I simply do not have to take a position concerning McCormack's ongoing critique of von Balthasar's account of when or even whether Barth made a transition from the dialectical to an analogical mode. In general, I think McCormack has developed an impressive case that makes clear there are profound continuities in Barth's work from beginning (the Romans commentary) to end. In fairness to von Balthasar, however, I think in many ways his account of Barth is quite similar to McCormack's. Like McCormack, von Balthasar sees that the issue is not really the dialectical or analogical character of Barth's theology but his increasing clarity, as well as his insistence that "the problem of analogy in theology must finally be Christological" (*The Theology of Karl Barth*, 55). In the preface to *Church Dogmatics* 4/2, the volume in which Barth develops the theme of the "Exaltation of the Son of Man" and his account of sanctification, Barth observes: "Perspicuous readers will surely notice that there is no break with the basic view which I have adopted since my parting with Liberalism, but only a more consistent turn in its development. To make this clear, I had to give particular careful expression to the christological section which stands at the head and contains the whole *in nuce*, speaking as it does of the humanity of Jesus Christ." *Church Dogmatics*, 4/2, trans. G. W. Bromiley (Edinburgh: T. & T. Clark, 1958), x.

Hans Frei, I think, is exactly right to suggest that dialectic and analogy were "devices" Barth used to express his conviction that the divine–human commerce described in the Bible and in the language of the church is "in the first place narrated, that it can indeed be redescribed, but only secondarily and fragmentarily, even appropriately, and that it cannot in the first place be argued. Barth's theology proceeds by narrative and conceptually descriptive statement rather than by argument or by way of an explanatory theory undergirding the description's real or logical possibility" (*Types of Christian Theology*, 160–161). Accordingly, Barth's discovery of analogy does not represent a major change in his position. Analogy was simply a new tool that helped Barth say better what he had been saying in a manner that did not play havoc with his Christology. My only disagreement with Frei, as I will try to show in the next lecture, is that I think Barth's way of working is an

Barth's "method," as well as on the changes his position may or may not have gone through, can make it appear his primary concern was to develop a "position"—and that is exactly what I want to avoid.

I am not suggesting that Barth did not care about intellectual consistency or coherence. The way he does theology in the *Church Dogmatics* is an ongoing attempt to show the interconnections between the various aspects of the Christian faith.[34] But Barth never thought that theology was to be done for its own sake. Barth's discovery that the proper subject of theology is God went hand and hand with his understanding of the cultural challenge facing Christians. That challenge, which he thought was unavoidably manifest in World War I as well as in the rise of National Socialism in Germany, was nothing less than a recognition that our world has become quite literally godless. Christendom, even a Christendom as pale as that represented by Protestant liberalism, had replaced the Christian worship of God, and the result could not help but be dire.[35]

Barth understood the connection between our knowledge of God and the omnipresent cultural practices that make us doubt knowledge altogether, not only of God but of ourselves. This understanding prepared Barth to recognize what few other Protestant theologians of his time

---

argument. Barth just cannot provide the kind of "knock down" argument so many desire; but that he cannot is both theologically and philosophically justified. For an extremely useful account of the role of narrative in Barth, see David Ford, *Barth and God's Story* (Frankfurt: Peter Lang, 1985).

34. Barth says: "The various departments of dogmatics do not lie alongside each other, but are implicated in each other, so that we cannot really work through any of them without expressly bearing in mind all the others to a greater or lesser extent, and certainly not without keeping them all in view. At what point, for example, does the doctrine of the Trinity cease to have any decisive importance of the doctrine of the Church, or of justification, or the return of Jesus Christ? It is just the same with the special doctrine of sanctification in which dogmatics directly and expressly becomes ethics." *Church Dogmatics*, 1/2, trans. G. T. Thomson and Harold Knight (Edinburgh: T. & T. Clark, 1956), 792.

35. Barth saw quite clearly that Christendom was dead and gone. He thought the rise of the "new age" began in the fifteenth century and was completed in the eighteenth century with the Enlightenment. The new age was characterized by the awakening of individual Christians to an awareness of their autonomy and particularity. Our age is no longer the new age; thus, according to Barth: "The idea of a Christianity which is automatically given and received with the rest of our inheritance has now become historically impossible, no matter how tenaciously it may linger on and even renew itself in various attempts at restoration by the Church and the world. The Christian West, i.e., the society in which Christian and non-Christian existence came together, or seemed to do so, no longer exists either in the city or in the peace of the remotest hamlet. Even in Spain it no longer exists. Hence a man can no longer be brought up as a member of it. His Christianity can no longer derive from the fact that he is a member of it. Whether he likes it or not, therefore, he is asked to-day whether or not this Christianity of his has some other basis than the scrap of tradition which may still remain as an anachronistic relic. It may thus be argued that to-day even from the historical standpoint there can be no escaping the startling

were capable of seeing, namely, that Feuerbach was right. If faith is but the realization of an individual's spiritual life and self-awareness, if faith is but the capacity of the infinite in the finite, then faith as the Christian's commerce with God can finally be no more than the Christian's commerce with herself. As a result, the truth of the gospel can be understood as an expression, a predicate, or a symbol of the Christian's inner experience. Barth argued that modern theology had accepted the Renaissance discovery that humans are the measure of all things, which meant that "there was no effective answer to be given to Feuerbach who eagerly invoked Luther's sanction in support of his theory that statements of the Christian faith, like those of all other religions, are in reality statements of more or less profound human needs and desires projected into the infinite."[36]

It may not be a fair reading, but it is certainly understandable that many people thought that Barth was doing nothing less than attempting

---

recognition that a man's being as a Christian is either grounded in his vocation or it is simply an illusion which seems beautiful perhaps in the after-glow of a time vanished beyond recall. And it is perhaps surprising that the most radical of the surviving Liberal theologians are the very ones who in a very old-fashioned way have been trying to deduce and explain the Christianity of self-understanding faith in terms of a Christian tradition supposedly still present and normative for us." *Church Dogmatics*, 4/3.2, trans. G. W. Bromiley (Edinburgh: T. & T. Clark, 1962), 524–525. Though this observation comes from Barth's later work, I think there is little doubt that his view on this matter was formed early. In any case, it is present already in *Church Dogmatics* 1/2, where Barth quotes Feuerbach to the effect, "The first stone of stumbling upon which the pride of egoism breaks is the Thou, the other ego." Barth observes: "Now in this matter Feuerbach must have been brought up upon a surviving scrap of Christian insight, the origin of which he had ceased to be aware of" (42).

36. Barth, *The Humanity of God*, 26. Barth wrote a close analysis of Feuerbach's work in 1920; it was published in *Theology and Church*, 217–237. In that article, Barth observes that theology's neglect of Christian hope and its spirit of "this worldliness" have at once separated it from the "*real man*" and made it "*all too human.*" As a result, Feuerbach represents the true reminder that Protestant theology's "highest idealism has fallen under the suspicion that its 'God' or its 'other world' side might be human illusion; on encountering it, one had better remain true to earth" (232). Barth's chapter on Feuerbach in *Protestant Thought from Rousseau to Ritschl*, trans. H. H. Hartwell (New York: Harper and Brothers, 1959), reads like a summary of the 1920 article.

Barth was probably wrong to accept Feuerbach's reading of Luther as the source of the problem. But Barth was surely closer to being right than the tendency of Protestant theologians, such as Philipp Melanchthon, to be more interested in the benefits of Christ than in Christ himself: surely one of the mistakes that prepared the way for the humanistic reduction of theology. See, for example, Barth's remarks on Melanchthon in *Church Dogmatics*, 2/1, trans. T. H. L. Parker, et al. (Edinburgh: T. & T. Clark, 1957), 259–260. Barth rightly thought that pietism and rationalism, though often appearing as enemies, in fact had far more commonalities than differences. Busch notes that in Barth's lectures at Bonn in 1933 he described pietism and the Enlightenment as "'two forms of the *one* essence, outwardly more different than they really were'; both were united in their attempt to 'incorporate God in the realm of sovereign human self-awareness'" (*Karl Barth*, 221).

to turn Feuerbach on his head. From such a perspective, Barth cannot help but appear as the sworn enemy of all forms of natural theology, which, of course, is exactly how Barth describes himself. In the foreword to *Church Dogmatics* 1/1, he explains that he abandoned the *Christian Dogmatics* in favor of the *Church Dogmatics* to avoid the slightest appearance that he was trying to give theology a basis or justification in the way of existential philosophy. He observes that he must avoid even the appearance of such a purpose because such an undertaking could be only a readoption of the theology that runs from Schleiermacher to Ritschl to Herrmann. Speaking of this line of thought, Barth says:

> I can only see the plain destruction of Protestant theology and the Protestant Church, because I can see no third possibility between play with the *analogia entis,* legitimate only on Roman Catholic ground, between the greatness and the misery of a so-called natural knowledge of God in the sense of the *Vaticanum,* and a Protestant theology self-nourished at its own source, standing upon its own feet, and finally liberated from secular misery. I can therefore only say No here. I regard the *analogia entis* as the invention of the Antichrist, and think that because of it one cannot become Catholic. Whereupon I at the same time allow myself to regard all other possible reasons for not becoming Catholic, as shortsighted and lacking in seriousness.[37]

This is a remarkable passage, and it has led many people to assume that what Barth says in the preface to *Church Dogmatics* 1/1 is an adequate summary of his position on natural theology. But this preface does not reflect Barth's most considered judgments on the subject, which arrive only when he is able to separate the question of natural theology from its association with Protestant liberalism. Of course, Barth never left behind his attack on the Protestant liberal attempt to ground our knowledge of God in experience, but he was able to recover a more adequate account of natural theology because the demands of his theological reflection led him in new directions. It was in fact Barth's Christological reflections that forced

---

37. Barth, *Church Dogmatics,* 1/1:x. It is at least worth noting, and it is seldom noticed, that in *Church Dogmatics* 2/1, Barth calls attention to two essays by Gottlieb Söhngen, who as a Roman Catholic gives an account of the *analogia entis* that challenges the presumption that the Roman Catholic position presumes an analogy of being that comprehends both God and us. Barth confesses that "if this is the Roman Catholic doctrine of *analogia entis,* then naturally I must withdraw my earlier statement that I regard the *analogia entis* as 'the invention of the anti-Christ'" (82). Barth, however, remains unconvinced that Söhngen's views are in fact the views of the Roman Catholic Church. Still, it is interesting to note that Barth was well aware that his views might not be that distant from how the Catholic tradition might be interpreted. As we shall see in the next lecture, these similarities with Catholicism make it all the more difficult to distinguish Barth's account of the *analogia fidei* from *analogia entis,* that is, his account of how our knowledge of God based in faith is different from knowledge of God based on being.

him to reconsider the possibility of a natural theology—a surprising development, perhaps, in the eyes of many defenders and critics of natural theology. Yet if what I suggested in the first lecture is true—that is, that natural theology makes Christian sense only as part of the whole doctrine of God—then Barth's recovery of natural theology as a Christological theme is exactly what we should expect.

Barth's Christological Recovery of Natural Theology

Bruce McCormack tells us that in May, 1924, Barth, preparing to deliver his first lectures in dogmatics, made a momentous discovery.[38] It was a surprising discovery because it was the result of reading Heinrich Heppe's *Reformed Dogmatics,* a work Barth later described as "out-of-date, dusty, unattractive, almost like a logarithm table, dreary to read, rigid and incredible on almost every page that I opened: in form and content very much like so many of the other writers of 'the old orthodoxy' on which I had heard lectures for years. Fortunately I did not dismiss it too lightly."[39] The discovery was the anhypostatic-enhypostatic Christological doctrine of the ancient church, that is, the doctrine that the humanity

38. Nothing Barth did seems without controversy. Since his appointment at Göttingen was "irregular," the Lutheran faculty disputed his right to give lectures in dogmatics. Accordingly, they specified that his lectures must be in Reformed theology. Barth gave in but then did what he wanted to do, assuming the attitude, "You can call it anything you want." Busch provides a vivid account of the incident (*Karl Barth*, 155–156). Barth knew he had to leave Göttingen as soon as possible, so the invitation to come to Muenster in 1925 was particularly welcome.

39. Ibid., 153. Barth continued throughout his life to read not only Heppe but Heinrich Schmid in order to inform his theological reflection. Barth was, in his own way, the Protestant parallel to the Catholic *ressourcement* movement—which resulted in his obscure references throughout his *Church Dogmatics* to Protestant scholastics unknown to anyone else. A study of Barth's use of these largely forgotten theologians will have to be made some day by someone with great patience. Barth was completely serious in his use of the Protestant scholastics. In *The Göttingen Dogmatics: Instruction in the Christian Religion,* trans. Geoffrey Bromiley (Grand Rapids: Eerdmans, 1990), Barth says that dogma is not humanly established, posited, or maintained but is discovered, acknowledged, and promulgated. What is given is not unchangeable and infallible—which means that all new dogmatic reflection must be established afresh: "Note how in Thomas dogmatics sought clarity on the whole sum of theological truths from the existence and trinity of God to the most detailed matters of the angelic world and the order of human life. These become the object of *Quaestiones* which can be answered only after regard is had to all the objections that Thomas himself can bring. Note that the classical form of Protestant dogmatics, too, is the play of question and answer in the catechism, which embraces everything as though nothing were for the time being fixed. This manner of instruction has the material significance of winning in order to have" (39–40). On the following page, Barth ends this reflection noting: "The vital interest of the church may be summed up again in the old war cry that the Reformers understood better and more profoundly than the humanists who first raised it: Back to the sources!"(41).

of Christ was without substance, or rather, that the substance of Christ's humanity was wholly dependent on his union with the Father. McCormack rightly suggests that Barth saw in this understanding of the Mediator a way to preserve the distinction between God and humankind without, as he had come close to doing in the Romans commentary, making the incarnation problematic.

Barth's use of the eternity/time dialectic in his earlier work threatened to become a metaphysical position that not only cut off any human pretensions to know God, but also made unclear how God could draw near to us, that is, how God is at once fully man and fully God in Jesus Christ. McCormack, drawing on the work of Michael Beintker, is surely right that Barth intended the eternity/time dialectic to be a soteriological theme and not an abstract metaphysical position, but it is also true that Barth had not yet developed the theological means to make clear that we do not know what we mean by eternity or time abstracted from cross and resurrection.[40] Barth feared that any account of humanity in the abstract, even of the humanity of Christ, could not help but be an invitation to return to Protestant liberalism.[41]

Barth's discovery of the anhypostatic-enhypostatic dynamic helped him see that the church had long before anticipated the problem of how to account for the full humanity of Christ without compromising the distance between God and God's creation, that is, without compromising that our very existence is grace. In *The Göttingen Dogmatics* Barth observes:

> The humanity of Christ, although it is body and soul, and an individual, is nothing subsistent or real in itself. Thus it did not exist prior to its union with the Logos. It has no independent existence alongside or apart from him. Those who want to see revelation in the idea of humanity as such are grasping at something that in itself is not just meaningless but

---

40. McCormack, *Karl Barth's Critically Realistic Dialectical Theology*, 12. McCormack refers to Michael Beintker's book, *Die Dialektik in der 'dialektischen Theologie' Karl Barth* (Munich: Chr. Kaiser Verlag, 1987). In *Church Dogmatics* 2/1, Barth himself criticizes the way he put the time/eternity dialectic (635–638). In particular, he expresses astonishment that in his exposition the one thing that continued to hold the field "as something tangible is the one-sided supra-temporal understanding of God which I had set out to combat" (635). What seems to have suggested to Barth that he must have made a mistake was Tillich's and Bultmann's embrace of Barth as an ally.

41. In "Karl Barth's First Lectures in Dogmatics: *Instruction in the Christian Religion*," an informative introduction to Barth's *Göttingen Dogmatics,* Daniel Migliore notes that Barth in *Church Dogmatics* 1/2 explicitly states that "human nature possesses no capacity for becoming the human nature of Jesus Christ, the place of divine revelation" (188). Accordingly, Barth acknowledges that he may have left the impression that the virgin birth is a condition for the new beginning of humanity rather than its sign. The crucial issue is always what Barth means by "human nature." Of course, human nature in the abstract can possess no "capacity" for revelation, but Barth could not tell the story of Mary without suggesting that her response to the good news of her pregnancy was "part" of *her* nature.

nonexistent. So are those who seek revelation in Jesus as a human individual. They are all necessarily groping in the void. This idea, the idea of humanity, and this individual who incorporates it, cannot for a single moment be abstracted from their assumption into the person of the Logos. The divine subject who unites himself with them makes them revelation. The human nature of Christ has no personhood of its own. It is *anhypostatos*—the formula in which the description culminates. Or, more positively, it is *enhypostatos*. It has personhood, subsistence, reality, only in its union with the Logos of God. . . . The one whom Mary bore was not an other or a second; he was nothing apart from being God's Son. He was in human nature, but this human nature was real only in the person of God's Son.[42]

Here we see the beginning of Barth's understanding of what he would later call "the humanity of God." God's deity is not a prison in which God can exist only for God's self; rather, it is

His freedom to be in and for Himself but also with and for us, to assert but also to sacrifice Himself, to be wholly exalted but also completely humble, not only almighty but also almighty mercy, not only Lord but also servant, not only judge but also Himself to be judged, not only man's eternal king but also his brother in time. And all that without in the slightest forfeiting his deity! All that, rather, is the highest proof and proclamation of His deity.[43]

God's deity cannot exclude God's humanity because it is exactly God's freedom for love that makes possible God's existence not only in and for God's self, but also with another distinct from God.[44] Barth can now say

42. Barth, *Göttingen Dogmatics*, 157.

43. Barth, *The Humanity of God*, 49. Barth's understanding of the Trinity obviously informs his account of "the humanity of God" and our knowledge of a God who would be known through Christ. In a characteristic passage in *Church Dogmatics* 2/1, Barth says: "A circular course is involved because God is known by God, and only by God; because even as an action undertaken and performed by man, knowledge of God is objectively and subjectively both instituted by God Himself and led to its end by Him; because God the Father and the Son by the Holy Spirit is its primary and proper subject and object. If it is also a human undertaking and action, if as such it also arrives at its goal, this is in consequence of the fact that God does not wish to know Himself without Himself giving us a part in this event in the grace of His revelation. . . . The first and the last thing to be said here too must consist in the fact that in the knowledge of God by God Himself we have to do with God Himself, and we have to do with Him in a matchless and incontestable certainty grounded on the faithfulness of God Himself. The beginning of all knowledge of God has now to be understood as its end and goal—God the Father and God the Son by the Holy Spirit as the object of the knowledge of God" (204–205).

44. Barth, *The Humanity of God*, 49. In *Barth's Moral Theology: Human Action in Barth's Thought* (Grand Rapids: Eerdmans, 1998), John Webster credits Hans Frei for being among the first to recognize that Barth's refusal to allow any synthesis of human aspiration and divine revelation was not grounded in the fact that God is *totaliter aliter*, "but in the fact that we are already inside a relation established by God—a point that, as Frei acutely perceives,

that eternity is not the opposite of time but "the quality of God in virtue of which he contains in himself the meaning of time."[45]

The truth that is Jesus Christ is, therefore, not one truth among others but

> *the* truth, the universal truth of God, the *prima veritas* which is also the *ultima veritas*. For in Jesus Christ God has created all things, He has created all of us. We exist not apart from Him, but in Him, whether we are aware of it or not; and the whole cosmos exists not apart from Him, but in Him, borne by Him, the Almighty Word. To Know Him is to know all.[46]

---

is the root of the deep continuity throughout Barth's work" (38). Webster is referring to Frei's 1956 Yale dissertation, "The Doctrine of Revelation in the Thought of Karl Barth, 1909–1922."

45. Barth, *Göttingen Dogmatics,* 436. Barth observes that from the days of Kant, time and space have been terms for the limits within which we exist as humans. But he argues that in dogmatics, space and time have nothing to do with philosophical idealism or realism. One can vacillate on whether time and space are ideal or real, but one cannot vacillate on the eternity and omnipresence of God, which means that time and eternity do not measure God; rather, God is the measure of time and eternity. Thus "it is only in the light of revelation . . . that we can speak meaningfully about these things. Our knowledge must be found at a place where all the knowledge of eternity and omnipresence in secular philosophy can find only offense and foolishness. The point here is that the eternal light has risen, and the circle of the whole world cannot contain what now lies in the virgin's womb" (*Göttingen Dogmatics,* 438). In *Church Dogmatics* 2/1, Barth displays the relationship between time and eternity in terms of creation by suggesting that "time is the form of creation in virtue of which it is definitely fitted to be a theatre for the acts of divine freedom" (464–465). Robert Jenson has developed Barth's account of time and eternity in an extraordinarily constructive fashion in *Systematic Theology,* vol. 1 (New York: Oxford University Press, 1997). Jenson observes that the dialectic between time and eternity powered Barth's critique of religion, but he overcame the abstractness of the dialectic by transposing it to Christology. Accordingly, time and eternity do not serve as a general boundary between God and creature but as the "event in one creature's conflicted existence; Christ's own suffering, not a principle, undoes religion's pretensions. The 'infinite qualitative difference' between God and us indeed obtains, but it is not a barrier between God and us; on the contrary, as this difference is enacted in the death and resurrection of Christ, it constitutes God's identification with us" (170). Barth's most extensive reflections on time occur in *Church Dogmatics* 1/2 under the heading "The Time of Revelation" (45–121). There he explicitly issues "a warning against certain passages and contexts in my commentary on Romans, where play was made and even work occasionally done with the idea of revelation permanently transcending time" (50).

46. Karl Barth, *Dogmatics in Outline,* trans. G. T. Thomson (New York: Harper and Row, 1959), 26. Some people may question my use of Barth's later work to spell out the implications of Barth's "discovery" in *Göttingen Dogmatics.* My attempt to explain Barth's earlier work in light of his later work is based not only on my sense that in the later work Barth says in a more concentrated manner what he had been trying to say all along, but also on the fact that reading Barth in this way helps us see why he developed a more positive attitude to natural theology. For example, Barth clearly states the implications of his Christology—present already in his early work—in the *Church Dogmatics* 2/1: "Man in the cosmos, who is confronted with God's revelation (long before he is aware of the fact, long before he has to make a decision and whatever this decision may be) becomes, as the man

An exploration of Barth's extraordinary claim that Christ is the truth by which all other truth is to be judged must wait for the next lecture.[47] At this point, I want to call attention to the fact that such christological reflections created for Barth the possibility of a more positive account of natural theology.[48]

Thus in the section in *The Göttingen Dogmatics* devoted to the knowability of God, Barth observes that his Protestant predecessors took no offense to the Roman Catholic article of faith, proclaimed at Vatican I in 1870, that God has made it possible by the light of natural human reason for us to know God from the things that are made. Acknowledging that he speaks at least partly "with his tongue in his cheek," Barth says that he has no more reason than his Protestant forebears to take exception to this defense of natural theology:

> The decisive point is that on the Roman Catholic view the claiming of reason for the knowledge of God is an article of faith, an assertion of the church that thinks in terms of revelation. The older Orthodox were thinking along the same lines, as we see from a statement of Maresius (d. 1673): Revelation does not exclude but includes natural religion, as a major includes a minor. Important, too, is the fact that a distinction is made in both Roman Catholic and the older Protestant dogmatics. The triune God, the God of real revelation, is not the object of this natural or rational religion, but the one God, the Creator of heaven and earth. Whether this distinction is tenable is another matter. The fact that the distinction was made shows an awareness of the problem.[49]

---

confronted by God's revelation, objectively another man. But this otherness of man is—always in the first place quite objectively—his truth, his unveiled reality: the truth and reality also of his cosmos. Revelation is indeed the truth: the truth of God, but necessarily, therefore, the truth of man in the cosmos as well. The biblical witnesses cannot bear witness to the one without also bearing witness to the other, which is included in it" (110).

47. In *How to Read Karl Barth: The Shape of His Theology* (Oxford: Oxford University Press, 1991), George Hunsinger provides a helpful analysis of Barth's understanding of truth as event, as mediated by revelation and salvation, and as encounter (67–184).

48. One might argue that even if the case I am trying to make is plausible, Barth did not explicitly associate his Christological reflections with his more positive account of natural theology. In *The Humanity of God,* however, Barth says: "The statement regarding God's humanity, the Immanuel, to which we have advanced as a first step from the Christological center, cannot but have the most far-reaching consequences. These result from the fact that we are asked about the *correspondence*—here the concept of analogy may come into its right—of our thinking and speaking with the humanity of God" (52). God's humanity, therefore, makes possible the analogical display that enables us to see how we, in our beginning and in our end, cannot help but manifest God's desire to have and to love us.

49. Barth, *Göttingen Dogmatics,* 344. Barth's deepest worry about natural theology was what kind of god it "proved." From Barth's perspective, you cannot begin by asking if God exists or if God can be known because any god that is the answer to such questions cannot but be "the World-Ground or the World-Soul, the Supreme Good or Supreme Value, the Thing in itself or the Absolute, Destiny or Being or Idea, or even the First Cause as the Unity of Being and Idea" (*Church Dogmatics,* 2/1:6). It is seldom noticed that Barth defended

As an example of the problem in question, Barth observes that we misunderstand Aquinas if we read his "proofs" for the existence of God in the Prima Pars of his *Summa Theologica* as the attempt to find an intellectual basis for belief in revelation. Aquinas understood that the existence of God does not depend on any proof because such a proof cannot help but submit God to human hands and, as a result, make God less than God.[50] We must remember, Barth notes, that the existence of God

the Roman Catholic position on natural theology against Brunner in *Nein!* Just as he does in *Göttingen Dogmatics*, Barth notes that no Roman Catholic theologian would, as Brunner alleges, assume that "*theologia naturalis* is derivable from reason alone." Any Roman Catholic theologian will reject such a claim because in Roman Catholic theology, "conditioned as it is by St. Thomas (and which therefore incorporates almost all of Augustine!), a true knowledge of God derived from reason and nature is *de facto* never attained without prevenient and preparatory grace. There can be no question of separating nature and grace 'neatly. . . . by a horizontal line.' Rather does nature presuppose grace, supernatural revelation as the sphere of relevant theological knowledge and statements, in the same way in which grace presupposes nature. According to the Roman Catholic, reason, if left entirely without grace, is incurably sick and incapable of any serious theological activity" (95–96). Barth begins these reflections by noting that he is sitting at an open window on the Monte Pincio in Rome from which he can see St. Peter's quite clearly.

For an extraordinary set of reflections that takes seriously the claim that we must hold in faith that God's existence can be established by reason, see Cornelius Ernst, O.P., *Multiple Echo: Explorations in Theology*, ed. Fergus Kerr, O.P., and Timothy Radcliffe, O.P. (London: Dalton, Longman, and Todd, 1979), 126–136. Ernst observes that the First Vatican Council did not endorse a philosophical proposition in which reason asserts its own powers: "However paradoxical it may seem, the teaching that we as Catholic Christians must accept in faith is that human reason, in the highest philosophical flight of which it is capable, the knowledge of God, is guaranteed by revelation. It is this revelation that allows us in faith to circumscribe the scope of reason. . . . Reason reflecting upon itself in faith is confronted with its own mystery within the mystery of God. It may be that I only believe that I can know God certainly by reason" (130). Ernst's ongoing analysis makes this stance more complex, but never in a way that would have prevented Barth from agreeing with Ernst's account of how reason can discover God's existence.

50. In lectures Barth gave during his time in Göttingen, he expresses a view not that far from the thought of Aquinas. He observes: "As ministers we ought to speak of God. We are human, however, and so cannot speak of God. We ought, therefore, to recognize both our obligation and inability and by that very recognition give God the glory." *The Word of God and the Word of Man*, trans. Douglas Horton (New York: Harper and Bros. Publishers, 1957), 186. In *That Jesus Christ Was Born a Jew: Karl Barth's Doctrine of Israel* (University Park: Pennsylvania State University Press, 1992), Katherine Sonderegger notes that this statement shows the continuity between the Barth of the Romans commentary and the later Barth. I have no doubt that she is right, but in the later Barth our "inability" to speak of God is christologically disciplined. Speaking of this aspect of Barth's work, Sonderegger observes that for Barth the particular can never be derived from the general; rather, the general must listen to and receive its form from the particular. Accordingly, all history for Barth is subordinate and confirmed by God's being, love, and freedom (151–153). Earlier in her book, Sonderegger says that for Barth "it is not so much that God acts in history as that history begins in God, and unfolds in our time the eternal election of the Son" (78). It may be that history becomes Barth's idiom, which was not the case for Aquinas, but it remains the case that for Aquinas and Barth our knowledge of God is knowledge of a mystery.

was simply not a "problem" for Aquinas; rather, it became a problem for modernity because of the presumption that somehow developments in natural science raise questions about God's existence. Barth points out that Aquinas, "standing with both feet in revelation," developed the proofs as a work of supererogation, thinking they were worthwhile as pointers to the problem and necessity of the concept of God.[51] Like Anselm, Aquinas knew that revelation comes first and that provability and the insights gained from the proofs come second. The proofs are but exemplifications of the declaration "I believe in order to understand."[52]

Barth's appeal to Aquinas is not just strategic. He was reading Aquinas to be instructed.[53] For example, in *The Göttingen Dogmatics*, as part of his discussion of God's attributes, and in particular the attribute

---

51. Barth, *Göttingen Dogmatics*, 347. I doubt that Barth appropriately appreciated the significance of Aquinas's claims that all we can know is *that* God exists not *what* God is. In an interesting way, Barth should have preferred Aquinas's argument that God can be known from things that exist exactly because such knowledge depends on the acknowledgment that all that is, is incomplete. Barth, at least at the time of *Göttingen Dogmatics,* seems to have assumed a "proof" is a "proof," not distinguishing between the ontological arguments and Aquinas's "proofs." One of Barth's problems is his failure to see that the "proofs" are not intended to prove God, but to "prove" that language/reason may find itself to be insufficient to testify to the God who is the beginning and end of all that is. Barth may be excused for thinking that Catholics, or at least the Catholics who produced the documents of Vatican I, think that God can be proved in a more robust sense. Vatican I is not as clear as it should be about what the "proofs" do. Barth's attacks on the *analogia entis* in *Church Dogmatics* 1/1 reflect his lack of clarity about whether Aquinas is Catholic or whether "Catholic" is synonymous with Vatican I. I am indebted to Lewis Ayers for these observations.

52. Barth, *Göttingen Dogmatics*, 347–348.

53. When Barth began to read Aquinas, and the extent of his reading, is not clear. According to Busch, Barth taught a seminar on Aquinas's *Prima Pars* in Muenster in 1928 (*Karl Barth,* 182), but he must have read Aquinas prior to that time, given his references in *Göttingen Dogmatics.* In *Karl Barth's Critically Realistic Dialectical Theology,* McCormack says that as early as 1923 Barth read Erich Przywara, who had criticized Barth for replacing the analogy between God and creature with pure negation. According to Przywara, Barth's one-sided account of God's relation to creation meant that no true unity of God with humankind was possible. As a result, both the incarnation and ecclesiology, which together help explain the continuing presence of God in the world, were not available to Barth. McCormack notes that Przywara wrongly attributed the way of pure negation to Barth, but Przywara at least challenged Barth to reconsider how his dialectics presented a problem for the doctrine of incarnation (319–322). Whether Barth learned how to read Aquinas from Przywara is not clear. Busch reports that Barth invited Przywara to his seminar in 1929, an experience that Barth described as "overwhelming." Barth says that Przywara was "an illustration of the way in which, according to his doctrine, the good God (at least within the Catholic church) overwhelms men with grace. The formula 'God in and beyond man from God's side' is the motto of his existence, and at the same time represents the dissolution of all Protestant and modernistic follies and constraints in the peace of the *analogia entis*" (*Karl Barth,* 183). We are in Eugene Rogers's debt for his extraordinary and thorough account of the similarity between Barth and Aquinas on the question of our knowledge of God. See *Thomas Aquinas and Karl Barth: Sacred Doctrine and the Natural Knowledge of God* (Notre Dame: University of Notre Dame, 1995).

of personality, Barth observes that we know God only as the living God, that is, as the God who makes God's self known as part of his very life. Barth then notes that life, according to Aquinas, is present where there is independent movement or activity. Following this definition, Protestant orthodoxy, Barth says,

> defined God's life as the actuosity of the divine essence. God's life is know-ing, willing, and loving as an act, indeed, as a pure act, that is, one that is independent, not conditioned from outside but from inside by the nature of the one who acts. This definition is important, and as thus defined this attribute is primary and basic. God is the one—and all the other attributes hang on this as on a nail—whom we know only as we know his indepen-dent and unconditioned act which is possible and actual only through himself; only as we know him as the living God.[54]

Such passages make it clear that Barth had learned to appreciate Aquinas, which is not to say that he was about to become a natural theologian.[55] Indeed, Barth tells us that he remains suspicious of the proofs and "for the time being" will not seek to bring them back into dogmatics, because it remains unclear how far their aim is really to give a proof—a necessary, cogent, and convincing pointer to God. If the proofs are to be of service in theology, they must lead us to the necessity of the actuality of revelation.[56] In the next lecture, we will see that, for Barth, Anselm's great accomplishment was precisely to lead us to the

54. Barth, *Göttingen Dogmatics*, 401–402. Whatever might be made of Barth's "occasion-alism," there is simply no question that in the essentials he is reading Aquinas correctly, as well as drawing the appropriate implications. See, for example, David Burrell's, *Aquinas: God and Action* (London: Routledge and Kegan Paul, 1979).

55. In several places, Barth goes to great lengths to separate Aquinas from what he takes to be the Roman Catholic position on natural theology. For example, in *Church Dog-matics* 2/1, he adopts Aquinas's claim that *Deus non est in genere* (God is not a genus). He then observes that "because *Deus non est in genere*, we must take exception to Roman Cath-olic theology when—in what seems an incomprehensible contradiction to this statement of Thomas Aquinas—it thinks it possible at every opportunity to fall back upon a concept of being which comprehends God and what is not God, and therefore at bottom to explain all the relations between God and what is not God in the form of an exposition of this general concept. Because *Deus non est in genere*, the doctrine of God in Kant is quite intoler-able, for in it the idea of God is put alongside other supreme ideas like freedom and im-mortality, and with them is subordinated to the crowning idea of reason" (310–311). Barth returns to this point in the same volume, observing that the ancient and medieval church worked out the uniqueness of God with great clarity, but "it was really the Reformation of the 16th century, above all the Calvinistic Reformation, which first brought into true focus the character of practical reason" (444). I have no doubt that Barth believed this lat-ter claim, but I find it hard to believe that Barth believed it, because he also thought that at least some aspects of the Reformation put Protestantism on the inevitable road that re-sulted in Protestant liberalism.

56. Barth, *Göttingen Dogmatics*, 348. In *Church Dogmatics* 2/1, Barth puts what he calls the "inner contradiction" of any "Christian" natural theology this way:

necessity and actuality of revelation through his proof of God's existence. According to Barth, this accomplishment made possible, if not necessary, an account of analogy in order to display how God's creation is never absent testimony to its creator.

For Barth, all of creation, and not humans alone, testifies in gratitude to the grace of the creator. Only God's revelation in Christ distinguishes humans from the rest of creation. "Man has been called to present to the Creator the gratitude of the creation," Barth says, but this does not mean that there are not other beings who, perhaps in a more perfect way than human beings, present gratitude to the creator. Accordingly, Barth observes, "we are certainly not always wrong, if we believe we hear a song of praise to God in the existence also of Sirius and the rock crystal, of the violet and the boa-constrictor."[57] For Barth, we differ from the violet or the star only to the extent that our gratitude to God can take the form of knowledge and service. We cannot have confidence in any creature, because we are required to have confidence in God alone, but "we can and should have confidence in every creature in its Creator and Lord."[58]

In "Church and Culture," an important essay written in 1926, Barth gives us some indication of what it means to have confidence not in any creature but "in every creature in its Creator and Lord." He observes that sin has not so wholly destroyed God's image in humans that God's

---

"As a 'Christian' natural theology, it must really represent and affirm the standpoint of faith. Its true objective to which it really wants to lead unbelief is the knowability of the real God through Himself in His revelation. But as a 'natural' theology, its initial aim is to disguise this and therefore to pretend to share in the life-endeavor of natural man. It therefore thinks that it should appear to engage in the dialectic of unbelief in the expectation that here at least a preliminary decision in regard to faith can and must be reached. Therefore, as a natural theology it speaks and acts improperly. And at this point—this betrays the contradiction—it is guilty of definite error, not only in regard to the subject, but also in regard to man, in regard to the world, in regard to unbelief. . . . Unbelief—just because it is unbelief towards God—is far too strongly and far too inwardly orientated to the truth, and (even if only negatively) interested in it, for us to be able to convince it of its wrongness and confront it with the truth by a skilful handling of what is after all, however preliminary and pedagogic in intention, further untruth. . . . If we proclaim the truth, which is indeed the task of the Church, but without telling it to him, we can only plunge him into new hatred against truth and increase the smart of his deprivation of the truth" (94–95).

57. Barth, *Knowledge of God,* 41.

58. Ibid., 43. In a wonderful letter written to Carl Zuckmayer in 1968, Barth observes: "I would not say with Max Born that natural science is responsible for the modern intellectual and spiritual debacle. On the contrary, I would gladly concede that *nature* does objectively offer a proof of God, though man overlooks or misunderstands it. Yet I would not venture to say the same of natural *science,* whether ancient or modern." *A Late Friendship: The Letters of Karl Barth and Carl Zuckmayer,* trans. Geoffrey Bromiley, preface Hinrich Stoevesandt (Grand Rapids: Eerdmans, 1982), 42. In the same letter, Barth reports: "An immature theological student from Canada came to see me this morning and asked—among other things—what reason means for my theology. Answer: I use it!" (43).

friendship is without an object. Human beings have not become sticks or stones but are still human, although only as sinners. It is to these human sinners that God, as a human, speaks in Jesus Christ and, in so doing, promises humanity to human beings. We are, Barth says, capable of taking part in this promise, "which is renewed with the assertion of the divine claim on man in Christ. The term *culture* connotes exactly that promise to man: fulfillment, unity, wholeness within his sphere as creature, as man, exactly as God in his sphere is fullness, wholeness, Lord over nature and spirit, Creator of heaven *and* earth."[59] For Barth, to speak of "culture," as of "humanity," is to speak not only of humans as sinners and of creation as fallen but of the unity and wholeness of creation as God's promise.

Consider Barth's comments on the consequences of sin in world history:

> In our more bitter moments we are tempted to think that they entail wholesale confusion—no more, but surely this is bad enough. Yet there is another side; for if through the confusion with nothingness which man has brought about, the goodness of the creation of God can be attained and discovered only in part, it declares itself the more plainly where it cannot be touched by man. In every age and place throughout world history, there has always been also the laughter of children, the scent of flowers, and the song of birds and similar things which cannot be affected by any confusion with nothingness. Nor have there been lacking poets and musicians and other noble spirits who have been able to look past or through the creation confused with nothingness and thus to perceive, and to make perceptible to others, its form as untouched by this confusion.[60]

By the time Barth moved from Muenster to Bonn in 1930, he had in place all the essential elements to write the *Church Dogmatics*, a work that, as I will argue in the next lecture, was nothing less than the attempt to develop a theological metaphysics and an ethic that witness to the God who is the beginning and end of all that is. In the late 1920s

---

59. Karl Barth, "Church and Culture," in *Theology and the Church*, 343. In a logically spare fashion, Barth makes the same claim in *Göttingen Dogmatics*. He says that he is maintaining only: (1) that God speaks to us; (2) that God does nothing in vain, and therefore (3) that we are possible hearers of his Word. "The first step here, divine revelation, the mighty presence of the Holy Spirit, is an act that does not take place everywhere, that is not self-evident, that is a matter of God's good pleasure. But the third step, which rests on the first two, expresses a conclusion which is always valid once it is drawn. If the reality of revelation is presupposed, then we must tell people, and hold them to it, that God has them in view, that he is seeking and finding them in his revelation, that it is possible for them to stand before God" (340). Though these passages come from Barth's early work, Barth expressed similar views throughout his work. Consider, for example, the passage from *Church Dogmatics* 4/3 that I quote just below in the text.

60. *Church Dogmatics*, 4/3.2:697–698.

and early 1930s (and, for many people, even today) Barth's endeavor appeared totalitarian and imperialistic.[61] Yet without such a theology, the church would have been even more devoid of resources in its confrontation with Hitler. I am not suggesting that because Barth wrote the Barmen Declaration we should, thereby, accept his account of our knowledge of God. Yet as I come to the end of this lecture, I cannot refrain from quoting what Barth wrote in the first paragraphs of that declaration. When we hear these words, we at least need to ask if they could have been written if God had not touched Karl Barth through Paul's letter to the Romans:

In view of the errors of the "German Christians" of the present Reich Church government which are devastating the Church and are also thereby breaking up the unity of the German Evangelical Church, we confess the following evangelical truths:

1. "I am the way, and the truth, and life; no one comes to the Father, but by me." (John 14:6)

"Truly, truly, I say to you, he who does not enter the sheepfold by the door but climbs in by another way, that man is a thief and a robber. . . . I am the door; if anyone enters by me, he will be saved." (John 10:1, 9)

Jesus Christ, as he is attested for us in Holy Scripture, is the one word of God which we have to hear and which we have to trust and obey in life and in death. We reject the false doctrine, as though the Church could and would have to acknowledge as a source of its proclamation, apart from and beside this one Word of God, still other events and powers, figures and truths, as God's revelation.[62]

---

61. I confess that I use the words "totalitarian" and "imperialistic" with some trepidation. They certainly do not do justice to the open character of Barth's work. He did not have a "system," which means that there can be no closure for those who follow him. That Barth's theology has an imperial "feel" does not derive from the work itself but from Barth's enemy. Barth's theology was written, as Timothy Gorringe suggests, against the hegemonic character of the cultural practices shaped by the presumption that we, and not God, exist. For people shaped by such practices—that is, I assume, for most of us—Barth's alternative can and should feel totalitarian. In an odd way, Barth's confrontation with Hitler—just one (admittedly severe) example of what the denial of God looks like—can distract us from Barth's more determinative political challenge against the autonomous presumptions of modernity. See Timothy Gorringe, *Karl Barth: Against Hegemony* (Oxford: Oxford University Press, 1999).

62. The Barmen Declaration can be found in Arthur Cochrane, *The Church's Confession under Hitler* (Philadelphia: Westminster Press, 1962), 172–178. Cochrane's book is a good account of the attempts to organize an opposition to the "German christian church" that led to the Barmen Declaration. Cochrane's book also offers a detailed analysis of what went

For Barth, the denial of natural theology as well as the discovery of the Christological center in theology were of a piece with his opposition to Hitler. His refusal to take the oath of loyalty to Hitler, which meant the loss of his position at Bonn, was inevitable, given his theological development. It may be thought that Barth's recognition of and opposition to a totalitarian regime had more to do with his personality than with his theology, but I have tried to show that we cannot separate Barth from his theology. That liberal Protestants, particularly in the beginning of Hitler's political ascendancy, failed to recognize much less op-

---

into the drafting of the text. Barth provides his own account of the Barmen Declaration in *Church Dogmatics*, 2/1:172–178, where he makes it clear that, at least as far as he was concerned, questions of our knowledge of God were at the heart of the challenge raised by the "German christians": "A natural theology which does not strive to be the only master is not a natural theology"; thus, conservative theologians like Abraham Kuyper and Adolf Stocker who sought to talk of revelation and reason and who used "happy little hyphens" between words like "modern" and "positive" or "religious" and "social" were naive (173). Or, as Barth put it in his 1933 essay "The First Commandment as an Axiom of Theology": Thus "said the eighteenth century: 'Revelation *and* reason.' Thus said Schleiermacher: 'Revelation *and* religious consciousness.' Thus said Ritschl and his disciples: 'Revelation *and* ethos of culture.' Thus said Troeltsch and his disciples: 'Revelation *and* history of religion.' Thus it is said in these days from every side: 'Revelation *and* creation.' 'Revelation *and* primordial revelation.' 'New Testament *and* human existence.' 'The commandments *and* the orders of creation.'" Barth goes on to observe that the creation of the *and* "began in the eighteenth century with the apology for a certain *petit-bourgeois* morality. Today it seems to end (or indeed does not seem content to end) with the apology for nationhood, morality, and the state." *The Way of Theology in Karl Barth: Essays and Comments*, 72–73.

Barth has been criticized for failing to make the persecution of the Jews the center of the Barmen Declaration. In a note in response to Friedrich Marquardt's criticism along these lines, Barth acknowledges that he was so preoccupied with the "Church Struggle" that he "neglected—I think of it today with shame—to powerfully point out this aspect directly." Barth's note is helpfully reproduced in Sonderegger, *That Jesus Was Born a Jew*, 136–137. Sonderegger rightly argues that Barth forced Christians to see the theological significance of Israel's election yet failed to provide a sufficient account of the theological challenge of Judaism. In fairness to Barth, no Christian theologian has yet to say what must be said about the Jews. Interestingly enough, Sonderegger points out that Barth was fond of quoting the response to the query of Frederick the Great for a proof of God's existence— "Sire, the Jews" (68). For a defense of Barth's views on Israel, see Eberhard Busch, "The Covenant of Grace Fulfilled in Christ as the Foundation of the Indissoluble Solidarity of the Church with Israel: Barth's Position on the Jews during the Hitler Era," *Scottish Journal of Theology* 52, no.4 (1999): 476–503; and Mark Lindsay, "Dialectics of Communion: Dialectical Method and Barth's Defense of Israel," in *Karl Barth: A Future for Postmodern Theology*, ed. Geoff Thompson and Christian Mostert (Hindmarsh, Australia: Australian Theological Forum, 2000), 122–143. In his wonderful letter to Eberhard Bethge on the publication of Bethge's biography of Bonhoeffer, Barth credits Bonhoeffer with raising the question of the Jews. Barth confesses: "For a long time now I have considered myself guilty of not having raised it with equal emphasis during the church struggle (for example, in the two Barmen Declarations I composed in 1934)" (*Fragments Grave and Gay*, 119). For an attempt to provide an account of election that constructively builds on Barth, see Scott Bader-Saye, *Church and Israel after Christendom: The Politics of Election* (Boulder, Colo.: Westview Press, 1999).

pose the Nazis may be thought to be a failure of political judgment rather than a failure of their theology. After all, few people in the beginning diagnosed who Hitler was or what he stood for. Yet this side of the Holocaust, Barth has surely earned the right to ask us all to see why his discovery of the strange new world of the Bible is necessary for us to name as well as to resist the demons unleashed in the name of humanity. There is no going back before Barth. Rather, there is only going forward through the *Church Dogmatics*. Thus it is that the *Dogmatics* is the subject of the next lecture.

7

The Witness
of the *Church Dogmatics*

Why the *Church Dogmatics* Has Neither Beginning Nor End

"We can only repeat ourselves."[1] For those who grow tired looking at, much less thinking about reading, the fourteen volumes of the *Church Dogmatics,* Barth's declaration that he can only repeat himself cannot but confirm their worst fears. Yet that Barth could only repeat himself is but an indication of his discovery that the God who has found us in

1. Karl Barth, *Church Dogmatics,* 2/1, trans. T. H. L. Parker, et al. (Edinburgh: T. & T. Clark, 1957), 250. I cannot resist calling attention to a similar remark by Ludwig Wittgenstein, but I do so forswearing any claims of how it may or may not illumine Barth's understanding of the necessity of repetition. In *Culture and Value,* ed. G. P. Von Wright, with Heikki Nyman, trans. Peter Winch (Chicago: University of Chicago Press, 1984), Wittgenstein says, in the context of a discussion of the Kantian solution to the problem of philosophy: "The limit of language is shown by its being impossible to describe the fact which corresponds to (is the translation of) a sentence, without simply repeating the sentence" (10E). In *Persons in Communion: Trinitarian Description and Human Participation* (Edinburgh: T. & T. Clark, 1996), Alan Torrance suggests that Wittgenstein's understanding that language creates and conditions thought illumines how Barth worked to show that theological speech acquires its meaning through the associations and connections necessary for a full account of the Christian faith. Torrance insists that Barth's method in this respect does not entail vicious circularity but invites a continuing investigation into how the form of our speech shapes what we say about God and how what we say about God shapes how we speak. Only after these lectures were in their final form did I discover, through the good agency of Christopher Seitz, Neil MacDonald's *Karl Barth and the Strange New World within the Bible: Barth, Wittgenstein, and the Metadilemmas of the Enlightenment* (Carlisle, Cumbria: Paternoster Press, 2000). MacDonald's argument is so important an elaboration of how Wittgenstein and Barth illumine one another that I felt I could not fail to mention his book in the hope that it will be read widely.

Jesus Christ is the subject of Christian theology. The *Church Dogmatics* is Barth's attempt to display the language of the faith in a such a way that the form of theology does not belie the subject of theology. As I will show—and it can only be shown—the *Church Dogmatics* became Barth's way to provide a compelling account of God and God's redemption of creation in a world constituted by practices that have made Christian speech unintelligible, particularly to those who continue to think of themselves as Christians.[2]

Barth explains that he can only repeat himself in *Church Dogmatics* 2/1 by observing that the answer to the open question of the *circulus veritatis Dei* can have nothing to do with an act of synthesis that we have executed. Rather, any answer that is truthful must be a witness to God's answer. In other words, theology cannot begin with our questions; rather, theology begins as an act of faith and is, therefore, capable of giving "factual proof of the truth of our knowledge of God." For Barth, such "factual proof" requires that we refer to Jesus Christ, but references to Christ cannot be the last word, because in respect to the *circulus veritatis Dei* there is no last word:

> We can only describe Him again, and often, and in the last resort infinitely often. If we try to speak conclusively of the limits of our knowledge of God and of the knowledge of God generally, we can come to no conclusion. We can only speak of it again and again in different variations as God in His true revelation gives us part in the truth of His knowing, and therefore gives our knowing similarity with His own, and therefore truth. And the question always remains whether we stand in faith so that this can be said of us, and therefore whether we are actually partakers of true knowledge of God. In this matter we have definitely no last word to speak. If we think we have, we have already pronounced our own judgment, because we have denied faith. For this very reason, the reference to Jesus Christ cannot and must not on any account try to have on our side the character of a conclusive word. Jesus Christ is really

2. The phrasing of this sentence should betray how much I have learned from Charles Taylor and, in particular, from *Sources of the Self: The Making of Modern Identity* (Cambridge: Harvard University Press, 1989). John Webster puts the challenge this way: "Part of the fate of Christian theology in the modern era has been its virtual displacement as a comprehensive account of the orders of nature and human history. Instead of furnishing an all-embracing interpretation of 'natural' reality through its doctrines of creation, human being, and providential governance (as they are shaped by a theology of redemption), Christian theology has found itself relativized by modes of inquiry apparently more universal in reach, less tradition-specific in their procedures." Webster notes that this situation has made apologetics seem unavoidable because Christian theologians assume that they must offer a foundation for subsequent theological claims by demonstrating within a theory of nature or history or human consciousness the necessity and legitimacy of theological categories concerning the necessity of the ultimate or the transcendent. Webster observes wryly that this was not Barth's way of doing theology. *Barth's Ethics of Reconciliation* (Cambridge: Cambridge University Press, 1995), 59–60.

too good to let Himself be introduced and used as the last word of our self-substantiation.[3]

If throughout the *Church Dogmatics* Barth can only say again what he has said already, it is because he is convinced, as Aquinas was, that the form of theology matters. In *Three Rival Versions of Moral Inquiry,* MacIntyre argues that the disputational form of the *Summa Theologica* is constitutive of Thomas's account of rationality.[4] Disputation denotes that rational inquiry cannot be closed because any answer, if it is a good answer, cannot help but produce further questions. Therefore, MacIntyre argues, the various parts of the *Summa* cannot be isolated from one another if the *Summa* is to have the practical effect Aquinas intended. The *Summa* is from beginning to end a work of instruction designed to develop in the reader the moral and intellectual virtues correlative to a proper understanding of God. Central to such understanding is the recognition that given the material content of the Christian faith, any attempt to display the rationality of this faith must be unending.

Obviously, the *Church Dogmatics* is not the *Summa Theologica;* and just as obviously, the challenges facing Barth were different from those facing Aquinas; nonetheless, Barth was engaged in a project quite similar to the one Aquinas attempted in the *Summa.* The *Church Dogmatics* is

---

3. Barth, *Church Dogmatics,* 2/1:250. In an appendix to his incomplete but final reflection on ethics, which was to be the climax of volume 4 of the *Church Dogmatics,* Barth observes that the special ethics he developed in *Church Dogmatics* 3/4 was shaped by the concept of freedom. Freedom is a "rich and beautiful concept," Barth says, because it is so appropriate to discussions of God and humanity and the covenant of grace. Yet, according to Barth, "in theology there can be no tyranny of concepts"; thus, he thought it advisable to look for a new basic concept for the second part of his special ethics. Given the unfinished character of Barth's final reflections, it is not clear if he made a final decision about this new concept, though certainly the concepts of witness and faithfulness are prominent. See Karl Barth, *The Christian Life: Lecture Fragments,* trans. Geoffrey Bromiley (Grand Rapids: Eerdmans, 1981), 277. I suggest below that Barth resisted any summary image in theology because he understood that to speak about God is to tell the story of God. That is why God is not only unprovable but also inconceivable. The Bible makes no attempt to define God or to grasp God in our concepts. Rather, in the Bible, God is named not as some timeless Being, as the philosophers do it, but as a working Subject who makes himself known: "The Bible tells the story of God; it narrates His deeds and the history of this God in the highest, as it takes place on earth in the human sphere." *Dogmatics in Outline,* trans. G. T. Thomson (New York: Harper and Row, 1959), 38. Barth provides no extended reflections on the place of narrative in theology, but his work presupposes that our knowledge of God not only takes the form of a story, but is a story. Thus, in *The Christian Life* he simply says: "Speaking about God's kingdom could only mean telling his story" (253). David Ford's *Barth and God's Story: Biblical Narrative and the Theological Method of Karl Barth in the Church Dogmatics* (Frankfurt am Main: Peter Lang, 1985) is the best account we have of the way Barth uses narrative, as well as of how the notion of narrative illumines Barth's work.

4. Alasdair MacIntyre, *Three Rival Versions of Moral Enquiry: Encyclopaedia, Genealogy, and Tradition* (Notre Dame: University of Notre Dame Press, 1990), 76–81, 127–138.

Barth's attempt to exhibit the conceptual and moral skills that we must have if we are to be adequate witnesses to the God revealed in the Bible. As it turns out, such conceptual and moral skills are inseparable, since our ability to live lives appropriate to the God we worship cannot be divorced from our ability to speak truthfully about and, more important, to pray to God. The *Church Dogmatics,* with its unending and confident display of Christian speech, is Barth's attempt to train us to be a people capable of truthful witness to the God who alone is the truth.

One might think that this description of the *Church Dogmatics* is obvious, that, indeed, it is but an exposition of Barth's own understanding of his project. After all, Barth argues that ethics is integral to the doctrine of God, which means—as he tells us in the foreword to *Church Dogmatics* 2/1—that he does not consider it right to treat ethics "otherwise than as an integral part of dogmatics, or to produce a dogmatics which does not include it."[5] My suggestion, however, is that even this understanding of "ethics" fails to indicate the practical character of the entire *Dogmatics*, not just its "ethical" sections. From the beginning to the end of the *Dogmatics* (the end being simply where Barth was forced to stop), Barth was attempting to show that Christian speech about God requires a transformation not only of speech itself but of the speaker.[6]

Barth himself exhibits this link between speech and speaker just to the extent that the *Dogmatics* became his life. Eberhard Busch observes that as the war drew to its end, Barth felt that his most important con-

5. Karl Barth, *Church Dogmatics*, 1/1, trans. G. T. Thomson (Edinburgh: T. & T. Clark, 1960), xiv. In *Church Dogmatics*, 1/2, trans. G. T. Thomson and Harold Knight (Edinburgh: T. & T. Clark, 1956), Barth explicitly denies that the distinction between "theoretical" and "practical" makes sense (787).

6. George Hunsinger provides an interesting comparison of Barth's and George Lindbeck's understanding of the self-involving character of speech about God. Hunsinger argues that although Barth and Lindbeck share much in common, Barth would not agree with Lindbeck's claim that the crusader's cry *"Christus est Dominus"* while cleaving the skull of the infidel falsifies the claim. Hunsinger thinks that Barth would see no reason why the meaning of what the crusader says should be determined by the use to which the crusader puts it. Barth certainly thinks that self-involvement is dependent on truth, but not that the truth is dependent on its self-involving character. Hunsinger, rightly I think, suggests that the basic difference between Barth and Lindbeck reflects their different understandings of nature and grace. According to Hunsinger, Lindbeck is closer to a Catholic understanding such as that of Aquinas, in contrast to Barth's view that "although the freedom of divine agency is independent of and external to that of human agency, the freedom of human agency is dependent on the internal to that of divine agency." "Truth as Self-Involving: Barth and Lindbeck on the Cognitive and Performative Aspects of Truth in Theological Discourse," *Journal of the American Academy of Religion* 61, no. 1 (spring, 1993): 41–56, esp. 52. Hunsinger goes over the same issue in *How to Read Karl Barth: The Shape of His Theology* (New York: Oxford University Press, 1991), 165–173. I am hesitant to express any disagreement with as able an expositor of Barth's theology as Hunsinger, but, as my account suggests, I think that Barth is closer to Lindbeck's position than Hunsinger allows.

tribution was to write his *Dogmatics*.[7] There can be no question that the *Dogmatics* took on a life of its own and that, in a sense, it took over Barth's life. Of course, this is not to say that Barth was any less engaged in the social and political events of the day than when he was dismissed from Bonn and returned to Basel. Barth's support of and advice for Christians in Communist countries, advice that many took to be a "betrayal" of the West, is but an indication that the work he was doing in the *Dogmatics* did not deter him from continuing his interventions in political and cultural affairs.[8]

That said, there still can be no question that the story of Barth's life became the *Dogmatics*. Hans Frei observes that the *Dogmatics* seems to go on and on because Barth, even for a theologian, "felt an unusual fascination with the sheer beauty, the sublime fitness and also the rational availability of the *loci* of Christian dogma."[9] Barth had what Frei describes as an "aesthetic passion," especially for those themes of Christian doctrine such as the Trinity and predestination that get short shrift in

7. Eberhard Busch, *Karl Barth: His Life from Letters and Autobiographical Texts*, trans. John Bowden (Philadelphia: Fortress Press, 1976), 322. Katherine Sonderegger, in her book *That Jesus Christ Was Born a Jew* (University Park, Pa.: University of Pittsburgh Press, 1992), notes that Karl Barth characterized his life and work as "engaged objectivity" (5). Barth thought that the work of the *Dogmatics* should continue through the war "as if nothing had happened." Such a remark can give one the impression that Barth withdrew from political and social questions, but nothing could be further from the truth. After the war, Barth was an opponent of the anticommunist crusade against the East, as well as a supporter of the State of Israel. I think Sonderegger is right, however, to caution against trying to interpret Barth's theology in terms of specific political positions he assumed. She rightly observes that Barth's "insistence on the goodness of the shadow side of creation, his lifelong critique of the liberal kingdom of God, do not make Barth a reliable political partisan" (85).

8. See, for example, Barth's essays in *Against the Stream: Shorter Post-War Writings, 1946–52*, trans. E. M. Delacour and Stanley Godman (London: SCM Press, 1954). Timothy Gorringe, in *Karl Barth: Against Hegemony* (Oxford: Oxford University Press, 1999), provides a helpful account of the correlation between what was happening in the world and how the various volumes of the *Dogmatics* reflect Barth's understanding of what was going on around him. Gorringe observes: "To read Barth as first and foremost a person of ideas is to do him a profound injustice. The very structure of the *Dogmatics,* the integration of theology and ethics, the refusal to separate law and gospel, is a sign of his determination not to allow so much as a knife blade between theory and practice" (8–9).

Barth's work on the *Dogmatics* was aided (probably far too weak a word) by Charlotte von Kirschbaum. Barth met her in 1925, and she became his theological assistant and close companion for the rest of his life. This relationship obviously placed a strain on Barth's marriage, though at least toward the end of his life Barth and his wife seem to have been reconciled.

9. Hans Frei, *Types of Christian Theology,* ed. George Hunsinger and William Placher (New Haven: Yale University Press, 1992), 158. Barth's use of Scripture and the classical creeds of the church was, I believe, his attempt to deal with the problem of authority. In the essay "Church and Theology," written in 1925, Barth calls attention to the exchange between Harnack and Peterson in which Harnack challenged Peterson to name which dogmas in which century for which church should have authority. Barth sides with Peterson,

modern theology. Indeed, one almost begins to think that the more absurd the doctrine from the perspective of modernity, the more Barth enjoyed showing why and how it must stand at the beginning of theology, as he did, for example, with the Trinity.

No doubt, Barth's aesthetic passion had something to do with the interminable character of the *Church Dogmatics*, but it is also crucial to remember, as Frei insists, that Barth was not a systematic but a dogmatic theologian. Barth calls attention to the difference in the foreword to the 1959 English edition of *Dogmatics in Outline*—the extraordinary lectures he gave in Bonn in 1946, quite literally amid the rubble left from the war. Barth says that the description "systematic theology" is recent and highly problematic:

> Is not the term "Systematic Theology" as paradoxical as a "wooden iron"? One day this conception will disappear just as suddenly as it has come into being. Nevertheless, even if I allow myself to be called and to be a "Professor of Systematic Theology," I could never write a book under this title, as my great contemporary and colleague Tillich has done! A "system" is an edifice of thought, constructed on certain fundamental conceptions which are selected in accordance with a certain philosophy by a method

---

maintaining that theology requires that the theologian identify with this or that confession of faith and this or that branch of the church, together with this or that presupposed affirmation of the ancient church on which the confession ultimately rests. Yet Barth confesses that the sad truth is that this answer is still *his* own, and however well grounded the answer may be, it remains *only* his answer. He continues: "Here the church must bear the responsibility for a considered answer—even if it be only a small regional church or a general synod which would be the legitimate representative of such a church. A fundamental cause of the weakness of our present-day theology is the fact that when we pursue theology we have no church behind us which has the courage to say to us unambiguously that, so far as we talk together, this and this is the highest concreteness. If the churches do not say this to us and yet demand that we learn and teach 'Dogmatics,' they are truly like King Nebuchadnezzar, who demanded that his wise men tell not only what his dream meant but also what he dreamed." *Theology and Church*, trans. Louise Smith (New York: Harper and Row, 1962), 290. By using the creeds and, of course, Scripture, Barth was attempting to be held accountable to the church's witness, but he knew that such recourse still did not solve the ecclesial problem. I cannot help but wonder if the massive character of the *Church Dogmatics* is not the result of Barth's realization that he could not solve the ecclesial challenge presented by Peterson. Peterson became a Roman Catholic. Barth wrote the *Dogmatics*, and, in effect, became a church father. For a wonderful account of the Peterson-Barth exchange, see Reinhard Hütter, *Suffering Divine Things: Theology as Church Practice* (Grand Rapids: Eerdmans, 1997), 95–115. Hütter sums up Barth's response to Peterson by noting: "The relation between Holy Spirit and church turns out to be the core problem. Although Barth did renew theology as a serious practice within the church, namely as 'church theology,' he was himself able to develop this theology only charismatically, that is, only in his own personal practice of it; yet he was unable to give it any pneumatological-ecclesiological foundation by demonstrating why this ecclesial discursive practice is necessary in the first place and in what way it is tied to church doctrine or makes such doctrine necessary" (13).

which corresponds to these conceptions. Theology cannot be carried on in confinement or under the pressure of such a construction. The subject of theology is the history of the communion of God with man and of man with God. This history is proclaimed, in ancient times and today, in the Old and New Testaments. The message of the Christian Church has its origin and its contents in this history. The subject of theology is, in this sense, the "Word of God." Theology is a science and a teaching which *feels itself responsible* to the living command of this specific subject and to nothing else in heaven or on earth, in the choice of its methods, its questions and answers, in its concepts and language, its goals and limitations. Theology is a free science because it is based on and determined by the kingly freedom of the word of God; for that very reason it can never be "Systematic Theology." . . . Directed by the witness of the Old and New Testaments, dogmatic theology is concerned with proving the truth of the message which the Church has always proclaimed and must again proclaim today.[10]

Barth's fear is that some people may think that reading *Dogmatics in Outline* can take the place of studying his *Dogmatics,* as if "the history of the communion of God with man and of man with God" can be systematized. Caustically responding to those tempted to such a shortcut, Barth quotes 2 Thessalonians 3:10—"If any one will not work, let him not eat." Barth says that anyone "interested only in the superficial impression given by pleasant or unpleasant catchwords cannot and will not be able to participate in *the truths* (of the dogmas) or *the truth* (of the dogma)." On the other hand, Barth promises that anyone willing "to delve more into detail" will discover "in this theological discipline and in theology in general a great amount of necessary, thrilling, and beautiful tasks which are fruitful for the Church and for the world."[11] This is an extraordinary claim, and it demonstrates that at least at one level Barth understood the *Church Dogmatics* to be a training manual for Christians, a manual that would instruct us that the habits of our speech must be disciplined by the God found in Jesus Christ.

For Christians to relearn the grammar of their faith requires, from Barth's perspective, nothing less than the recognition that, as Frei puts it, "the whole substance of Christian theology could be mirrored in a distinct way in every one" of the church's major and quasi-independent

10. Barth, *Dogmatics in Outline,* 5. Barth delivered these lectures without a manuscript, which gives them a freshness and directness that one can miss in the *Church Dogmatics.*

11. Ibid., 6. Barth is certainly correct that *Dogmatics in Outline* is no substitute for reading the *Church Dogmatics,* but I believe this small book to be one of the great books of our century. Indeed, I think it is one of Barth's singular accomplishments. No one can read this book and think that Barth was just another "theologian." That Barth came to Bonn in 1946, to the university from which he had been dismissed for his opposition to Hitler, to help Germans understand the relation between their worship of false gods and the war exemplifies at once his courage and humility. The setting of these lectures gives not only their form but their content an unmistakable beauty.

topics.[12] Barth thought that there could "be no vitality and freshness in theology where there is only one insight, no matter how true and important it may be in itself."[13] Thus, any one volume of the *Church Dogmatics* requires a display of every part of the Christian story—exactly because the *Dogmatics* is itself a story. Barth makes the point, which rests at the heart of his understanding of the Christian faith, this way:

> We can think of Jesus Christ only as the living and eternal Lord of temporal life. The Father loves the Son and the Son is obedient to the Father. In this love and obedience God gives Himself to man. He takes upon Himself man's lowliness in order that man may be exalted. When this is done, man attains to freedom, electing the God who has already elected him. But all this is history. It cannot be interpreted as a static cause producing certain effects. As the content of eternity before time was, it cannot remain beyond time. *Per se* it is in time as well as before time. And in time it can only be history. Who and what Jesus Christ is, is something which can only be told, not a system which can be considered and described.[14]

"Who and what Jesus Christ is, is something which can only be told, not a system which can be considered and described." The gospel, according to Barth, is just that simple, but because it is just that simple it requires a complex telling, since we are telling a story about the beginning of all beginnings whose end has come and yet is still to come.[15] It is

---

12. Frei, *Types of Christian Theology*, 158.

13. Barth, *Church Dogmatics*, 2/1:636. Barth's comment comes as part of his discussion of the discovery of the eschatology of the New Testament, which produced the "theology of crisis." Barth observes that although this movement created a certain excitement, it could not sustain interest because it lacked freshness and vitality. He makes the further interesting comment that secularization follows "hot foot" on such systematization just as the tedious follows on the "all too interesting."

14. Karl Barth, *Church Dogmatics*, 2/2, trans. G. W. Bromiley, et al. (Edinburgh: T. & T. Clark, 1957), 188.

15. That Barth has no place to begin theology has led some to identify him as a precursor for what is now called "nonfoundationalism." William Johnson, for example, argues that Barth was a nonfoundationalist, at least if the term designates more a style of thinking than a set of epistemological claims. According to Johnson, nonfoundationalists share the common goal of putting aside all appeals to presumed self-evident, noninferential, or incorrigible grounds for their intellectual claims. Johnson argues that Barth was certainly a nonfoundationalist on all counts involving our knowledge of God. *The Mystery of God: Karl Barth and the Postmodern Foundations of Theology* (Louisville: Westminster/John Knox Press, 1997), 3.

In *Barth's Ethics of Reconciliation*, John Webster also identifies Barth as a nonfoundationalist, on the grounds that he refused to locate "faith, church, and their intellectual expressions within a larger class of realities ('knowledge,' 'religion,' 'history'), realities of which the particulars of Christian conviction are examples and into which they may be by and large resolved as contingent expressions of generic states of affairs. In this sense at least, the Barth of the early *Dogmatics* is no foundationalist: he is entirely reluctant to sever the identity between 'the absolute' or 'that which is of ultimate significance' and the content of

this complex simplicity that makes every volume of the *Church Dogmatics* at once so similar to and so different from every other volume.[16] Just as you cannot tell any story "all at once," the story that is the story of God requires many tellings. Each telling remains the same story of the same God, but differently told. The Christian name for this difference is Trinity; or, as Barth puts it, "Trinity" names the discovery that "He who makes Himself ours in His revelation—is really God."[17]

Of course, at times in the *Dogmatics*, Barth's complex telling of the Christian story seems tortuously obscure. When it does so, you can see Barth straining to put into formal terms his understanding of how God makes God's very self known. Thus passages like the following are not rare:

> God is who He is in His works. He is the same even in Himself, even before and after and over His works, and without them. . . . But He is who He is without them. He is not, therefore, who He is only in His works. Yet in Himself He is not another than He is in His works. In His works He is

---

the Christian faith, above all its trinitarian and Christological content. Underlying all this is Barth's theological *realism*. His rejection of non-theological prolegomena to dogmatics, his 'maximization of the difference between *Wissenschaftslehre* and theology,' is much more than an attempt to secure cognitive privileges for the theologian by separating theology from the 'non-theological' disciplines. It is grounded in an assertion of the *ontological* supremacy of God in his self-manifestation" (26). I do not think you can describe Barth's position on these matters any better than Webster has done.

16. Barth calls *Church Dogmatics* 1/1 a "prolegomena," but it is not the kind of prolegomena characteristic of nineteenth-century theology. As Barth puts it: "Prolegomena to dogmatics are possible only as a portion of dogmatics itself. The syllable pro- in the word prolegomena is to be understood figuratively; what is in question is not the things that must be said previously but the things that must be said first" (45). Robert Jenson characterizes Barth's "method" by noting that with each new volume of the *Dogmatics* "Barth begins his reflections anew. It is therefore possible to begin reading at the beginning of any major section; none absolutely requires its predecessors to be understood." See "Karl Barth," in *The Modern Theologians: An Introduction to Christian Theology in the Twentieth Century,* 2d ed., ed. David Ford (Oxford: Blackwell, 1997), 28.

17. Barth, *Church Dogmatics,* 1/1:436–437. Barth's account of the doctrine of *perichoresis* is quite interesting in respect to his understanding of the unity and difference in the Godhead. He regards the doctrine as one important form of the dialectic required to express how the three persons of the Trinity "indwell" in one another, but in the common mode of one God who posits God's self from eternity to eternity (*Church Dogmatics,* 1/1:425–426). Unlike many theologians, Barth was never impressed with claims about "monotheism," identifying it as an "idea which can be directly divined or logically and mathematically constructed without God," at least without the God of Jesus Christ (*Church Dogmatics,* 2/1:448–450). Alan Torrance argues that Barth rightly maintains that the "revelation event" is, in Gilbert Ryle's terms, necessarily a "success event." Torrance, however, contends that Barth's "revelational model" of the Trinity overdetermines his account just to the extent that this emphasis fails to give an account of how the persons of the Trinity, and therefore how we, participate in the Trinity. Torrance acknowledges that the developments Barth makes in the fourth volume of the *Dogmatics* qualify his critique of Barth's trinitarian views in *Church Dogmatics* 1/1.

Himself revealed as the One He is. It is, therefore, right that in the development and explanation of the statement that God is we have to keep exclusively to His works—not only because we cannot elsewhere understand God and who God is, but also because, even if we could understand Him elsewhere, we should understand Him only as the One He is in His works, because He is this One and no other.[18]

Such complex passages often frame the simplicity of Barth's work—the heart of which he displayed on his trip to America, where, when asked to give a summary of his theology, he said, "Jesus loves me, this I know, for the Bible tells me so."[19]

For Barth, the narrative character of Christian theology follows from the incarnation of the Word, which assures that the story of God and the story of humanity—that is, of history theologically understood—are one and the same. God's Word is *hic et nunc* (here and now); thus, names like Pontius Pilate are part of the story Christians tell. Accordingly, Christians have no reason to fear Lessing's question of how an "eternal truth of reason" can be based on an "accidental truth of history":

God's history is indeed an accidental truth of history, like this petty commandant. God was not ashamed to exist in this accidental state. To the factors which determined our human time and human history belong, in virtue of the name Pontius Pilate, the life and Passion of Jesus as well. We are not left alone in this frightful world. Into this alien land God has come to us.[20]

In an attempt to characterize Barth's complex telling of the simple story that in Jesus God has come to us, Hans Frei observes that "Barth was about the business of conceptual redescription: He took the classical themes of communal Christian language molded by the Bible, tradition and constant usage in worship, practice, instruction and controversy, and he restated or redescribed them, rather than evolving arguments on their behalf."[21] Frei is right that Barth did not evolve arguments on behalf of the language of the church. But what Frei fails to see is that as Barth uses it, the language of the church is itself already an argument just to the extent that his descriptions and redescriptions cannot help but challenge our normal way of seeing the world. Earlier I said that the *Church Dogmatics* is a manual designed to train Christians that the

18. Barth, *Church Dogmatics*, 2/1:260.

19. In the epilogue to Karl Barth, *Fragments Grave and Gay,* trans. Eric Mosbacher, with a foreword and epilogue by Martin Rumscheidt (London: Collins, 1971), Rumscheidt reports that Barth said these words in response to a student's question at Union Theological Seminary in Virginia (124).

20. Barth, *Dogmatics in Outline*, 109.

21. Frei, *Types of Christian Theology*, 158. For a similar view of Barth's "method," see Johnson, *The Mystery of God*, 58–60.

habits of our speech must be disciplined by the God found in Jesus Christ. I can now add that this training, which requires both intellectual and moral transformation, enables Christians to see the world as it is, and not as it appears.

Barth helps us understand that if we get our theology wrong, we get the world wrong; or, to place the point in the context of the Apostles' Creed, as Barth does, if Christians isolate the first article of the creed from the second, then whatever we say about creation will be mistaken. If Christians, in an effort to make our faith generally available, try to provide an account of creation abstracted from election in Christ, we will deceive not only those outside the faith, but, worse, ourselves:[22]

> What the meaning of God the Creator is and what is involved in the work of creation, is in itself not less hidden from us men than everything else that is contained in the Confession. We are not nearer to believing in God the Creator, than we are to believing that Jesus Christ was conceived by the Holy Spirit and born of the Virgin Mary. It is not the case that the truth about God the Creator is directly accessible to us and that only the truth of the second article needs a revelation. But in the same sense in both cases we are faced with the mystery of God and His work. For the Confession does not speak of the world, or at all events it does so only incidentally, when it speaks of heaven and earth. It does not say, I believe in the created world, nor even, I believe in the work of creation. But it says, I believe in God the Creator. And everything that is said about creation depends absolutely upon this Subject.[23]

22. For example, Barth observes: "In modern theology, when the theologian neither could nor would prove the existence of God, he attempted at least to prove that of man, i.e., his distinctive being of man in the cosmos. As we saw, he was forced to defend the Christian position at this point. And it is certainly relevant to acknowledge that modern theology did defend itself and was not prepared to surrender at this point. There can be no doubt that to the scientific as to every world view the No and Yes of Christian faith, insight and confession had to be plainly spoken. It was essential to contradict the forgetfulness and denial of the specifically human for which man himself showed a strange capacity and inclination. To try to deny man his humanity, and to understand him as the expression of a universal dynamic, was to do something which could only avenge itself, and has done so, and will probably do so further. These Christian apologists of man may have had a foreboding of this coming damage when they opposed to this theory what they thought to be a better [theory]. The remarkably optimistic tone so characteristic of their writings might of course be taken to suggest that basically they were as little aware as their adversaries of the danger which threatened. But however that may be, here they made their stand. They came down on the right side. This is to be noted, however critical may be our attitude to the way in which they tried to do it." *Church Dogmatics*, 3/2, trans. Harold Knight, et al. (Edinburgh: T. & T. Clark, 1960), 84. It is hard to think that Barth did not have William James in mind when he wrote this passage, but as far as I can tell Barth never engaged James.

23. Barth, *Dogmatics in Outline*, 50. Here Barth is only expressing the argument he began as early as *The Göttingen Dogmatics*, namely, that election must precede creation as a topic in dogmatics. Accordingly, in the second volume of the *Church Dogmatics*, which is devoted to

Through his *Dogmatics,* Barth was trying to help his readers acquire the skills necessary to see that all that is, is so by God's grace. Our knowledge of God is, thus, but a correlative to our willingness to obediently accept our lives as gifts. These are not just "pious" sentiments but reality-making claims. Barth was well aware that, in a time like ours, his theology could not help but be read by Christian and non-Christian alike as one assertion after another. It should now be clear, however, that he could not attempt to "explain" what he was doing without ceasing to do the very thing that begged explanation. But that does not mean that he did not seek ways to show that theology was not simply "confessional" or, worse, subjective. Indeed, as I read it, the *Church Dogmatics* is Barth's attempt not only to train his readers in the proper use of Christian speech but also, and at the same time, to develop a theological metaphysics, that is, an account of all that is. Nowhere is this aspect of Barth's theology more apparent than in his account of the *analogia fidei* as an alternative to the *analogia entis.*

Analogia Fidei as an Expression of God's Being

I am aware that to return at this point to Barth's attempt to distance himself from natural theology and, in particular, from what he took to be the Catholic doctrine of the *analogia entis* is to risk going over ground covered by the previous lecture. Hopefully, however, the suggestions that I have made about the character of the *Church Dogmatics* provide a richer context for Barth's understanding of the doctrine of the *analogia fidei.*

I have no intention of trying to determine to what extent Barth's characterization of the *analogia entis* is a fair presentation of the Catholic position, partly because it is unclear if there is one Catholic position. Nor do I intend to argue in detail, though I think it to be true, that when all is said and done there is little difference between Aquinas's and Barth's understanding of analogy.[24] More interesting than either of these matters is Barth's recognition, as von Balthasar observes, that

---

the doctrine of God, Barth argues that he must discuss election before creation because God "in the primal and basic decision in which He wills to be and actually is God, in the mystery of what takes place from and to all eternity with Himself, within His triune being, God is none other than the one who in His Son or Word elects Himself, and in and with Himself elects His people" (*Church Dogmatics,* 2/2:76). When Barth explicitly takes up creation in the *Church Dogmatics,* he continues to insist that the topic is not creation alone, but creation and covenant—thus the famous formula that creation is "the external presupposition of the covenant," and the covenant is "the internal presupposition of creation." See *Church Dogmatics,* 3/1, trans. W. Edwards, O. Bussey, and Harold Knight (Edinburgh: T. & T. Clark, 1970).

24. In *Church Dogmatics* 1/1, Barth again distances his views from Brunner's account of the necessity of a "point of contact" between God and humanity, because such a "point" can

"the concept of analogy is in fact unavoidable." The relation between God and creature can in no way be one of identity. "Identity would either mean that God had ceased to be God or conversely that man had himself become God." But the relation cannot be one utterly lacking in resemblance either. For if we *re*-cognize God, this must mean that we see God using our prior views, concepts and words; thus we see God not as something totally Other. But in and with these means of images, concept and words (the only ones we have), we truly do see God.[25]

---

become real only in faith. Barth observes, however, that to describe how the possibility as well as reality of our knowledge of God is possible he uses the expression "conformity with God." He then observes: "That is also expressed by the concept of the *imago Dei*. We must be quite clear that that puts us into hairbreadth proximity to the Catholic doctrine of the *analogia entis*. But even if and because of this proximity our doctrine will have to be quite a different one from that. We certainly regard the analogy, similarity or equiformity between God and man which in fact requires asserting here, not as an *analogia entis,* as an analogy in a synthesis from the standpoint of an onlooker. Not a being which the creature should have in common with the Creator in spite of all the dissimilarity, but the action inaccessible to any mere theory, the human decision, in faith, amid all its dissimilarity, similar to the decision of the grace of God" (274). George Hunsinger is right to suggest that the decisive issue for Barth was what he took to be the presumption of the *analogia entis* doctrine that we shared a common "being" with God, which denied the gratuitous character of God's creation and redemption. In contrast, the *analogia fidei* assumes an analogy between a human action (faith) and a divine action (grace) in just a situation where no ontological commonality is conceived to exist (*How to Read Karl Barth,* 283). See also, George Hunsinger, *Disruptive Grace: Studies in the Theology of Karl Barth* (Grand Rapids: Eerdmans, 2000). In an essay in that book originally published in 1987 and entitled "Beyond Literalism and Expressivism," Hunsinger argues that the basic difference between Barth and Aquinas is that for Barth the emphasis is on God as known, whereas for Aquinas it is on God as unknown. Accordingly, for Aquinas the status of analogy in theological discourse leads to an emphasis on the "performative" aspect of theological truth; in contrast, for Barth the emphasis is on the more "realistic" side of analogy. Hunsinger explains this contrast by noting that "Aquinas finally seems to stress that we are to respond as if the analogies held true, whereas Barth stresses that because the analogies hold true we are to respond accordingly" (220–221).

The recent interpretations of Aquinas's account of analogy by Norris Clarke and David Burrell, as well as Eberhard Jungel's attempt to develop Barth's position, have made many of the past formulas and stereotypes comparing "Catholic" and "Protestant" views on analogy not only wrong but irrelevant. For an indispensable analysis as well as a comparison of Clarke's, Burrell's, and Jungel's interpretations, see Philip Rolnick, *Analogical Possibilities: How Words Refer to God* (Atlanta, Ga.: Scholars Press, 1993). Rolnick ends his close analysis of the arguments concerning analogy with the observation that "analogy has long been employed to express relation, and it is eminently suited to expressing the relation between creation and cross, wherein 'grace upon grace' is received. *Analogia entis* and *analogia fidei* are different, but they are hardly incompatible" (300).

25. Hans Urs von Balthasar, *The Theology of Karl Barth,* trans. Edward T. Oakes, S.J. (San Francisco: Ignatius Press, 1992), 109. The internal quotations are from *Church Dogmatics* 2/ 1:225. In *The Göttingen Dogmatics,* Barth does not develop any extended treatment of analogy, but in his account of the attributes of personality he discusses the relation between God's knowledge and will and he observes "we come up against facts on which our con-

Barth's appeal to the *analogia fidei* (which, interestingly, he rarely mentions explicitly in the *Church Dogmatics*) is his way of exploring the inseparable connection between God's being as act and our ability to speak of God.[26] In his book on Anselm, Barth had attempted to explore the grammar of what it means to say that only God can act without loss. Ironically, his account of why it is that only God exists in a manner such that nonexistence is unthinkable brought Barth very close to Aquinas's claim that only in God are existence and essence one.[27]

Barth's elegant analysis of Anselm helped him understand that Anselm was not attempting to "prove" God by showing that God, as the most perfect being, cannot not exist. Rather, Anselm's proof calls attention to the fact that our knowledge of God, especially the knowledge called "revelation," is by necessity analogical. As Barth puts it: "The name of God demands that his existence, even if it is denied, cannot (and incidentally this renders its denial impossible) be conceived merely as an existence in fact, but only as one that is necessary."[28] Anselm's argument does not make existence a predicate but reveals that existence

---

cepts break, as they are broken they still tell us things about the facts that break them." He at least sensed that disanalogies are as important as positive analogies. *The Göttingen Dogmatics: Instruction in the Christian Religion,* trans. Geoffrey Bromiley (Grand Rapids: Eerdmans, 1990), 412.

26. I am not suggesting that because Barth seldom mentions *analogia fidei* it is unimportant; rather, I take his lack of interest in the term itself to reflect his view that *analogia fidei* is but a name for what he is doing all the time.

27. This, at least, is David Burrell's interpretation of Aquinas. For Aquinas on this point, see *On Being and Essence,* translated and interpreted by Joseph Bobik (Notre Dame: University of Notre Dame Press, 1965). For Burrell's account of Aquinas, see *Aquinas: God and Action* (London: Routledge and Kegan Paul, 1979). Barth's conclusions are ironic because of the general presumption that due to Aquinas's criticism of the ontological argument any defense of Anselm must involve a disagreement with Aquinas. Barth responds explicitly to Aquinas's criticism of Anselm in *Anselm: Fides Quaerens Intellectum* (Cleveland: World Publishing Co., 1962), 136–137, 153. Lewis Ayres provided me with a wonderful shorthand way to display the similarity and difference between Barth and Aquinas:
Barth—Acts is being is christological therefore creation is included.
Aquinas—Being is acts is also christological therefore creation is included.

28. Barth, *Anselm,* 148. Bruce McCormack, as usual, puts the matter well, suggesting that Barth says that Anselm was "not seeking to prove *that* God exists. That much is known on the basis of revelation. Anselm is asking what else we must say about the existence of God, given the truth of the *Credo.* The existence of God figures here as the unknown article *x* to be investigated. The formula with which Anselm reasons about the existence of God ('something beyond which nothing greater can be conceived') is not of his own contrivance. It is a revealed name in the form of a prohibition. It forbids him to conceive of God in any way which would allow him to conceive of anything else that is greater. Anselm uses this 'rule of thought' as a key by means of which to explicate the meaning of God's existence. And that is what 'proof' finally means, as Barth understands it: it means *explicatio.*" *Karl Barth's Critically Realistic Dialectical Theology: Its Genesis and Development, 1909–1936* (Oxford: Clarendon Press, 1995), 433–434.

itself is an analogical concept. Barth explains that it is not, therefore, "the existence that God has in common with beings who are different from him, but rather that peculiar, indeed unique and in the end only true existence which, over and above this general existence, applies only to him."[29]

Barth's reading of Anselm is correlative to his understanding of why "reality" is ontologically "actuality." In his 1929 essay "Fate and Idea in Theology," Barth argues that the very concept of revelation alerts us to the fact that if theology is appropriately "realistic," it must understand God as an actuality. To understand God in these terms is to understand that our lives are not fated, even if our judgments about reality, which are predicated on the indissoluble connection between our perceptions of self and world, make it appear as if, indeed, everything is subject to fate. Fatedness makes the world necessary, but our knowledge of God and the world cannot be other than gift, that is, our knowledge is always contingent on God's actuality. Thus, Barth says, "act means being, and being can only mean act." God's action, however, cannot be understood in terms of efficient causality; for God "is the reality through which and in which the reality of self and world is real. As the preeminent reality God is *causa prima, ens relissimum* and *actus purus*, the reality of all reality. Yet precisely as such, *in similitudine,* God is an object of our experience, experience always understood in the twofold sense of outer and inner."[30]

Barth's recourse to the notion of God's actuality is of a piece with his account of the *analogia fidei,* which is the means he uses to display that God is at once both supreme necessity and supreme contingency;[31] that

29. Barth, *Anselm,* 149. Interestingly, we can now see that Niebuhr's objections to Barth mentioned in the last lecture do indeed go to the heart of the matter—that is, the Christian faith is false if our existence is self-explanatory, that is, if existence is not itself an analogical concept. In other words, we know "person" only from God's trinitarian life, not from a general anthropology.

30. Karl Barth, "Fate and Idea in Theology," in *The Way of Theology in Karl Barth,* ed. Martin Rumscheidt, intro. Stephen Sykes (Allison Park, Pa.: Pickwick Publications, 1986), 36–37. This article is Barth's most concentrated argument against what Christoph Schwöbel calls the modern inversions of being and knowing and actuality and possibility. Schwöbel makes the point that against these modern inversions, Barth argued that the being of God is the ground for any knowledge of God and that the actuality of the Word of God determines the possibility of theology. See Christoph Schwöbel, "Theology," in *The Cambridge Companion to Karl Barth,* ed. John Webster (Cambridge: Cambridge University Press, 2000), 17–36. Barth's analysis of how realism and idealism (in quite different ways) represent attempts to make God ontologically and noetically the fate of humanity seems to be profoundly right. It is interesting that he does not suggest further how the process of construing Christianity in realistic or idealistic terms results in Christianity becoming a form of disguised Stoicism. Yet Barth rightly sees that Christian hope is not "just a virtue" but a metaphysical draft of the universe that denies we are creatures subject to a closed causal system.

is, only God is capable of acting in a manner such that action is being. As Barth puts it:

> Only in the illusion of sin can man ascribe this being to himself. Whenever God confronts him in His revelation, this illusion is destroyed, and this being is denied to him and to the whole world. In the light of the judgment and grace which come to him as God's revelation, man must ascribe this being to God and to God alone. Now, if the being of a person is a being in act, and if, in the strict and proper sense, being in act can be ascribed only to God, then it follows that by the concept of the being of a person, in the strict and proper sense, we can understand only the being of God. Being in its own, conscious, willed and executed decision, and therefore personal being, is the being of God in the nature of the Father and the Son and the Holy Spirit.[32]

Barth's account of God's actuality counters the mistaken notion that our lives are fated, that we are trapped in a closed universe. Barth's account of the *analogia fidei* makes the same point differently. "Only in the illusion of sin," Barth says, can we suppose that our existence is *ours,* that our lives are reducible to our actions, and that everything else is fate. Revelation destroys this illusion because it alerts us to the fact that our existence is contingent on the One who is revealed as Trinity, that is, on the God whose being is action—and whose action is speech. It should come as no surprise, given what I have said so far about Barth, that when he describes God and God's illusion-destroying revelation, he does so in terms of God's speech:

31. Barth, *Church Dogmatics,* 2/1:548. Barth explains that the "supreme contingency in the essence of God which is not limited by any necessity, the inscrutable concrete element in His essence, inscrutable because it never ceases or is exhausted—is His will. He not only is and lives and has power and knows. But in all this He wills, and in doing this He finally reveals and confirms the fact that He is a person, a spirit. Because He wills, He is not only God, but there is a Word of God and a work of God, and He is to be sought and found in His Word and work and not elsewhere." As Barth puts it earlier in this volume: "God has limited Himself to be this God and no other, to be the love which is active and dwells with me at this point and in this way in Jesus Christ. God has bound himself in His own Son to be eternally true to his creation" (518).

32. Barth, *Church Dogmatics,* 2/2:271. The oft made criticism of Barth's "actualism," which seems to entail an occasionalism (a critique that I did not begin but did my part in continuing), is, I am increasingly convinced, misplaced. Although one might wish that Barth had found a more adequate conceptual means to describe God's activity, I think Gorringe is right to suggest that what Barth's "actualism" is trying to do is deny that God is *Ursache* (the first cause) because God is rather the *Ursprung* (the origin). Barth's "event" language is his attempt to find a way to talk of God without implying that God is the first of a chain of causes (Gorringe, *Karl Barth,* 58–59, 135).

Church proclamation is language. Holy Scripture is also language. But revelation itself and as such is language too. If we hold to the Word of God in the three forms in which in fact it is heard in the Church, if we do not think beyond the Church to things which God could have willed and done, but once and for all has not done, at all events in the Church, and therefore has not willed either, we have no reason for not taking the concept "Word of God" in its primary and literal sense. 'God's word' means, God speaks. . . . We shall have to regard God's speech also as God's act, and God's act also as God's mystery. But as only God's act is really God's mystery (and not any other sort of mystery), so only God's speech is really God's act (and not any other sort of act).[33]

Barth's development of the *analogia fidei* was not an attempt to develop a theory or method of analogy based on prior metaphysical claims but an attempt to display the metaphysical claims intrinsic to theological speech. From Barth's perspective, metaphysics is not a mode of investigation with a subject matter peculiar to itself. Rather, we speak, and in speaking we discover that we are caught up, together with that about which we speak, in an endeavor that must be described as "metaphysical." What it means to speak of metaphysics in these terms is illuminated by John Milbank's argument that "only theology overcomes metaphysics."[34] Of course, Milbank does not mean to deny that theological speech is inherently metaphysical; rather, like Barth, he insists that a theological metaphysics cannot pretend to be more determinative than God. Without making too much of the similarities between Barth and Milbank, I think it is fair to say not only that Barth thought that theology overcomes metaphysics, but that the *Church Dogmatics* is this overcoming.

Not surprisingly, the overcoming of metaphysics is also the overcoming of epistemology. In *Three Rival Versions of Moral Enquiry*, MacIntyre

33. Barth, *Church Dogmatics*, 1/1:150–151. In *Dogmatics in Outline*, Barth says eloquently: "Church proclamation is language, and language not of an accidental, arbitrary, chaotic and incomprehensible kind, but language which comes forward with the claim to be true and to uphold itself as the truth against the lie. Do not let us be forced from the clarity of this position. In the Word which the Church has to proclaim the truth is involved, not in a provisional, secondary sense, but in the primary sense of the Word itself—the Logos is involved, and is demonstrated and revealed in the human reason, the human *nous*, as the Logos, that is, as meaning, as truth to be learned" (22). In other words, "Jesus is Lord" is a true proposition, but the truth it is, is the truth of a language implicated in the practices of a community. The truth of the proposition, however, still "corresponds" to the way the world is.

34. John Milbank, *The Word Made Strange: Theology, Language, Culture* (Oxford: Blackwell, 1997), 36–52. For the idea that Barth was developing a theological metaphysics, I am indebted to Robert Jenson, who suggests that the *Church Dogmatics* is an immense metaphysical system, "a huge doctrine of being, which offends against the previous tradition of Western thought by putting an individual, the risen Jesus Christ, as the Ground of Reality" ("Karl Barth," 34–35). Fergus Kerr, in his chapter on Barth in *Immortal Longings: Versions of Transcending Humanity* (London: SPCK, 1997), describes Barth's work as a "Christological metaphysics" (23–45). Kerr also credits Jenson with helping him see the logic of Barth's work.

argues that the great mistake of nineteenth-century Thomists such as Kleutgen was to read Aquinas as if he was responding to the same questions that plagued Descartes and Kant, as if, that is, his primary concerns were epistemological. In fact, Aquinas simply did not begin by trying to secure, in principle, a place to begin. Indeed, MacIntyre argues that such epistemological questions have "no place in Aquinas's own scheme of thought." For this reason, Aquinas is the cornerstone of MacIntyre's attempt to circumvent the "doom" "of all philosophies which give priority to epistemological questions."[35] In a similar fashion, Barth is the pivotal figure in my narrative because he was engaged in a massive attempt to overturn the epistemological prejudices of modernity. As John Webster observes, for Barth, revelation is not an epistemological doctrine because Barth saw that any attempt to furnish an answer to the question "How do we know God?" is dependent on an answer to the question "Who is God?"[36] The oft made claim that Barth is a "revelational positivist" mistakenly assumes that Barth is trying to answer a question that he thought should not be asked.[37]

The fourteen volumes of the *Church Dogmatics* represent Barth's attempt to overturn epistemology and to overcome metaphysics. In place of the questions and answers that circumscribe these pursuits, Barth had a single concern: to use every resource at his disposal to show that our existence and the existence of the universe are unintelli-

35. Alasdair MacIntyre, *Three Rival Versions of Moral Enquiry,* 68–81, esp., 75. MacIntyre puts the change occasioned by the epistemological focus of modernity this way: "The philosophy of craft-tradition presented the mind as inadequate until it had conformed itself to the object which theology presented for its attention. And where the philosophy of the encyclopaedia made epistemology primary—for the philosophy of craft-tradition, knowledge is a secondary phenomenon to be understood in the light of the objects of knowledge and not vice versa. The whole epistemological turn of philosophy is thus from this point of view the outcome of a mistake, that of supposing that the skeptics' challenge was to be met by some vindication of rationality-in-general in which what was evident to any mind whatsoever could furnish an adequate criterion for truth" (69).

36. Webster, *Barth's Ethics of Reconciliation,* 24. Webster makes the same point earlier in his book, observing that "no view of Barth is adequate which construes his understanding of revelation as simply 'epistemological,' in the sense of a deposit of knowledge of essentially a- or pre-temporal states of affairs or divine acts" (6). In other words, Barth is a historicist all the way down, insofar as he assumes that there is no place to begin but *in medias res.*

37. Barth understood one of the tasks of theology to be the silencing of certain questions. That is one of the reasons he admired Anselm's work, just to the extent that Anselm helped the fool see that to ask more questions of the revealed Word of God is to fail to see how that Word calls into question the form of our question (Barth, *Anselm,* 28–29). Bonhoeffer's offhand description of Barth's theology as "revelational positivism" betrays the deep continuity between Barth and Bonhoeffer, particularly in terms of their theological metaphysics. See, for example, Charles Marsh, *Reclaiming Dietrich Bonhoeffer: The Promise of His Theology* (New York: Oxford University Press, 1999), and Andreas Pangritz, *Karl Barth in the Theology of Dietrich Bonhoeffer* (Grand Rapids: Eerdmans, 2000). Pangritz provides a close analysis of the charge of "revelational positivism" and why it does not apply to Barth.

gible if the God found in Jesus Christ is not God. Among the resources at Barth's disposal was the *analogia fidei*. Barth knew that our ways of speaking of God (which, to be sure, entail metaphysical claims) are far too diverse to be captured by a *theory* of analogy. If Barth had a theory of analogy, then that theory is nothing other than the full sweep of *Church Dogmatics* itself. The *Church Dogmatics* was Barth's attempt to show how our speech is at once a witness to God and a revelation of our nature as God's creatures. In that sense, the *Church Dogmatics* is a theological metaphysics.

Of course, Barth always maintained that we can never be sure that God will make our speech God's speech.[38] The *Church Dogmatics*, however, is good evidence that God has done just that. And if our God is the God who has made himself known through the promise of Israel and the life, death, and resurrection of Jesus, we should not be surprised that when our speech becomes God's speech, that is, when we participate in God's revelation, we find ourselves involved in a story.

Our participation in God's revelation consists in our offering thanks; such is the very condition of our speaking truthfully about God and ourselves. In every aspect of our lives, we cannot try to be anything other than a grateful response to God's revelation. As Barth says: "The work of the knowledge of God as man's participation in the veracity of the revelation of God certainly involves a witness, a question and a summons to all other works. But it takes place as such, as human work, with the same unpretentiousness with which they must take place, and alone can take place as good works."[39]

---

38. When I discuss Barth's understanding of sanctification below, I will explore this issue more fully. For Barth, the question of the status of our speech about God is correlative to the status of Christ's humanity. In "Fate and Idea in Theology" Barth says: "The Word became flesh, but flesh is not for that reason the Word. The relationship is irreversible. Flesh is the Word only because and only to the extent that the Word became flesh in a particular instance" (46). Barth's refusal to suggest how Christ remains actually present in the church is reflected not only in his understanding of our language about God but also in his views about the sacraments and our sanctification. Obviously, I am trying to show that Barth's practice in this respect is richer than his theological hesitancy.

Henri Bouillard put the issue well when at the end of his study of Barth, *The Knowledge of God* (New York: Herder & Herder, 1968), he observes: "Throughout the three chapters which make up this book on the knowledge of God we have in fact said only one thing, just as Barth on this subject says only one thing. Every Christian will admit that we know God through God on the foundation of biblical revelation and within the faith; but it is necessary to admit that it is *we* who know him. Consequently, the very knowledge of faith includes a natural knowledge of God capable of being demonstrated in a 'proof'; and human language, including the language of the Bible, is not fittingly brought to bear on the incomprehensible God except by means of the internal negation which is the characteristic of analogical attribution. If these precisions are accepted, one can accept the validity of the positive contributions of Barthian thought" (127).

39. Barth, *Church Dogmatics*, 2/1:216.

To speak of participation in these terms means, for Barth, that no metaphysics—even a theological metaphysics—can be intelligible without the witness of the church. The world is so constituted that God's nature can be manifest *in speculo, per similitudine, per analogiam* even if in fact it is manifest to no one. However, "with its knowledge of God the Church actualizes a possibility open to mankind but of which mankind as such cannot avail itself in practice because of the Fall—yet, for that very reason, a possibility whose reality must be insisted upon, and which within the Church can be realized."[40] Thus, any account of Barth's understanding of the possibility of our knowledge of God must end by attending to his understanding of the church's witness to God, as well as to his understanding of the moral life that the church makes possible.

As I suggested in the last lecture, however, to attend to Barth's account of the church is, first, to notice that it is not sufficient to display the implications of his understanding of analogy. Of course, Barth thought that the task of the church is to be a witness to Christ, but as Joseph Mangina observes, in Barth "it is not clear that the church *as a configuration of human practices* makes much difference to this task."[41] As a result, according to Mangina, Barth's understanding of the church seems to oscillate between claims about what is essential (Christ *is* his body, the church) and claims about the merely accidental and empirical, that is, about those aspects of the church that, for Barth, are largely indifferent and without theological significance.

Given this understanding of the church, Barth cannot account for why and how the church is necessary for our knowledge of the world. For example, in *Church Dogmatics* 3/4.2, in the paragraph on "The Holy

---

40. Barth, *Anselm*, 117. Barth says that the knowledge of God "can" be realized in the church; I would say that it "must" be so realized. And in spite of Barth's explicit "can," there are many passages in his work that seem to suggest that the church, indeed a concrete empirical church, must exist. He has little use for any visible/invisible distinction. For example, in *Dogmatics in Outline*, he says: "It is best not to apply the idea of invisibility to the Church; we are all inclined to slip away with that in the direction of *civitas platonica* or some sort of Cloud-cuckooland, in which the Christians are united inwardly and invisibly, while the visible Church is devalued. In the Apostles' Creed it is not an invisible structure which is intended but a quite visible coming together, which originates with the twelve Apostles. The first congregation was a visible group, which caused a visible public uproar. If the Church has not this visibility, then it is not the Church. . . . We believe in the existence of the Church—which means that we believe each particular congregation to be a congregation of Christ" (142–143). For a similar passage, see *Church Dogmatics*, 2/1:199–200.

41. Joseph Mangina, "Bearing the Marks of Jesus: The Church in the Economy of Salvation in Barth and Hauerwas," *Scottish Journal of Theology* 52, no. 3 (1999): 278. Mangina notes that his views on Barth's understanding of the church have been shaped by Reinhard Hütter and Nicholas Healey. See Hütter's *Suffering Divine Things: Theology as Church Practice,* and Nicholas Healey, "The Logic of Karl Barth's Ecclesiology: Analysis, Assessment, and Proposed Modifications," *Modern Theology* 10, no. 3 (July, 1994).

Spirit and the Sending of the Christian Community," Barth says that we may venture three statements: "1. the world would be lost without Jesus Christ and His Word and work; 2. the world would not necessarily be lost if there were no Church; and 3. the Church would be lost if it had no counterpart in the world."[42] If the world is not necessarily lost without the church, then it is by no means clear what difference the church makes for how we understand the way the world is and, given the way the world is, how we must live. To gain a sense of how Barth thought we should live, given the world as it is described in his theological metaphysics, let me turn to Barth's understanding of ethics.

"A Strangely Human Person": Barth's Ethics of Witness

William Johnson suggests that it is not accidental that ethics forms the summit of each of the volumes of the *Dogmatics*. "Even though Barth's own preferred vineyard was that of conceptual, doctrinal analysis, the broad trajectory of his thought suggests that ethics becomes the primary sphere in which his theology should be validated."[43] "Validated" is not a word that one would associate with Barth's understanding of theology.[44] Yet Johnson even suggests that the interplay Barth opens up between theology and ethics envisions an "implicit possibility (and perhaps obligation) for the theologian to test theological claims pragmatically. The proof of one's theology, that is to say, must be made in the living."[45] Though I will not put the matter quite the way Johnson

42. Karl Barth, *Church Dogmatics*, 3/4, trans. G. W. Bromiley (Edinburgh: T. & T. Clark, 1962), 826.

43. William Johnson, *The Mystery of God*, 8.

44. As Barth puts the matter in "Fate and Idea in Theology": "Theology claims to say more than philosophy can say. It claims to offer and to be human knowledge that rests upon a recognition of divine revelation. Yet theology can in no way make the truth of its claim directly visible, to say nothing of making it verifiable, simply because theology can never be and offer itself as anything other than human knowledge" (27–28). In *Church Dogmatics* 1/1, he puts the matter as forcefully as it can be put: "The Word of God over and to the Church is not susceptible of any proof, not even and least of all this proof by the faith present in the Church" (300). Barth's account of witness does not entail a disavowal of these claims; rather, the significance of witness for Barth helps us see that theology does not lack resources to make claims about the way things are.

45. Johnson, *The Mystery of God*, 155. Johnson suggests that Barth's validation of theology through the prism of ethics indicates a shift away from both the ontology-based approach of premodernity and the epistemological-based approach of modernity toward an ethical-based openness that is postmodernity. Obviously, I do not think Barth represents a movement away from ontology, and I have no idea why postmodernity is identified with "ethics." If anything, modernity represents the ethical reduction of theology. John Webster provides the most discerning account of Barth, modernity, and postmodernity in *Karl Barth: A Future for Postmodern Theology*, ed. Geoff Thompson and Christian Mostert (Hindmarsh, Australia: Australian Theological Forum, 2000), 1–69. Webster observes that at the

does, I am, in general, sympathetic with his suggestion of the significance of Barth's ethics.

"Barth's ethics," however, is a description begging for specification. We obviously have the explicit ethical paragraphs on ethics in *Church Dogmatics* 2/2 and 3/4. However, if the argument I have made about the character of the *Church Dogmatics* is right, then it is a mistake to identify Barth's "ethics" only with those sections that he explicitly identifies as such. All the volumes of the *Dogmatics* are Barth's "ethics," because Barth rightly saw that the truthfulness of Christian speech about God is a matter of truthful witness.[46] That many people assume the question

---

beginning of the *Church Dogmatics,* Barth makes clear that dogmatics does not have to begin by inventing the standards by which it is measured. Such standards are given by the church. Thus, Barth says in *Church Dogmatics* 1/1: "It is given in its own peculiar way, as Jesus Christ is given, as God in his revelation gives Himself to faith. But it is given" (12). Webster comments: "'It is given': virtually the whole of what I have to say about Barth's relation to postmodernism is summed up in those three words. Construed through trinitarian and incarnational categories as the free, self-manifesting majesty of God's presence, that 'givenness' for Barth made possible a kind of theological activity whose primary concern was not questions of its own feasibility in a culture of disarray, but with the sheer actuality of God's act of revelation, which as it were had already set theology on its path, thereby requiring the theologian to follow its given—spiritually given, but nevertheless given—presence and movement. Unlike much postmodern theology, Barth did not feel the need to maintain a suspicious bearing towards the church and its traditions of speech" (18–19). Graham Ward provides the best account of what it might mean to say that Barth anticipated some of the themes now associated with postmodernism. Ward rightly insists that Barth's nonfoundationalism is a form of philosophical skepticism made possible by his theological realism. According to Ward, neither Barth nor Wittgenstein are, contrary to many interpreters, linguistic idealists. "Barth, Modernity, and Postmodernity," in *The Cambridge Companion to Karl Barth,* 274–295.

46. John Webster, who is without peer as an interpreter of Barth's ethics, observes that Barth's insistence that Christian ethics is properly located in dogmatics is "incomprehensible without reference to a set of theological and ontological convictions about the being and activity of God as the defining context for ethical theory." As a result, according to Webster, theological ethics in Barth's hands is "neither agnostic nor skeptical about the existence of the good, nor reluctant to undertake a positive description of its character. Indeed, the primary task of theological ethics is just that: a steady description of what is taken to be the case by Christian faith. Such description is generally undertaken in close proximity, and by extensive appeal, to the language of Christian confession: Barth's use of the Lord's Prayer as a framework for expounding the Christian life is no mere incidental device. For theological ethics is not transcendental or critical inquiry into morals. Theological ethics, like all theology, is dominated by the question: 'To what extent is reality as the Christian believes it to be?'" (*Barth's Ethics of Reconciliation,* 218–220). Nigel Biggar's book *The Hastening That Waits: Karl Barth's Ethics* (Oxford: Clarendon Press, 1993) is also an invaluable guide to Barth's understanding of ethics. Those familiar with my past discussions of Barth and, in particular, my criticism of Barth's "occasionalism" may find it curious that I do not return to that topic in this context. I have not done so partly because I think Webster and Biggar have to some extent provided a defense of Barth on this issue. Also, and more important, I am convinced by Joseph Mangina's suggestion that those who have criticized Barth's understanding of temporality, as I have, have failed to see that their criticism is

"What ought we to do?" is the question that makes ethics *ethics* is understandable, and Barth rightly makes that question his own in *Church Dogmatics* 2/2. Yet Barth's account of why and how such a question should be asked as well as answered makes clear that the question itself must be bounded by the more determinative witness to which God has called Christians.[47]

Ethics, therefore, is but a motif Barth uses to display one of the forms the Christian obligation to be a witness takes. The opportunity to witness, moreover, is not something Christians do subsequent to our salvation; rather, it is constitutive of our redemption as well as of the redemption of the world. Barth puts the matter as simply and directly as it can be put—"God is known in the world thanks to the ministry of Christianity."[48] That Christians exist, of course, is not their own doing; but

---

"better stated as a *pneumatological* worry and specifically a worry about the role played by the church in the economy of salvation. In brief, is the church merely a human echo or analogy of Christ's completed work, as in Barth? Or is it also somehow the herald of new activity in which God is engaged between now and the eschaton?" ("Bearing the Marks of Jesus," 282).

47. For Barth's famous discussion of the question "What ought we to do?" see *Church Dogmatics*, 2/2:641–661. In *Church Dogmatics*, 4/3.2, trans. G. W. Bromiley (Edinburgh: T. & T. Clark, 1992), Barth observes that the liberation of the Christian consists "in the fact that he no longer has to exist in the dialectic of the moral and immoral, but may now exist in that of forgiveness and gratitude. Or, as we might also put it in the more familiar terms, he no longer has to live under the Law, but may now live under the Gospel." Barth notes that it is a mistake to think that a genuine act of obedience, even if stained by sin, is made a good and obedient act by morality. Barth observes that if the "act of the Christian were really good and obedient in this sense, it would correspond exactly to what every serious and careful Jew, Hindu, Mohammedan, pedagogue or psychologist usually describes as a good act, but it would not correspond in the very least to the divine act of reconciliation, to the justification and sanctification of the sinner accomplished in Jesus Christ, the knowledge and attestation of which are what makes the Christian a Christian" (670). This kind of claim makes it clear that Barth, although not denying that something called "morality" exists, teaches that the Christian story challenges and transforms "morality" by placing our lives in a more encompassing narrative. Accordingly, Barth's ethics cannot be limited to the ethical sections of the *Dogmatics*.

48. Barth, *The Christian Life*, 119. "Witness" is one of Barth's ways of displaying what it means for us to participate in the life of the Trinity. As Johnson puts the matter: "God is both the acting subject that enables humanity's redemptive experience and the very act itself. God is both the subject and predicate of God's own revelatory deed." Johnson adds: "One can hardly imagine a more radical way of formulating this than Barth's: God is what God achieves in human beings (*KD* I/1, 315, *CD* 299)" (*The Mystery of God*, 50). Apparently, Johnson is paraphrasing Barth here, since a review of both the German and English versions of the texts Johnson cites seems to indicate that Barth did not put the matter quite this way. In any event, Johnson certainly captures one side of Barth's claims, but his formulation fails to indicate that for Barth although God achieves our unity with God in Christ, we are not identical with Christ's person. I suspect that Barth would think Johnson's paraphrase crosses a boundary, making the witness of Christians equivalent to that to which they witness. In *Church Dogmatics* 1/1, Barth was always careful to distinguish

that they exist witnesses to the God who makes their existence not only possible but necessary. Christians and the church are often unfaithful, of course, but that does not make their existence any less necessary. Through baptism, Christians are made different so that even in our unfaithfulness we may be for the world witnesses to the God who would not abandon creation:

> The God whom the Christian confronts is the true God who is also true man. Confronting him, man is confronted by his creature, the neighbor, the fellow man who is God's child with him and hence his own brother. As he confronts God and is in covenant with him and responsible to him, not only atheism and religiosity and nostrification but also the inhumanity which in the world can compete so strangely with the knowledge of God, and therefore with humanity, can be no alternative for him. In his acts he simply cannot take part in the great vacillation between his being without or against his fellows and his being for them. It is thus most striking that he presents himself to other men of the world as a nonconformist, as one who is zealous for God's honor, as a witness to what he, who is also a man of the world, has to advocate to others of his kind. He does this by offering to them the image of a strangely human person.[49]

To speak of a "strangely human person" is Barth's way of displaying what it means for Christians to be sanctified. Sanctification is "the separation, claiming, commandeering, and preparation of a person" with a view to the higher purpose destined for them, which is nothing less

---

God's speech from the effects of that speech. As he puts it, "where God speaks, it is meaningless to cast about for the corresponding act" (162). Barth exercises the same caution when he deals with questions of witness and ethics. For example, in *Dogmatics in Outline* Barth maintains that our knowledge of God is not idle knowledge: "The conclusion of revelation time is not the end of a spectacle, where the curtain falls and the onlookers may go home, but it ends with a challenge, with a command. The salvation even now becomes a bit of world event." But then he adds: "It should not be said that the work of Jesus Christ simply continues in the life of Christians and the existence of the Church. The life of the saints is not a prolongation of the revelation of Jesus Christ upon earth" (127).

In a fascinating response to von Balthasar's work on the saints, Barth notes that von Balthasar has grasped clearly and finely a whole field of "possible and actual representations" of the history of Jesus Christ, "the repetitions or reenactments of His being and activity by the saints" or by those who achieve some measure of sanctity. Indeed, Barth says that von Balthasar has presented the saints with such positive and stimulating force that Barth finally has an inkling of what von Balthasar meant when he "mildly rebuked" Barth for "christological constriction." Yet, Barth counters, "we must bring against him the counter-question, whether in all the spiritual splendor of the saints who are supposed to represent and repeat Him Jesus Christ has not ceased—not in theory but in practice—to be the object of the Christian faith." As hopeful as the "christological renaissance" in Catholicism may be, Barth says, it is in danger of absorbing the doctrine of justification into sanctification. *Church Dogmatics*, 4/1, trans. G. W. Bromiley (New York: Scribner's Sons, 1956), 768.

49. Barth, *The Christian Life*, 203–204.

than dedication to the service of God.[50] Accordingly, for Barth, a Christian cannot help but be "a lonely bird on the housetop" (Ps. 102:8), but nonetheless content. The song the Christian must sing is not an old, familiar, or popular one but a strange song that will not necessarily result in great choirs joining in the refrain. On the whole, Christianity, as Barth describes it, is an exalted but "forlorn hope," with few or no chances to achieve the triumphant status of membership in the so-called world religions.[51]

For Barth, to be a Christian, to anticipate here and now the future, universal praise of God, is to be a member of a limited and prophetic

50. Ibid., 150. That Barth had an extensive account of sanctification is often overlooked. Joseph Mangina, in "The Practical Voice of Dogmatic Theology: Karl Barth on the Christian Life" (Ph.D. diss., Yale University, 1994), has provided a wonderful account of Barth's understanding of sanctification. In his chapter on Barth's understanding of sin, Mangina helpfully contrasts Barth and Niebuhr. Unlike Niebuhr, Barth rightly insisted, according to Mangina, that any account of sin must be christologically determined (127–143). Mangina suggests that, nonetheless, Barth's account of the "existential phenomenology of sin" is in some ways quite similar to Niebuhr's account of pride and sloth. Mangina observes that although Barth, unlike Niebuhr, offers no privileged anthropological clue to sin, his descriptions reference our world in which the concept of sin has to be applied. Thus, Barth in *Church Dogmatics* 4/1 describes pride as the desire to be the "judge" of our own life: "The history of every person is, in fact, the history of a specific view of what is right. And the history of all people is the history of their many and constantly arising and mutually contradictory intersecting views. To live as a human being means in effect to be at some point on the long road from the passionate search for a standard by which to judge our own human affairs and those of others, to the discovery of such a standard" that is then hardened into a certainty that betrays the fact that we cannot judge ourselves much less others (447). Mangina thinks that this account of pride is an example of what Frei characterizes as Barth's *ad hoc* apologetics (155). That may be the case, but whatever such passages indicate about Barth's understanding of sin, I think it is far more important to see that he refused to let sin become a controlling category of his theology.

51. Barth, *The Christian Life*, 96. That Barth uses music to suggest how Christians witness to God is, of course, not accidental given his love of music and, in particular, Mozart. Indeed, Barth's most "purple" passages concerning the witness God makes possible in creation use music as the means to display how we become part of God's song. For example: "What is lacking to the self-attestations of the creature as such . . . they can acquire as and when God Himself begins to speak and claims and uses them in His service. . . . They can blend their voices with that of God. He could hardly be the God who has lent them these voices if they could not do this as commanded and empowered by Him. What they say can so harmonize with what He Himself says that to hear Him is to hear them, and to hear them to hear Him, so that listening to the polyphony of creation as the external basis of the covenant . . . is listening to the symphony for which it was elected and determined from eternity and which the Creator alone has the power to evoke, yet according to His Word the will also. Nor has He only the will. For when He speaks His one and total Word concerning the covenant which is the internal basis of creation, this symphony is in fact evoked, and even the self-witness of creation in all the diversity of its voices can and will give its unanimous applause." Karl Barth, *Church Dogmatics*, 4/3.1, trans. G. W. Bromiley (Edinburgh: T. & T. Clark, 1961), 1059–1160. That Barth sees that we must "blend" our voices at least suggests that "the lonely bird on the housetop" may in fact be a flock. I am indebted to Rev. Michael Baxter, C.S.C., for reminding me that birds often come in flocks.

minority. Here and now, Christian praise takes the form of prayer, for it is the good news of the gospel that Jesus told his followers: "Pray then like this."[52] Such prayer is prophetic because the world does not know that it was created for praise, nor does or can the world know without the witness of prayer the One to whom such praise should be directed. The Christian ministry of witness, therefore, will disturb some people, and they will react to the pressure of the witness with counterpressure. Though no doubt such "pressure" will take different forms, "real Christians" are always those who are oppressed by the surrounding world. Indeed, Barth says that it may even be the case that no one can be a Christian without falling into affliction; for what the "world perceives when it hears the witness of the Christian is the opinion of a fanatic who has obviously broken his bridges and burned his boats behind him and demands that it should do the same."[53]

Barth, of course, did not think that Christians could be witnesses as individuals. The individual Christian is always in the church. That the Christian is in the church is not just accidental or incidental:

> He is not in it merely in the sense that he might first be a more or less good Christian by his personal choice and calling and on his own responsibility as a lonely hearer of God's Word, and only later, perhaps optionally and only at his own pleasure, he might take into account his membership in the church. If he were not in the church, he would not be in

---

52. Barth, *The Christian Life*, 70. For Barth, the Christian is not only someone who prays but someone who has become prayer. For example, in what almost appears an offhand remark in *Church Dogmatics* 2/2, Barth says: "God's eternal will is the act of prayer in which confidence in self gives way before confidence in God" (180). The significance of Barth's discussion of the holy day, confession, and prayer before he begins his "special ethics" has been insufficiently appreciated. See *Church Dogmatics*, 3/4:47–116. Prayer is the form our acknowledgment of God must take if our obedient response to God's command is to be free.

53. Barth, *Church Dogmatics*, 4/3.2:623. This paragraph paraphrases Barth's remarks in the section of this volume entitled "The Christian in Affliction," 614–647. In *The Mystery of God*, Johnson suggests that at least one aspect of Barth's rejection of Troeltsch was Barth's perception that Troeltsch's approach to religion served to buttress the sociopolitical consensus of a middle-class and conservative life style (15–20). I have no doubt that Barth, as Johnson maintains, possessed a general disdain for the bourgeoisie, but I do not think that Barth confused the peculiarity of the Christian witness with his own dislike for the bourgeoisie (Johnson may not think this either, though one can get that impression from his book). Barth did think that one of the dangers of natural theology was that of making the gospel respectable. For example, in *Church Dogmatics* 2/1, he says that the triumph of natural theology in the church, which can be "described as the absorbing and domesticating of revelation, is very clearly the process of making the Gospel respectable. When the Gospel is offered to man, and he stretches out his hand to receive it and takes it into his hand, an acute danger arises which is greater than the danger that he may not understand it and angrily reject it. The danger is that he may accept it and peacefully and at once make himself its lord and possessor, thus rendering it innocuous, making that which chooses him something which he himself has chosen, which therefore comes to stand as such alongside all the other things that he can also choose, and therefore control" (141).

Christ. He is elected and called, not to the being and action of a private person with a Christian interest, but to be a living member of the living community of the living Lord Jesus.[54]

According to Barth, then, individuals as witnesses are part of the larger witness of the church, and the church, as this witness, must be visible. The Word became flesh; this is the original and controlling sign of all signs. In relation to this sign stand all forms of creaturely testimony to God's eternal Word. Such testimony does not exist everywhere, Barth says, but only where the Word has chosen and called witnesses. Thus, there exists, as Barth puts it, "a testimony by the word of the prophets and apostles of this Word; by the visible existence of His people, His Church; by the Gospel which is delivered and to be heard in it; by the sacraments in which this Gospel has also a physically visible and apprehensible form; and finally, by the existence of us who believe this testimony."[55] For Barth, a church may be thoroughly orthodox in its doctrine, which in itself is a good thing, but it will cease to be the church if it lacks faithful witnesses.[56]

54. Barth, *The Christian Life*, 188. A few pages later, Barth continues this theme, noting that the Christian cannot break solidarity with other Christians but must accept responsibility for "actualizing his zeal for God's honor as a member of the church. He cannot make a separate peace with God or wage a separate war for his honor. He stands or falls with the cause of the church" (190).

55. Barth, *Church Dogmatics*, 2/1:199. Barth, of course, never tires of reminding us that the visibility of Christ and the church cannot in any fashion compromise God's hiddenness. God's hiddenness, for Barth, is not simply a claim about our inability to comprehend God. What makes God incomprehensible is not God's remoteness but God's nearness in Jesus Christ. As Barth puts it: "The very hiddenness in which He is revealed is only the mark of the grace of His revelation, with the knowledge of which our knowledge of God must begin and from which it must never depart. But in the revelation of God there is no hidden God, no *Deus absconditus*, at the back of His revelation, with whose existence and activity we have also occasionally to reckon beyond His Word and His Spirit, and whom we have also to fear and honour behind His revelation" (*Church Dogmatics*, 2/1:210). However, the issue remains, as Reinhard Hütter has argued, whether Barth's refusal to maintain the bond between the Spirit and particular church practices does not weaken his ecclesiology and ethics. See Hütter's *Evangelische Ethik als kirchliches Zeugnis: Interpretationen zu Schlussel-fragen theologischer Ethik in der Gegenwart* (Neukirchener Verlag: Neukirchen, 1993). Webster responds on Barth's behalf to Hütter's criticism by arguing that Hütter fails to appreciate that Barth did not desire to burden the church with responsibility that is properly God's affair; see John Webster, *Barth's Moral Theology: Human Action in Barth's Thought* (Edinburgh: T. & T. Clark, 1998), 146, 170. I would like to agree with Webster's defense of Barth and, in particular, with his account of Barth on agency, but I remain unconvinced. Barth set his sail clearly on these matters as early as *The Göttingen Dogmatics*, in which he distanced himself from the Catholic view of sacraments (168–173). Barth, as far as I know, never wavered from the position he took there. I am not alone in noticing how Barth's Zwinglian view of the sacraments at least mirrors his hesitancy concerning Christian sanctification. See, for example, Torrance, *Persons in Communion*, 116–119.

56. Barth sounds this theme numerous times in *The Knowledge of God and the Service of God according to the Teaching of the Reformation*, trans. J. L. M. Haire and Ian Henderson (London: Hodder and Stoughton Publishers, 1938), which is not surprising for someone who

Christian orthodoxy cannot be Christian truth without living Christians. In the absence of living Christians, orthodoxy cannot help but give birth to and be opposed by mystical, liberal, existential Christianity without Christ.[57] The church's struggle to produce truthful witnesses is an ongoing task; to the extent that such witnesses exist, by their fruits you shall know them. For Barth, therefore, the question of the distinctive character of the Christian life as a witness to God is inseparable from, in fact is the necessary condition for, any account of the truth of Christian convictions:

> Because the election of Jesus Christ is the truth, then the difference of those who are chosen in Him (their calling) is *the* witness to the truth besides which there is no other. There and there alone the truth is testified—there and there alone it finds expression—where in and with the election of Jesus Christ the election of man is proclaimed to him, and where he may have assurance of it through faith in Him. Thus the difference of the elect from others, their isolation and foreignness among them, is *the* witness to the truth.[58]

The truth that makes Christians distinct is not a truth that is peculiar to them. It is not *their* truth but *the* truth for anyone. The vocation of a Christian, Barth says, which takes quite different forms in quite different lives, "determines the situation of every man to the extent that it is the future or *telos* of his existence; this implies a responsibility of every man and thus compels the Christian to see and understand not only himself but also the non-Christian in his responsibility, and to address him in terms of it."[59] The Christian, in other words, cannot address the

---

engaged in the battle with the German "christians." As he puts it: "The true church lives on the truth and in the truth, and truth will not admit of fusion with its contrary, error" (167).

57. Barth, *Church Dogmatics*, 4/3.2:656.

58. Barth, *Church Dogmatics*, 2/2:345–346. I am aware that Barth's account of truth is designed to drive philosophers to distraction. Moreover, an attempt like that of Hunsinger to clarify Barth's understanding of truth is unlikely to help: "Barth's view of theological truth is multidimensional. Truth is at once miraculously actualized and yet textually stabilized, objectively efficacious and yet existentially authenticated, unique in kind and yet habituated in the midst of the ordinary. It is always entirely subjected to divine validation, and yet its human reception and assertion are open to coherentist modes of justification with a web of communal belief and practice" (*How to Read Karl Barth*, ix). A "coherentist mode of justification" may sound far too much like "warranted assertability" for philosophers with realist commitments, and in any case, I do not think that either Barth or Hunsinger would be satisfied with a "coherentist" position. I do think, however, that Barth is committed to some account of the self-involving character of claims that would make any attempt to separate what is asserted from the speaker problematic. Obviously, such an account would need to be displayed. My point is simply that Barth's position on theological truth at least requires that Christians must be who they say they are—and that is not without significance for questions of truth.

59. Barth, *Church Dogmatics*, 4/3.2:494.

non-Christian on the basis of a general or human responsibility interpreted as the responsibility to conscience or to supposed or real orders and forces of the cosmos. Rather, every person is to be addressed as one who exists and stands in the light of Jesus Christ.[60]

According to Barth, the Christian knows that the will of God has been fulfilled outside the church. To the shame of the church, in fact, the will of God has often been better fulfilled outside the church than within it. That this has been the case is not an indication of some general goodness of humanity but of the fact that Jesus has risen from the dead and sits at the right hand of God as the Lord of the world.[61] Still, Barth says, the Christian must recognize the "*worldliness* of the world," that is, the self-evident way in which the world "accepts the desecrating of the name of God by the system and regime of balance, which finds its true triumph there outside and with the establishment and preservation of which man knows only too well how to comfort and justify and safeguard himself."[62]

According to Barth, there are two extremes that must be ruled out as Christian responses to the "worldliness" of the world: first, the negative view of the world that results in either monasticism or the crusade; second, the positive view of the world that, on the basis of the correct notion that the world has already been reconciled to God in Christ, simply accepts the secularity of the world by way of the Christian "approximation and assimilation" of the attitudes and languages of the world.[63] Both alternatives are closed to the Christian because each in its own

60. In the midst of the lectures we now know as *Dogmatics in Outline,* Barth pauses to address a question that he was asked several times in the course of giving the lectures: "Are you not aware that many are sitting in this class who are not Christians?" Barth reports that when asked this question: "I have always laughed and said: 'That makes no difference to me.' It would be quite dreadful if the faith of Christians should aim at sundering and separating one man from the others. It is in fact the strongest motive for collecting men and binding them together. And what binds is, quite simply and challengingly, at the same time the commission which the community has to deliver its message. If we consider the matter once more from the standpoint of the community, that is, from the standpoint of those who seriously wish to be Christians—'Lord, I believe: help Thou mine unbelief!'—we must remember that everything will depend upon the Christians not painting for the non-Christians in word and deed a *picture* of the Lord or an *idea* of Christ, but on their succeeding with their human words and ideas in pointing to Christ himself" (93–94). Barth had sounded this note earlier in the lectures when he recommended that "everyone who has to contend with unbelief should be advised that he ought not to take his own unbelief too seriously. Only faith is to be taken seriously; and if we have faith as a grain of mustard seed, that suffices for the devil to have lost his game" (20–21).

61. Barth, *Church Dogmatics,* 2/2:569.

62. Barth, *The Christian Life,* 197.

63. Ibid., 197–199. I am indebted to Bill Werpehowski for correcting my identification of Barth's position with this second option in an earlier draft of this lecture. Barth gives several reasons for rejecting both of these positions. Those who adopt the first view, according

way entails the loss of the humility, modesty, and courage that must characterize Christian witness.

As Barth sees it, Christians must steer a middle course between these two extremes. However, Christians cannot try to "square the circle" by uniting these extremes but must maintain their "freedom to take a few steps or even to go a good way along either path as need requires."[64] Christians will, therefore, be willing to expose their lives to the charge of fanaticism on one side or libertinism on the other. Christians are people of the world who have heard the Word and thus been enabled through divine revelation to "pierce and conquer and rule the world." And yet, Barth says, though this conquering and ruling may "under God be the growing fruit of . . . human action . . . it cannot be its meaning and purpose. It would be better if precisely at this point Christians would confine themselves to speaking only about what may be said and done at a human level."[65]

Barth fails to specify the material conditions that would sustain his "middle way." Of course, Barth intentionally depicts the "middle way" as unstable, but instability is as likely to lead to unfaithfulness as faithfulness. Barth's attempt to steer a "middle course" between monasticism and the liberal embrace of the secular is but the other side of his overly cautious account of the role of the church in the economy of God's salvation. Because the church cannot trust in its calling to be God's witness, Barth seems far too willing to leave the world alone. For example, at the very beginning of the *Church Dogmatics,* he argues that theology cannot justify itself before other sciences because to put itself in a systematic relationship with other sciences would require theology to regard its own special existence as necessary. But that is exactly what theology cannot do, for to do so would be to regard itself as a member of an ordered cosmos, when in fact it is only a stopgap in an unordered cosmos.[66]

As a statement of Barth's contention that theology must be determined by its own object, there is nothing surprising in his contention

---

to Barth, underrate the objective knowledge of God in the world, overrate their own confidence in confronting the world as teachers or conquerors, obscure the positive content of the witness Christians owe the world, and deny that witness remains purely human. Those who adopt the second view assume the opposition to what God has done in Jesus Christ is not severe enough to preclude God from ranging himself with it, think they must keep quiet about the fact that Christianity has something new to show the world, obscure the No that gives form to God's gospel, and forget that the Christian zeal for God's honor demands that special action is required of the Christian. Werpehowski provides a helpful overview of Barth's "politics"; see "Karl Barth and Politics," *The Cambridge Companion to Karl Barth,* 228–242.

64. Barth, *The Christian Life,* 200–201.
65. Ibid., 201.
66. Barth, *Church Dogmatics,* 1/1:9

that theology as a science has no stake in imitating or even conversing with other sciences. It does not follow, however, as Barth seemed to think, that Christian faithfulness should not involve challenging false notions of science, morality, or art on theological grounds. According to Barth, only the presumptions of a "victorious modern Christendom" gave birth to phrases like the "Christian" view of the universe, "Christian" morality, "Christian" art, "Christian" families, "Christian" newspapers, "Christian" societies, endeavors, and institutions.[67] Barth may well be right that Christendom produced such phrases, but we no longer live in Christendom, so why does Barth assume that the church has no stake in producing knowledge that is congruent with the knowledge that is faith?[68]

67. Karl Barth, *The Holy Spirit and the Christian Life: The Theological Basis of Ethics*, trans. Birch Hoyle, with a foreword by Robin Lovin (Louisville: Westminster/John Knox, 1993), 37–38. In *Church Dogmatics* 4/3.2, Barth advises against any attempt to develop a Christian philosophy of history (713–715) or a sacred language (735).
Of course it is not just "knowledge" that is at stake but, more important, questions of how the Christian is to negotiate social and political matters. Barth consistently argued that the question of the "state" belongs to the second article of the creed, which means that the church does not act in relation to the state as if we lived "in a night in which all cats are grey." Yet I think it is fair to say that Barth simply did not have the resources to develop the implications of this promising theological claim; thus, in what might be called his theological politics, he gave the state far too much independence. This is an odd result, I admit, for the writer of the Barmen Declaration. Nonetheless, I fear that this is Barth's final position. Barth's "theological politics" is best displayed in three essays edited by Will Herberg and collected in *Community, State, and Church* (Garden City, N.Y.: Anchor Books, 1960). Barth's comment about "a night in which all cats are grey" can be found on page 119 of that collection. The essays in Barth's *Against the Stream* suggest that Barth's political judgments were often better than his explicit theological account of those judgments. John Howard Yoder's *Karl Barth and the Problem of War* (Nashville: Abingdon Press, 1970) remains the best critique of Barth, not only on the issue of nonviolence but on Barth's understanding of the status of the state. David Matzko McCarthy argues that Barth's relativization of all earthly kingdoms, which provides the basis for the analogy between God's mercy and the church's claim that the burden of proof is always on those who would use violence, is undercut when Barth looks to the state as the place where these analogies are made social. "When he looks for a natural form to co-humanity, he is diverted from the history of martyrs, saints, and common folk who have lived by Christ and the Spirit and continue to make peaceable, gracious human community a reality in the world." D. M. McCarthy, "Hazarding Theology: Theological Descriptions and Particular Lives" (Ph.D. diss., Duke University, 1992), 206.
68. Toward the end of *The Mystery of God*, Johnson observes that Barth failed to show us what it would look like "to craft a theology that was not only 'dogmatic' but 'practical' as well" (174). There is some truth to Johnson's observation, but I worry about the distinction between "dogmatic" and "practical." Barth rightly thought that his dogmatics was practical. Johnson observes that Barth did not distinguish theoretical and practical reason, which I think is true just to the extent that Barth assumed that all his work was "practical." But Barth would have helped his case if he had developed a more fulsome account of practical reason. That he did not do so played havoc with some aspects of his ethics because he lacked the resources to display why actions cannot be separated from agency.

Of course, such a question may simply indicate that the challenges Barth faced are not ours, and that, therefore, there are limits to how we might use his work. Certainly, Barth never desired to spawn Barthians. Rather, he sought to free theology to be the joyful discipline it must be if it is to witness to the God who is the beginning and end of our existence. However different from Barth we may turn out to be, I am convinced that the difference, if it is marked by faithfulness, will be the result of Barth's extraordinary work. If nothing else, Barth taught us what it might mean not only to think but to live when God is acknowledged as the beginning and end of our existence. It seems fitting, therefore, to end my account of Barth with words he wrote just before his death:

> How do I know whether I shall die easily or with difficulty? I only know that my dying, too, is part of my life. . . . And then—this is the destination, the limit and the goal for all of us—I shall no longer "be," but I shall be made manifest before the judgment seat of Christ, in and with my whole "being," with all the real good and the real evil that I have thought, said and done, with all the bitterness that I have suffered and all the beauty that I have enjoyed. There I shall only be able to stand as the failure that I doubtless was in all things, but . . . by virtue of his promise, as a *peccator justus*. And as that I shall be able to stand. Then . . . in the light of grace, all that is now dark will become very clear.[69]

Such was the witness of Karl Barth.

---

69. Quoted in Busch, *Karl Barth*, 499.

8

The Necessity
of Witness

No Witness, No Argument

The bare outline of the story I have told goes like this:

Lord Gifford, heir of a church which had already ceded the intellectual and moral marketplace to modernity and its presumptions, provided for a series of lectures to illumine, via an appropriate variation of the scientific method, "The Infinite, the All, the First and Only Cause . . . the Sole Being," etc. He did not realize that no "non-traditioned account of rationality can be given that is sufficient to make natural theology a subject analogous to natural sciences." James, in a curious combination of Darwinism and pragmatism, utterly fulfills Lord Gifford's stated wishes. He turns natural theology—the discovery of God in God's creation—into religious psychology—the discovery of humanity's worth in human subjectivity. A young Niebuhr adopts James pragmatism and his "empirical approach" to religion, little realizing that his Christology would have to empty itself fully in order to be compatible with a methodologically atheist approach to theism. The god he discovers is the ultimate fulfillment of human needs, who, conversely, sets a standard so perfect that attempts to adhere to it are but "a new form of egoism, namely, pharisaic pride." Barth, in contrast, begins not with human reason or human religious experience or human scientific discoveries, but by talking about God, insisting that God is the subject of theology—natural or otherwise. The theology that God reveals (and not vice versa) makes claims on persons' lives—it has something to say about humans, though it begins with God, and it tells humans who they are and how they should be.[1]

1. This summary overview was written by Mrs. Sarah Conrad Sours, who was a student in a course I taught on the Gifford Lectures in which we read lectures 1 through 7

I hope this story is not only truthful but also, as good stories should be, entertaining. Of course, even if the story I have told is truthful and entertaining, some people may think that the very form of my presentation precludes it from amounting to anything so grand as an argument. Modern philosophers and theologians generally do not think stories can do the work of argument. Yet I agree with John Milbank that "narrating," exactly because narration is the "science" of the particular, is a more basic category than either explanation or understanding.[2] Such a view does not presume that all stories are created equal but that any narrative that claims to be true cannot but invite different tellings. Whether I have told the story well will be known, therefore, only to the extent that others seek to tell the story differently, no doubt with different characters who will change the shape as well as the substance of the narrative.

I have tried to tell the story of the fate of Christian theology in the twentieth century, but I cannot pretend that this has been my only aim. Since Barth has been the hero of my story, any modest ambition is impossible. And yet, because Barth is the hero of my story, it is also the case that my full ambition runs into difficulty. I focused on Barth because he, more than most theologians in modernity, helps us see why "natural theology" is unintelligible when abstracted from a full doctrine of God. Even if my account of Barth served that purpose, however, this may not be good news in a time such as ours—either for the church or for individual Christians. We live in times when many people believe that Barth is but the name that confirms the judgment that Christian theology is not capable of rational justification, particularly in the light of the character of the knowledges that constitute the modern university. Barth's refusal to submit theological claims to nontheological standards can seem to make Christian theology and Christian practice an entirely self-referential as well as a self-justifying enterprise. If this is indeed the case, then the story I have told simply confirms what James and Niebuhr, each in their own way, understood: Christianity makes sense only as a disguised humanism. As anything else, it can appear only as nonsense.

along with James, Niebuhr, and Barth. I am extremely grateful to this class not only for their criticism, but for helping me better understand what I was trying to say. Mrs. Sours's summary was part of her seminar report in response to an early version of my lectures. I have used her summary not only because I think it is better than one I would probably produce, but also because I think it is always better to hear from another what you have written rather than to presume that as the author you know better than your reader what you have said. Of course, sometimes that may be the case, but not always. I am grateful to Mrs. Sours for permitting me to use her account of the story I have told.

2. John Milbank, *Theology and Social Theory: Beyond Secular Reason* (Oxford: Basil Blackwell, 1990), 264–267.

The burden of my argument in this last lecture, and the overarching ambition of all of my lectures, is to show that Christian practice and theology are neither self-referential nor self-justifying. Christian practices and beliefs cannot be self-justifying because Christians, as Barth insists, must be witnesses to the God who is the Father, Son, and Holy Spirit. Just as the Son witnesses to the Father so the Spirit makes us witnesses to the Son so that the world may know the Father.[3]

If what Christians believe about God and the world could be known without witnesses, then we would have evidence that what Christians believe about God and the world is not true. All that is, all that is creation, is a witness to the One alone who is capable of moving the sun and the stars as well as our hearts. If we and the world existed by necessity, then no witness, no story of creation, would be required. But God did not have to create, much less redeem; yet we have it on good authority that God has created and redeemed. Creation and redemption constitute the story necessary for us to know who we are. Such knowledge comes only through the telling of this story.

Calling attention to the necessity of witnesses suggests to many people, particularly those of the philosophical bent, the end of argument. For Christians, however, "witness" names the condition necessary to begin argument. To be a witness does not mean that Christians are in the business of calling attention to ourselves but that we witness to the One who has made our lives possible. Witness, at least the witness to which Christians are called, is, after all, about God and God's relation to all that is.

To speak of witnesses, then, is not the end of argument; however, what Christians believe about God and God's relation to the world requires that the form and manner of our arguments have a particular shape. For example, Bruce Marshall observes that "Christian theologians have long maintained, that there is no hope of generating what William James calls 'coercive arguments' for the church's chief convictions (though the Christian community expects that it will be able, at least in the long run, to meet almost any argument which is brought against these beliefs, by showing that objections to them are not rationally coercive,

---

3. I am indebted to Bruce Marshall for this formulation. As he puts it: "The triune God grants us true beliefs in order to give us a share in his own life. Countless beliefs about creatures are tied up with beliefs about the triune God and his purposes in the world, and there is probably no clear or effective way to draw a line between those which are and those which are not. The Spirit cannot, it therefore seems, lead us into the life of God without seeing to it that we hold most true beliefs, not only about God, but also about everything else. Since we hold beliefs at all only insofar as they fit with the rest of what we suppose to be true, this is to say that the Spirit guarantees that our beliefs are generally—though of course not always—true when we take them to be." *Trinity and Truth* (Cambridge: Cambridge University Press, 2000), 281.

either)."[4] According to Marshall, the Spirit's work is to teach us how to believe and judge all things in accordance with claims whose denial will always be rationally plausible.[5] In other words, it is the work of the Spirit to teach Christians that their claims about the way things are, though always susceptible to being refuted on rational grounds, are not without persuasive power and/or the support of argument.

That there can be no "coercive arguments" for Christian convictions is but an elaboration of Aquinas's discussion of whether sacred doctrine is a matter of argument. Against those who argue that doctrine is not a matter of argument, Aquinas quotes from Paul's letter to Titus, which states that a bishop should "embrace that faithful word which is according to doctrine, that he may be able to exhort in sound doctrine and to convince the gainsayers."[6] Aquinas explains that just as other sciences do not argue in proof of their principles but from their principles to demonstrate other truths in the sciences, so proceed arguments from doctrine. Accordingly, doctrines, which are the articles of faith, do not argue in proof of their principles but from them go on to prove something else. Aquinas notes, however, that "it is to be borne in mind" that inferior (philosophical) sciences "neither prove their principles nor dispute with those who deny them" but leave such proofs and disputes to the highest science in philosophy, which is metaphysics. Metaphysics, however, is not the highest science, for higher still is what Aquinas calls the divine science.

4. Ibid., 181. Of course, one of the great failures of Christians in modernity has been, as Alasdair MacIntyre observes, to offer the atheist less and less to disbelieve. See Alasdair MacIntyre, with Paul Ricoeur, *The Religious Significance of Atheism* (New York: Columbia University Press, 1969), 24. Christians owe it to themselves and their neighbors to put descriptions of the world that presume that God does not exist into what MacIntyre calls "epistemological crisis." The great failure of Christians in modernity is our willingness to make peace with the world.

5. The phrase "judge all things" has a similar status to the locution I used in the first lecture, that is, that theology must be able to give some account of "the way things are." "Judge all things" and "the way things are" may be regarded as stand-ins for the more philosophical notion of existence. As Aidan Nichols suggests, the habit of theology entails the willingness to be stimulated by appropriate objects. Such objects can be arranged in three concentric circles: (1) "existence"; (2) "sacred history"; and (3) "the Bible." "Existence" is the largest of the circles, which often leads some people to think that it is the most important "object," which in turn means that theology depends on the development of an adequate metaphysics. Nichols, however, suggests that "existence" is but shorthand for "anything you care to mention." Unfortunately, theologians have too often thought that by developing an account of being *qua* being—that is, an account that mimics the mistaken view that philosophy has a subject peculiar to itself called "being"—they can avoid having to come to terms with "anything you care to mention." Precisely as a way of avoiding this mistake, I have enlisted colloquial phrases like "the way things are." See Aidan Nichols, *The Shape of Catholic Theology* (Collegeville, Minn.: Liturgical Press, 1991), 18.

6. St. Thomas Aquinas, *Summa Theologica*, trans. the Fathers of the English Dominican Province (Westminster, Md.: Christian Classics, 1948), 1.1.8. Thomas is quoting Titus 1:9.

According to Aquinas, if an opponent in a dispute concerning the first principles of a science will make some concession, then an argument is possible; but if the opponent concedes nothing, there can be no dispute, though the science "can answer his objections." Therefore,

Sacred Scripture, since it has no science above itself, can dispute with one who denies its principles only if the opponent admits some at least of the truths obtained through divine revelation; thus we can argue with heretics from texts in Holy Writ, and against those who deny one article of faith we can argue from another. If our opponent believes nothing of divine revelation, there is no longer any means of proving the articles of faith by reasoning, but only of answering his objections—if he has any—against faith. Since faith rests upon infallible truth, and since the contrary of a truth can never be demonstrated, it is clear that the arguments brought against faith cannot be demonstrations, but are difficulties that can be answered.[7]

These remarks are not meant to be a protective strategy to insure that Christian doctrine can evade objections that may be brought against it.[8] Rather, Aquinas assumes that he is simply providing an account of the

7. Aquinas, *Summa Theologica*, 1.1.8. Aquinas's claim that first principles are necessary for argument is, of course, not widely accepted by contemporary philosophers. For a defense of Aquinas's (and Aristotle's) understanding of first principles, see Alasdair MacIntyre, *First Principles, Final Ends, and Contemporary Issues* (Milwaukee: Marquette University Press, 1990). MacIntyre argues that the contemporary philosophical habit of ignoring first principles is closely related to the exclusion of a *telos* necessary to describe the activity of particular beings. According to MacIntyre: "Genuine first principles can have a place only within a universe characterized in terms of certain determinate, fixed, and unalterable ends, ends which provide a standard by reference to which our individual purposes, desires, interests and decisions can be evaluated as well as badly directed" (7). MacIntyre notes that first principles are analytic, but that does not mean that they can be known to be true *a priori*; rather, first principles are judgments grasped intellectually through participation in the activity in which they are embedded. MacIntyre's understanding of first principles is crucial for understanding his account of how traditions of inquiry can, when confronted by alternative accounts of the way things are, be put in an "epistemological crisis." Such a crisis is but a reminder that theoretical achievements are rooted in practices that entail narrative display. My emphasis on witness as a constitutive aspect of Christian convictions is an attempt to display how theological inquiry works, if, indeed, MacIntyre's understanding of inquiry is, as I take it to be, correct.

8. On the notion of a protective strategy, see Wayne Proudfoot, *Religious Experience* (Berkeley: University of California Press, 1985), and Matthew Bagger, *Religious Experience, Justification, and History* (Cambridge: Cambridge University Press, 1999), 103–104, 133–134. Bagger, following Proudfoot, characterizes a protective strategy as one designed by philosophers of religion to exclude critical inquiry from outside religion. Put differently, it is the attempt to sustain accounts of religious experience and/or belief by showing that they can be neither justified nor falsified. Though I think Bagger is right to criticize this "strategy," he does not appreciate why it is so tempting for theologians in modernity, namely, because of the cultural presumption, which has no particular warrant, that theological claims bear the burden of proof. "Protective strategies" are often attempts to resist that presumption.

conditions necessary to have an argument, not only in theology but in any subject. Nothing in Aquinas's remarks commits him to the view that the Christian faith is just another set of beliefs incapable of justification. Christians do not seek to justify what they believe out of fear that it may not be true. Rather, justification is inherent in the material convictions that constitute what Christians believe exactly because they are required by what they believe to be witnesses.[9] The witness of Christians may or may not take the form of argument at different times and places, but if the Holy Spirit does not witness to the Father and Son through the witness of Christians, then Christians have no arguments to make.[10]

Christian argument rests on witness, and both argument and witness are the work of the Spirit. Thus, as Marshall argues, acquiring a Christian view of the world

> calls for a persistent willingness to overturn the epistemic priorities (though not the totality of belief) we would otherwise be inclined to have.

9. Marshall rightly notes that the martyr's blood may provide evidence for others of the truth of his or her beliefs, but that cannot be true for the martyr. The martyr "dies because he believes the gospel and loves the gospel's God, not in order to believe it. So participationist versions of the pragmatic thesis end up in a paradox: the more excellently or successfully a person participates in the church's practices, the less need he has to treat those practices as evidence for the church's beliefs (or would have, were practice susceptible of being treated this way in the first place). Whatever epistemic bearing the saint's life has—and it surely, as the New Testament insists, has one—is for others, and not for the saint; however the saint comes by his convictions, it seems not to be by way of his own sainthood" (*Trinity and Truth*, 190–191). One might object that I am confusing issues of justification with the question of truth, but given my purposes, I have not thought it necessary to maintain a strict distinction between justification and truth. Marshall, however, provides a helpful account of the difference between a justified and a true belief (*Trinity and Truth*, 7–9, 105–106, 223–226). For an extraordinary confirmation of Marshall's account of martyrdom, see Brad Gregory's *Salvation at Stake: Christian Martyrdom in Early Modern Europe* (Cambridge: Harvard University Press, 1999). Gregory notes that martyrdom exposes many of the methodological shortcomings in recent accounts of religion just to the extend such accounts assume everyone willing to die because they believe what they believe is true must be "vocational." He notes that "Nietzsche is not so shocking; he is passé. Meanwhile, the aftermath of indifference has helped embed athiestic assumptions so deeply in the status quo that skepticism and unbelief are mistaken for neutrality. Institutionally and intellectually, our world is one that committed early modern Christians and could have imagined. I am certain they would not have wanted to live in it" (352).

10. James McClendon entitles the third volume of his "systematic theology" "Witness" because this last volume deals with issues traditionally associated with missiology, that is, with the delineation of the mission field and the strategy and tactics of the mission to that field. Accordingly, he takes up questions once associated with the relation of Christianity and culture, as well as questions about how Christian convictions can be justified. I think McClendon has it just right; issues of justification are, indeed, a subset of Christian witness. See, in particular, the last chapter of McClendon's book, which is entitled "A Theology of Witness" and offers a wonderful account of how and why "witness" is tied to the Christian understanding of our place in the world. James McClendon, *Witness: Systematic Theology*, vol. 3 (Nashville: Abingdon Press, 2000).

In at least this sense, ordering one's beliefs such that Jesus Christ has un-restricted epistemic primacy requires a change of heart and not simply a change of mind. The gospel of Jesus Christ, it seems, proclaims a truth which cannot be known unless it is also loved (see 2 Thess. 2:16).[11]

That the truth of Christian convictions requires witnesses is but the "pragmatic" display of the fact that the God who has created and re-deemed the world has done so from the love that constitutes the life of the Trinity. That is what it means to say that witness and argument are the work of the Spirit, and that truth involves the heart as well as the mind. The truth of Christian convictions can be known only through witnesses because the God Christians worship is triune. If the truth of

11. Marshall, *Trinity and Truth*, 181. Marshall's qualifier, "though not the totality of belief," is extremely important. No one can doubt all one's beliefs at once. The gospel does not re-quire that we doubt everything we believe but that everything we believe be reordered. Marshall, like anyone dealing with these matters, has to fight linguistic habits that seem to suggest that "beliefs" can be isolated from "changed hearts." The truth that is loved is not a "belief" that provides the basis of a subsequent love. Rather, the love that changes our hearts is knowledge. Appreciative as I am of Marshall's work, I think his commitment to the account of truth conditions set forth by Alfred Tarski and Donald Davidson makes it appear as though he believes that propositions and/or sentences can be judged apart from the speaker. To his credit, Marshall is well aware of this problem: "A Tarski-Davidson ap-proach cannot by itself be adequate for a theological account of what truth is, because it gives us no clue about how to connect truth to a person as its bearer" (245). Marshall makes this comment as he explores the necessary theological claim that Jesus Christ is the truth.

Fergus Kerr also questions Marshall's use of Tarski-Davidson, just to the extent that their account of truth may fail to acknowledge Aquinas's ontological understanding of truth. Kerr notes that for Aquinas truth is found not only in sentences and in formal iden-tity between thoughts and things, but also in the relationship of the world to God. There-fore, for Aquinas, even if there were no human minds, things would still be "true" in rela-tion to God's mind: "Thus, while 'the way of truth for us' is indeed 'demonstrated' in Christ our Savior, Thomas supposes that logically prior to that, any truth whatsoever is brought about by a mind/world identity, which is grounded in the participation of cre-ated beings in God's own being." Fergus Kerr, "Book Symposium: Bruce D. Marshall, *Trin-ity and Truth*," *Modern Theology* 16, no. 4 (October, 2000): 503–509. In his response to Kerr, Marshall says that he doubts whether Thomas holds that any truth, including the truth that creatures have by virtue of their likeness to God, is logically (or ontologically) "prior to the way in which Jesus Christ is the truth." Bruce Marshall, "Theology after Cana," *Modern Theology* 16, no. 4 (October, 2000), 517–527, esp., 524. I do not share Marshall's judg-ment that the Tarski-Davidson account of truth is "the best philosophy available to us," though he may be right that this account does not exclude the kind of ontological claim to which Kerr calls attention. On the other hand, I do share what I take to be Marshall's "Barthian" reading of Aquinas. Marshall rightly argues that Barth's great achievement was to see that Christian talk of the Trinity is not a metaphysical proposal about divine unity but a way of calling attention to what Christians are talking about when they speak of God. Talk of the Trinity is not, according to Marshall, a theological stipulation about what Christians ought to believe "but an empirical judgment warranted by an analysis of pub-lic Christian practices." As I intimated in my second lecture, James displays how such judgments work for helping us understand what we do when we say as Christians what we believe is not only what we believe, but what we believe is true.

Christian convictions could be known without witnesses, then that truth would no longer be the work of the Trinity, and those who espoused it would no longer be Christians.[12] William James rightly thought that lives matter. Unfortunately, he too often failed to understand how the people who lived the lives he thought mattered actually meant what they said about the God who had made their lives possible. In other words, James did not understand that the lives he admired were the lives of witnesses, and that there can be no witnesses without the One to whom they witness.

Witnesses must exist if Christians are to be intelligible to themselves and hopefully to those who are not Christians, just as the intelligibility of science depends in the end on the success of experiments. Indeed, Marshall argues that the Christian martyr's willingness to die for his or her faith in Christ is similar to the scientist's commitment to experimental results, though any pragmatic similarity that can be drawn between science and theology is inexact. Thus, martyrs—who are but the most determinative display of what being a witness entails—go to their deaths convinced that the gospel is true, but scientists do their experiments in order to become convinced that a hypothetical set of beliefs is true. Moreover, for the scientist the failure of predicted results may disconfirm the theory that shaped their experimental designs; but Christians believe that they should trust the gospel even when they fail to live lives congruent with it, and even when such trust requires that they die.[13] Christians behave in this way because they understand themselves to have become characters in the story that God continues to enact through the ongoing work of the Holy Spirit. Lives that seem like failures do not disconfirm the gospel, because Christians learn to confess their sins by being made part of the work of the Spirit.

Still, like scientists, Christians can never deny that successful Christian practices must remain open to explanations other than the ones given by those who engage in those practices. Marshall notes that Christians have no grounds to deny, for example, that the martyrdom of St. Maximilian Kolbe, a Catholic priest who voluntarily took the place of a condemned prisoner at Auschwitz, might be open to a nontheistic account of Kolbe's action. Such an account could acknowledge that Kolbe thought the beliefs that led him to his martyrdom were true, but deny that such beliefs are in fact true. Christians must be open to such alternative explanations, but, like scientists, they also must be able to distinguish when such explanations have completely altered what they were trying to describe in the

12. To put it as forcefully as I can, if there were a "knock-down" argument capable of demonstrating the truth of what Christians believe about God and the world that made witness irrelevant, then we would have evidence that what Christians believe is not true.

13. Marshall, *Trinity and Truth*, 185–186.

first place. As Marshall notes, alternative accounts of the practices of Christians often cease to be descriptions of Christian practice.

Alternative accounts of Christian practice often fail to do justice to events because such accounts divorce practice from belief. Marshall argues, for example, that psychoanalytic accounts of actions like Kolbe's often diminish "the inextricability of practices and their description from the larger web of belief in terms of which practices are described."[14] In other words, to say that St. Maximilian's death is rightly described as martyrdom, that is, as an act by which one shares in the self-sacrificial love the triune God shows to the world through the cross, is a description not only of that act but also of a complex set of beliefs about God and how God acts in the world. Therefore, whether the description of St. Maximilian's death is rightly described as martyrdom involves questions of how that description fits in the larger web of beliefs. According to Marshall, then, the description of *a* practice alone cannot be decisive for an epistemic assessment of the larger system of belief.[15] Put differently, the truthfulness of Christian convictions cannot be abstracted from the politics that supports the practices necessary "to fix the meaning of the community's most central beliefs."[16]

According to Marshall, a "pragmatic thesis," that is, the view that "successful practice on the part of the Christian community and its members helps to *justify* the community's central beliefs," seems entailed by funda-

---

14. Ibid., 188. The "inextricability of practices and their description from the larger web of belief" has been the animating center of how I have tried over the years to "do ethics." Ethics, as a theological discipline, but names for me the attempt to make the connections Christians need to make if our lives are to be located within the story that is the gospel. Accordingly, I have tried to do little more than elicit simple questions, such as: "If Christians come to think that abortion is morally acceptable, what does that mean for our understanding of Mary's "Here am I, the servant of the Lord; let it be with me according to your word"? I am not suggesting that Mary's response should determine everything that Christians have to say about abortion, but it is surely a good place to start.

15. Ibid.

16. Ibid., 202. Marshall elaborates: "The Spirit instructs the church—and thereby also the world—in the meaning of its own beliefs by his total mastery of the practical situations in which the community and its members (and indeed all human beings) speak. Since the Spirit creates and rules the total situation in which the relevant utterances are made, the meaning of those utterances depends primarily on the action of the Spirit himself, and only secondarily on the free human agents who make them. As the immediate agent of the unitary action of the Trinity in the world, the Spirit is the total cause of all that is not God: of, as the Nicene Creed says, 'all things, visible and invisible.' 'All things' presumably includes the free acts of human beings as well as occurrences which have other sorts of causes; God, transcending the distinction between causes which produce their effects with necessity and those which produce them contingently, is free to create what exists in its totality, including the manner (necessary or contingent) in which each thing is" (203). For an elaboration of Marshall's position along the lines I am developing, see Nicholas Healy, *Church, World, and the Christian Life: Practical-Prophetic Ecclesiology* (Cambridge: Cambridge University Press, 2000), 115–128.

mental Christian convictions.[17] The idea that the practices of a community justify its beliefs may suggest that Christianity functions according to a "pragmatic definition of truth," that is, Christians can make the world anything they want it to be if they just work hard enough at it. But Marshall's pragmatic thesis in fact suggests something else.

The work of the Spirit is not to create evidence for the truth of what Christians believe, because there can be no "evidence" for beliefs beyond the totality of beliefs to which any contested claims might be brought. Thus, the Spirit does not, as Marshall puts it, "persuade by adding something to the totality of belief, by giving us reasons or evidence we do not already have, but by eliciting our assent to a way of structuring the whole."[18] In other words, that martyrs die for their faith does not *prove* that Jesus is risen; on the other hand, that some people have assented to a totality of belief that includes the belief that Jesus is risen surely means that martyrs will die for their faith.[19]

To put Marshall's pragmatic thesis in the idiom of this lecture: Christianity is unintelligible without witnesses, that is, without people whose practices exhibit their committed assent to a particular way of structuring the whole. That such witnesses exist, however, cannot and should not be sufficient to compel others to believe what Christians believe. Witnesses are not evidence; rather, they are people whose lives embody a totality of beliefs and, accordingly, make claims about "how the world is arranged."[20] To understand what the church believes is to know what the world is like if these beliefs are true. Just to the extent that witnesses such as Maximilian Kolbe live as if these beliefs are true, they show us what the world is like.

That Christians come to hold beliefs that the world is structured in a certain way depends, as Marshall puts it, "on the attractiveness and the habitability of the world they describe." But as attractive as a world created and redeemed in love may be, such an attraction is not and, more important, should not be sufficient to convince anyone that such a world exists. Attractive worlds can often turn out to be no more than fantasies. The needed incentive not just to entertain but to live Christian convictions requires the display of a habitable world exemplified in the life of the Christian community. As Marshall puts it: "Communal success at holding these beliefs and living accordingly—the encounter with actual public willingness to suppose that the world described by these beliefs is not simply desirable but real—encourages and prompts its like."[21]

17. Marshall, *Trinity and Truth*, 182.
18. Ibid., 204.
19. Ibid., 188.
20. Ibid., 194.
21. Ibid., 205.

Marshall's account of the relationship between Christian belief and practice reminds us that when Christians get their theology wrong, they cannot help but get their lives and their accounts of the world wrong as well. Or rather, more accurately, Christians often get their theology wrong because they have gotten their lives wrong. In part, Barth refused to use natural theology as a way of attracting those not already convinced by Christianity because he understood that, for Christians, everything is related to everything else and that, therefore, the only truthful way to make Christianity attractive is through witness. Barth understood that to get our theology right, we have to have our lives in order. For Barth, Christianity is not a "position," just another set of beliefs, but a story at once simple and complex that encompasses all that is. Christians, therefore, are people who, via a community called church, witness to the creator of all that is. However, as I suggested in the last lecture, Barth was hesitant to provide a fulsome account, as Marshall argues we must, of the practices necessary for the witness the church is—the practices, that is, that make the world as Christians describe it habitable.[22] To that task I now turn.

From Barth's Witness to Witnessing Barth

Almost as an aside, Marshall observes that attempts to provide justifications of Christian practices in an "earlier day" tended to regard those practices "as closely bound up with the distinctive achievements of modern Western culture, and so took the development of the West as part of

22. Katherine Sonderegger is right to suggest that Barth's "idealism" was decisively qualified by his understanding of Israel. Barth's theology found its own voice, a voice she characterizes as "medieval in character and tone, canonical, and anti-Judaic," separate from his indebtedness to idealism. The discovery of that voice enabled Barth to liberate theology from the constraints of modern culture. In lecture 6, I footnoted Barth's fondness for Frederick the Great's comment about the Jews as proof of God's existence. In *Church Dogmatics*, 2/2 (Edinburgh: T. & T. Clark, 1957), Barth comments on Israel's rejection of Christ, noting that "even in this way it really gives to the world the very witness that is required of it. How it is with man, the nature of the burden which God in His great love assumes, the nature of the curse which God has made Himself for the good of man, man himself by whom and for whom Jesus was crucified—these things and all that they mean it reveals even in this way, even in and with its unbelief, even in the spectral form of the Synagogue. The existence of the Jews, as is generally recognized, is an adequate proof of the existence of God. It is an adequate demonstration of the depths of human guilt and need and therefore of the inconceivable greatness of God's love in the event in which God was in Christ reconciling the world to Himself. The Jews of the ghetto give this demonstration involuntarily, joylessly and ingloriously, but they do give it. They have nothing to attest to the world but the shadow of the cross of Jesus Christ that falls upon them. But they, too, do actually and necessarily attest to Jesus Christ Himself" (209). For Sonderegger's account of this passage, see *That Jesus Christ Was Born a Jew: Karl Barth's "Doctrine of Israel"* (University Park, Pa.: Penn State Press, 1992), 68–69.

the practical evidence for the truth of Christianity."[23] In contrast, according to Marshall, the theological attempts to make the gospel intelligible in our time have been countercultural. Certainly, theologians have often styled themselves as countercultural, but I think Marshall is wrong. Most recent Christian theology and practice is not countercultural. Indeed, it is my contention that the reason Christian convictions have lost their power for many Christians and non-Christians alike is that many Christians, and in particular most Christian theologians, have failed to challenge the cultural accommodation of the church to the world.

Marshall, however, seems to think that when Christian theology is done in faithfulness to the gospel, it cannot help but appear "against the grain" of the world. Marshall observes: "Christians will inevitably encounter a kind of epistemic affliction, because they not only hold true, but insist on treating as epistemically primary across the board, beliefs which will be rationally contestable until the end of time."[24] Marshall does not tell us which beliefs create this ongoing affliction for Christians, but I am sure he is right that Christian convictions become unintelligible when Christians uncritically submit their beliefs to the epistemic requirements of "the world," that is, to the requirements of everything that uses the time God's patience creates not to acknowledge God. I have suggested that the project Lord Gifford wished to support in the name of natural theology at once reflected and reproduced a Christianity far too accommodated to this world. In short, Lord Gifford's understanding of natural theology was but one of the desperate attempts used by a dying Christendom to maintain not only its intelligibility but its power in liberal social orders.

Karl Barth challenged the accommodation of Christian theology to the presumed conditions of truthful speech set by the world. His was a stunning intellectual performance, but it was just that—an intellectual performance. Like the music of his beloved Mozart, Barth's work can too easily give the appearance of springing from the head of Zeus.[25] That is why Barth's achievement cannot help but languish without witnesses such as John Howard Yoder and John Paul II. I am aware that

23. Marshall, *Trinity and Truth*, 184.

24. Ibid., 216. The way Marshall puts the matter may privilege the idea that this situation is peculiar to Christians. But it would be an odd position, if it is one of substance, that did not involve "contestable beliefs." Christian beliefs may or may not be found to be "epistemically afflicted," and in differing ways, from time to time. Different kinds of affliction, moreover, are crucial in order for Christians to understand what it is they believe. That is why the heretics are blessed; without them, we would not know what we believe.

25. See, for example, Barth's wonderful reflections on Mozart in his *Wolfgang Amadeus Mozart*, trans. Clarence Pott (Grand Rapids: Eerdmans, 1986). John Updike provides an extremely insightful foreword to this little book. Of course, Barth loved the beauty of Mozart's music, but I think he also loved Mozart because he was the embodiment of God's grace, insofar as there could be no easy explanation how such music came from him.

this selection of witnesses may appear arbitrary, if not perverse. Pairing a Mennonite with the pope is strange enough, but to suggest that John Paul II may stand in some continuity with Barth seems incredible. However, just as war makes strange bedfellows, so in this time after Christendom, we Christians should not be surprised to discover that those who we once thought enemies are in fact friends. John Howard Yoder and John Paul II represent the recovery of the politics necessary for us to understand why witness is not simply something Christians "do" but is at the heart of understanding how that to which Christians witness is true. If lives like theirs did not exist, then my argument could not help but appear as just another "idealism."

John Howard Yoder and John Paul II are particularly important for my argument just to the extent that their lives and their works are unintelligible abstracted from their ecclesial contexts. Yoder and the pope are not "thinkers," though Yoder had and John Paul II has extraordinary intellectual gifts; rather, both men are representative figures of churches that have challenged the presumptions of modernity. In particular, these churches have called into question attempts, such as those represented by James and Niebuhr, that in the name of rationality and democracy relegate God to "what we do with our privacy." Not only are Yoder and the pope the kind of witnesses that Barth's theology requires—they are the kind of witnesses who must exist if Christians are to recover the confident use of theological speech that Barth exemplifies so well. Moreover, because confident Christian speech has been compromised by the disunity of the church, it is important, as I hope to show, that John Howard Yoder and John Paul II are one in their witness to the One who moves the sun and the stars and is to be found in a manger.[26]

Of course there are many witnesses I could have chosen other than John Howard Yoder and John Paul II. Theologians and popes are seldom

---

26. Bruce Marshall, for example, argues that the unity of the church is a necessary condition for holding the gospel to be true: "The gospel of which the world is supposed to be convinced by the church's unity is that Jesus is eternally loved by the Father, and just for that reason temporally sent by the Father for the redemption of the world. One outcome of this love and mission is supposed to be a visible eucharistic community that comes to be, and be one, as God freely but genuinely grants human beings a share in the divine being and unity constituted by that love and enacted in that mission. But this means that the gospel necessarily includes or implies the existence of this visible eucharistic community: If the gospel is true, there will be such a community in space and time. Thus the credibility of the gospel (holding it true) depends on the visibility in the world of the love that is the life of the triune God, that is, on the eucharistic unity of that ongoing communal history that makes visible in the world what it is that the gospel talks about, namely the missions of the Son and the Spirit from the Father, enacting that love in time." "The Disunity of the Church and the Credibility of the Gospel," *Theology Today* 50, no. 1 (April, 1993): 82. Marshall observes that the credibility of the gospel, therefore, depends not on its content alone but on the contingent empirical shape of the communal history in

counted among the most determinative witnesses to the gospel—a point, no doubt, that Yoder and the pope would be the first to make. I am sure that they would both argue that the countless nameless Christians that have lived lives faithful to the gospel are more likely subjects than either of them for witnessing the faith. I have no reason to doubt that they would be right to direct attention to others. But John Howard Yoder and John Paul II are theologically articulate witnesses whose witness has required them to say why the truth of what the church proclaims cannot be known as truth without witnesses; thus, given what I have tried to articulate in these lectures, they are particularly good witnesses.

John Howard Yoder and the Politics of Jesus

The very title of these lectures, "With the Grain of the Universe," indicates my indebtedness to Yoder's work. Furthermore, the account of James, Niebuhr, and Barth I have given is background necessary to understand why Yoder's work is significant for any attempt to reclaim the truthfulness of Christian convictions in the world in which we find ourselves. Of course, Yoder would have been puzzled that anyone would find his work important for addressing the questions the Gifford Lectures represent.

We have no reason to think that Yoder regarded such questions as unimportant, nor should we conclude that such questions are absent from his work because of Barth's negative portrayal of natural theology, though, indeed, Yoder studied with Barth and signs of Barth's influence appear throughout his work. Like Barth, Yoder, I suspect, thought that the questions of natural theology were ill formed, but Barth did not teach Yoder to avoid natural theology. What Yoder learned from Barth was to do theology with the confidence and skill you can learn only from a master—a master who desires to produce not disciples who will be called Barthians but theologians who will be faithful to Christ and

---

which it is proclaimed (84). Thus, the violence the disunity of the church entails is not simply a "moral" problem but a problem at the heart of the Christian doctrine of God. No one has pressed this issue more forcefully than Ephraim Radner, in *The End of the Church: A Pneumatology of Christian Division in the West* (Grand Rapids: Eerdmans, 1998). Drawing on the work of Richard Popkin, Radner correlates the rise of skepticism with the disunity of the church begun in the Reformation. Indeed, Radner quite effectively shows that many of the criticisms of Christianity now associated with "secularism" began as anti-Catholic polemics by Protestants. For extremely helpful accounts of Radner's difficult book, see Bruce Marshall, "The Divided Church and Its Theology," *Modern Theology* 16, no. 3 (July, 2000): 377–396, and "Who Really Cares About Christian Unity," *First Things* 109 (January, 2001): 29–34; see also, Joseph Mangina, "Review Essay: Ephraim Radner, *The End of the Church: A Pneumatology of Christian Division in the West,*" *Pro Ecclesia* 9, no. 4 (fall, 2000), 490–496.

his church.[27] If Yoder never took up questions of natural theology, it is for the simple reason that no one asked him to. In his faithfulness, Yoder always did what he was asked to do because he understood himself to be a servant called to respond to the challenges confronting those committed to Christian nonviolence.[28] Just for this reason no one has helped us see better than Yoder why questions of the truthfulness of Christian convictions are inseparable from the witness that the church is, as well as why that witness must be nonviolent.

Yoder assumed that Christians will always encounter what Marshall calls an "epistemic affliction." Such an affliction for Yoder is not simply epistemic but more fundamentally an eschatological and, therefore, political reality. The gospel cannot be at home in the world, because the church that is called into existence through the work of the Spirit exists to witness to the God found in the life, death, and resurrection of Christ. For Yoder:

> Christ is *agape;* self-giving, nonresistant love. At the cross this nonresistance, including the refusal to use political means of self-defense, found its ultimate revelation in the uncomplaining and forgiving death of the innocent at the hands of the guilty. This death reveals how God deals with evil; here is the only valid starting point for Christian pacifism or nonresistance. The cross is the extreme demonstration that *agape* seeks neither effectiveness nor justice, and is willing to suffer any loss or seeming defeat for the sake of obedience.[29]

27. Yoder studied with Barth at Basel, but his doctoral thesis was written under Ernst Staehelin on the controversies between the Anabaptists and the Reformed in Strasbourg. Yoder often said that his field of competence was in the history of the early Anabaptist movement. However, Yoder did what his community asked him to do, so he became an "ethicist." In truth, Yoder had extraordinary logical and conceptual gifts that are evident in all he did.

When Yoder heard Barth's lectures on what became *Church Dogmatics* 3/4, he wrote a critique of Barth on war called *Karl Barth and the Problem of War* (Nashville: Abingdon Press, 1970). This book was a reworking of a paper Yoder had written during his studies at Basel. When he published the book, he was careful to note Barth's reactions to his original paper. He argued, and Barth did not dissent, that Barth was a pacifist in everything but name, since he believed that in most past, present, and future wars Christians collectively should have been and should be conscientious objectors (104–105).

28. The best account of Yoder's life is the first chapter of Mark Thiessen Nation's dissertation, "The Ecumenical Patience and Vocation of John Howard Yoder: A Study in Theological Ethics" (Ph.D. diss., Fuller Theological Seminary, 2000). A version of this chapter also appears as "John H. Yoder, Ecumenical Neo-Anabaptist: A Biographical Sketch," in *The Wisdom of the Cross: Essays in Honor of John Howard Yoder,* ed. Stanley Hauerwas, Chris Huebner, Harry Huebner, and Mark Thiessen Nation (Grand Rapids: Eerdmans, 1999), 1–23.

29. John Howard Yoder, *The Original Revolution* (Scottdale, Penn.: Herald Press, 1971), 59.

Yoder's case for Christian nonviolence is compelling because his understanding and justification of nonviolence cannot be separated from the Christian conviction that God is our creator and redeemer. In other words, Yoder forces us to see that the doctrines of God and nonviolence are constitutive of one another. That God has chosen not to be without us, that God has chosen not to redeem the world without us, is how and why we know that God's kingdom is one constituted by nonviolence. The good news the gospel is becomes good news through its reception by us.[30] Nonresistance but names the way God has chosen to redeem us. Accordingly, Christian nonresistance has its basis in the character of God as revealed by Christ. As God is in the world, so Christians are in the world, which means, as Yoder puts it, that the calculating link between "our obedience and ultimate efficacy has been broken, since the triumph of God comes through resurrection and not through effective sovereignty or assured survival. The relationship between the obedience of God's people and the triumph of God's cause is not a relationship of cause and effect but one of cross and resurrection."[31]

That Christians are committed to nonviolence does not entail, as is often assumed, that Christians must withdraw from the world. The church of Jesus Christ must be in the world as he was in the world. Indeed, without the church there can be no world because, as Yoder puts it, the church precedes the world epistemologically; for Christians believe that we know more fully the way things are from the confessed faith in Christ than from any other source. Accordingly, the meaning and validity and limits of concepts like "nature" or "science" cannot be allowed to be self-justifying but must be governed by the confession of the lordship of Christ. The church, moreover, precedes the world not only epistemologically but also axiologically. The lordship of Christ is the center that guides all that Christians do and all they hold dear. Christians, therefore, must subordinate or even reject those desires and loves that make it impossible for them to be disciples of Jesus.[32]

Attempts to defend the cause of the church before—or by using—secular standards and processes cannot help but betray the presumption

---

30. As far as I know, Yoder never reflected on how this emphasis on the necessity that the gospel be received distanced his position from that of Barth. Of course, it is not easy to know how deep this difference might go because Barth's position, as we have seen, is not easy to pin down. Yoder, like Barth, would insist that the gospel creates the conditions for its reception, but it is also the case that Yoder sometimes specifies those "conditions" in a manner that might make Barth uncomfortable.

31. John Howard Yoder, *The Politics of Jesus* (Grand Rapids: Eerdmans, 1972). The first sentence of this quotation comes from page 246, the second from page 238. I took the liberty of bringing them together because I think together they make Yoder's point powerfully.

32. John Howard Yoder, *The Priestly Kingdom: Social Ethics as Gospel* (Notre Dame: University of Notre Dame Press, 1984), 11.

that the true meaning of history is to be located somewhere else than in the church. According to Yoder, the view that what God is doing is being done primarily through the framework of society as a whole and not through the Christian community is the presumption that lies behind the Constantinian accommodation of the church to the world.[33] Put simply, Constantinianism is the attempt to make Christianity necessary, to make the church at home in the world, in a manner that witness is no longer required.

To be sure, Constantinianism has taken many different forms throughout history, but the common thread that constitutes the family resemblance between its various forms is that the validity of the church, of Jesus Christ, and of the New Testament is to be judged by standards derived from the world. According to Yoder, "secular revelation" originally was assumed to come by way of the power of the emperor of Rome. But for those of us constituted by the secularism of modernity,

33. John Howard Yoder, "Christ, the Hope of the World," in *The Royal Priesthood: Essays Ecclesiological and Ecumenical*, ed., with an intro., Michael Cartwright (Grand Rapids: Eerdmans, 1994), 198. In his introduction to this collection of essays, Cartwright notes that Yoder does not assume that "Constantinianism" began with Constantine's legalization of Christianity. Yoder was well aware that what we call Constantinianism began long before Constantine and has assumed many different forms. For example, Yoder suggested that the kind of "neo-Constantinianism" that emerged after the so-called "wars of religion" in 1648 was in many ways far more pernicious than the kind of identification of church and society in the Middle Ages; for after the "wars of religion," the church was linked to particular national governments that weakened the ability of the church to criticize such identifications in the name of the unity to be found in the Holy Roman Church. After the Reformation, churches no longer claim to be servants of humanity but justify themselves by serving a particular society.

That said, I do not deny that accusations of Constantinianism can invite a kind of "name calling" that fails to do justice to forms of Christian Constantinianism that may be more faithful to the gospel than forms of nonviolence. Yoder would be the first to acknowledge that nonviolence does not in itself result in faithfulness. For an extremely important exploration of these issues, see Gerald Schlabach, "Deuteronomic or Constantinian: What Is the Most Basic Problem for Christian Social Ethics," in *The Wisdom of the Cross*, 449–471. Travis Kroeker also develops an appreciative criticism of Yoder's account of Constantinianism; see, "Why O'Donovan's Christendom Is Not Constantinian and Yoder's Voluntariety Is Not Hobbesian: A Debate in Theological Politics Re-Defined," in *The Annual: Society of Christian Ethics* (Washington, D.C.: Society of Christian Ethics, 2000), 41–64. Kroeker thinks Yoder is right to identify Constantinianism with a falsely realized eschatology that results in the scandalous Christological "marks" of the church becoming invisible, but he thinks Yoder does not stress how the church is called into the world to be of service to the world. Kroeker rightly questions my criticism of O'Donovan's eschatology as too realized, because my critique depends on Yoder's standard criticism of Constantinianism as too realized. Kroeker suggests that the problem is not that O'Donovan asks too little from the state, but that on Yoder's grounds he should ask more. Craig Carter provides a helpful chapter on Yoder's understanding of Constantinianism in *The Politics of the Cross: The Theology and Social Ethics of John Howard Yoder* (Grand Rapids: Brazos Press, 2001), 96–111.

this "revelation" is captured in the presumption that our only alternative is to believe in the fantastic capacity of our democratic and technocratic societies to make things work, or else in the conviction that everything is so bad that revolution is the only meaningful imperative.[34]

It is a mistake, therefore, when, in the interest of "justifying" our convictions or of being socially "responsible," Christians think that we must translate our language into the dominant language of our surroundings. The early Christians did not ask, "Shall messianic Jews enter the Hellenistic world and adjust to its concepts?" Their question could not be whether or not to enter the world of Hellenism, but *how* to be there. Their question, as Yoder says, was "how in the transition to render anew the genuine pertinence of the proclamation of Christ's Lordship, even in a context (*particularly* in a context) where even the notion of such sovereignty is questionable."[35] As the early Christians did, so must we do now, which is not to say that we should become Hellenist Christians. The last thing we should do is try to translate the early church's understanding of, for example, the notion of preexistence or the participation of the Son in creation into the "pluralist/relativist" language of our time.[36] As Yoder says, that would be like

> asking whether with the bases loaded you should try for a field goal or use a number three iron. What we need to find is the interworld transformational grammar to help us to discern what will need to happen if the collision of the message of Jesus with our pluralist/relativist world is to

34. Yoder, "Christ, the Hope of the World," 198.

35. John Howard Yoder, "'But We Do See Jesus': The Particularity of Incarnation and the Universality of Truth," in *The Priestly Kingdom*, 56. Yoder wrote this essay for a conference at Boston University that was to address the question of the "foundation of ethics." It is one of the few times Yoder addressed what may be considered fundamental "methodological" issues. Yoder was extremely suspicious of all attempts to get clear on "method" before saying what you have to say. From his perspective, "methodological considerations" too often take the form of endless throat-clearing. In the introduction to *The Priestly Kingdom*, he observes that although he is not disrespectful of "the authentic self-critical ministry of conceptual analysis," he is skeptical about the possibility that such exercises can come first. You cannot start by trying to provide the conditions for meaningful discourse between two cultures or communities. There is simply no "scratch" to which "one can go back to begin, anymore than there is any 'onion per se' to be reached by peeling off one after another the layers of flesh. What must replace the prolegomenal search for 'scratch' is the confession of rootedness in historical community" (7).

36. Yoder's use of "pluralist/relativist" is purely descriptive. In other words, he is offering no theory-laden account of pluralism or relativism. He is well aware that such theories exist, but he prefers to use these descriptions at a more common sense level. They simply name the way the world is. Moreover, Yoder has no stake in the attempt to defeat relativism by offering foundationalist theories of truth. I suspect that Yoder assumes such theories are exactly what makes "relativism" such a compelling philosophical position. From Yoder's perspective, attempts to develop knock-down arguments against relativism do little to affect the actual relativism that constitutes our lives. I also suspect that Yoder

lead to a reconception of the shape of the world, instead of rendering Jesus optional or innocuous. To ask, "Shall we talk in pluralist/relativist terms?" would be as silly as to ask in Greece, "Shall we talk Greek?" The question is what we shall say. We shall say, "Jesus is Messiah and Lord"; but how do you say that in a pluralist/relativist language? If that language forbids us to say that, do we respect the prohibition? Or do we find a way to say it anyway? We won't play with the utopia of getting out of our own pluralist/relativist skins by going either backward or forward. It is within these skins that we need to restate whatever our claims are. Since for some even the phrase "truth claims" evokes echoes of theocratic compulsion or of pretensions to infallibility, let us use the more biblical phrases "witness" and "proclamation" as naming forms of communication which do not coerce the hearer.[37]

We are not called on to translate what our forbears said of Christ's lordship after their encounter with Hellenism but to emulate their exercise. Just as the early Christians laid claim to Hellenist cosmologies as a way to instantiate the peace of God's creation, so Christians today should find in the pluralistic/relativistic world a way to restate the truth of Christian claims. The world of pluralism/relativism may be confusing, but it is not alien. Such a world is, after all, as Yoder reminds us, a child of the Jewish and Christian intervention in history. We must remember that the world as we find it is at least partly the result of the missionary mobility of the church, the Christian love of enemy, the church's relativizing of political sovereignty, the charismatic vision of the many members of the church, and the Christian disavowal of empire and theocracy. Of course, the relativism that is at least partly the result of Christian witness has had a corrosive effect on those who would witness the good news in Christ. Yet, according to Yoder, it is still the case that the world that seems to make relativism unavoidable is part of the ripple effect of the gospel's impact.[38]

It is also the case, Yoder says, that in spite of the extent to which it is a stumbling block to effective witness, relativism profoundly threatens

---

assumes attempts to develop philosophical arguments against relativism too often fail to see that the problem is not philosophical because, quite simply, no matter how convinced someone may be that relativism is true, no one can live it. In this respect it would be fascinating to compare and contrast Yoder's understanding of relativism with that of Alasdair MacIntyre's in *Whose Justice? Which Rationality?* (Notre Dame: University of Notre Dame Press, 1988), 352–356. MacIntyre rightly historicizes the notion of relativism by suggesting that "relativism" becomes a real option only with the development of cosmopolitan cultures and the philosophical justifications that such cultures produce. For a constructive use of MacIntyre and Yoder that provides a theological account of relativism with which I am in large agreement, see Brad Kallenberg, "The Gospel Truth of Relativism," *Scottish Journal of Theology* 53, no. 2 (2000): 177–211.

37. Yoder, "'But We Do See Jesus,'" 56.
38. Ibid., 59–60.

two kinds of politics with correlative epistemologies that are or should be enemies of the church. Relativism threatens the epistemology of the establishment, which is validated by placing the power of political authority behind a particular belief system. Yoder notes that this epistemology is still normative among those who seek a monocultural unity in order to remove "subjective" choice from belief. Christians often have desired a peace conceived as "unity," but when we have done so we confuse the peace of Christ with worldly order, which, as Yoder points out, is exactly what happened when the church of Rome became the great Constantinian church.

The other political and epistemological option that relativism threatens is the one that has underwritten the apologetic strategy of dominant Christianity and, in particular, mainstream Protestantism. Because the church perceives itself to lack political power, the search for some operation—linguistic, statistical, logical—is undertaken in an effort to secure a solid ground that will no longer be subject to the objections of others or to our own self-doubt. Such a strategy seeks to deny particularity, Yoder says, in the "vain effort to find assurance beyond the flux of unendingly meeting new worlds, or to create a metalanguage above the clash, in order to renew for tomorrow the trustworthiness and irresistibility of the answers of the past."[39] Reinhold Niebuhr's distinction between permanent and primitive myths is but one form of this mistaken strategy.[40]

Both of these epistemological strategies cannot help but deny that Jesus Christ is Lord. Christians may, therefore, be tactical allies of the

---

39. Ibid., 60.

40. Yoder wrote an appreciative but critical evaluation of Reinhold Niebuhr as early as 1955. See his "Reinhold Niebuhr and Christian Pacifism," *Mennonite Quarterly Review* 29 (April, 1955): 101–117. Yoder clearly saw that Niebuhr remained a liberal Protestant. For example, in Yoder's *Christian Attitudes toward War, Peace, and Revolution: A Companion to Bainton* (unpublished lectures, 1983), Yoder characterizes Niebuhr's theology as "applied anthropology": "All of the great theological themes in the classic tradition are transposed into ways of saying something about human nature or human hope. The doctrine of the trinity, the doctrine of creation, the doctrine of the fall, and other more complicated doctrines such as the proofs of the existence of God, are all transposed into what they mean for human nature and what human nature means for ethics today. So Niebuhr is still a liberal, in the sense that theological and cultural liberalism in the middle of the first half of this century meant being open minded and reasonable and letting all of the arguments speak for themselves, and then making your own decisions. Niebuhr happens to have been more honest than some other liberals with the negative data, i.e., with the positive readings you get about the evil in man and in culture, if you read the data straight and don't let yourself be brainwashed by evolutionary or enthusiastic optimism" (345). Yoder's book *The Christian Witness to the State* (Newton, Ks.: Faith and Life Press, 1964) was at least partly his attempt to free Mennonites from accepting Niebuhr's account of them as "vocational pacifists." In "The Ecumenical Patience and Vocation of John Howard Yoder," Mark Nation reports that Yoder sent his essay to Niebuhr, but Niebuhr never responded.

pluralist/relativist questioning of the secular orthodoxies that promise certainty through coercion, but Christians must also challenge every attempt to make relativism a new monism. The Christian confession that God has placed the Messiah above every cosmology and culture means that Christians affirm that the cosmos will find its true coherence in the lordship of Christ. Fired by such a conviction, Paul claimed in his letter to the Colossians that the powers are not merely defeated in their sovereignty but are reenlisted in the original creative purpose of service to humanity and praise of God. Yoder notes that in a similar fashion, in the Johannine corpus,

> the *logos/sophia* vision of the rationality of the universe and of history is not only dethroned but is also put to work illuminating everyone who comes into the world, and empowering sons and daughters. To know the Lamb who was slain was worthy to receive power not only enables his disciples to face martyrdom when they must; it also encourages them to go about their daily crafts and trades, to do their duties as parents and neighbors, without being driven by cosmic doubt. Even before the broken world can be made whole in the Second Coming, the witnesses to the first coming— through the very fact that they proclaim Christ above the powers, the Son above the angels—are enabled to go on proleptically in the redemption of creation. Only this evangelical Christology can found a truly transformationist approach to culture.
>
> We still do not *see* that the world has been set straight. We still have no *proof* that right is right. We still have not found a bridge or a way to leap from historical uncertainty to some other more solid base that would oblige people to believe or make our own believing sure. As it is, we do not see everything in subjection to him. *But we do see Jesus,* revealing the grace of God by tasting death for everyone (Heb. 2:8–9).[41]

This is John Howard Yoder's witness, which, as is true of all good witness, does not call attention to itself. Rather it directs attention to the witness of his Anabaptist forbears and to the God who made their lives and deaths possible. If their witness to the power of nonviolence had not existed, then Yoder would have no basis to make the claims he makes. Yet if the Anabaptists had not been witnesses to the Christians across time who had lived faithfully to Christ, then their witness would not have been possible. And the witness of Christians across time would not have been possible if God had not vindicated Christ's sacrifice on the cross through resurrection and ascension. On the basis of such witnesses, Christians can rightly claim that to bear the cross is not a confession peculiar to them; rather their lives reveal the "grain of the universe."

41. Yoder, "'But We Do See Jesus,'" 61.

John Paul II: The Non-Constantinian Pope

To say that lives that bear the cross reveal the grain of the universe is an outrageous claim to be sure, but one that is increasingly accepted by many Christians—not the least being John Paul II. I am not suggesting that the pope has become a pacifist, though I think any honest reading of his encyclicals suggests that he has been moving in that direction. Rather, I believe that Yoder was right to suggest that Vatican II began a process through which the church of Rome has given up Constantinian ambitions. As George Weigel makes clear, this Polish pope has embedded the process begun at Vatican II in the heart of the Roman church.[42] Indeed, Weigel goes so far as to characterize John Paul II as the first "post-Constantinian Pope."[43] John Paul II's post-Constantinian stance, according to Weigel, is evident in the spirit he has brought to the papacy, both through his travels that help Christians understand that we are

42. George Weigel, *Witness to Hope: The Biography of Pope John Paul II* (New York: Harper Collins, 1999). Weigel provides a helpful account of Karol Wojtyla's engagement with the Second Vatican Council, noting that he attended every session. In particular, Wojtyla had a hand in debates around *Dignitatis Humanae* and *Gaudium et Spes*. In regard to the former, it is particularly interesting that Wojtyla argued that the declaration should present religious freedom "substantially as revealed doctrine, which is entirely consonant with sound reason" (165). That he did so means that he stood against the American Jesuit John Courtney Murray, who preferred a natural-law defense of religious freedom.

In almost all of John Paul II's encyclicals, some reference is made to Vatican II. For example, in *Dives in Misericordia* he observes: "The more the Church's mission is centered upon man—the more it is, so to speak, anthropocentric—the more it must be confirmed and actualized theocentrically, that is to say by being directed in Jesus Christ to the Father. While the various currents of human thought both in the past and the present have tended and still tend to separate theocentrism and anthropocentrism, and even to set them in opposition to each other, the Church, following Christ, seeks to link them up in human history, in a deep and organic way. And this is also one of the basic principles, perhaps the most important one, of the teaching of the last council. Since, therefore, in the present phase of the Church's history we put before ourselves as our primary task *the implementation of the doctrine* of the great *Council*, we must act upon this principle with faith, with an open mind and with all our heart." *The Encyclicals of John Paul II*, ed., with introductions, J. Michael Miller, C.S.B. (Huntington, Ind.: Our Sunday Visitor Publishing Division, 1996), sec. 1, par. 4, p. 111.

43. Weigel, *Witness to Hope*, 295–299. I am not suggesting that Weigel believes that John Paul II is "post-Constantinian" in the exact manner in which Yoder is "non-Constantinian," but, as I will argue, given Yoder's understanding of the background epistemological assumptions that shape the various forms of Constantinianism, John Paul II is much closer to Yoder (and Barth) than he is to theologies shaped by Constantinian intellectual habits. In "The Papacy and Power," *First Things* 110 (February, 2001): 18–25, Weigel has developed in greater detail how John Paul II represents the search by popes in modernity to find a politics to resist the allure of the nation-state. In this essay, Weigel identifies Constantinianism as "the deep entanglement of the Church and the papacy with state power, and the papacy's tacit acceptance of criteria for political judgment that were sometimes incompatible with the evangelical function . . . this state of affairs was the product of both a

members of a universal church, and, most of all, through his unrelenting christological focus.

John Paul II's first encyclical, *Redemptor Hominis*, begins: "The Redeemer of man, Jesus Christ, is the center of the universe and of history. To him go my thoughts and my heart in this solemn moment of the world that the Church and the whole family of present-day humanity are now living."[44] Weigel notes that *Redemptor Hominis* introduced to a global audience a theological analysis of the contemporary human condition that Karol Wojtyla had been refining for thirty years.[45] In this encyclical, John Paul II holds out hope not only for Christian unity but for how that unity portends the unity of all in Christ. Such unity, moreover, is to be found through nonviolence:

> It was not without reason that Christ said that "the Kingdom of heaven has suffered violence, and men of violence take it by force" and moreover that "the children of this world are more astute . . . than are the children of light." We gladly accept this rebuke, that we may be like those "violent people of God" that we have so often seen in the history of the Church and still see today, and that we may consciously join in the great mission of revealing Christ to the world helping each person to find himself in Christ, and helping the contemporary generations of our brothers and sisters, the peoples, nations, States, mankind, developing countries and countries of opulence—in short, helping everyone to get to know "the unsearchable riches of Christ," since these riches are for every individual and are everybody's property.[46]

God's peaceable people cannot but appear to the world as "violent people" just to the extent that they challenge the normality of violence. That is why there is nothing naive about John Paul II's understanding

---

distinctive history and a strategic judgment: that the Church's truth claims and public position required the buttressing of something like 'Christendom'" (20). For a wonderful response to Weigel's article that supports my reading of John Paul II's papacy, see Paul Griffiths's contribution to "The Future of the Papacy: A Symposium," *First Things* 111 (March, 2001), 34–35. Griffiths argues that the pope "is the most powerful man in the world" exactly because "his power is in the judicious use of weakness." Griffiths explains: "The idea that real power can only be had by renouncing its counterfeits (army and money) is fundamental to Christian thinking. It is a central part of the story of Jesus' temptations, and it is enshrined forever in the figure of Christ on the cross. In its ideal form (which is never its actual form), the papacy serves as a sacramental sign of this truth and, thus, as a sacrament of the power of weakness. The pope is the only actor on the world stage whose understanding of power is (ideally) self-emptyingly pacific. This, then, is why the pope is the most powerful man in the world: the understanding that he represents will endure, while the others inevitably curve in upon themselves and expire of their own contradictions" (35).

44. John Paul II, *Redemptor Hominis*, in *The Encyclicals of John Paul II*, sec. 1, par. 1, p. 46.

45. Weigel, *Witness to Hope*, 288.

46. John Paul II, *Redemptor Hominis*, sec. 11, par. 5, p. 62. "The violent people of God" are, of course, the nonviolent ones who have refused to defend God's kingdom with violence.

of the call for unity that is to be found in Christ. After all, this is the pope who lived in the belly of the beast, suffering and surviving first the Nazis and later the Communists. As he later put it, "I participated in the great experience of my contemporaries—humiliation at the hands of evil."[47] The hope John Paul II offers is a hope that has no basis other than the work of Christ made present in the church through the Spirit. He observes that the church, "which has no weapons at her disposal apart from those of the spirit, of the word and of love, cannot renounce her proclamation of 'the word . . . in and out of season' (2 Timothy 4:2)." The pope declares that the church, therefore, cannot cease to implore states, in the name of God and in the name of humanity, not to make war on one another: "Do not kill! Do not prepare destruction and exter- mination for men! Think of your brothers and sisters who are suffering hunger and misery! Respect each one's dignity and freedom!"[48]

For John Paul II, the church is the alternative to violence just to the extent that the church is the agent of truth. In *Redemptor Hominis* he strikes the theme that is central to every encyclical he has written, namely, what the church owes the world is to be and say the truth, which is nothing less than "Jesus is the Christ." The Second Vatican Council made clear that the church appears before the world as the so- cial subject responsible for divine truth:

> With deep emotion we hear Christ himself saying: "The word which you hear is not mine but the Father's who sent me." (John 14:24) In this affirma- tion by our Master do we not notice responsibility for the revealed truth, which is the "property" of God himself, since even he, "the only Son" who lives "in the bosom of the Father," (John 1:18) when transmitting that truth as a prophet and teacher feels the need to stress that he is acting in full fidel- ity to its divine source? The same fidelity must be a constitutive quality of the Church's faith, both when she is teaching it and when she is professing it. Faith as a specific supernatural virtue infused into the human spirit makes us sharers in knowledge of God as a response to his revealed word.[49]

In *Redemptor Hominis* John Paul II not only holds Christ up as the source of hope, but also provides on the basis of that hope his extraordi- nary analysis of the pathology of modernity. He notes that fear charac- terizes modern life. As modern people, we are afraid of what we pro- duce, particularly that part of our making that is the result of our genius and initiative. We fear that our creations will turn against us and be- come the means for our unimaginable self-destruction.[50] In later encyc-

---

47. Weigel, *Witness to Hope*, 87.
48. John Paul II, *Redemptor Hominis*, sec. 16, par. 11, p. 74.
49. Ibid., sec. 19, par. 1, pp. 81–82.
50. Ibid., sec. 15, par. 2, pp. 67–68.

licals, he describes our condition as a "culture of death" that is nowhere more evident than in our unwillingness to receive into this world our own children, exactly because we fear our calling to be God's good creatures. Abortion is but the sign that we fear the truth and as a result are attracted to destruction and death. We are attracted to death for no other reason than that the consciousness of our deaths confirms that at least for a moment we existed, which produces the wan hope that perhaps our existence might matter.[51]

John Paul II says that a church confronted by a culture of death cannot afford to entertain a distinction between faith and morality. The separation of faith from morality has led many people, even many Christians, to live as if God does not exist. Therefore, it is all the more urgent, the pope says, for Christians to rediscover that the Christian faith is not simply a set of propositions to be accepted by the intellect; rather, "faith is a lived knowledge of Christ, a living remembrance of his commandments, and a *truth to be lived out*. A word, in any event, is not truly received until it passes into action, until it is put into practice."[52] According to John Paul II, the life of the Christian cannot avoid becoming the life of a witness, and a witness is always a potential martyr: "Charity, in conformity with the radical demands of the Gospel, can lead the believer to the supreme witness of *martyrdom*."[53]

Perhaps it is odd to think it remarkable that a pope might rediscover the connection between martyrdom and matters that confront daily Christian practice: that abortion is not a moral alternative, that suicide is not an option, that both capital punishment and war are problematic. Nonetheless, I find it extraordinary that John Paul II sees the connection. Martyrdom, he says, bears witness to the holiness of God's law and is the sign of the holiness of God's church. By spawning martyrs, the church serves civil society well, warding off the headlong plunge into the most dangerous crisis that can afflict humanity: "the *confusion between good and evil*, which makes it impossible to build up and to preserve the moral order of individuals and communities."[54] In most times, the pope admits, few Christians will be called to martyrdom, but

there is nonetheless a consistent witness which all Christians must daily be ready to make, even at the cost of suffering and grave sacrifice. Indeed, faced

---

51. John Paul II develops this line of thought most fully in his encyclicals *Veritatis Splendor* and *Evangelium Vitae*. See in particular *Evangelium Vitae*, in *The Encyclicals of John Paul II*, sec. 58–63, pp. 846–853. For a similar analysis of the necrophilia that grips our lives, see Catherine Pickstock, *After Writing: On the Liturgical Consummation of Philosophy* (Oxford: Basil Blackwell, 1998), 101–118.

52. John Paul II, *Veritatis Splendor*, in *The Encyclicals of John Paul II*, sec. 88, par. 4, pp. 746–747.

53. Ibid., sec. 89, par. 2, p. 747.

54. Ibid., sec. 93, par. 1, pp. 749–750.

with the many difficulties which fidelity to the moral order can demand, even in the most ordinary circumstances, the Christian is called, with the grace of God invoked in prayer, to a sometimes heroic commitment.[55]

I do not pretend to have even scratched the surface of John Paul II's witness.[56] Nor have I tried to compare and contrast the life and work of John Paul II and John Howard Yoder. Yet as different as an obscure Mennonite theologian may be from the pope, it is clear that John Paul II and John Howard Yoder represent a recovery of the Christological center of the church's life and witness. That center, moreover, requires and entails that the church be a witness to the peace that is an alternative to the death that grips the life of the world. What John Paul II and John Howard Yoder share over and above their differences is exemplified by a life that joins what they each hold dear. The name given to that life is Dorothy Day.

Dorothy Day was an obedient and pious Catholic, a pacifist, and committed to the daily practice of the corporal works of mercy.[57] She and Peter Maurin, who together founded the Catholic Worker, were too radical to be Marxist or socialist. They established Houses of Hospitality because they saw no alternative.[58] Because Dorothy Day existed, we can know that the church to which John Paul II and John Howard Yoder witness is not some ideal but an undeniable reality. Moreover, such a church must exist if indeed the cross and not the sword reveals to us the very grain of the universe.

55. Ibid., sec. 93, par. 1, p. 750. In the next paragraph of *Veritatis Splendor*, in a quite wonderful example of "natural theology," John Paul II suggests that Christians are not alone in their conviction that their moral commitments may require martyrdom. He quotes Saint Justin to the effect that "the Stoics, at least in their teachings on ethics, demonstrated wisdom, thanks to the seed of the Word present in all peoples, and we know that those who followed their doctrines met with hatred and were killed" (sec. 94, p. 751).

For an insightful exploration of the complex relation between Christian martyrdom and heroism, particularly in an age that denies both, see Brian Hook and R. R. Reno, *Heroism and the Christian Life: Reclaiming Excellence* (Louisville: Westminster/John Knox Press, 2000).

56. I confess that making John Paul II part of my narrative was not my idea but that of my friend and dean, Greg Jones. I remain convinced that John Paul II is a crucial witness for the case I want to make for witness, but I feel nothing but frustration as I come to the end of this section. I know I have not done justice to John Paul II, or to John Howard Yoder for that matter. I feel less frustration about Yoder because I have written on him in the past, but John Paul II's life and work is so rich that any brief (or lengthy) treatment of him is bound to make anyone feel inadequate for the task.

57. Dorothy Day's autobiography, *The Long Loneliness* (New York: Harper and Row, 1952) remains the best source for an account of her life. I am indebted to Charlie Reynolds for reminding me of the significance of Dorothy Day for my account of witness.

58. In her introduction to Peter Maurin's *Easy Essays* (Chicago: Franciscan Herald Press, 1977), Day describes how they got into the practice of hospitality. She notes that Maurin had written a series of essays addressed to the bishops, pointing out to them that

The Church and the University

To suggest that witnesses like John Howard Yoder and John Paul II are crucial for understanding the rationality of Christian convictions may well try the patience of those who expect the Gifford lecturer to provide philosophically compelling arguments for the existence of God. I am sure that the brief allusion to Dorothy Day can only confirm the judgment of some people that the argument I have tried to make in these Gifford Lectures is nothing more than a nice example of special pleading. For those inclined to so dismiss my argument, I have no decisive response other than to ask if they represent practices that can produce a Dorothy Day.

Yet if there is no standpoint external to the practice of Christianity for assessing the truth of Christian convictions, then why should anyone trust their lives, in Marshall's terms, to an "epistemologically afflicted" set of convictions? Lives may be required for assessing Christian convictions, but can such lives be anything more than attractive or unattractive? Does the truth of Christian convictions depend on the faithfulness of the church and, if so, how do we determine what would constitute faithfulness? Am I suggesting that the ability of the church to be or not to be nonviolent is constitutive for understanding what it might meant to claim that Christian convictions are true? Do I think the truthfulness of Christian witness is compromised when Christians accept the practices of the "culture of death"—abortion, suicide, capital punishment, and war?

Yes! On every count, the answer is "Yes." Moreover, if I am right, there is a way to respond to the challenge that the argument is hopelessly circular. Christians betray the grammar of the Christian faith when we try to answer the charge of circularity by divorcing what we believe from the way our beliefs are embedded in our lives and, more important, from the way our lives are embedded in the church. In short, I am suggesting that Christians in modernity have lost the ability to answer questions about the truthfulness of what we believe because we have accepted beliefs about the world that presuppose that God does not matter. The problem for Christians and non-Christians alike is the Christian inability to live in a way that enables us to articulate what difference it makes that we are or are not Christian.

I noted in the first lecture that there are many reasons for the inability of Christians to articulate what makes them Christian, but surely

---

canon law called for the establishment of hospices in every bishopric. "When a reader who had been sleeping in the subway came into *The Catholic Worker* office one day and disclosed her need (the apartment and the office were already full), Peter's literal acceptance of 'If thy brother needs food or drink, feed him, and if he needs shelter, shelter him' meant that we rented a large apartment a block away which became the first House of Hospitality for women." The pages of Day's introduction are not numbered.

one of the most important reasons is the failure of Christians to maintain universities that are recognizably Christian.[59] Indeed, our very ability as Christians to lead lives of witness has been compromised by our inability to sustain a Christian intellectual witness worthy of the martyrs.[60] At best, in the universities shaped by the practices and knowledges required by a democratic social order, Christian presence has been relegated to the realm of "values" associated with courses in ethics or involved with issues in "student life." It has simply become unthinkable that Christian convictions might have something to do with the actual content of the curriculum and with pedagogical practice.

By directing attention to the university as a site where Christians might rediscover the difference that being Christian makes for claims about the world, I do not mean to overvalue the importance of universities for Christians. Given the character of the modern university, we should not be surprised that the most significant intellectual work in our time may well take place outside the university.[61] Moreover, the Christian practice of hospitality embodied by Dorothy Day and the challenges of church unity that have been central for John Paul II are more important for the Christian understanding of the habitability of

---

59. How and why Christians have lost the ability to sustain the universities they created is a complex tale. See, for example, George Marsden, *The Soul of the American University: From Protestant Establishment to Established Nonbelief* (New York: Oxford University Press, 1994); Douglas Sloan, *Faith and Knowledge: Mainline Protestantism and American Higher Education* (Louisville: Westminster/John Knox Press, 1994); James Burtchaell, C.S.C., *The Dying of the Light: The Disengagement of Colleges and Universities from Their Christian Churches* (Grand Rapids: Eerdmans, 1998); and Julie Reuben, *The Making of the Modern University: Intellectual Transformation and the Marginalization of Morality* (Chicago: University of Chicago Press, 1996).

60. In the terms Charles Taylor has taught us to use, Christians have simply become inarticulate, and not only in the face of those who do not share our practices. Even more important, we have lost the skills necessary to understand ourselves. To be articulate, according to Taylor, requires the ability to reason in "the transitions." Such reasoning involves arguments that have their source in biographical narratives; for it is through such narratives that we are able to make the connections that render our beliefs coherent. For example, how Christians think about questions of violence is inseparable from their worship of the God revealed in the cross and resurrection of Jesus. For Taylor's account of how modernity has made Christian and non-Christian alike inarticulate, see *Sources of the Self: The Making of Modern Identity* (Cambridge: Harvard University Press, 1989).

61. In particular, I am thinking about Wendell Berry, who quite self-consciously stands apart from the university. He does so because the modern university is organized to divide the disciplines in a manner that insures that the university need pay little or no attention to the "local and earthly effects" of the work that is done in them. According to Berry, if the university sponsored authentic conversation between disciplines, the college of agriculture would have been brought under questioning by the college of arts and sciences or medicine. Berry confesses that he has no wisdom about how the disciplines might be organized but observes only that at one time, a time when the idea of vocation was still viable, the disciplines were thought of as being useful to one another. However, once the notion of vocation is lost, the university has no other purpose than to insure that the rich or powerful are even more successful. Berry wryly notes he does not believe that

the world than our ability to maintain universities.[62] Nonetheless, by attending to the university, I can at least suggest how Christians and non-Christians can discover useful disagreements. And it should become clear as I proceed that the question for me is not whether a university can be Christian, but whether a church exists sufficient to sustain a Christian university.[63]

---

a person was ever "called" to be rich or powerful. The hallmark of the contemporary university is, of course, the professionalism whose religion is progress, and "this means that, in spite of its vocal bias in favor of practicality and realism, professionalism forsakes both past and present in favor of the future, which is never present or practical or real." Wendell Berry, *Life Is a Miracle: An Essay Against Modern Superstition* (Washington, D.C.: Counterpoint Press, 2000), 129–130. Berry's criticism could fruitfully be compared to John Paul II's understanding of the culture of death. For example, Berry observes that the story that dominates our age is the story of freedom from reverence, fidelity, neighborliness, and stewardship. Strikingly, he suggests that the "dominant story of our age, undoubtedly, is that of adultery and divorce. This is true both literally and figuratively: The dominant *tendency* of our age is the breaking of faith and the making of divisions among things that were once joined" (133).

62. Hospitality and questions of the church's unity, however, do have everything to do with the ability of Christians to maintain a culture of excellence that includes the work of scholars. Christianity, by its very nature, requires that some people be set aside to think hard about our faith. The work of those so set aside will differ in different times, but part of such work requires those who do it to struggle to understand their relation to the work done in the past. It is sometimes assumed that the radical accounts of Christian convictions represented by people like John Howard Yoder, Dorothy Day, and Peter Maurin provide no space for such work. That is simply not the case. Peter Maurin, for example, loved nothing more than a good argument and was deeply committed to the life of the mind. In his essay entitled "Back to Newmanism," he joined President Hutchins of the University of Chicago to complain that students no longer knew the "great books of the Western World." Maurin quoted Newman: "If the intellect is a good thing, then its cultivation is an excellent thing. It must be cultivated not only as a good thing, but as a useful thing. It must not be useful in any low, mechanical, material sense. It must be useful in the spreading of goodness. It must be used by the owner for the good of himself and for the good of the world" (*Easy Essays*, 126–127). Maurin's attitude toward the modern university was quite similar to Wendell Berry's critique of the curriculum of the contemporary university (see the previous note).

63. My reflections on the university are informed by James McClendon's last chapter in *Witness*: "Theology and the University," 387–420. I believe McClendon is right to note that what we need is not Christian universities or secular universities but universities that are identified by the beauty of their practices. McClendon identifies such practices: (1) conflict resolution, (2) interethnic inclusiveness, (3) economic leveling, (4) a division of labor based upon acknowledgment of vocation, and (5) a voice for all (403–406). Such universities would not feel the need to exclude theology, according to McClendon, but would discover that just to the extent that they are universities, they *cannot* exclude theology. See also John Milbank's "Theology and the Economy of the Sciences" in *Faithfulness and Fortitude: In Conversation with the Theological Ethics of Stanley Hauerwas,* Mark Thiessen Nation and Samuel Wells, eds. (Edinburgh: T. & T. Clark, 2000), 39–57. Milbank argues a stronger position than the one I take—namely that unless the "other disciplines are (at least implicitly) ordered to theology (assuming that this means participation in God's self-knowledge—as in the Augustinian tradition) they are objectively and demonstrably null and void, altogether lacking in truth." (45).

234 The Necessity of Witness

It is not surprising that John Howard Yoder and John Paul II refuse to accept the relegation of Christian knowledge to the "soft side" of the university. For example, Yoder argues that if the relationship between the obedience of God's people and the triumph of God's cause is not a relationship between cause and effect but one of cross and resurrection, then it must surely be the case that how history is done by Christians will be different than how it is done by those who assume that God has nothing to do with our lives.[64] Therefore, history must be taken back from the grasp of military historians and chroniclers of battles and dynasties so that a society's character will be described and thus judged by how those "without a role in history" were treated. Thus, Yoder asks: "Instead of reading history as proof of a theory of political science, i.e., the definition *sine qua non* of the state as its monopoly of physical coercion, could we study the story with some openness to the hypothesis that genuine power is always correlated with the consent of the governed or legitimized in some other way?"[65]

Yoder does not mean to suggest that Christian historiography should be done in isolation from how others conceive of and write about history. He is not recommending a state of affairs in which Christians get to say, "You have your story, and we have ours." Rather, he is suggesting that if Christian witness is to be faithful, then how Christians tell their story, as well as how they tell the stories of others, cannot be based upon the presumptions that govern non-Christian historiography. Furthermore, only by writing history on their terms can Christians learn to locate the differences between the church and the world. Of course, it may be the case that Christians will discover deep continuities between their account of events and the accounts of others, but this is simply evidence that the

64. The first part of this sentence is a paraphrase of a passage from *The Politics of Jesus* (238), and the second part is from "Christ, the Hope of the World," 208.

65. Yoder, "Christ, the Hope of the World," 208. Yoder is not equating the "consent of the governed" with democracy, nor does he assume that democracies are intrinsically less violent. See, for example, "The Christian Case for Democracy," in *The Priestly Kingdom*, 151–171. In "Christ, the Hope of the World," Yoder provides a fascinating example of the kind of historiographical practice for which he is calling. He contrasts the response of the native Indians of North America to the European invasion with that of the natives in Latin America. The North American natives fought and were defeated, with the result that their culture was degraded; the Latin American natives, lacking the means to defend themselves, were rolled over, with the result that they not only saved much about their lives but shaped the resulting culture (213). I am sure Yoder would not want too much to be made of this example, as it obviously needs to be "thickened" with detailed descriptions of the similarities and differences between the North American and Latin American invasions. His point, however, still stands, as is increasingly clear by the development of so-called subaltern histories of the colonial period. See, for example, Dipesh Chakrabarty's extraordinary book, *Provincializing Europe: Postcolonial Thought and Historical Difference* (Princeton: Princeton University Press, 2000). Chakrabarty observes that the "time" of modern history is "godless, continuous and, to follow Benjamin, empty and homogeneous" (73).

church does not exist in isolation from the world. Given the God we worship as Christians, we should not be surprised when evidence of that God shows up in work that assumes our God does not exist.

Yoder's position—which may seem quite challenging to Christian and non-Christian alike—pales in comparison to the stance John Paul II takes toward philosophy in his encyclical *Fides et Ratio*, though just how radical the pope's stance is may not be apparent immediately.[66] John Paul II asserts that in spite of the various meanings of the term "philosophy" and the variety of philosophical systems, there exists a core of philosophical inquiry in which Christians have a stake. For example, he asks us to consider

> the principles of non-contradiction, finality and causality, as well as the concept of the person as a free and intelligent subject, with the capacity to know God, truth and goodness. Consider as well certain fundamental moral norms which are shared by all. These are among the indications that, beyond different schools of thought, there exists a body of knowledge which may be judged a kind of spiritual heritage of humanity. It is as if we had come upon an *implicit philosophy*, as a result of which all feel that they possess these principles, albeit in a general and unreflective way. Precisely because it is shared in some measure by all, this knowledge should serve as a kind of reference point for different philosophical schools.[67]

Accordingly, John Paul II claims that the church cannot help but value philosophy as that which names the activity through which our lives are rendered more worthy. Indeed, he goes so far as to claim that "the Church considers philosophy an indispensable help for a deeper understanding of faith and for communicating the truth of the Gospel to those who do not know it."[68]

None of this seems radical, but John Paul II goes on to say that because the church is confident of its competence to bear the revelation of Jesus Christ, and because the Second Vatican Council insisted that the bishops are a "witness of divine and catholic truth," criticism must be leveled at philosophy that "rather than voicing the human orientation toward the truth, has wilted under the weight of so much knowledge and little by little has lost the capacity to lift its gaze to the heights, not daring to rise to the truth of being."[69] From John Paul II's

66. John Paul II, *Fides et Ratio* (Boston: Pauline Books and Media, 1998).

67. Ibid., pp. 12–13, par. 4. It is fascinating to wonder what Barth would have made of these claims about philosophy. I think it is a mistake to assume that he would have dismissed them outright. After all, the pope is not suggesting that philosophy can give us knowledge of Jesus Christ.

68. Ibid., p. 13, par. 5.

69. Ibid., p. 14, par. 5.

perspective, modern philosophy has made a philosophical mistake by trying to develop epistemologies that insure that our knowledge is true. In the process, modern philosophy has forgotten that existence is prior to knowledge and thus determines how we know what we know.[70]

At the end of the twentieth century—a century that at least in the Northern Hemisphere had become increasingly secular—we find the pope, of all people, defending the activity of reasoning. Moreover, we find him honoring the good of philosophy as a discipline. Yet we also find him arguing that although the results of reasoning may be true, they "acquire their true meaning only if they are set within the larger horizon of faith: 'All man's steps are ordered by the Lord: how then can man understand his own ways?'" (Proverbs 20:24).[71] In other words, the truths discovered through philosophy must be tested and judged by the truth known through revelation; for the latter is not the product or consummation of arguments devised by human reason but comes to us as the gift of life, Jesus Christ. That gift gives purpose to the work of reason by stirring thought and seeking acceptance as an expression of love.[72]

John Paul II, therefore, assumes that how philosophy is done in Catholic universities may well be different from how it is done in more secular institutions. Of course, much of what Catholic philosophers do will

70. It would be an extremely instructive enterprise to compare John Paul II's account of modern philosophy and MacIntyre's account in *First Principles, Final Ends, and Contemporary Philosophical Issues*. MacIntyre suggests that philosophers who are committed to a Thomistic-Aristotelian mode of philosophy, that is, a view that by training we can be made adequate to understand the way things are, must approach contemporary philosophy in a manner akin to a Nietzschian genealogist. Genealogists try to explain why their antagonists have come to an impasse and why they cannot recognize or extricate themselves from the impasse on their own terms. Accordingly, a Thomist must try to show that the predicaments of contemporary philosophy, both analytic and deconstructive, are the result of the long-term consequences of rejecting the Aristotelian and Thomistic teleology at the threshold of the modern world (59).

71. John Paul II, *Fides et Ratio*, p. 32, par. 20.

72. Ibid., p. 26, par. 15. Later in the encyclical, John Paul II suggests that the best way to conceive of the relationship between theology and philosophy is that of a circle: "Theology's source and starting point must always be the word of God revealed in history, while its final goal will be an understanding of that word which increases with each passing generation. Yet, since God's word is Truth (cf. John 17:17), the human search for truth—philosophy, pursued in keeping with its own rules—can only help to understand God's word better. It is not just a question of theological discourse using this or that concept or element of a philosophical construct; what matters most is that the believer's reason use its powers of reflection in the search for truth which moves from the word of God toward a better understanding of it. . . . This circular relationship with the word of God leaves philosophy enriched, because reason discovers new and unsuspected horizons" (pp. 92–93, par. 73).

It would be fascinating to compare MacIntyre's understanding of the relation of philosophy and theology to John Paul II's understanding of that relation. I am sure that MacIntyre would accept the pope's account in general, although the claim that theology not

be indistinguishable from philosophy done by non-Catholics. Indeed, Catholic philosophers will have much to learn from their non-Catholic counterparts. The pope clearly respects the kind of specialization in philosophy and in other disciplines that makes it difficult to locate a strong difference between Catholics and others. But what he refuses to accept is the fragmentation of the curriculum characteristic of modern universities. This fragmentation is but an expression of our cultural presumption that there is no order to what we know, nor to how we know it.[73] From John Paul II's perspective, philosophers have a particular responsibility for the intellectual work necessary for the ordering of our knowledge and, thus, of the curriculum.

Given this understanding of the relation of faith and reason, it comes as no surprise that John Paul II thinks that a university can and should be fully Catholic without in any manner compromising its activity as a university.[74] In *Ex Corde Ecclesiae,* he makes it clear that not only does the church have a stake in the work of the university, but the work of the university is best done when the Truth, who is God, is acknowl-

---

only judges philosophy but adds content to the subject of philosophy seems to go beyond what MacIntyre has said explicitly. John Paul II identifies exemplars of his understanding of philosophy and theology: St. Gregory of Nazianzus, St. Augustine, St. Anselm, St. Bonaventure, and St. Thomas, and, more recently, John Henry Newman, Antonio Rosmini, Jacques Maritain, Étienne Gilson, and Edith Stein—a list, I suspect, that MacIntyre would approve. What is interesting, however, is that most of the people named made no hard and fast distinction between philosophy and theology.

73. In a number of his essays, MacIntyre has noted that one of the characteristics of modern life that makes the moral life, at least the moral life as conceived by a Thomistic-Aristotelian, impossible is the compartmentalized character of our lives. The fragmentation of the university curriculum at once reflects and reproduces this compartmentalization. As a result, education cannot do what an education should do, that is, transform the desires students bring to their studies. Of course, the modern university does, in a certain sense, provide moral training, just to the extent that the fragmentation of the curriculum reinforces the fragmentation of student lives, making it impossible for students to think of their lives as whole. This kind of training is justified insofar as the university is expected to produce the kind of "personality type" necessary to sustain liberal democracies, that is, people who believe that in the name of fairness they are capable of understanding and appreciating without prejudice any and all people and positions. For MacIntyre's account of compartmentalization, see "Social Structures and Their Threats to Moral Agency," *Philosophy* 74, no. 289 (July, 1999): 311–328.

74. Put more strongly, I suspect that John Paul II assumes that any university that has the ambition to be a university, whether it is officially sponsored by the church or not, cannot help but exhibit the characteristics of a Catholic university, which may mean that only Catholic universities in our time have the potential to be universities just to the extent that they are committed to the rational possibility of giving a coherent account of themselves. As Reinhard Hütter has suggested: "God matters for the university because only a university in and for which God matters can be an enterprise that can give a comprehensive account of what it is all about" (personal correspondence). The Catholic university should be capable of such a witness to the extent that it gains its intelligibility from the witness that is the church.

edged. In other words, the university has a stake in the church. Thus, Catholic universities are called to continuous renewal both as universities and as extensions of the Catholic Church, for the very meaning of the human person is at stake in their common task. Theology must play a particularly important role in Catholic universities because "it serves all other disciplines in their search for meaning, not only by helping them to investigate how their discoveries will affect individuals and society, but also by bringing a perspective and an orientation not contained within their own methodologies."[75]

In the last chapter of *Three Rival Versions of Moral Enquiry,* MacIntyre suggests that the modern university confronts the Thomist with a problem. Any attempt to embody Thomism "requires both a different kind of curricular ordering of the disciplines from that divisive and fragmenting partitioning which contemporary academia imposes and the development of morally committed modes of dialectical enquiry, for which contemporary academia affords no place."[76] Therefore the Thomist, particularly a Thomist like John Paul II, cannot avoid asking what the modern university is for, as well as what particular goods the modern university serves. But those are just the questions, according to MacIntyre, that the modern university must repress in order to preserve the illusion that the university transcends conflict. Like James's famous hotel corridor, the modern university has become all things to all people (who have money) by looking away, as James puts it, from "first things, principles, 'categories,' supposed necessities; and [by] looking towards last things, fruits, consequences, facts."[77]

75. John Paul II, *Ex Corde Ecclesiae,* in *Origins* 20, no. 17 (October 4, 1990): 269. John Paul II also observes that interaction with other disciplines enriches theology by making theological research more relevant to current needs. I have no intention of entering the debates surrounding questions concerning the implementation of *Ex Corde.* For the text of the implementing document, see *"Ex Corde Ecclesiae:* An Application to the United States," in *Origins* 30, no. 5 (June 15, 2000): 65–75. As a Protestant, I can only stand in awe at the clarity with which the pope seems to understand the challenges before the modern university. He is not about to let theology be relegated to "ethics" or, even worse, to "values." John Paul II thinks that theology and philosophy involve claims about the way things are that have implications across the curriculum. Julie Reuben's *The Making of the Modern University* could serve as a commentary on what happens when theology is no longer thought to entail claims about the way things are and is reduced at best to "morality."

76. Alasdair MacIntyre, *Three Rival Versions of Moral Enquiry: Encyclopaedia, Genealogy, and Tradition* (Notre Dame: University of Notre Dame Press, 1990), 220.

77. William James, *Pragmatism and the Meaning of Truth,* intro. A. J. Ayer. (Cambridge: Harvard University Press, 1996), 32. George Marsden uses this quotation from James to justify the possibility as well as the existence of Christian scholarship in the university; see *The Outrageous Idea of Christian Scholarship* (New York: Oxford University Press, 1997), 45–46. Many people think that Marsden's defense of "Christian scholarship" is radical. From my perspective, Marsden is not nearly radical enough, as his use of James's image makes clear. Christians do not desire just a place at the "table," particularly a table that has been set by the modern university. Christians do not want a *place* at the table; they want

In contrast, MacIntyre argues that universities ought to be where "conceptions of and standards of rational justification are elaborated, put to work in detailed practices of enquiry, and themselves rationally evaluated, so that only from the university can the wider society learn how to conduct its own debates, practical or theoretical, in a rationally defensible way."[78] Accordingly, MacIntyre suggests that we need, as an alternative both to the premodern university of enforced and constrained agreements and to the modern university of alleged unconstrained agreements, a university of constrained disagreements.[79] MacIntyre's university would have faculties of encyclopaedists, genealogists, and traditionalists, that is, all of the various options for serious inquiry would be included. In time, this arrangement might well result in the establishment of a set of rival universities. Such a result would present to the wider society rival claims, as each university advanced its own inquiries on its own terms and secured agreements to ensure the progress of its inquiries by its own set of exclusions and prohibitions.[80]

MacIntyre's analysis of the character of the modern university makes clear why what Yoder says of history and what the pope says of philosophy are not simply curricular suggestions. Rather, both Yoder and the pope are making claims about what Christian practice entails if we are rightly to know our world. Moreover, both Yoder and the pope are making the claim that such knowledge can be rationally sustained only by a politics called church. The question is not whether Christian claims about the way the world is make it impossible for Christians to enter

---

both to build and set the table itself. See, for example, Mike Baxter, C. S. C., "Not Outrageous Enough," *First Things*, 113 (May, 2001), 14–16.

78. MacIntyre, *Three Rival Versions of Moral Enquiry*, 222.

79. Ibid., 230–231. MacIntyre acknowledges that some people might think his suggestion utopian, but he asks those who would do so to consider that "the degree to which it is difficult to envisage the restructuring of the university so as to make systematic debate concerning standards of rational justification between such points of view as the genealogical and the Thomistic a central preoccupation of our shared cultural and social life, is also the degree to which the structures of present society have exempted themselves from and protected themselves against being put in question by such systematic intellectual and moral enquiry. What are accepted as the *de facto* standards of argumentative justification in the established forums of political and bureaucratic negotiation are to a remarkable degree now protected against subversive challenge because the legitimacy of any particular challenge is measured by those self-same standards" (235).

I should hope that MacIntyre's university of constrained disagreements would have a place, as the University of Notre Dame did, for John Howard Yoder in the Department of Theology.

80. Ibid., 234. MacIntyre knows that such encounters are always dangerous just to the extent that "knowing how to read antagonistically without defeating oneself as well as one's opponent by not learning from the encounter is a skill without which no tradition can flourish" (233). Those people the church sets aside to do this kind of work obviously must be formed by the virtues necessary to have their souls so tested.

debates with those who hold alternative views. Instead, the question is
whether the church can produce people capable of sustaining the arguments that Christians and non-Christians so desperately need to have
with one another. From this perspective, Christians and non-Christians
alike should despair when it becomes difficult to distinguish the church
from the world. Of course, for Christians, despair is a vice that robs us of
our ability to see what is before our eyes—that is, lives with names like
John Howard Yoder, John Paul II, and Dorothy Day.

In the long run (and the long run is all there is), when everything is
said and done, James was right: by their fruits we will know the truthful ones. James however, failed to follow his own best pragmatic commitments. Shaped by the practices of American culture, James limited
the context of willing to an agency that remains ultimately individuated and, thus, abstracted not only from the community of knowers but
from the traditions, histories, and narratives out of which the community must work. Niebuhr, too, limited himself to an individuated
agency abstracted from the contexts that make agency intelligible, and
thus, like James, he failed to follow his own best commitments, though
these were not so much pragmatic as theological. Of course, the abstractions that characterize the works of both of these Gifford lecturers are
the same abstractions that determined the presuppositions on which the
Gifford Lectures are based.[81]

In the twilight of Christendom, Christianity could not help but become invisible to itself as well as to those who wanted nothing more
than for it to disappear completely. That invisibility made James's and
Niebuhr's work at once intelligible and incoherent. Karl Barth, in a
manner that defies the imagination, refused the crumbs that modernity
offered to sustain an attenuated Christianity. Reclaiming the scriptural
and theological resources of the Christian tradition, Barth imagined the
visibility of the gospel after Christendom. Barth was able to do so because he taught himself and, hopefully, those who follow in his foot-
steps how to do theology without reservation.

Barth sought not to convince but to witness and, of course, by witness to convict, yet his witness requires further witnesses. Indeed, if ad-
ditional witnesses were not required, then Barth's work would not have
the power it does. The appeal to such witnesses is not an attempt to
avoid the arguments we must have as Christians in this time between
the times. Christians believe that God has given us all the time we need
to address one challenge, one argument at a time. We can take our time

---

81. I am in debt to Peter Ochs for this way of summarizing the story I have tried to tell.

to make our arguments because we know that our lives are not our own; thus it is possible for us to live without our living being no more than a hedge against death, that is, it is possible for us to live as witnesses. I have said that without witness, there is no argument. But it does not follow that arguments always accompany witness. Sometimes witnesses are all Christians have to offer, and sometimes witnesses are enough; for what could be more powerful than the discovery that human beings have been made part of God's care of creation through the cross and resurrection of Jesus of Nazareth.

Index